RUSH'S LANCERS

Rush's Lancers

The Sixth Pennsylvania Cavalry in the Civil War

Eric J. Wittenberg

WESTHOLME
Yardley

Published by Westholme Publishing, LLC

904 Edgewood Road, Yardley, Pennsylvania 19067

ISBN: 978-1-59416-355-5

Visit our Web site at www.westholmepublishing.com

Printed in United States of America.

*To the men who followed the guidon of the
6th Pennsylvania Cavalry*

*To my parents, Joseph and Leah Wittenberg,
for encouraging me to study and learn*

CONTENTS

PREFACE

MAJOR ROBERT F. BECKHAM's Confederate horse artillery was about to have a very difficult morning. As the sun began rising on June 9, 1863, the snoozing artillerists awoke to the sound of gunfire crackling just yards away from their camps. Through the ghostly mist of early dawn, Brig. Gen. John Buford's division of the Army of the Potomac's Cavalry Corps splashed across the Rappahannock River at Beverly's Ford, near Culpeper, Virginia, surprising the Southern cavalry pickets posted there. The blue-clad horse soldiers and their commander soon found themselves entangled in the largest cavalry battle ever fought on the North American continent, the Battle of Brandy Station.

Brushing aside Capt. Bruce Gibson's squadron of the 6th Virginia Cavalry at the crossing, the Yankee wave thundered up the Beverly Ford Road toward the camps of Beckham's batteries. Col. Benjamin Franklin "Grimes" Davis led Buford's advance. His brigade drove quickly up the road, until Davis received a mortal wound in a duel with a lone Confederate trooper. Now leaderless, the brigade hesitated and fell back to regroup. Upon hearing of the death of Davis, Buford crossed the river and assumed personal command, pressing his troopers further up the hill. Unsure of what force lay before him and now harassed by Confederate artillery, Buford positioned his division in a thick wood facing the enemy line of battle. Approximately one-half mile away, the Southerners were thinly strung out atop a ridge, with the wooden structure of St. James Church anchoring the left of the line. Beckham's cannons unlimbered in front of the church and belched fire and shell at the Yankee lines taking shelter in the trees. Buford wanted those guns captured.

Buford ordered Maj. Charles Whiting, commanding the Reserve Brigade of the Army of the Potomac's Cavalry Corps, to direct the skirmishers of the 6th Pennsylvania Cavalry to clear the field in front of the woods. Whiting, in turn, sent an orderly to deliver the instructions to Maj. Robert Morris, Jr., the commander of the 6th Pennsylvania Cavalry. [1]

Without hesitation Morris formed up his five companies and began moving forward. It was no small task to hold a steady line while moving around trees and other obstacles under fire, but each trooper and horse handled this maneuver with the skill of a Regular. Nearing the edge of the wood, the command "Draw!" echoed down the lines, then

"Sabers!" The exhilarating metallic clang of hundreds of blades being drawn from scabbards and carried to shoulder rang out.

A few Confederate skirmishers, still deployed in the field far in advance of the main Rebel line, spotted the bright morning sunlight flashing off the blades of the Yankees. They wasted little time retreating back up the hill to the safety of their lines. The Southern gunners on the ridge had also seen the flashes and paused to see what would develop. This sudden halt in firing caused an unnerving quiet to drift over the battlefield.

Confederate eyes and ears strained to gain a sense of what was happening in the wood. The sounds of tramping hoofs, snapping twigs, rattling scabbards, and stretching leather broke the silence and then grew louder. These sounds could mean only one thing: the movement of massed cavalry into position.

As the Pennsylvania horse soldiers emerged from the tree line, they closed up boot-to-boot and redressed their lines. Major Morris, the great-grandson of Robert Morris, a financier of the Revolutionary War, stiffened with resolute pride as he watched his battalion step out onto the field. Seeing this, the Confederate cannoneers resumed firing, large plumes of smoke rising from the ridgeline across the field. Lead whistled a deadly tune as bullet and canister found their marks on men and horses. Major Morris could see that the once thin lines of gray had been reinforced. His Philadelphians now faced a large force of enemy carbines blasting away at his flanks while bursts of canister from Beckham's guns rent great gaps in his front ranks as they dashed across the field.

The popping of Southern carbines increased in intensity as Major Morris gave the command, "Forward, guide right, march!" The two waves of blue lines moved out in concert with each other. After advancing some twenty paces, Morris shouted, "Trot, march!" Sod flew from the horses' hooves. Some sixty paces later, the major called out, "Gallop, march!" Buglers echoed the command above the ever-increasing din of battle. As the pace of the horse soldiers quickened, so did the pace of canister that blasted in their faces. Now closing quickly on Beckham's cannons, Major Morris pointed his saber and cried, "CHARGE!"[2] Union bugles sounded, his men raised their sabers, and a resounding cheer rivaling that of the rebel yell carried along the lines as the 6th Pennsylvania put spurs to horse. For a moment, the grand charge transfixed the Southern artillerists, but they were hardened veterans and soon grabbed whatever weapons they could find and prepared to defend their guns. Samuel L. Gracey, chaplain of the 6th Pennsylvania, later wrote, "The Philadelphia men rode hard across the open field toward their date with destiny, their company guidons snapping in the warm spring breeze."[3]

The Pennsylvanians found glory that June day in 1863. Such everlasting glory however, had not always been theirs. The boys from Philadelphia first had to become trained cavalry troopers. Early in their formation, they mastered a strange, outdated weapon, and endured the laughter and ridicule it brought upon them from the rest of the Army of the Potomac. Long periods of boredom tested their wills, and the rigors of the campaign tested their bodies. They suffered from sickness and lack of food and felt the pain of the loss of a good horse or a trusted comrade. On picket lines and battlefields and in numerous skirmishes that no one much remembers, their mettle was tested. They died in surprise guerrilla ambushes, horrible prison conditions, and in hospitals far from their beloved Philadelphia. When it was over, the lucky survivors carried the memories of the glory and the savagery of war home with them.

This is their story, the history of the men of Rush's Lancers, also known as the 6th Pennsylvania Cavalry.

Recruits Wanted!

FOR COL. RUSH'S 70th P. V. REGIMENT OF

LANCERS.

$152 BOUNTY $152

RECRUITING STATION,
S. W. cor. Chestnut and Eighth Street.

Lieut. MITCHELL,
" ODENHEIMER, | *Recruiting Officers.*

Recruits will be received at No. 620 Chestnut Street.

KING & BAIRD, Printers, No 607 Sansom Street, Philadelphia.

(Mitch McGlynn)

Chapter One

FORMATION OF THE
SIXTH PENNSYLVANIA CAVALRY

I N 1860, THE DAWN OF A NEW DECADE, the City of Philadelphia had a population of 565,529, which made it the fourth largest city in the world, behind only London, Paris, and New York.[1] It had a distinguished history as the cradle of independence and the first capital of the United States, and Philadelphians were justifiably proud of their revolutionary heritage.[2] The city's status as the "first city" of the United States began slipping during the administration of President Andrew Jackson, however, when Jackson, who was vehemently opposed to the idea of a national bank, got into an ugly public dispute with the president of the bank, prominent Philadelphia businessman Nicholas Biddle. When Biddle refused to knuckle under to Jackson's demands, Jackson vowed to kill off the national bank. He diverted federal funds from the bank, and then arranged for it to be moved from Philadelphia to New York, all of which ultimately triggered the Panic of 1837.[3]

By 1860, Philadelphia was no longer the political or financial center of the United States. However, its population still connected with its revolutionary history and still maintained an important place in American society. Its economy hummed along, driven by manufacturing enterprises such as locomotive works, cigar factories, carpet mills, textile mills, and other similar ventures.[4] There was also a strong merchant class, with dry goods dominating the city's economy. The Port of Philadelphia offered a gateway to the wave of European immigrants streaming across the Atlantic Ocean. The City of Brotherly Love's teeming streets bustled with activity.

The city's population was diverse. Two-thirds of the citizenry was native born. Most of its immigrants came from Ireland (16.7 percent of the population) and Germany (7.5 percent). Blacks made up less than 4 percent of the population.[5] In 1861, there were four hundred churches in the city, and twice that number of organized lodges, clubs, and beneficial associations. There were also street gangs of rough thugs, fraternal societies, organized fire companies, and other similar citizen networks and clubs. Not surprisingly, the large population was almost evenly split along political lines. In 1856, Democrat James Buchanan received 53 percent of the city's votes, the American Party candidate 36 percent, and Republican candidate John C. Frémont only 11 percent. In 1860,

Republican candidate Abraham Lincoln received 52 percent of the Philadelphia vote, with the balance divided between Democrat Stephen Douglas and independent candidate John C. Breckinridge.[6]

At the same time, the City of Brotherly Love had a large class of wealthy, blue-blooded aristocrats who dated back to, and whose fortunes were tied to, William Penn and to the patriots who founded the nation, such as the Biddles, Barclays (both influential banking families), Rushes, Carpenters, and other rich and powerful families. The schisms between the social classes were stunning, as the gaps in income and standard of living were wide. The coming conflict would, however, erase these divides and bring them all together as proud Philadelphians.

The city's population also reflected the divisions regarding the issue of slavery that ultimately drove the North and South apart. A significant percentage of Philadelphia's native-born population was Quaker. The Society of Friends preached pacifism, and was strongly opposed to slavery in any fashion. However, the Quakers were not in the majority, and "defenders of racial equality were in a distinct minority in the City of Brotherly Love." In fact, many Philadelphians were sympathetic to the Southern cause when the secession crisis of 1860 developed. Most denounced the forceful coercion of the disloyal states, and most hoped to avoid war.[7]

All of this changed when war finally broke out in April 1861. A wave of patriotic fervor crashed over the city of Philadelphia. Chestnut Street, the city's main commercial thoroughfare, was "a sight; flags, large & small flaunt from every building," observed Sarah Butler Wister, whose father was a Southern sympathizer. "The dry-goods shops have red white & blue materials draped together in their windows, in the ribbon stores the national colors hang in long streamers, and even the book sellers place the red, white, and blue bindings together."[8] When President Abraham Lincoln called for 75,000 volunteers, the city responded enthusiastically. "The town is in a wild state of excitement," recorded diarist Sidney George Fisher, a member of the city's social elite, "Everybody is drilling."[9] As young men flocked to join the army, another diarist noted, "most every other man in the street is in some kind of uniform."[10] In the opening months of the war, forty-one regiments of infantry, five batteries of artillery, and twelve regiments of cavalry were formed, with the men signing up for three-year terms of service. Nearly 90,000 men answered the initial calls for volunteers.[11]

Thirty-seven-year-old Richard Henry Rush was tall and slender with dark hair, dark eyes, a mustache, and a regal bearing. He carried himself as one would expect a member of the city's elite would. His grandfather, Dr. Benjamin Rush, was not only a prominent physician and educator; he was also a well-known patriot who had signed the Declaration of Independence. Richard Henry's father, Richard Rush, served as the United States ambassador to England. Young Richard received an appointment to the United States Military Academy at West Point in 1842, and graduated with the legendary class of 1846. Richard's class included his fellow Philadelphians George B.

McClellan and John Gibbon, Virginians Thomas Jonathan "Stonewall" Jackson, Ambrose Powell Hill, and George E. Pickett, New Yorker George Stoneman (who would be Rush's commander in 1863), and a number of other officers who achieved the rank of general during the Civil War.[12]

After graduating from West Point, Rush was commissioned as a brevet second lieutenant of artillery. He served honorably in the Mexican War, winning promotions to second lieutenant and first lieutenant for his conduct in the war. Rush resigned his commission in the Regular Army for unknown reasons on July 1, 1854, and returned to Philadelphia, where he became involved in various business ventures.[13] He was well respected for his service in the artillery during his eight-year career in the Regular Army.

Responding to President Lincoln's initial call for volunteers in May 1861, Rush sought a commission as a brigadier general and command of the Commonwealth of Pennsylvania's volunteer artillery units. When Pennsylvania Governor Andrew Gregg Curtin denied that request, Rush asked for permission to raise a regiment of light artillery. Ten days later, Rush learned that "the Governor would raise no artillery reg't. & if I desired active service, he would advise me to apply to the War Department." On July 24, 1861, Rush offered his services to the Federal government as an alumnus of West Point.[14]

One of his supporters wrote, "Rush is not only in every aspect highly qualified for the command, but a gentleman of high tone, calculated to raise the character of the troops under his lead, if to reflect more honor on the state than the office can confer upon him."[15] Another soldier recalled, "Col. Rush was an excellent organizer and instructor, having but few superiors, if any. . . . He was well versed in all the requirements of the Quartermaster, Commissary and Ordinance Departments. . . . His memory was excellent; he could call every member in the regiment by name. He was exacting as to neatness and a quick appreciation of the qualities necessary for an ideal soldier."[16]

Despite these qualifications, Rush's application was rejected. A frustrated Rush enlisted help from Clement Biddle Barclay, a member of the prominent Biddle and Barclay families of Philadelphia and New York. These two families were involved in banking and finance, and they carried a lot of political clout. Barclay had great political influence with Governor Curtin, serving as his unofficial aide and good-will ambassador to the troops.

Although he was unable to wrangle a commission in the artillery for the West Pointer, Barclay persuaded Curtin to authorize Rush to raise a cavalry regiment, the Philadelphia Light Cavalry. A dispute about the proper name for the new unit arose. The troopers wanted to be called the Philadelphia Light Cavalry, with no state designation, while Governor Curtin wished to number them with the rest of the state's volunteer regiments, in which case, they would be the 70th Regiment of Pennsylvania Volunteers or the 6th Pennsylvania Cavalry.

The debate raged for several weeks, with a number of letters being exchanged in an effort to resolve the issue. Finally, on October 13, Maj. C. Ross Smith and the regimental adjutant, Lt. Frederic C. Newhall, paid a call on Pennsylvania Attorney General William Meredith, another politically powerful Philadelphian. Newhall's father, a prominent Germantown businessman, penned a letter of introduction to Meredith for the two soldiers. "Our community is very much interested in the success of this Regiment," wrote the elder Newhall, "Colonel Rush you are well aware is highly esteemed and is eminently the right man in the right place. Many of your old friends have sons among his officers, who are anxious to serve their country, and it will be truly unfortunate if Col. Rush is not allowed to carry out his original plans of taking to Washington a thorough military organization that will do honor to State and City." Despite these persuasive arguments, Meredith insisted that the regiment adopt a name associated with the Commonwealth of Pennsylvania, and not the City of Philadelphia. Curtin withdrew the appointment of two doctors for the regiment, and permitted Rush to appoint his own regimental surgeons.[17]

The dispute about the new regiment's name having been resolved, the regiment now had two specific designations—the 70th Regiment of Pennsylvania Volunteers, and the 6th Pennsylvania Cavalry—because it was the seventieth regiment of the Pennsylvania Line raised in response to the crisis and also the sixth regiment of cavalry. The two designations were sometimes used interchangeably, but always referred to the same unit. Barclay assisted in forming, organizing, and outfitting the new unit, raised money to aid in arming it, and used his personal fortune to look after the comfort of its troops. His indelible fingerprint stayed on the regiment throughout its service.[18]

Rush mustered into the 6th Pennsylvania Cavalry for a term of three years on August 15, 1861,[19] and he immediately set about developing his new regiment, and opened a recruiting office at 833 Market Street in downtown Philadelphia. On September 1, the colonel advertised in several local newspapers, seeking recruits for the Philadelphia Light Cavalry, which was an unofficial designation for the 6th Pennsylvania Cavalry that played on Philadelphia's civic pride. To entice men to join up, the ad included the pay scale, which ran from $13 per month for a private to $22 per month for a sergeant major, chief bugler, or quartermaster sergeant, princely sums for the times.[20] In addition, enlistment bounties of $152 per soldier were to be paid. All things considered, signing up was not only patriotic; it was also profitable.[21]

The advertising campaign was successful. Colonel Rush personally recruited most of the 1,000 members of the regiment. "Young men filled with patriotic feelings, left their workshops and counting houses and joined some military organization for the defense of our common country, and the preservation of the Union," recounted Sgt. Lewis J. Boos of Company B.[22] Recruiting was brisk. After just a few days, a Philadelphia newspaper reported, "so fast have men applied for enlistment at the rendezvous that the regiment is now almost full."[23] Rush's high reputation was at least partly responsible. "Col. Rush is well known as an able officer, and his regiment will, no doubt, be one of the most complete yet formed in our city," recounted the *Philadelphia Public Ledger*.[24] "The desire of the recruit seemed to be as great to conceal his physical defects as it became in the days of the 'draft' to magnify them," wrote Chaplain Samuel L. Gracey, "The spirit was at its height, and numerous regiments for all arms of the service were recruiting at the same time, and all filling up rapidly. In spite of competition and haste, the material of the regiment was far above the average."[25] On September 25, the newspaper noted, "This regiment is nearly filled up to the regulation number of men."[26]

Nine of the regiment's ten companies were raised in Philadelphia. Most of the men constituting those companies came from the city or from its neighboring Chester, Montgomery, Bucks, and Delaware counties. Aristocratic young gentlemen from Philadelphia's finest families mixed with Quakers and rough-hewn immigrants, creating a regimental melting pot. In October, Company G, also known as the Reading Dragoons, joined the regiment. Raised in nearby Reading by Capt. George E. Clymer, most of the men came from Berks County and were of German descent.

A typical Civil War cavalry regiment formed in 1861 consisted of ten companies of 101 men each, for a total of 1,010 officers and men. Each regiment had a colonel, a lieutenant colonel, three majors, ten captains, ten first lieutenants, and ten second lieutenants. Later in the war, two additional companies were added, raising the full complement to twelve companies. Each regiment had a quartermaster, and each company had a quartermaster sergeant who was responsible for making sure that the men were properly supplied. Each company also had a blacksmith and a farrier, who was tasked with caring for the horses' equipment. Each man had to have a horse, and each horse required a saddle, a bridle, stirrups, reins, and a blanket. Each man also required a full complement of weapons: a saber, a pistol, and a carbine. It could cost as much as $500,000 to raise and mount a regiment of cavalry in 1861; a typical regiment of infantry cost only about $100,000. Many of these men were unfamiliar with horses, and knew nothing about their care and upkeep. The cavalry would have a lot to learn before they could expect to take the field as an effective force.[27]

In addition, a regiment of cavalry provided additional logistical problems for quartermasters. Not only did the men require food and water; so did their horses. Thus, logistics played an even bigger role with mounted units than they did with infantry units. Because of the cost involved, and also because of the lag time to train men and horses, the War Department at first resisted the raising of regiments of volunteer cavalry, and it did not initially embrace them once raised. Thus, units such as the newly formed 6th Pennsylvania Cavalry faced institutional resistance on top of the logistical hurdles already described. That they took the field at all is something of a miracle.

Perhaps to mollify Rush for not granting him the coveted commission in the artillery, Governor Curtin permitted Rush to choose his own officers. Typically, the men of a newly formed regiment would elect their officers, meaning that Curtin gave Rush an extraordinary degree of latitude. The colonel had almost completely filled the ranks of his officer cadre before the recruiting offices even opened. Fortunately, as history has shown, Rush made wise choices for his officers.[28]

Rush's officers included twenty-five-year-old Maj. Robert Morris, Jr., a great grandson of the Revolutionary War financier Robert Morris and former first sergeant of the First City Troop, who was described by a member of the regiment as "a boy who does not let the grass grow under his feet."[29] Also recruited were Capt. Charles E. Cadwalader, scion of one of Philadelphia's most influential families and whose great-grandfather had been a major general in the Revolutionary War; Capt. James H. Starr, a Harvard-trained lawyer who had also served in the First City Troop; Lt. Emlen N. Carpenter, a direct descendant of Quaker merchant Samuel Carpenter (a close associate of William Penn); Lt. Frank H. Furness, a young architect and son of a well-known abolitionist minister; Lt. Frederic C. Newhall, a member of a prominent Germantown family who would write several important historical accounts of the regiment's service; Lt. Robert Walsh Mitchell, who came from a socially prominent Philadelphia family (his brother S. Weir was a famous physician), and was an adventurer and ne'er-do-well who had killed a man in a duel in Mexico;[30] and Lt. Thomas Gregg, first cousin of the governor of Pennsylvania and younger brother of Brig. Gen. David M. Gregg, who commanded a division of the Army of the Potomac's Cavalry Corps for much of the war.

Many of the new regiment's officers had served in an elite militia unit called the First Troop Philadelphia City Cavalry, which traced its roots to the American Revolution. The original First City Troop, as it was known during the Revolution, was organized in 1774 to serve as George Washington's personal bodyguard. "The gentlemen of the Light Horse of Philadelphia were professional men, shipowners, importers, or traders, generally of conspicuous prominence in the affairs of the day," noted the official history of the Troop.[31] The original Troop had covered the Continental Army's retreat from the Battle of Trenton, and had served honorably throughout the entire Revolutionary War. None of its members accepted pay for their service. The next generation of troopers served with distinction during the War of 1812. Membership in the First City Troop was by election only, and was highly desired by members of the city's social elite. "The Philadelphia City Troop," noted a local newspaper in 1861, "has signalized itself in deeds of bravery and valor whenever required."[32] As a member of the First City Troop, Clement Barclay undoubtedly brought the promising young men of the Troop to Rush's attention.[33]

The First City Troop was called into active service in the spring of 1861. Sixty new members were elected, and the Troop was mustered into ninety days' service on May 13, 1861. After seeing action in the Shenandoah Valley under command of Philadelphian Gen. Robert Patterson, the Troop returned to Philadelphia amid great fanfare and mustered out on August 17. "The efficiency and discipline of the Troop, as exhibited on all occasions, clearly show that the reputation established for it by its original founders, embracing among its numbers some of the most distinguished men of the country, has not been tarnished by a single act of unworthiness," noted the *Philadelphia Inquirer* upon the Troop's return from the Valley.[34] Forty-five members of the Troop then joined other volunteer regiments and served as officers during the Civil War. Thirteen of those men joined Rush's so-called Philadelphia Light Cavalry, many of them joining Company E. Three of these gifted young men went on to command the regiment later in the war. All of them lent experience and discipline to the new regiment.[35]

Other officers of the 6th Pennsylvania Cavalry served in a militia unit called the Philadelphia Light Horse, which was composed of young men from a suburb of Philadelphia called Germantown, and commanded by William R. Wister. About twenty of the city's social elite formed a militia company and set up a drill field, where they practiced the evolutions of the U.S. Army's cavalry tactics manual. Virtually all of these young gentlemen ended up being commissioned in various volunteer cavalry regiments. William P. C. Treichel, Frederic C.

Col. Richard Henry Rush. (USAMHI)

Newhall, William W. Frazier, Emlen N. Carpenter, and Osgood Welsh all served in the Philadelphia Light Horse before receiving commissions in Rush's new regiment.[36]

Still others served in Company A, 1st Pennsylvania Artillery, a Philadelphia militia unit that dated back to 1844. On April 19, 1861, the unit was reactivated, and Chapman Biddle—who later commanded a Union infantry brigade—was elected captain. "This command included in its membership many of the best known and most affluent citizens of that period." When Biddle resigned after being appointed colonel of the 121st Pennsylvania Infantry, Henry D. "Harry" Landis, a prominent Philadelphia attorney and merchant and brother-in-law of Col. John F. Reynolds, a former West Point commandant and a career artillerist, was elected captain of the company.[37] The company soon became known as Landis' Battery. Frank H. Furness and Charles E. Cadwalader both served in this company, which was frequently activated for emergency duty during the Civil War, giving its members invaluable military experience prior to joining the Lancers.[38]

One of the regiment's officers from farther afield was Capt. Joseph H. McArthur of the 5th U.S. Cavalry, a member of the West Point class of 1849. McArthur served honorably in the West, where he fought Comanche Indians as a member of this legendary regiment. Just promoted to captain in August 1861, he resigned his Regular Army commission, accepting an appointment as lieutenant colonel of the 6th Pennsylvania. His experience and discipline gave Colonel Rush an added resource for teaching and training his new charges their trade as cavalrymen. McArthur returned to the 5th U.S. Cavalry in February 1862. Although his tenure with the 6th Pennsylvania was short, McArthur made a lasting mark on the regiment he helped to form.[39]

The officer cadre also included Capt. Henry C. Whelan, who left behind a stirring personal account of his participation in the great cavalry battle of Brandy Station on June 9, 1863. Counting young George Meade, who joined the regiment in 1862, five officers from the Lancers served as staff officers at the Army of the Potomac's headquarters. More of Maj. Gen. George G. Meade's staff officers came from the Lancers than from any other regiment.[40] Most of these dashing young men were college educated, and many were graduates of the University of Pennsylvania. Dr. William Moss, the regimental surgeon, exemplifies the literate and intelligent men that molded the nascent regiment. The twenty-eight-year-old Moss, who might have been the regiment's only Jewish member, was a graduate of the University of Pennsylvania and of the Jefferson Medical College, and had continued his studies in Europe. He was erudite, worldly, and very competent.[41]

When the regiment mustered in 1861, the following men made up its original officer roster:

> Colonel Richard H. Rush
>
> Lieutenant Colonel John H. McArthur
>
> Majors C. Ross Smith, Robert Morris, Jr.
>
> Adjutant Frederic C. Newhall
>
> Quartermaster Thomas E. Maley
>
> Surgeons William Moss, Charles M. Ellis
>
> Chaplain Washington R. Erben
>
> Captains George E. Clymer, William P. C. Treichel, John H. Gardiner, Henry C. Whelan, Joseph Wright, J. Henry Hazeltine, Robert Milligan, Benoni Lockwood, James Starr, Howard Ellis
>
> 1st Lieutenants Augustus Bertolette, R. Walsh Mitchell, Charles L. Leiper, Henry P. Muirhead, Samuel Hazzard, Jr., G. Irvine Whitehead, Charles E. Richards, Charles E. Cadwalader, Oswald Jackson, John W. Williams
>
> 2nd Lieutenants William B. Call, William W. Frazier, Jr., Emlen N. Carpenter, Charles B. Davis, J. Newton Dickson, J. Hinckley Clark,

Edwin L. Tevis, William Odenheimer, Frank H. Furness, Thomas W. Neill.

Although there would be many changes over the course of the war, these men provided solid leadership to the new regiment.[42]

Inevitably, tension developed between the aristocratic officers and the rougher ranks of the enlisted men. "Ever since we have been in service our officers (the majority of whom are Beardless Boys and Belong to the Class generally known in Philadelphia as the Ginger Bread Aristocracy) have been trying to get the Regiment accepted as Regulars," noted an enlisted man who was an upholsterer by training, and who had little in the way of formal education. He continued that the officers "have Tyronised over the men and Ground them down more than any Regulars which it has been my luck to meet with yet."[43] These class differences would continue for the duration of the regiment's service, although the enlisted men eventually came to respect the courage of the officers who led them into battle.

The War Department established a large training facility called Camp Meigs in the Nicetown section of northeast Philadelphia. Rush chose a pleasant wooded grove for his camp and training grounds. The camp featured long rows of baggage wagons, each with a team of four mules on one side, and with neat rows of white tents on the other. Six new cavalrymen, along with their saddles and other gear, occupied each tent. Sentinels patrolled the camp's perimeter. These sentries carried only sabers and pistols, but they provided effective security for the environs of Camp Meigs.

Each erstwhile horse soldier spent three weeks on kitchen duty, so that the members of the regiment "all are initiated into the cooking art, thus providing for casualties and death," observed a Philadelphia newspaper. "The cooking arrangements would amuse Philadelphia housekeepers, accustomed as they are to so much space and such a multitude of small comforts and conveniences." A trench in the ground, "from which a fire heats rows of iron pots, is the kitchen range." The equipment was functional and not showy, and the pots were kept boiling most of the time.[44]

In addition to learning kitchen duty, nearly all of the raw recruits had to learn their new trade—including how to care for their horses, and how to execute difficult weapons drills—before they could even consider venturing into the field. Dismounted drills commenced on September 7 because no horses had yet arrived in camp. The men also received Colt army revolvers and sabers. Unfortunately, those sabers were "defective in temper and . . . of objectionable pattern." The new cavalrymen had to overcome these hurdles in learning their new skills. Each company also received twelve carbines, obviously nowhere near enough for the new soldiers to master the art of marksmanship. Problems with supplies plagued the Union cavalry as a whole for the first two years of the war. The army had never fielded a large mounted force, and the hard lessons of logistics had yet to be learned.[45]

The men of the 6th Pennsylvania Cavalry presented a unique and interesting appearance. The quartermaster's department issued the men uniforms that often did not fit properly. "After a while we did find out that a No. 2 man in a No. 4 jacket, with the collar chafing his ears and a loose overloaded belt dragging it awry; in trousers a world too large, a slouching cap and enormous boots, is not seen to the best advantage," wryly noted Chaplain Gracey.[46] The original uniform for the regiment featured heavy brass shoulder scales. It also included an unusual hat with flaps over the ears made of heavy materials and of a large size. "What a dreadful load it was to carry, and how the wearer's head would throb under the weight . . . the stoutest knight of old could not have hewn through this helmet, had he hewn with all his might, any more than he could have carried it about on his head all day." Needless to say, these hats did not last long, and were soon traded in for standard issue kepis and forage caps.[47]

The army's quartermaster department had been trying to find reasonably priced and suitable mounts for the 6th Pennsylvania Cavalry since mid-August. Appropriate horses cost $140 each, meaning that mounting the entire unit would cost nearly $150,000 for the horses alone (about $2 million in modern dollars). Officers were required to purchase their own mounts, at a cost of $150-180 per animal. Rush wanted either sturdy Morgan horses from Vermont or Kentucky thoroughbreds for his regiment, but he did not get his wish. While Rush had no personal stake or financial interest in the procurement contract, he earnestly wanted "to have a well mounted regiment, and of course an effective one." Quartermaster General Montgomery Meigs eventually granted the request for mounts, although not for quality thoroughbreds, and sufficient horses for the entire regiment were rounded up in Vermont and New York.[48]

The first horses arrived on September 20, and by September 25, most of the new troopers were learning how to manage them.[49] Many of these animals were ill or had serious defects, but the government had purchased them anyway. The rookie troopers learned their drills and maneuvers on these wretched beasts, many of which were not suited to the vicissitudes of cavalry service. Company A received the first horses. "There was mounting in hot haste, even before the saddles arrived; and meantime there was some rapid dismounting, too, of luckless riders pitched over picket ropes as the horses came galloping madly up from watering." The men first learned how to take care for the animals, and then how to ride them and fight on them.[50]

Camp Meigs was always bustling, with numerous daily visitors milling about "for the purpose of witnessing the evolutions of the Cavalry." Colonel Rush made public requests that visitors keep clear of the horses, and not bring young children to Camp Meigs "for fear of accidents, as among so many untrained horses and riders, runaways are likely to occur."[51]

On October 2, Rush reported to Governor Curtin on the regiment's progress. By that time, six companies of ninety men each were in camp, "undergoing constant drill, mounted & dismounted, & subjected to strict military discipline in every particular."

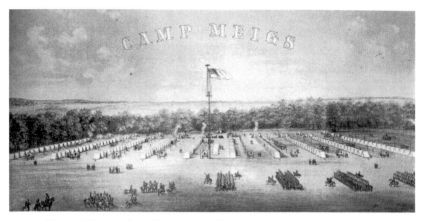

Camp Meigs, Philadephia. (Author's Collection)

Four of the six companies had already been supplied with saddles, bridles, and other necessary cavalry equipment, but no arms had arrived. More than 350 horses and 80 mules were on hand, along with twenty wagons. Rush indicated that he expected recruiting of the remaining companies to be completed shortly, and concluded that "my regiment will be in marching order, & will prove of a character to effect credit upon the State," by November 1.[52]

By October 7, the new troopers had progressed enough in their intensive drilling that Rush scheduled a parade through the city's teeming streets. "Colonel Rush's Light Cavalry presented a very creditable appearance," reported a local newspaper. "The men were on horseback, and managed their steeds with the dexterity of veterans."[53] Another newspaper noted that the cavalrymen "attracted general attention, not only for the soldierly appearance of the men, but also for the skill and training of the troops and their horses."[54] This martial showing spurred ongoing enlistments, and the size of the regiment continued to swell, as "young men of good families, who entertaining a high opinion of the Colonel and his subordinates, gave their consent to press the war with vigor."[55]

The troopers received their full complement of weapons during the first two weeks of October.[56] Each man received a saber, a pistol, and a carbine, which was a short-barreled rifle. Most cavalry carbines were breechloaders. They were highly accurate and could be reloaded quickly, but they had a limited range as a result of their short barrels. The men drilled three times each day, twice mounted and once on foot. The morning drill ran from 8:30 to 10 o'clock, with the men putting their horses through various maneuvers set out in the tactics manual, and also in practicing their pistol marksmanship while mounted and honing their fencing skills. After an hour break, the men then drilled dismounted for an hour. After a lunch break, mounted drill resumed from 2:30 until 4:00. The weary troopers then got a respite until sundown, when they repaired to their tents for dinner. They were free to visit and socialize until 9:30, when "lights out" sounded. This tedious but necessary routine quickly whipped the raw recruits into a respectable cavalry unit.[57]

Ready for action or not, on October 28, 1861, Secretary of War Simon Cameron directed the regiment to come to Washington, D.C., and report to McClellan for orders.[58] Two days later, the *Philadelphia Inquirer* reported, "A part of Colonel Rush's Philadelphia Cavalry Regiment, which is now recruited to nearly one thousand men, has been ordered to Washington, and will leave this week."[59]

On October 30, 1861, the unit received its regimental flag and a set of guidons at Camp Meigs in a stirring patriotic ceremony that featured a speech by Col. Rush.[60] Hundreds of citizens attended, and nearly a thousand horsemen, now bedecked in handsome new and well-fitting uniforms, "were drawn up in column, and stood with all the silence and precision of military discipline."[61] William R. Wistar, commander of the Philadelphia Light Horse and member of a wealthy and prominent family of Dutch descent that traced its roots back to the earliest settlers of eastern Pennsylvania, representing the ladies of Germantown who had made the flag and guidons, also addressed the crowd from a dais. "Soldiers, you are in arms in response to the call of your country; at that call you have left your peaceful avocations, your friends, and your families to defend that country and the Constitution which for more than seventy years has given happiness to the people, the good name and fame of which have penetrated beyond the confines of civilization," exhorted Wistar to the cheers of the throng.[62]

When Wistar finished speaking, the captains of the ten companies simultaneously dismounted. An orderly advanced to the bridle of each horse, while the captains and Rush advanced one foot toward the dais and received the company guidons from the ladies while the colonel received the regimental colors. The captains then returned to their companies and remounted. Rush handed the new standard to the chosen color bearer and advanced to the podium. He thanked the ladies for their generous gifts and said, "If we cannot, in the hour of trial, do all that is expected of us, we will do our best. But I must request you not to expect too much from those thus willing to do their best." His remarks reflected the strict discipline typically practiced by graduates of West Point: "It is easy to collect men together in masses, dress them in uniform, and invest them with the surroundings of military life; but it is not thus alone that soldiers are made. It is only discipline—regular, steady, rigid discipline—which can form the soldier to be relied on in the hour of need." After concluding his remarks, Rush descended from the dais, marched to his horse, mounted, and proudly led his regiment in mounted drill. "The whole regiment reflects great credit on the officers," gushed a reporter from the *Philadelphia Inquirer*. "The men are fine looking, young and athletic, and ride well. The officers are all fine horsemen, from the Colonel to the youngest Lieutenant, and all men of high character and principles."[63]

On November 4, the *Inquirer* reported, "It was expected that the regiment would leave yesterday for the seat of war, but the means of transportation were not at hand. The men and horses will doubtless be forwarded in a few days."[64] While the men waited and

Lancers, first row: Eugene Bertrand*, Henry Brighton*, unidentified†; second row: Charles Cadwalader†, William Carey‡, Emlen Carpenter*; third row: George Clymer†, John Coover†, William Dager*. (*Ronn Palm, †USAMHI, ‡Author)

Colonel Rush made his final preparations for the move to Washington, D.C., he heard from his old friend, fellow Philadelphian, and West Point classmate, Maj. Gen. George B. McClellan. McClellan and Rush had served together during the Mexican War and knew each other's abilities well. Not long after the Union army's embarrassing defeat at the Battle of Bull Run in July 1861, McClellan had taken command of the main army in the east, which he dubbed the Army of the Potomac. McClellan's resume included representing the United States in the 1850s as an official observer of the Crimean War, where he became particularly enamored of Napoleonic tactics. European cavalry made extensive use of lances, and Little Mac had studied their use and tactics at length while in Europe.

The *Army and Navy Journal*, a popular publication for those interested in military affairs, explained the value of the mounted lancer in an article published in the fall of 1863. After pointing out that there was not a single lance unit in the Federal mounted service, the commentator correctly observed, "And yet in the European services the lancers have been a favorite corps, and the lance a useful weapon. The philosophy of it in charging *au fond* upon infantry in line or square is evident. The bayonets of the infantry, added to the length of the horse's neck, keep the trooper at such a distance that he cannot use his sabre; while the lancer, with a weapon from eleven to sixteen feet long, overcomes the distance, and impales the footman in spite of his bayonet."[65] Such was the rationale. It remained to be seen whether this weapon would be useful in America. McClellan was determined to find out.

McClellan sent a note to Rush that asked, "How would you like to organize your regiment as lancers." Rush responded immediately, "Your wishes would be my choice. The material of my regiment is fully equal to the lance. I would consider the selection an honor."[66] Rush had little choice but to accede to McClellan's request. "Most of us heard of it with enthusiasm; and those of us whose opinion was asked pondered how the points should be sharpened and how the shafts should best be tapered to the downfall of all opposers." Another wrote, "We cannot conceive why lances should not be quite as efficient as sabers; and cavalry, armed with sabers only, has been one of the principal wants of the present war. We are not soldiers enough to decide what arm would be most effective in the hands of such gallant soldiers as those in Col. Rush's command; but we feel assured that under any and all circumstances they will do honor to the cause of the Union and its flag."[67] The first shipment of lances arrived in Camp Meigs on November 30, and the men immediately began drilling with them.[68]

Each man received a nine-foot-long wooden lance, with ferules at one end and an eleven-inch steel blade at the other. The lances, copies of an Austrian pattern and unique in the Civil War, each weighed about eight pounds, and were topped by a scarlet pennant, which later became a handy target for Confederate sharpshooters. "They were a trifle awkward to handle at first, perhaps, and we used to wonder how St. George managed to kill the Dragon, but we made no doubt that in time we should be able to ride a tourney with great success."[69] Lt. Frank Furness of Company I rushed off to his tent after seeing the lances for the first time. Furness drew a caricature of the cavalrymen, before and after being armed with the lance. "A cavalryman with a sabre rode into a charge and pierced one foe and carried him off in triumph on his sword," wryly noted

Lancers, first row: Charles Davis*, J. Newton Dixon†, Rudulph Ellis†; second row: James Foster‡, W. W. Frazier†, John Gardner†; third row: Herbert Gee*, Christian Geisel†, Samuel Gracey†. (*Author, †USAMHI, ‡Ronni Foster)

Furness, "but a lancer rode in by his side, and transfixed half a dozen foes, and bore them off on his lance gaily."[70]

This weapon would soon prove cumbersome and impractical in the wooded terrain of the eastern seaboard; Cpl. Joseph Blaschek of Company M later recalled that the lances were "a decided nuisance in a wooded country."[71] Another trooper wrote, "The officers like it, but the men do not, and the officers wouldn't if they had to use [it]."[72]

Certainly, their lances set the men of the regiment apart from the other cavalry units assigned to the Army of the Potomac, and they proudly bore the name Rush's Lancers.

However, the role of the Lancers remained undefined. McClellan believed that it would take two years to adequately train volunteer cavalry, and few in 1861 expected that the Rebellion would last that long. Consequently, there was a major debate among the high echelons of the Federal command about how to properly use and arm the many volunteer cavalry regiments being raised in the summer of 1861. McClellan was biased against volunteer cavalry, and believed in late 1861, "For all present duty of cavalry in the upper Potomac volunteers will suffice as they will have *nothing to do but carry messages & act as videttes.*" A week later, McClellan requested that no more volunteer cavalry regiments be raised throughout the North, since their role was unclear, and there were questions about the army's ability to mount and arm the new recruits.[73]

Still awaiting orders to move south, the Lancers marched and drilled, while hundreds of curious Philadelphians visited their camp to watch them. Wagons ran from the busy intersection of Second and Girard Avenues every ten minutes, permitting "a great many who have not the time to go out to the camp during working days, avail themselves of the Sabbath." Enthusiastic spectators thronged to watch the new soldiers perform the intricate maneuvers of the lance manual. Rush posted guards around Camp Meigs in order to protect his men from the visitors that flocked there daily.[74] On November 21, Rush invited Governor Curtin to come to Camp Meigs to "review and inspect his Regiment, at any time most convenient and agreeable." He indicated that "his Regiment is not yet armed, nor has as yet had that amount of instruction and practice, to enable it to make a very perfect display." In spite of the regiment's incomplete training with their new lances, its proud colonel still wanted Curtin to see how far they had come. Unfortunately, Curtin was unable to make it to Philadelphia until just before the Lancers departed for Washington.[75]

"Our busy days carried us into the autumn fast, and the woods on the border of our camp were painted with brilliant hues," wrote Chaplain Gracey. "Then the leaves fell, and we nestled under the shelter of the great trees from the chill November gales. Then mud came, and cold, and the fair weather friends of summer left us almost alone." The horse soldiers worried about missing the war as the fall turned to winter. They had no idea what niche they might fill in the great army assembling around Washington. "Our feelings were somewhat mixed, perhaps, owing to our isolated condition and the sort of arms we carried, and we did not know whether to take it for granted that we should be a centre from which all other troops would radiate, or to fear that General McClellan would move away with the rest of his army and forget us."[76]

Nevertheless, morale remained high as the regiment continued its seemingly endless drilling.[77] "The health of the camp is good, and the horses look remarkably well considering the amount of wet weather they have been exposed to and the exercise they have to take every fine day in morning drill and afternoon regimental drill," reported Capt.

Robert Milligan of Company F. After dinner, when the men had the run of the camp for a few hours, large campfires blazed, officers and men socialized, their cigars glowing in the darkness, as they listened to the airs of the regimental band. The entire regiment then devoted an hour or two to the study of cavalry tactics every night before lights out.[78]

On Thanksgiving Day 1861, the regiment gave a full dress parade and invited the entire city of Philadelphia to review it. "The regiment looked well," observed a correspondent from one of the local newspapers. "The men were all uniformed, and

The Regimenal Flag of the Sixth Pennsylvania Cavalry. (Mitch McGlynn)

paraded with their blankets and overcoats strapped on horseback. They were about eleven hundred strong. One of the companies had black horses—as fine a looking set of animals as could be got together. The regiment was accompanied by a mounted band. The corps extended over a distance of about three-quarters of a mile," marveled the reporter. Their shiny new lances made quite an impression on the admiring throngs lining the city streets.[79]

A welcome visitor, the army paymaster, visited Camp Meigs on December 3. The men drew up before the paymaster's tent in companies, and then came forward one by one to receive their first pay since joining the army three months earlier. It took nearly forty-five minutes per company to pay the men. Each private received $28, noncommissioned officers received from $32 to $40, and commissioned officers received between $200 and $600. The paymaster, Maj. David Taggart, disbursed a total of $26,000 among the men and officers of the regiment. Major Taggart complimented the Lancers by saying that they were "the best looking set he ever had the pleasure of paying off." Once paid, each member of the Lancers received a pair of army blankets, and new Sibley tents, which could accommodate sixteen men apiece. Each tent contained an army stove that warmed the entire tent. The fully equipped Lancers were now ready to take the field.[80] Their departure was less than two weeks away.

On December 4, the Lancers again paraded through the streets of Philadelphia. "This was one of the finest cavalry displays ever witnessed in [Philadelphia]," recorded Chaplain Gracey. "The lance being new and highly burnished; the scarlet pennon bright and attractive; the new uniform, and the tidy appearance of men and horses, all combined to render it a brilliant and imposing pageant."[81] Nearly three thousand newly trained infantrymen joined the parade. The entire column passed in review before Governor Curtin and an array of dignitaries.

After the politicians reviewed the troops, Governor Curtin made a lengthy and patriotic speech, stating, "You go to vindicate the history of the past, and to make that of the present."[82] Colonel Rush made a few brief remarks in response. "I trust that the regiment will be worthy of the wishes expressed for it in anticipation. Nevertheless, I may be forgiven in saying that a little time is required to complete the thorough organization of a regiment of cavalry," proclaimed Rush. "The combination of horse and leader is a difficult task, and requires much training on the part of the attack. If we do not, at an early day, give a good account of ourselves, due allowance may be made, and we must not be judged harshly."[83]

Although Rush was ordered to "bring . . . [his] regiment with its organization . . . to Washington without delay" in October, it took more than six weeks for the command to march. On December 10, Rush scheduled a third parade of the full regiment through the streets of Philadelphia. A newspaper noted, "Col. Rush has, at the request of many of our citizens, ordered a parade of the regiment in the city, to give all an opportunity to see a full regiment of Lancers." Accompanied by their mounted band, the proud troopers carried their scarlet-tipped lances so that the citizens of the City of Brotherly Love could see them one final time before their trip south.[84]

When the time for departure finally came, the first battalion, consisting of Companies A, B, C, and D, headed for Washington on December 13, and the other two battalions followed within a few days. As the first battalion, including its horses, embarked on the trains, the regimental band played the national anthem to the cheers of the assembled throng.[85] They rode the train to Baltimore, where they disembarked and mounted up. They passed silently through the streets of Baltimore to another train depot, where they then embarked on another train that carried them to Washington.

The men of Company K boarded the trains the next day, passing through Wilmington, Delaware. Sgt. Hamilton Ballentine had fallen asleep as the train left the station in Philadelphia. However, the cheers of an enormous crowd awakened him in Wilmington. He made his way to the platform of the car and then climbed down to the ground. He had scarcely gotten down from the train when a "very fine young lady" ran forward and shook hands with him. She said she wanted to go with the Lancers. Ballentine was disappointed that she could not accompany them. The Lancers had serious work ahead of them, and a pretty girl would be quite an unwelcome distraction.[86]

These young men had finally begun the greatest adventure of their lives. Many of those lives would be forever changed.

Chapter Two

LEARNING TO BE SOLDIERS

A FTER RIDING THE TRAINS DOWN from Philadelphia, the Lancers finally reached Washington early on the morning of December 14, 1861. They partook of a "splendid breakfast" prepared for them by the citizens of District of Columbia, and were then dismissed until noon. Most of the Lancers had never been to the national capital, so they used the opportunity to take in the sights. After lunch, they remounted and marched another two miles, the sounds of the cheering citizenry ringing in their ears, with their scarlet pennons fluttering in the late fall breeze.[1]

The energized Lancers traveled to Meridian Hill in the far northwest quadrant of Washington, D.C., where they established Camp Barclay, named for their patron. The camp sat near Columbia College, on Fourteenth Street, in a remote area in the northwest quadrant of the District of Columbia.[2] They occupied ground that had previously served as the camp for another regiment of cavalry.

By December 16, the entire regiment had reached Washington and established residence in their new camp. Meridian Hill "was a first rate site for an encampment of cavalry," observed a member of the regiment. "There is a stream of water a short distance from our camp, so that it is quite handy for us to water our horses." However, the wet December weather turned the parade ground into a deep, clay-laden bog, causing the horses to sink to their knees in the thick mud. The men also had to slog through the goo, necessitating "such constant labor to secure proper drainage, that many of the command were unavoidably exposed to the severity of the weather, and much sickness resulted." Some of the men took great pleasure in seeing the young gentlemen of the regiment's officer cadre suffering. "It would be a pleasure for some of us to see our Chestnut Street dandies tiptoeing it through the mud," noted the same soldier.[3]

The muddy conditions required the Pennsylvanians to exercise some ingenuity in order to make their surroundings more comfortable. The men cut down thin, young chestnut trees, split them half, and trimmed them into five-foot lengths. They then dug trenches the size of their tents and put the poles in the trenches, tamping down dirt around them. They then pitched the tents atop the poles and filled the cracks with the thick, gooey mud, sealing holes and placing their sleeping quarters above the soggy ground. "We have fine winter quarters now," reported a farrier of Company C.[4]

In spite of the miserable conditions and the resulting sickness that spread throughout the camp, Brig. Gen. George Stoneman, the Army of the Potomac's chief of cavalry, paid a visit to Meridian Hill. Stoneman, a crusty old Regular horse soldier who was one of Rush's West Point classmates, inspected and favorably reviewed the Lancers. He proclaimed them ready to take the field.[5]

By Christmas, the men were homesick. Many had never been away from home before, and they desperately missed their families. Lt. Theodore Sage of Company B wrote on December 24: "All the boys in the tent are setting around wishing that they could be in Philadelphia for a few hours but wishing will not do much." The men did the best that they could to enjoy their first Christmas away from home, and then earnestly resumed their preparations to become soldiers.[6] Colonel Rush called the regiment together that morning, and the regimental chaplain preached a Yuletide sermon, easing some of the men's unease at being away from home for the holidays.[7] The new cavalrymen understood that political pressures would bring a spring campaign for the newly christened Army of the Potomac, and that they had to be ready for the rigors of service in the field.

The Lancers rang in 1862 with style, parading through Washington with their new weapons proudly on display.[8] The parade provided a distraction from the daily routine of drilling and training, but tedium quickly settled back over Camp Barclay once the parade was over. "Colonel Rush's Light Cavalry Regiment paraded here today," reported the *Philadelphia Inquirer*. "They made a magnificent entrance."[9] Tedious or not, the men of the 6th Pennsylvania Cavalry were slowly growing accustomed to life in the army. Although homesickness ran rampant in the camp, they were not alone in their misery—nearly all of the volunteer soldiers in both armies had these experiences.

The regiment also suffered its first fatality on New Year's Day. Pvt. Andrew Snaw, of Company F and Luzerne County, died after a short but severe illness. Snaw received full military honors and was interred in the cemetery attached to the Soldier's Home, about a mile from the Meridian Hill camp. Snaw's comrades from his company served as his funeral escort.[10]

Much of the early allure of soldiering had worn off by January 1862. Several major battles had been fought, but nothing had been resolved. Many young soldiers on both sides realized that the war was going to last longer than anyone had expected in those heady days of the summer of 1861. The untried Lancers settled into a boring routine of waiting for the weather to break and finding ways to relieve the tedium. The weather was miserable. "We have had very rough weather for the last week. There is about 4 inches of snow on the ground now and you may believe our horses suffer very much, we have Burried 6 Horses out of our company since we have been here." At least the new horse soldiers enjoyed good food. "Our grubb is getting somewhat better as we have had fresh

CAMP BARCLY, Meridian Hill D.C.
1st LANCERS 6th PENNA CAVALRY .
Col. R.H. Rush—Lt.Col. J.H. McArthur – Major, C.Ross Smith – Jun.Major, Robert Morris jr.

Camp Barclay, Washington, DC. (USAMHI)

Beef twice in the last 7 Days," reported a member of Company I, "and we have fresh Bread 2 Days out of 5."[11]

On January 8, Company B went on provost duty in the city, and Company A assumed the same role the next day. The two companies alternated days on provost duty until the 12, when they both assumed the role together. "This [duty] does not seem to give satisfaction to many of our men," noted a Lancer, "who are anxious to get in active service on the other side" of the Potomac River. The entire regiment was originally to rotate in and out of this duty, but the arrival of the 4th Pennsylvania Cavalry on February 5 altered those plans.[12]

The tedium of camp life continued unabated. Minor events provided the bulk of the regiment's excitement. "Colds and injuries from kicks and falls are the prevalent afflictions of those who are on the doctor's list," wrote a trooper at the end of January.[13] The men of the regiment received smallpox vaccinations during the second week in an attempt to keep the men healthy.[14] However, the miserable winter weather still had not broken, the Army of the Potomac had not left its winter camp, and life for the men of the 6th Pennsylvania consisted of drilling, when the weather permitted, and guard duty. "We drill morning and afternoon," reported Henry Cowan of Company K on January 8. "We are watching every day for orders to march southward. I would like so Col Rush's Lancers have one good lick at the traitors to their country."[15]

However, it was winter, and conditions were not conducive for green troops to campaign. "We have had the most awful weather," reported an officer. "Rain, hail, sleet, snow, mud knee deep. Horses covered with ice."[16] Their trusty steeds stood out amidst the elements, exposed to "cold, wet, and snow," without any shelter except such as some of the boys have put up themselves." At the end of January, they received new horse blankets, made from the tents of Camp Meigs, which made "our horses look much more comfortable."[17]

Without the allure of female callers, Camp Barclay took on a different look from Camp Meigs. "Our boys, excepting the sick, present a robust, healthy and martial appearance: the greater part of them have discarded the razor, thereby luxuriating in a goodly growth of hirsute appendages," observed a trooper in letter published in a Philadelphia newspaper. The only women in camp were servants looking for work doing laundry for the officers and men.[18]

A member of the regiment wrote home on January 26, "The mud has been ankle deep, indeed, in some places knee deep; still we have managed to keep our tents dry and warm. . . . When the weather was fair, our officers let no time go by unemployed, but for the last two weeks, in consequence of the inclemency of the weather, the drill has been almost entirely dispensed with. It has been exceedingly disagreeable in camp since the rain set in."[19]

On February 6, the noncommissioned officers of the regiment, accompanied by the regimental band, presented Colonel Rush with a handsome ceremonial sword on the regiment's parade grounds. "It all looked mighty fine," noted a sergeant of Company K. Forged by a Philadelphia craftsman, the blade was ornamented with beautiful designs and patriotic expressions, and inscribed with the initials "R.H.R." and "Presented to Colonel R. H. Rush, of the Philadelphia Light Cavalry, by the non-commissioned officers of his regiment," using twenty-seven gold coins provided from their own pockets. It had a solid silver rip, bound with gold lace, and gold leaves adorned the sheath. Sgt. Maj. Eugene P. Bertrand, a Frenchman, made a presentation speech, and Rush responded with a few remarks in acceptance of the gift, praising the officers' good taste in selecting such a fine sword. He also told them that without them, his command would be seriously handicapped and that the non-commissioned officers of the Lancers were more highly esteemed than lieutenants in some other regiments. Lieutenant Colonel McArthur and Majors C. Ross Smith and Robert Morris, Jr., also made brief speeches.[20]

The presentation ceremony marked only a short respite from the miserable weather and tedium of camp life. At the end of February, Lieutenant Colonel McArthur left the Lancers. He received orders to report to his old company with the 5th U.S. Cavalry, and reverted to his Regular Army rank of captain. McArthur's departure caused a shakeup in the officer cadre of the 6th Pennsylvania. The men missed McArthur. "He was a blunt, honest, open-hearted officer, and was fast winning his way into the affections of the men," observed an enlisted man. C. Ross Smith was promoted to lieutenant colonel, meaning that, for the time being, the regiment would have only one major instead of the usual complement of two.[21]

The men generally seemed to like their officers. "All the officers are popular, with very few exceptions," bitterly noted a Lancer. "These 'exceptions,' in spite of their aristocratic ideas, should remember that privates have some feelings of manhood about them, and it might be well for them to learn that these very privates possess the power of keen discrimination in the matter of those officers who deserve their esteem and those who do not." This thinly veiled threat evidently accomplished its goal, as grousing about the regiment's officers decreased significantly after this letter was published in the *Philadelphia Sunday Dispatch*.[22]

Washington, D.C., was a land of opportunity for profiteers during the early phases of the Civil War. Lincoln's first Secretary of War, Pennsylvanian Simon Cameron, proved to be one of the most corrupt politicians in the country. Cameron's primary objective was lining his own pockets. It was often said of Cameron's Washington, "You can sell anything to the government at almost any price you've got the guts to ask."[23] Cameron's greed helped create an environment in which opportunistic shopkeepers took advantage of the naive young soldiers. Corrupt merchants often sold both the government and the soldiers serving it their shoddy goods.

Cpl. Thomas W. Smith described such an incident in a letter home. "The Store Keeppers and People in general are nothing but a set of Thieves and sharpers and their main object is to cheat the soldiers out of their money," he reported. Smith went to a barbershop for a shave, shampoo, and haircut. When he asked the price, the barber asked for $1.25. Smith "gave him 50 cents and told him to go to the Devil."[24]

As spring neared, the Lancers grew excited about the prospect of getting away from the stagnation of Camp Barclay. Capt. Robert Milligan wrote, "We are more ignorant of what is going on immediately round you in quiet, stupid Wilmington [Delaware]."[25] Finally, however, rumors of an impending movement reached Camp Barclay, welcome news to the ears of the Lancers. The captains called their companies out and instructed the men to get their things in order for a move across the Potomac River. Capt. James Starr, commander of Company I, informed his men that "we might go in an hour or that we might not go for three weeks," recounted a member of the company. "We are to take no tents nor nothing but one Blanket and our Over Coats. He said we might come back and if not that our tents and Property would be sent on to us." The excited horse soldier noted, "I think we will see a Battle before Long."[26] It was, unfortunately, just a rumor. Nothing came of these orders, and the men returned to the ordinary tedium of drilling. "All are looking forward anxiously for the call to advance," reported one of the Lancers at the end of January, "We earnestly hope that when the call is extended, we may be numbered among the participants in the coming contest."[27]

On February 19, 1862, the men received new scarlet pennants for the ends of their lances, a gift from the women of Philadelphia.[28] By mid-February, the weather had improved sufficiently to permit the men to resume drilling in earnest. Suitably outfitted, the men continued trying to master their clumsy lances. In the morning, they performed the mounted saber drill, and in the afternoon, they did mounted saber and lance drills. "All the drill that we have had in the Lance Exercise is Charge Lance and Carry Lance. The Saber and Pistol exercise we are very good on."[29] Employing French tactics, the men slogged through the knee-deep mud.

Colonel Rush used creative means to keep up the morale of his men. On February 22, the 130th birthday of George Washington, Rush mustered the regiment for inspection. Once the inspection ended, the regimental adjutant read Washington's farewell address to his troops to the assembled group, which re-ignited the fires of their patriotism.[30]

The next morning, the men assembled on the regimental parade ground and several deserters were brought before the assembled men and their court-martials read to the regiment. One man, who was caught in Philadelphia, was required to wear a twelve-pound ball and chain attached to his ankle and sentenced to hard labor for three months. He was branded with the deserter's letter "D" on his left hip, had his head shaved, and was drummed out of the service in the presence of his own regiment. Others were punished by wearing a barrel over their head with their head and arms through the barrel, some by the ball and chain, and some by forfeiting pay. Discipline was tough, but it had to be.[31]

At the beginning of March, the regimental chaplain distributed pocket Bibles to all of the members of the 6th Pennsylvania Cavalry. Those Bibles "may be seen in the hands of a soldier in almost all parts of the camp," noted Henry Cowan. With the terrors of combat yet to come, it comes as no surprise that the men turned to their faith for courage.[32]

The winter weather broke for a few days at the beginning of March, and the regiment's officers took advantage of the improved conditions. The Lancers drilled two or three times each day, "perfecting ourselves in the use of the lance, sabres, & pistol." The men were proud of their appearance. "To those who have never witnessed a lance drill it is exceedingly novel and interesting. That grove of slender and polished shafts, with their small, blood-red streamers, now motionless in line of battle anon whirling through the intricate mazes of squadron and company evolutions, reminds the spectator of the olden days of tilt and tournaments. It makes one proud to belong to the Lancers," proclaimed an enlisted man. The regiment's mounts were slowly becoming accustomed to the sound of pistol shots from their backs and of fighting at close quarters.[33] However, as one trooper observed, "We have fun. The horses get very fractious."[34] Their hard work was beginning to pay dividends. The regiment was slowly becoming proficient at the art of war.

Like the men in the ranks, the horses also required constant drill. "We are busy training our horses to stand fire," noted one Lancer. "Some of them, mine in the number, were pretty firey themselves at first and several men were thrown and severely hurt. When we were making a charge some days ago we fired a volley from our pistols when two men were thrown broke their lances, one of them is in the hospital." The same discipline that governed the men applied to their mounts as well. That discipline would pay off later.[35]

As the Union high command planned the spring campaign, elements of the regiment performed various ceremonial duties in the nation's capital. When Brig. Gen. Frederick W. Lander died of pneumonia on March 1, 1862, he received an elaborate funeral in

*Lancers, first row: Charles Gulager, James Hazeltine, John Hendricks; second row: Bernard Herkness, E. D. Hughes, William Kirk; third row: Charles L. Leiper, Benoni Lockwood, Archer Maris. (*USAMHI, †Ronn Palm, ‡Civil War Museum and Library)*

Washington that involved the 104th Pennsylvania Infantry, a section of a Regular battery, and a company of the Lancers.[46] These occasions gave the Lancers an opportunity to show off their discipline, exotic weapons, and smart appearance, and they made the most of those events.

The hard work, poor conditions, and bad weather took their toll on the Lancers. In spite of this, the men realized that a movement by the entire army loomed just ahead. "The oft-repeated query is heard on all sides, 'When shall we move?'" asked a Lancer, "No one can satisfactorily answer, but we all impatiently wait."[37] On March 8, the sick men of the regiment were transferred to various hospitals around Washington, and the Lancers prepared to take the field with the Army of the Potomac.

On March 9, Rush inspected the regiment in full traveling kit, with saddles packed, ready to move. The men were not allowed out of the range of sound of a bugle call, as the orders to march could arrive at any moment. "We cannot take anything with us but what we really need," complained one member of Company K. "We may not have any tents for the summer."[38] The colonel gave a stirring speech to his assembled men. He said that certain Congressmen had suggested that the their regiment was armed with sticks with a red rag on the end, and that "when he leads us to battle if he does not redeem the credit of this regiment he will not bring a man out of it."[39] The long-awaited orders to march finally arrived on March 10.[40]

The bulk of the Army of the Potomac was encamped near the old Bull Run battlefield at Manassas, Virginia, and the Lancers received orders to join the army there. They moved out a few days later. Chaplain Samuel L. Gracey wrote, "The regiment presented a fine appearance as, with colors flying, and band playing, they passed through the city, and started out for active service. The men were in buoyant spirits as they bid farewell to winter quarters, and took the field for earnest work."[41] The Lancers marched across the Chain Bridge and advanced about ten miles into Virginia, where they joined the Fourth Corps of Gen. Erasmus D. Keyes. This combined force then moved forward to Prospect Hill, intending eventually to attack the large Confederate camp at Manassas Junction. "Our spirits were buoyant as we received these orders, for many of us had already become tired of the dull monotony of camp life, and were longing for something more active and stirring," remembered Sgt. Lewis Boos.[42]

Although the first night began enjoyably enough with the men laughing and telling stories around their campfires, it soon began to rain, saturating their blankets and making sleep impossible. They spent a sleepless night huddling for warmth, telling stories, and waiting for the dawn. "By that time our hearts were ready for a spree like hounds after horses," noted Sgt. Hamilton S. Ballentine of Company K. "For my part I was ready to take things as they came. What came was the shrilling of the bugle and every man to the critters."[43] Unfortunately, the attack never materialized.

The Lancers instead spent several unpleasant days at Prospect Hill, waiting for further orders. When orders finally came, the Lancers returned to Chain Bridge, "where we were to wait for further Orders. We waited there untill nightfall and no orders came. It then began to rain and we were ordered to unpack our Horses and Picket them in the woods and make ourselves as comfortable as possible. We staid there untill Saturday night at 7 o'clock when General Keys gave orders that if we wished we could go to camp and wait there for further orders. Our bugle blown saddle up and our Boys were soon in their way to Camp which we Reached about 11 o'clock."[44] Sergeant Ballentine and his friend Sgt. George Stroud bunked together with their pistols and sabers by their sides, and forty rounds of ammunition. By 2 a.m., the raid had soaked through. "We gathered our wet blankets around us and made up our minds that this was a soldier's life and we had to take it," complained Ballentine. "At last like drowned muskrats we had to crawl out."[45] Nobody understood why the advance had been aborted, and the uncertainly harmed the regiment's morale.

The Lancers did not enjoy their first foray into the field. Their bivouac was cold, wet, and miserable from the heavy rains. "We have been one whole week living in the rain and mud without tents," recounted Capt. Milligan.[46] Finally, they marched back to Camp Barclay, where they "rejoiced to find tents still standing, and dry shelter awaiting them. This being our first trip to 'Dixie,' was a very rough introduction to field service, and has been remembered in the regiment as the Prospect Hill 'Mud March.'"[47] However, their tents held six inches of water, and the men had to suffer that way until morning, when they could clean them out.[48]

The Lancers resumed the familiar and monotonous routine of camp life. They awaited their long overdue pay, and tried to figure out where fortune would lead them next. "We are hourly expecting marching orders," wrote Cpl. Smith, "Our Colonel told us yesterday that when we march from here again it will be by water, he didnt say where we are going to, but I think it will up the Rappahanock River."[49] Others speculated that they would join Maj. Gen. Ambrose E. Burnside's amphibious expedition in the Outer Banks of North Carolina.[50] Rumors of the impending movement to the Virginia Peninsula by the entire Army of the Potomac for a grand assault on Richmond eventually reached the camp of the Lancers, causing a great stir among the unhappy and impatient men.

Several of the Lancers took an unauthorized trip to Washington on March 29, and they paid for it dearly. Some got drunk, several were badly hurt, and one man was killed. The Lancers had received their pay when many other regiments had not. Soldiers of other regiments, desperate for money, waylaid the unfortunate men of the Lancers for their cash. One man was shot through the leg when he returned from a trip to mail his pay home. Sergeant Ballentine found a horse with his equipment running loose, and led the animal home to camp. Ballentine later heard that the horse's owner had been beaten and robbed.[51]

On March 30, the orders to march again finally arrived. The Lancers saddled up for their journey, marched through rain and mud across the Long Bridge, and proceeded on to Alexandria, Virginia, where they encamped near Fort Ellsworth, named for the slain Zouave hero, Col. Elmer Ellsworth. "After getting over [the Long Bridge] we found the roads in dreadful condition," recalled a sergeant. "We were mud turtles."[52] The men set up shelter tents, but heavy winds blew them down almost as soon as they went up, leaving the men in a frigid pouring rain. They gathered around the campfires until morning, spending a cold restless night.[53] They also learned that the Rebels had evacuated Manassas Junction and had retreated to Yorktown, where they took up a position on the old Revolutionary War battlefield, meaning that it was likely that the focus of the war would shift.[54] The Pennsylvanians camped at Fort Ellsworth for three days before receiving orders to embark on schooners for the journey down the Chesapeake Bay on April 3. Pvt. Charles H. Masland of Company E found the sight of the army's pending departure incredible. "The Potomac River is full of vessels between here and Alexandria for to transport troops south." He also noted, "We are all anxious to have a chance at the rebels."[55]

"At noon we saddled up and went to town to ship but we only got four companeys aboard by dark and the Rest of us had to go back and lay on the old ground again until Thursday morning when we went to town again. Our Company was the last one that got aboard," recounted Cpl. Smith. "We got the whole Company aboard one schooner the Marryland and at dark we Dropped out into the River and anchored over night."[56] Each schooner could accommodate sixty men and their mounts. They required seventeen schooners and a number of tugs to convey the entire regiment in addition to its horses and wagons.[57]

The city boys, many of whom had never been aboard a ship before, found the ocean trip very unpleasant. Not long after the ships departed, a heavy storm blew up. The tug lines for the ships broke, and they spent a day drifting aimlessly. Finally, the wind died down enough for the little flotilla to anchor off Fortress Monroe, a vast masonry fort guarding the entrance to the critical harbor at Hampton Roads. "We were to land here but it seems there had been a Battle fought at Yorktown on the York River and our forces have got the worst of it and want Reinforcements," reported Smith. "There was a steamer sent up the Bay to stopp all transports of troops, and tell them to turn in at York River, but they missed our Company and that accounts for us being the only Company our of the Regiment that arrived here." The rough weather prevented the horse soldiers from unloading, an unhappy turn of events for the seasick and hungry soldiers. As they waited to unload, the troopers spotted the *Monitor*, a "curious looking affair she is, all that is to be seen of her is a Round Iron Tub" anchored about one hundred yards away. The U.S. Navy's newest ship had steamed into Hampton Roads to protect the naval base from the threat of the Confederate ironclad *Merrimack*.[58] "I wish she would come so that we could see the fun," said one member of Company K.[59]

Before departing Fortress Monroe several days later, the horse soldiers witnessed a once-in-a-lifetime spectacle. The *Merrimack* steamed into the harbor with seven gunboats escorting her, and the Lancers headed for the shore and front-row seats for the impending action. Cpl. Thomas W. Smith noted "the shores were Black with men and the Rigging of the Shipping were crowded." Assuming any position that offered a decent view, they watched the titanic struggles of the *Monitor* and *Merrimack* as the world's first ironclad warships engaged in combat. Federal warships pulled back to safety as the

Monitor, described by one of the Lancers as "our Little Cheese Box," moved in to battle. The little Confederate flotilla captured three old Federal schooners that were unable to get out of their way, and then moved toward the *Monitor.*[60]

This engagement, the first battle between ironclad warships, ended inconclusively. On March 8, 1862, the *Merrimack* had steamed into Hampton Roads and sank the USS *Cumberland* and then ran the USS *Congress* aground. She then turned her sights on the already crippled USS *Minnesota,* but the *Monitor* attacked before she could sink the *Minnesota.* Their epic battle lasted for four and a half hours, when the *Merrimack* finally withdrew due to falling tides. The *Monitor* did not pursue because of a crack in her gun turret. Consequently, neither side could claim victory. Four hundred and nine Union sailors were casualties in this fight, while the Confederacy lost twenty-four sailors. These two ships were destined to meet again; one would have to destroy the other for the question to be settled.[61]

Private Masland reported on the epic encounter in a letter to his parents. "There was a great excitement here yesterday. The Rebels' steamer Merrimack came down from Norfolk accompanied by other armed steamers," he wrote. "They captured two brigs and one schooner that were in Hampton Roads. I ascended the rigging of a schooner and had a good look at the huge monster. The Monitor came up from the fort and fired several shots at her and she returned fire. It is supposed that several balls struck the Merrimack."[62]

Despite the entertainment of the epic duel of the ironclads, the men were thoroughly sick of being aboard ship. "We would like to disembark soon be we dread going ashore on such a day as this," complained Sergeant Ballentine. "It is very wet and cold besides landing among our enemies. We would risk it though to get off. We have been on board nearly six days. The horses have plenty to eat but not too much to drink but salt water. For our part we can't lie down not to mention the other hardships we have had since we left Camp Barclay." Ballentine had only had about twenty pieces of hardtack and a portion of pork fat since boarding the ship, and he was hungry. He would have to wait a few more days before seeing land again.[63]

On April 8 and 9, the regiment came ashore. Companies E and I marched to Hampton, which had been destroyed by the retreating Confederates. This squadron of Lancers camped there to await the arrival of the remainder of the regiment. The last two companies arrived at Fortress Monroe that evening after an especially trying journey. The men and horses of Company G had gone without provisions for more than forty-eight hours. Hampton presented a grim sight for the rookie soldiers. It was the first time any of them had seen the devastation of war up close. "The town of Hampton, Va. is a complete ruin," a member of Company K told his father. "Before deserting it the rebels burned every house to the ground there being nothing left but the walls. You can form an idea of it if you were to enter Philadelphia and see the houses with nothing standing but walls—there is not a house in the town that escaped burning."[64] They waited in the ruined town until all companies had arrived. Once the regiment reunited, it prepared to advance up the Peninsula with the rest of the Army of the Potomac.[65]

The Lancers joined the Army of the Potomac's Cavalry Reserve, commanded by Brig. Gen. Philip St. George Cooke, the U.S. Army's senior cavalry officer. Cooke, the father-in-law of Confederate cavalry chief J.E.B. Stuart, was considered the founder of the U.S. cavalry. By the outbreak of the war, Cooke had already served in the Army for thirty-four years. Despite his excellent reputation as a cavalryman, Cooke's time probably had come and gone. Capt. Emlen N. Carpenter of Company G of the 6th Pennsylvania astutely observed, "Gen. Cooke is an old man & has not the *vim* necessary to maneuver against [Stuart]."[66]

Cooke's Cavalry Reserve consisted of two brigades. The First Brigade, commanded by Brig. Gen. William H. Emory, consisted of the 5th and 6th U.S. Cavalry regiments, and the Lancers.[67] The 5th and 6th U.S. were part of the U.S. Army's Regular mounted force, although the 6th U.S. was a new regiment, formed during the summer of 1861. Emory was a fifty-two-year-old West Pointer who had served in the Regular Army for nearly thirty years by the outbreak of the Civil War. A cavalryman from Massachusetts noted that Emory was "a fine specimen of the old United States army officer."[68] He was a hero of the Mexican War, and was commanding cavalry for the first time. Profane and eccentric, the men called him "Old Brick Top" for the color of his hair. The troopers who served under Emory did not like him.[69] One officer wrote home, "The General is grossly neglectful of us."[70]

The Cavalry Reserve represented the first time that cohesive brigades of cavalry were formed in the history of the United States Army. The Lancers were fortunate to be grouped with the Army's professional horse soldiers. McClellan generally did not trust the volunteer cavalry regiments, and formed the Cavalry Reserve to provide a cohesive command structure for the Regular cavalry regiments. The Regulars would perform the bulk of the army's traditional cavalry roles, such as scouting, picketing, and screening the advance of the army.

The Regulars did not receive the new horse soldiers warmly. Their lances made the men of the 6th Pennsylvania Cavalry something of a laughingstock among the rest of the Federal army. Maj. Alexander Biddle of the 121st Pennsylvania Volunteer Infantry, another former member of the First City Troop, wrote home to his wife, a first cousin of Richard Rush, "I was told today that their little pennants are called 'hospital flags' derisively."[71] Others dubbed the Pennsylvanians "Lances Rushers."[72]

Capt. John C. Tidball, who was a Regular Army artillerist and West Point alumnus, was suspicious of the Lancers. "The regiment was a crack one, coming from Philadelphia, and numbering in its organization many who were of the blue blood of that aristocratic city," he wrote. "As it was armed with lances it was entirely useless for combative purposes and was therefore employed for fancy duty, in which the men, dashing about on their fine horses, carrying their long lances with the gay pennants attached, attracted much attention and sometimes a little ridicule."[73] The men were being criticized for a weapon foisted upon them by McClellan, and they resented it.

The Regular cavalrymen sniffed at the newcomers. They believed that the Lancers were nothing but "fancy boys" from Philadelphia. "They were an awfully nice-looking set of fellows on parade. A thousand of them made about as dashing a show as can be imagined when galloping along in line or column," wrote a Regular. "It was expected that these long poles with the sharp spears on the ends would be just the thing to charge on an enemy. The boys called them 'turkey-drivers,' probably because of the red patch on the end of the pole," he continued.[74]

As the erstwhile Lancers trotted through the Virginia countryside, their scarlet pennons flapping in the spring breeze, the Union infantrymen "would yell and gobble at them in such a ridiculous way that they had to be suppressed. I have heard as many as 10,000 men in the camps in the woods gobble at the turkey-drivers, as if it were droves of wild turkeys, every time the Lancers would ride along." The Regulars enjoyed the misery of the Philadelphians, who refused to dignify the mocking. "We of the Regular cavalry at headquarters were, of course, pleased to witness the frequent discomfiture of the turkey-drivers, probably because we were a little bit jealous of them and feared that their bright, dashing appearance might give them a preference over us as the headquarters favorites," he concluded.[75]

In spite of the jeers, they were confident. "Success will be certain where Rush's Lights become engaged," declared Henry Cowan of Company K.[76] Their daily routine consisted of caring for their horses and drilling.[77] However, the countless hours of hard and repetitive drilling and the severe discipline imposed by Rush had instilled an unshakeable belief in their own abilities in the men of the 6th Pennsylvania Cavalry. They were ready to take the field.

On April 19, the *Philadelphia Inquirer* reported, "several changes have taken place recently in Col. Rush's Sixth Pennsylvania Cavalry. Lieutenant John Williams has been appointed Assistant Adjutant-General to General Ricketts, with the rank of Captain; Quartermaster Thomas Maley has received a position in the Fifth Cavalry; Lieutenant A. G. Bertolet has tendered his resignation; and Henry Graffen, who entered the regiment as private, has been promoted to a Lieutenancy."[78]

The regiment's long waiting period was nearly over. As the Lancers prepared to make their first foray into battle, they were in good spirits, and they believed in themselves. They would soon see combat as McClellan's giant army advanced up the Virginia Peninsula toward the Confederate capital at Richmond. There, at long last, they would face the enemy for the first time.

Chapter Three

THE LANCERS IN MCCLELLAN'S 1862 PENINSULA CAMPAIGN

MAJOR GENERAL GEORGE B. MCCLELLAN believed that he could capture the Confederate capital at Richmond by assaulting it from the east, moving along the finger of land protruding into the Chesapeake Bay between the York and James Rivers. Two corps of infantry stayed behind to protect the army's lines of supply and communication, while the balance of the Army of the Potomac advanced up the Peninsula, cutting loose from its base of operations at Fortress Monroe. McClellan's grand army of more than 100,000 men moved at a glacial pace, as McClellan erroneously insisted that the Confederates, who actually had less than half his available manpower, outnumbered his force.

McClellan believed that this massive enemy army blocked his route to Richmond, and that belief soon permeated the ranks of his army. "There are now 250,000 men concentrated around Yorktown on both sides and I expect there will be a hard fight there," reported Pvt. Christian Geisel.[1] Instead of moving aggressively, McClellan besieged the small Southern garrison. Little Mac's pause in front of the Revolutionary War battlefield at Yorktown delayed his advance two full weeks, giving Confederate Gen. Joseph E. Johnston time to rally his forces in front of Richmond. "I have been through the Rebel camps and forts and I think if the Rebels had stayed and fought," observed Charles Masland of Company E, "there would have been a great battle with great loss of life."[2] The retreating Confederates left behind large quantities of land mines called torpedoes that took a toll on the advancing Northerners. Geisel avoided the torpedoes, but watched in horror as two of his comrades were "blown up by shells which the Confederates have buried all around their works." The Lancers held their positions near Yorktown for several days, encountering angry local bushwhackers. Geisel noted that two Lancers "were found tied to a tree and their brains blowed out."[3] The delay also cost the Army of the Potomac its opportunity to capture the Southern capital easily.

Although the men were beginning to suffer from the diseases carried by the mosquitoes that plague tidewater Virginia, duty remained fairly pleasant for the Lancers. On May 3, the men of Company K rode their horses four or five miles out into the surrounding countryside before stopping to unsaddle. They rode the horses into the water, swam them to wash the thick Virginia mud from them, and then went for swim themselves in the hope of getting clean. They let the horses graze a while and then had a leisurely ride back to camp. Henry Cowan had an especially fast and nimble horse. "There are but few horses (if any) that can beat him. I have called him Gen. Zollicoffer which I think is a very appropriate name for he can run like a deer which is generally the style of rebel generals," he reported, his tongue planted firmly in his cheek.[4]

That night, the Confederates evacuated their trenches at Yorktown. About daylight on May 4, the Federals discovered that the enemy lines were empty. The Lancers, along with the 5th and 6th U.S. Cavalry, moved out to pursue the retreating Confederates. They followed all day, and stopped only after dark. Fearing that the enemy was lurking about, the men received orders to stand to their horses all night, meaning that after they fed their mounts, the men reformed line of battle and then remained in the position "prepare to mount" until daylight the next morning, when they resumed the march. They were almost at Williamsburg when the Lancers received orders to halt and wait for their supply wagons to come up while the Regulars continued on. When the Regulars encountered a large force of the enemy, they called for reinforcements, and the Lancers mounted up and headed out again. However, the fight had already ended by the time that they arrived. They had missed a prime opportunity to see combat for the first time.[5]

The Federal advance also paused in front of the colonial capital at Williamsburg, where a small force of Rebel infantry again delayed them. On May 6, 1862, the regiment received word that disaster had befallen the Federal troops of General Joseph Hooker at Williamsburg on the 5th, and the Lancers received orders to march. They spent the night standing to horse in a downpour.[6] After the fierce battle in front of Williamsburg, McClellan finally shook himself free of the stubborn Confederates and marched on Richmond. The Lancers were finally about to get their first opportunity to prove their worth.

The men went on scouting excursions and continued drilling. On May 7, Maj. Robert Morris, Jr., led a squadron of Lancers out of its camp near Yorktown, marching until 1 a.m. on the 8th. They struggled over almost impassable roads running through thick woods until they reached a large Confederate fort at Mulberry Point on the James River, opposite Yorktown. The fort was filled with burned-out Southern cannon and caissons. They also found nearly two hundred seven-inch cannonballs, and "a lot of spades, picks, wheelbarrows, and timber ready for use" in a second, smaller fort being constructed in a nearby swamp. "I was informed that the enemy advanced their works and camps on Friday last," reported Maj. Morris, "and all the residents about this point have left." Two gunboats kept watch over the little contingent of cavalrymen, but "as they displayed no flags, it is impossible to say on which side they belong." The reconnaissance had been a success.[7]

However, the Lancers drew the critical eye of Colonel Rush, who did not approve of their appearance. In early May, Rush called a snap inspection of the entire regiment by him and Stoneman. The men hastily returned to camp, and stood for inspection with horses and men covered with mud. When Stoneman expressed his displeasure with the appearance of the regiment, Rush dressed the men down and ordered them to spend three hours per day cleaning their horses—ninety minutes in the morning and another ninety minutes after the day's drill. "Ever since the Inspection Rush has Played the Tyrent to Perfection. One day last week while the Regiment was on Drill he sent a guard around and found 10 men off Drill most of them were washing," complained Corporal Smith. "He called a drum head court martial, and had them fined to the amount of $61 sixty one dollars to be taken out of their Pay."[8]

Smith recounted another episode regarding Colonel Rush. Whenever an officer ranking major or higher approached the regimental guardhouse, custom required the guards to turn out and present arms in salute. When Rush visited the guardhouse, the enlisted man in front failed to call out the guard. "Rush got into one Hell of a Pashion, put the man in the Guard House and not satisfyed with this fell to cursing all the men who were there." Smith related that Rush's opening salvo was "you are a God Damn pretty number one you Damn Sons of Bitches you," and that the colonel ranted at the whole regiment for nearly ten minutes as a result of the mistake of one man.

The Lancers were brigaded with the 8th Pennsylvania Cavalry. Col. David McMurtrie Gregg of the 8th Pennsylvania, a first cousin of Governor Curtin, commanded the newly formed brigade. Smith speculated that Rush was unhappy at being passed over for command of the brigade in favor of the governor's cousin. "This is what galls Rush so much," he concluded.[9]

Smith's observations about Richard Rush were not unique. Maj. Alexander Biddle of the 121st Pennsylvania Infantry, married to one of Rush's cousins, observed, "Rush is . . . a very unnecessarily mean and severe officer, as regards his treatment of officers in presence of the men. I hear constantly of complaints of treatment which nothing could sanction and I fear he has raised feelings of bitterness which operate up against him."[10] The colonel's reputation as a martinet ultimately cost him the affection of his regiment, and harmed his career. Although Rush was advanced as a candidate for brigadier general of volunteers on several occasions, the promotion never followed. Perhaps his difficult personality factored into that decision.

The Lancers scouted and picketed the area around Yorktown until May 9, when they finally received orders to join Brig. Gen. William H. Emory's Second Brigade of the Army of the Potomac's Cavalry Reserve. Progress on May 11 and 12 was not good, as wagon trains blocked the roads. "For we found out that the Road from Yorktown to Williamsburgh 13 miles was completely blocked up with Troops and waggon Trains, so we had to go back to our old Camp Ground and lay there over night," recounted Smith.[11] The Lancers finally joined their brigade on the night of May 12. That night, Capt. Joseph

Wright, the commander of Company D, died of typhoid fever, the first casualty in the regiment's officer cadre. Charles E. Cadwalader was promoted to captain and took command of Company D a few weeks later.[12]

As the Lancers moved from Yorktown to Williamsburg, they got their first look at the ravages of a pitched battle. "As we passed over the Battlefield or the Plain of Williamsburgh as they are called the ground was strewn with armes and clothing of every Description dismounted guns Broken waggons muskets sabers boye knives knapsacks belts &c.," reported Smith. "All along the Road from Yorktown where the Reble army Retreated, the Road Bears Indications of the haste in which they left. Gun carriages ammunition waggons and vehicles of every Discription are left standing in the Road, but

Maj. Gen. George B. McClellan. (Library of Congress)

they always took good care to cut the spokes out of the wheels before abandoning them."[13] The sight of Williamsburg houses filled with dead and wounded Rebels shocked the Lancers.[14]

They also got their first look at the Confederate infantry when prisoners of war marched past them on their way to captivity. "Of all the dirty ragget filthy looking men that it was ever my ill fortune to see I think they would take the Prize," sniffed Smith. "Some of them had not enough Rags to cover their nakedness and one Poor Devil had nothing on but a pair of ragget pants and an great ragget Coat that trailed on the Ground it was the Hottest day we have had. They were so dirty that they Really stunk as they passed us."[15] The Pennsylvania horse soldiers would soon learn to respect the tatterdemalions they sneered at.

John P. Kepner of Company I wrote home on the night of May 12, relating his experiences to date. "I had a fine view of them and such a set of mean uncombed unwashed lousy-looking and destitute set of human beings I never saw. I could scarcely sit upon my horse as they passed. I felt as though I could take the heart-blood out of everyone of them. It was with difficulty I could retrain my feelings," he declared. "As soon as they stand we will undoubtedly have a fight. And where we have it I made up my mind that should I have a chance I will never take a rebel prisoner. I'll shoot every bloody one I can ever catch."[16] His chance would come.

On May 13, they marched to Cumberland, where they spent a couple of days camped on the farm of a Confederate officer. On the 17th, Rush's troopers marched to

White House Landing on the Pamunkey River. They then encamped on a portion of an estate owned by Col. W. H. F. Lee, the middle son of Confederate General Robert E. Lee and commander of the 9th Virginia Cavalry.[17] Rumors circulated through camp that Richmond had been evacuated, and the men were in high spirits, awaiting orders to capture the empty Rebel capital.[18]

While the Lancers still had not seen any combat, they had to endure miserable living conditions. "I never was so thoroughly uncomfortable in my life," announced Capt. Robert Milligan. "No money no clothes except one change, two towels, no tooth brush. No whiskey, no smoking tobacco, no letter paper, no envelopes, no postage stamps, no pen, and no ink. And no definite prospects of matters getting any better as far as I can see."[19]

On May 18, the Lancers moved to the Richmond and York River Railroad, where they again camped, awaiting further orders. On the 20th, they marched another six miles and encamped at Confederate fire-eater Edmund Ruffin's farm Marlbourne on the Pamunkey River, near Old Church. There, they were finally in close proximity to the Confederate lines, and their excitement grew as they anticipated their first encounter with the enemy.[20] Although there had yet to be a large-scale engagement, Milligan optimistically wrote, "I think this hellish Rebellion is pretty much played out. I certainly wish so. I am thoroughly sick and tired of soldiering."[21]

The men remained confident. "I expect that by the time you receive this our regiment will be in the would-be capital of the Confederate states," boasted Pvt. Henry Cowan of Company K on May 21. At the time, the regiment was a mere twelve miles from Richmond.[22]

On May 22, the Lancers searched for a contingent of Rebel cavalry thought to be operating in the area around New Castle and Hanovertown Ferries. Colonel Rush led the entire regiment out, and after a lengthy march, found no enemy. "I questioned by detached parties all houses within sight of the roads," reported Rush, learning that Southern horse soldiers had passed through the area a few days earlier. "The country I have passed through is very rich, and the farms are all stocked—sheep, cattle, &c., rich fields of grain and grass, and the ladies and families at home." Rush interviewed the son-in-law of Edwin Ruffin "and learned much from him." After finding no evidence that the enemy was operating in the area, the Lancers returned to camp.[23]

The next day, they briefly skirmished with an enemy contingent near Hanover Court House. That same day, Colonel Rush interviewed Mrs. Robert E. Lee, whose husband had sent her away from Richmond to escape the advancing Yankee horde, believing that the countryside provided safety from the Union army's advance. Rush reported to McClellan, "The admission of Mrs. Lee that the U.S. Troops were not expected this way, by her family, is so important an item that I deem it proper to report the fact to you at once."[24]

The arrival of the Lancers that day made quite an impression on the locals. "Five or six lancers, with their red streamers, rode slowly by our gate this evening," noted Mary

Brockenbrough Newton, of the Summer Hill farm near Hanover Court House, in her diary. The next day, Richard Rush himself appeared. Judith McGuire saw "an officer in the front porch, and a squad of cut-throat looking fellows on the steps; while a number, with their red streamers and lances, were dashing hither and thither; some at the stable, some at the kitchen, others around the servants' quarters and at the barn, while the lane was filled with them." Rush introduced himself and rudely demanded the production of her grandson, Edward Brockenbrough. "The child was aroused from his sleep," she noted, "and hastily dressed himself, but not quickly enough for our impatient Colonel, who walked to the staircase and began to ascend, when [her sister-in-law, Catherine Nelson Brockenbrough] called to him, 'Colonel Rush, do you mean to go to a lady's chamber before she is dressed? The boy is in his mother's room'." When two young boys appeared, Rush took them and questioned them, and later released them, but not after calling them "little rebels." Not surprisingly, the locals quickly grew to hate the sight of the men's distinctive red pennons.[25]

A few weeks later, Mrs. McGuire's sister, Mary Brockenbrough Newton, vented her spleen in her diary. "Wagons passing to Dr. [Newton]'s for corn, guarded by Lancers, who are decidedly the worst specimens we have seen," she declared. "Compared with them, the regulars are welcome guests. It is so strange that Colonel Rush, the son of a distinguished man, whose mother belonged to one of the first families in Maryland, the first-cousin of James M. Mason, and Captain Mason of our navy, of Mrs. General Cooper and Mrs. [Sidney Smith] Lee [General Robert E. Lee's brother, who was a naval officer], should consent to come among his nearest of kin, at the head of ruffians like the Lancers, to despoil and destroy our country!" She concluded, "I suppose that living in Philadelphia has hardened his heart against us, for the City of Brotherly Love is certainly more fierce towards us than any other." Their reputation among the civilian populace stood in stark contrast to the Lancers' reputation with their comrades in arms in the Army of the Potomac. It also stood in stark contrast to that of the Regular cavalrymen of the Reserve Brigade.[26]

The men were eager to see action. "We found, on May 23, the enemy were very strong at Hanover Court House and instantly sent word to [Maj. Gen. Fitz-John Porter, commander of the Fifth Corps] upon which information General Porter ordered us to destroy all the ferries and bridges along the Pamunkey, which the squadrons that were picketed along the ferries instantly did," reported Colonel Rush.[27] The Lancers had finally contributed to the Union cause by locating the Confederate force at Hanover Court House in one of the first combined force operations of the war, consisting of cavalry, infantry, and artillery. "We are 18 miles from Richmond on the extreme right of the army. We was out this morning within 12 miles of Richmond and drove in the rebel pickets," noted Trooper Charles Masland of Company E on May 23. "We expect to attack them every day." They would not have long to wait.[28]

Seven companies of the Lancers made a reconnaissance on May 24. Not long after heading out, they scattered some enemy cavalry pickets and spurred off in pursuit of them. Colonel Rush, who personally led the scouting expedition, came under fire. A Confederate hiding in a stand of woods opened up on the column of Lancers as it passed. Rush had a close call when a Confederate ball grazed his cheek, but he shrugged it off and continued his scouting expedition.[29]

"Our Squaddron drove in a line of the Enemies Pickets, untill we came within sight of their mane Picket Guard when we Retreated slowly to try and draw them out," recounted Corporal Smith. "But they would not come. They were encamped in a large piece of woods and one of them who we captured and also a Negro told us they were in strong forse, and had Artillery which we had not. So we had to return to Camp for fear of them cutting off our Retreat. . . . Our first Squadron distroyed a Rope ferry, and sunk the ferry Boat and captured three Prisoners."[30] Lt. Theodore Sage noted, "The column returned after being absent about four hours. Our regiment drove in their pickets about two miles when they fell back on their reserve and we returned to camp losing one and no one being injured. There is every probability that there will be some warm work for us in our advance."[31]

During this advance, Company C of the 6th Pennsylvania made a mounted charge with their lances, scattering Confederate cavalry pickets and capturing a few. A few days later, Northern soldiers, taunting the Southerners, accused them of running away. "O it wasn't you we run from," responded one of the prisoners, "it was the Fellows with them long Poles." The lances had proved to be an effective weapon of terror. "So far the Speer has turned out to be the best weapon we have got," declared Smith.[32]

The reconnaissance by the Lancers had actually uncovered the presence of a strong Confederate force located near Hanover Court House, just a few miles from Richmond. This force consisted of Brig. Gen. Lawrence O'B. Branch's brigade of North Carolina infantry. After the Lancers had reported their intelligence find, McClellan dispatched a strong force of cavalry, Fifth Corps infantry, and artillery to confront the Confederates. "I assume that this morning there was a force at Hanover Court House of not less than 3,000 infantry, six pieces of cannon, and 300 cavalry, four regiments of infantry having arrived day before yesterday," reported Rush on May 24. "I further think that they are now in sufficient force to move upon us at this point with success, and would suggest at least four pieces of artillery and another regiment of infantry to make this place up to the Hanover Ferry secure."[33] Based on such solid intelligence, Porter followed this suggestion, and the Federal force was augmented enough to make it formidable.

Reports reached McClellan that a force of 17,000 enemy infantry was moving toward Hanover Court House in an effort to outflank the Army of the Potomac. These reports came from a local civilian and were unreliable, but McClellan accepted them as the truth and reacted. He worried about the presence of a large enemy threatening his

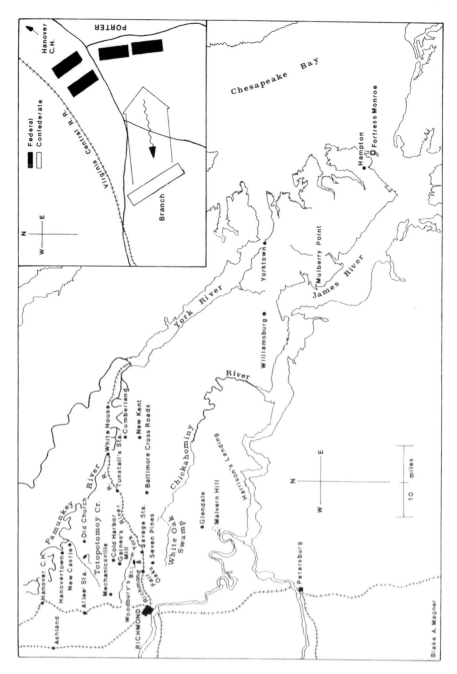

Map 1. The Peninsula and Hanover Court House.

rear, and moved quickly to clear his flank. McClellan gave this important job to Maj. Gen. Fitz-John Porter and his Fifth Corps.[34]

The Battle of Hanover Court House occurred on May 27.[35] The Lancers set out at dawn that day, accompanying Col. Gouverneur K. Warren's brigade of Fifth Corps infantry command in the northern arm of a pincer movement intended to trap the Confederates. Rush ordered his men to travel light: they carried two days' rations, their canteens, a clean undershirt, their rain ponchos, and a single blanket that doubled as a saddle blanket. Porter's infantry led the Federal advance. In a heavy engagement that lasted most of the afternoon, the Fifth Corps defeated Southern infantry, supported by cavalry and artillery. Hanover Court House marked the first engagement of the Fifth Corps's sterling career in the Civil War, and the Army of the Potomac's first victory over the Southern infantry.[36]

The Lancers did well in the Battle of Hanover Court House. Along with elements of Warren's infantry, they captured an entire company of the 28th North Carolina Infantry. At the end of the day's fighting, the Lancers pursued the fleeing Tarheels down the road to the Pamunkey River, and rounded them up at lance point.[37] "We were then in hopes that the enemy would stop the pursuit, but we were now sadly mistaken," recounted one of the Tarheels. "At the end of the lane it was near a half mile across the river bottom to the bridge. We pushed on & tried to do it as the enemy's cavalry was just behind us. I filed off to the right in a wheat field. As I did this I looked back & seen many of our broke down men behind in every direction, slipping through the wheat doing all they could to get out of the way of the enemy." This officer, along with fifteen enlisted men, tried to escape, but they could not outrun the charging Lancers. "As the sun was setting & its last bright rays were kissing the tops of the trees, on came the furious cavalry charging upon us, to whom we had to surrender, or be destroyed, as there were only 15 of us & 60 of them and just at the river & over 1,000 in sight. Here I had the most awful feelings I ever have had in my life," he concluded.[38]

The pursuit was vigorous. "We turned and run our horses a distance of three miles through a scorching sun to take part in the fight," recounted Henry Cowan of Company K. "We then began pursue the enemy much on the style of 'fox-hunting' through woods and over fences. We soon came up with a Captain of a North Carolina regiment with 30 men they threw down their arms and surrendered. We kept on here and there picking up a straggler." The men then stood to horse all day, waiting for their next assignment.[39] Pvts. Daniel Aulrich and John Zayzer were wounded during the fighting.[40]

The performance of the Lancers caught the attention of a correspondent of the *Philadelphia Inquirer.* "The Lancers had done good previous service in destroying bridges, scouring the country and dispersing guerrilla band, but this was their first regular engagement. They went into action with the coolness and steadiness of veteran troops, and, at a critical moment of the day, when the cavalry were ordered to charge, heading the regulars, they rode solidly and fearlessly down on an overwhelming force of

Lancers, first row: *Charles Masland*, unidentified†, Robert Milligan*; second row: Robert Mitchell‡, Isaac Moffett*, Albert Morrow*; third row: H. P. Muirhead*, Thomas Neill*, George Pepper*. (*USAMHI, †Ronn Palm, ‡Author)*

the Rebels, under a galling fire, and scattered them like sheep," declared the correspondent. "This charge decided the fortune of the day on that wing. Their conduct excited the special comment of the Division commander, from faint praise is honor, who applauded in the highest terms their gallantry and discipline." The correspondent concluded his report with high praise for the Lancers. "We could expect nothing but success, however, from the fine material, careful organization and thorough drill of the Lancers, and hope that in their next battle the Rebels will delay their flight sufficiently long to embrace an opportunity of testing the practical effects of a *bayonet charge on horseback*."[41] In the end, they would not have many such opportunities.

The 6th Pennsylvania Cavalry also participated in an expedition to destroy the railroad bridges over the Pamunkey, which the combined arms force accomplished along with its objective of locating the Rebel flank. The demolition of the bridges had a major impact on the outcome of the campaign—Stonewall Jackson's force, coming from the Shenandoah Valley to join Lee's army in front of Richmond, had to take a different route and was late arriving.[42] "We got the Order Forward, March yesterday at 10 o'clock and started off at a gallop as the Rebbles were Retreating," recounted Cpl. Thomas W. Smith. "We chased them across a Stream of water about 5 miles, burnt the bridges and a Railroad Bridge and cut the Telegraph wires. We took 32 Prisoners including 7 Cavelrymen." Lt. Albert P. Morrow of Company B narrowly escaped when Confederate cavalrymen opened fire on him at point blank range. All somehow missed their mark.[43]

During this expedition, the Lancers spent fourteen hours in the saddle and covered forty miles. "Both our Horses and ourselves completely worn out with Fatigue. We lost 37 Horses out of the Regiment while gone. They were run to death and even my Gallant Nag showes the Effects of Being over exposed and his Back is all Raw. He will not be able to ride again for a Week at Least," concluded Smith.[44]

General Porter commended the role of Rush's men in rounding up Confederate prisoners.[45] One Regular recorded, "On the left stood, formed in a long line across the field, the 6th Pennsylvania Cavalry, then armed with lances . . . and making a fine display, reminding me of the engravings I had seen once of the Mexican cavalry at the war of 1848."[46] The Lancers wanted to make a lance charge, but the opportunity never presented itself. "I dont think that our Lances will ever be of any use in this war unless we should get a chance to charge in an open Field. In that case, they would be a most Powerful weapon," complained Cpl. Smith. However, the lance was not as popular with the rest of the men of the regiment as it was with Smith, and it remained the subject of much jesting in the ranks of the Army of the Potomac. As Maj. Alexander Biddle, of the 121st Pennsylvania Infantry, wrote home to his wife, Julia, "[the Lancers] are made much fun of."[47]

Col. Gouverneur K. Warren, of the 5th New York Infantry, commanded the combined arms expedition to the bridge over the Pamunkey River. "Thrown together as my command was for the first time I have special reason to speak of the promptness and energy with which the different commanders obeyed my orders and seconded me in all my endeavors to carry out [my] instructions," praised Warren. He also noted the toll taken on the 6th Pennsylvania Cavalry's horses by this expedition: "Two of Colonel Rush's horses gave out and died from exhaustion on the pursuit toward the Pamunkey."[48]

"This was the first engagement in which any part of our regiment was recognized as being a participant, and is so mentioned in the report of Colonel Rush to Governor Curtin," recalled Chaplain Gracey. "The 6th regiment was sent on the extreme right of the advance, and by its active demonstrations in that quarter, served to distract the attention of the enemy from our main infantry column. We were under fire most of the day, but no opportunity offered for the regiment to be used in the charge."[49] Colonel Rush noted, "The regiment was under fire for the first time, and all the officers and men behaved most gallantly."[50] "This ten days' scout was a very hard one, though we lost no men," stated Rush in his report to Governor Curtin, "Thirty-four horses were killed or maimed."[51]

The Confederates abandoned Ashland on May 29 and retreated toward Richmond. On the following day, the Lancers reconnoitered toward Ashland, where they drove the grayclad pickets, took a number of prisoners, and burned a railroad bridge.[52] During the expedition, the Lancers took a total of eighty prisoners and eighteen horses, good work for a regiment seeing its first action.[53] Two days later, a squadron of the 6th U.S. Cavalry and two squadrons of Lancers marched to the Pamunkey to burn boats and to reconnoiter King William County. Capt. August V. Kautz of the 6th U.S. commanded this foray. As the ferry across the wide river had been destroyed, they did not get far, and Kautz dispersed his three squadrons to search for information on the dispositions of the enemy. After torching as many boats as possible, Kautz and the Lancers returned to camp after a successful excursion.[54]

On May 31, Gen. Joseph E. Johnston was badly wounded in the shoulder at the Battle of Seven Pines. Maj. Gen. Gustavus W. Smith, the next ranking officer in the Confederate army, assumed command, but Smith was unable to stand the pressure of the position. He suffered something akin to a nervous breakdown and was relieved of command. Gen. Robert E. Lee, a fifty-six-year old Virginian, who had been serving as President Jefferson Davis' military advisor, replaced Smith on June 1. The Army of Northern Virginia would never be the same again.

On June 4, the regiment established its camp at Johnson's farm, where the Lancers rested for a few days. On the 10th, Maj. Morris led two squadrons (Companies A, H, I, and K) of Lancers on a reconnaissance toward the Pamunkey River. Over several days, they scoured the countryside all the way to Hanover Court House, but found nothing of importance other than rounding up a few prisoners. They returned on the 12th and resumed picketing the army's flanks.[55]

The Lancers paid another visit to the Brockenbroughs on June 11. They stopped at Mary Page Newton's barn, ripped off the planks, and helped themselves to fodder for their horses. "The door was opened by the overseer, but that was too slow a way for thieves and robbers," complained Mary Brockenbrough Newton. They encamped for the night in front of her home. Her niece, Catherine Brockenbrough, was detained by bad weather, meaning that the Lancers "took that opportunity for searching everything.

While they were filling the wagons at the barn, four officers went over every part of the house, even the drawers and trunks. They were moderate in their robberies, only taking some damask towels and napkins from the drawers, and a cooked ham and a plate of rolls from the pantry. These men wore the trappings of officers!"[56]

Brig. Gen. J.E.B. Stuart, Lee's cavalry commander, had urged Lee to move on McClellan's left flank for more than week. On June 10, Lee called Stuart to his headquarters and instructed him to assemble a reconnaissance in force to examine the ground beyond and behind the Union right flank, held by the Fifth Corps. Stuart was to pay special attention to a ridgeline between the Chickahominy River and Totopotomoy Creek in order to find out whether McClellan was shifting farther to the right. Stuart suggested that instead of simply scouting the flank, he would continue on, make a complete circuit of McClellan's army, and return to Richmond via the James River shoreline.[57]

On June 12, Stuart and his command set off on their excursion. They safely rode all the way around the Army of the Potomac. Along with the rest of the Federal cavalry, most of the 6th Pennsylvania pursued Stuart's troopers. Brig. Gen. Philip St. George Cooke, Stuart's father-in-law, led the Yankee pursuit but failed miserably, much to the frustration of his men. The Confederate horse soldiers made a clean escape with almost no losses, humiliating Cooke and the Northern cavalry. "Gen. [Cooke] did not attach much importance to the [first reports of the raid] thinking it was only a foraging party, never dreaming in his listlessness that [Stuart] would have the audacity to attack him," bitterly noted Capt. Emlen Carpenter of Company E. "The whole affair was a . . . disgraceful failure on the part of Cooke to prevent it. . . . I hope he will do better next time."[58]

On June 13, fifteen hundred of Stuart's horsemen and four batteries of horse artillery fell upon two squadrons of the 5th U.S. Cavalry near Old Church. The Regulars, commanded by Capt. William B. Royall, were out searching for the enemy cavalry. "The Rebels had come in force, from three Different Directions, and surrounded a Squadron of the 5th Regulars who were on Picket at Old Church and cut them all to pieces," reported Thomas W. Smith. The Confederate horsemen surrounded Royall's squadrons and moved in for the kill. Royall called his men together, formed them in line, and charged at the Confederates to try and cut their way to safety. Royall was wounded in five places, including three saber cuts, a pistol wound, and one carbine wound, demonstrating the ferocity of the engagement. Eventually Royall recovered and returned to duty. Two-thirds of his men were captured, but the rest escaped from the enemy trap.[59]

By noon, the Lancers were in the saddle, pursuing Stuart and looking to help Royall out of his scrape. They marched all night, and only stopped to rest near Tunstall's Station on the morning of June 14. "Here we found evidence of his presence, in a general destruction of cars, wagon trains, sutler's and commissary stores, and all Government property accumulated at the Station," reported a Lancer. Stuart's horsemen attacked a Federal supply train as it pulled into the station, but the engineer fortuitously escaped with his train. Instead, the Confederates contented themselves with destroying the train depot and the supplies stored there. Advancing Federal infantry drove off the raiders. A large force of Union cavalry lit out in pursuit, with Maj. Morris and a squadron of the Lancers at their head.[60]

Spurring off, Morris spotted fresh tracks from a large body of horses and wagons. He stopped at a house and learned that a large force of enemy troopers had passed by during the night. Hot on the trail, Morris pushed on toward White House Landing, where he believed that a large force of Confederates was plundering the Federal supply depot. Still following the tracks of the Southern horses, Morris pursued them to Baltimore Cross Roads, where he received orders from Emory to continue tracking Stuart and his men. Morris pressed on with

Brigadier General J. E. B. Stuart. (Library of Congress)

his tired horses, still following the enemy horse tracks. Finally, a galloper reached Morris and instructed him to wait there for the rest of the regiment to come up. Soon Colonel Rush and the regiment spurred up. The united command advanced toward the Chickahominy River, where the men spotted tendrils of smoke rising above the river.[61]

The Southern horse soldiers constructed a temporary bridge over the rain-swollen Chickahominy. This project significantly delayed their march and allowed the Lancers to catch up to their rear guard. As the end of Stuart's column torched the bridge, the Pennsylvanians had the satisfaction of firing the only shots at Stuart's raiders during their entire excursion around McClellan's army. One of Stuart's staff officers, Maj. Heros von Borcke, recounted, "The rear guard, under Col. W. H. F. Lee, had meanwhile moved down steadily from the high ground, and defiled across the bridge."[62] "Rooney" Lee, as the colonel was known, was a Harvard classmate of Capt. James Starr of Company I of the Lancers. Starr's men were the ones to squeeze off a few shots at Stuart's fleeing column, although it is unlikely that either of the old friends realized the fraternal nature of the incident.[63]

As the hooves of the rear guard clattered off the end of the bridge, "shots resounded on the opposite bank of the stream, and Colonel Rush thundered down with his Lancers to the bank. He was exactly ten minutes too late. Stuart was over with his artillery, and the swollen stream barred the way, even if Colonel Rush thought it prudent to 'knock up against' the one thousand five hundred crack cavalry of Stuart. His men banged away at Colonel Lee, and a parting salute whizzed through the trees as the gray column slowly disappeared."[64] Capt. Emlen Carpenter noted, "the bridge over the Chickahominy had been burnt & they swam their horses. Stewart [sic] was crossing when we came up into the field. Alas we were too late—the enemy got safely onto their own territory and we only got one horse and killed one."[65]

The frustrated Pennsylvanians began marching back to camp. A disappointed Rush stopped for refreshment along the way at a house near New Kent. The owner of the house asked the weary colonel if his men had caught Stuart. Rush replied, "No, he has gone in at the back door. I only saw his rear guard as it passed the swamp."[66] Back at camp, the Lancers received credit for locating the retreating Southern column and for giving the Federals the chance to bring the withdrawing Rebels to bay. When he penned his report of this frustrating foray, Rush noted, "Great credit is due Major Morris for the prompt manner in which he found and followed the trail of the retreating rebels in the morning."[67]

The Lancers lost a couple of men captured during this expedition. Lt. Albert P. Morrow of Company B and Lt. Charles B. Davis, the acting regimental quartermaster, along with two servants, were returning from the main Federal supply depot at White House Landing and were near Old Church when they met a teamster who warned them of fighting ahead. Davis and Morrow disregarded the warning and rode out toward Old Church, and were captured by Stuart's troopers. Twenty-year-old Morrow, tall, slender, handsome, with sparkling blue eyes, was a bookish sort. The son of a schoolmaster, Morrow considered himself to be something of an expert on Shakespeare. He had enlisted in a ninety-day militia regiment in April 1861. He mustered out with the rest of his regiment in August 1861 and then enlisted in Company C of the Lancers as a sergeant in September. A few weeks later, he was promoted to first sergeant of Company L. In February 1862, he was promoted to sergeant major of Company F.[68] Morrow, who had just received his third promotion in less than six months, spent two months in Richmond's notorious Libby Prison before he and Davis were exchanged and returned to the regiment.[69]

On June 16, the Lancers marched to Cold Harbor, a crossroads near a large mill. Along with the 1st, 5th, and 6th U.S. Cavalry, the 8th Pennsylvania Cavalry, and the 1st New York Cavalry, they established a comfortable camp there, and settled down for a couple days' rest. Company A stood picket duty while the rest of the regiment relaxed and recuperated. On June 18, Rush received orders to detach four companies—B, C, G, and H. Under command of Maj. George Clymer, the two squadrons reported to Maj. Gen. George McCall, commander of the Pennsylvania Reserve Division of the Fifth Corps, which held the extreme right of the Army of the Potomac's position near Mechanicsville. This detachment encamped near Beaver Dam Station and picketed and patrolled the roads from Mechanicsville to Atlee's Station.

On June 19, two more squadrons, consisting of Companies A, D, I, and K, under command of Lt. Col. C. Ross Smith, picketed the area around Hanover Court House.[70] "We reached here about noon," recounted Thomas W. Smith, "and the 1st Squaddron were sent out on picket, and we encamped in the woods about one mile from Mechanicsville. By climbing a tree, we can see the Smoke of the enemies camp coming out of the woods on the other side of the Chickahominy. We can see their Baterys, and with a Glass we can see them digging their last Ditch. Their pickets are within three quarters of a mile of our Camp. This morning one of Company B's Pickets traded his canteen of coffee, for a canteen of whiskey, with one of the Rebel Pickets."[71]

Colonel Rush's West Point classmate, Maj. Gen. Thomas J. "Stonewall" Jackson, commanded the Confederate forces in the Shenandoah Valley of Virginia. Jackson's army had bewildered the Union forces assigned to the Valley in an aggressive campaign that spring. After his victories at Cross Keys and Port Republic, Lee ordered Jackson to come east to join the Confederate armies defending Richmond. The arrival of Jackson and his command would increase Lee's strength to nearly 92,000 men, almost evening the odds between him and the Army of the Potomac. Jackson's army, which had to detour as a result of the destruction of the railroad bridge over the Pamunkey at Hanover Court House, unexpectedly appeared in front of Smith's little outpost. The Lancers fell back to Old Church, where they reported to Stoneman. The chief of cavalry recognized the threat to the main supply depot at White House Landing, and he sent a strong column of cavalry, including the Lancers, there to protect the army's provisions.[72]

McClellan continued his slow advance until his army could see the church steeples of Richmond. The stage was now set for the series of battles that have become known as the Seven Days, which commenced on June 25 with the Battle of Fair Oaks. Robert E. Lee launched a series of ferocious attacks intended to drive McClellan's army from the gates of Richmond. Although McClellan won each of the battles, he had already decided to withdraw, and was fighting a retrograde action. He lost the initiative to Lee, and never regained it. McClellan slowly pulled back until his army reached the banks of the James River and the protection of his big naval guns.

Stuart's cavalry moved toward Cold Harbor to link up with Lee's army. Capt. William W. Blackford, Stuart's engineering officer, got his first glimpse of the Lancers that day. The reputation of the Pennsylvanians preceded them, and the Confederates were eager to find out what sort of men they were. The Lancers "had been gotten up regardless of expense," and were "called in the Northern papers 'the finest body of troops in the world,'" recalled Blackford. "And so they were, as far as their tailors could make them, and they were certainly well-mounted," he added drolly. Blackford spotted the splendid Lancers drawn up in line of battle two hundred yards away, the steel tips of their lances glistening in the bright sunshine. "I must confess I felt a little creeping of the flesh," Blackford admitted. "To think of these being run through a fellow was not at all pleasant. The appearance they presented was certainly very fine, with a tall forest of lances held erect and at the end of each, just below the head, a red pennant fluttering in the breeze."

Stuart threw a regiment into line, and the two lines of battle stared each other down from across the field. With a rousing Rebel yell, the Southern horse soldiers charged at the Lancers. "They lowered their lances to a level and started in fine style to meet us midway, but long before we reached them the gay lancers' hearts failed them and they turned to fly." With the mocking jeers of the grayclad cavalrymen echoing, Blackford and the Southern horsemen chased the Lancers for a couple of miles before giving up the pursuit. "The road was strewn with lances thrown away in their flight," he recounted, "and nothing but the fleetness of their horses saved them all from capture."[73] Their first encounter with Stuart's vaunted horsemen was anything but auspicious, and the Lancers now had a score to settle. Their chance to redeem their reputation would come.

During the great fight at Gaines's Mill on June 27, the Federal cavalry made its first mark in the war. Guarding the flank of the Fifth Corps, Cooke had a strong force of cavalry, including eight companies of Lancers, five companies of the 5th U.S. and four companies of the 1st U.S., drawn up in a mounted line of battle, protecting the Army of the Potomac's left flank. "Their fluttering pennons, their guidons, their bright sabres and lances, give an additional charm to the martial spirit of the picture," admired a member of the 1st New York Cavalry.[74] Savage Confederate attacks crushed the Union left, and Cooke ordered the 1st and 5th U.S. Cavalry to make a massed mounted charge into the teeth of the advancing Confederate infantry. Cooke hoped that his Napoleonic charge would blunt the ferocious Southern advance that threatened to sweep the Fifth Corps from the battlefield. One of Cooke's staff officers, Lt. Wesley Merritt, spurred up and unlimbered a battery there to support the cavalry charge. The battery commander asked, "Who will support me, Lieutenant?" "The Lancers," responded Merritt. The battery commander replied, "Very well: if *they* will stand by me, here goes."[75]

With three squadrons of the Lancers to protect them, the Federal guns belched canister at the advancing Confederate infantry. Before long, things got too hot for the artillerists to remain, and they withdrew, freeing some of the Philadelphians to join the charge of the Regulars.[76] The Regulars spurred ahead, their colorful guidons flapping as they galloped. "On came that splendid body of cavalry at breakneck speed," recalled a Confederate, "while our boys calmly waited until they were within seventy five yards, and then there shot out from that ragged line a continuous sheet of flame, emptying many a saddle and hurling back the charging squadron in wildest confusion."[77] The Lancers took about twenty-five casualties, including Pvt. George Pinkerton, who was killed in the charge.[78] Pvt. Charles H. Masland had his horse shot out from under him. The bullet came within a whisker of hitting Masland's leg.[79] Even though they took heavy losses, the Federal horsemen blunted the Confederate attack and permitted Porter and his Fifth Corps to escape to safety.[80]

Colonel Rush had every reason to be proud of his Lancers. "My regiment was the last to leave the left of the field, where our troops had given way, and the perfect coolness and admirable behavior of officers and men enabling me to maneuver the regiment in close column of squadrons and to take advantage of the character of the ground, I was enabled to cover my regiment and prevent a heavier loss in killed and wounded," he wrote in his report of the action. "My men and horses were worn down with previous picket and outpost duty. Some of the companies had not been unsaddled for a week."[81] When he penned his report of the fight at Gaines's Mill, Cooke praised the Lancers' role, noting, "From the first opening of the fight until its close, after 8 o'clock, the 6th Pennsylvania Cavalry behaved like veterans."[82]

Maj. Gen. Fitz-John Porter.
(Library of Congress)

Quite undeservedly, the Lancers received negative press about their performance at Gaines's Mill. Maj. Gen. Fitz-John Porter, the commander of the Fifth Corps, disingenuously blamed Cooke's charge for the failure to hold the battlefield at Gaines's Mill, or to bring off the Federal artillery and his wounded men.[83] In addition, some accused the Lancers of cowardice for breaking and running from the field after the repulse of the 5th U.S. Cavalry, and these accusations made it into the Philadelphia newspapers, much to the anger and chagrin of the Lancers. "The 5th were shot to pieces before they reached the enemy," argued an angry Lancer, who took great pains to quash those rumors in a letter to the editor of one of the Philadelphia newspapers. "Any man who was on the field and says that the Lancers ran away, or that they flinched under the heavy fire, or that they did not march off the field in good order, and slowly, and that they were not the last to leave," fumed the indignant trooper, "simply lies."[84]

A contingent of twelve wounded and sick Lancers, including Surgeon Charles M. Ellis and Pvt. Henry I. Cowan of Company K, was taken prisoner when Stuart's cavalry overran the Union field hospital near Cold Harbor. The Rebels raided the hospital's store of medicines and supplies, and carried off every man who could walk. "There seemed to be a special demand for quinine," reported Trooper Thomas A. Russell of Company A, "and Dr. Ellis had great trouble in retaining a single bottle for his own sick." The Confederates left Ellis and a few nurses behind to care for those unable to travel. The rest marched off to the misery of Richmond's Libby Prison.[85]

Sgt. Louis J. Boos of Company B stood picket duty around Cold Harbor during the first days of June. One night, while on picket, a Rebel ball hit Boos in the shoulder. He had been recuperating in the field hospital near Cold Harbor when the Confederates captured the convalescents. "The first intimation we had of capture was the driving in of our pickets immediately after which we saw the advance guard of the rebels consisting of one company of the Cobb Legion Cavalry, who riding up to our hospital with drawn sabres, pistols cocked, ready to shoot, demanded the surrender of the place," recalled

Boos. "Dr. Ellis . . . in a calm and dignified manner quickly handed over the keys of the house, whereupon they dismounted and made a rush for some 12 or 15 sabres, which were gathered together in one of the rooms, after which three or four of the rebels came into each room where the sick were, and one of them pointing a revolver at me, ordered me to collect all the arms that were in the room." Realizing that discretion was the better part of valor, Boos complied with the request. After the Southern horse soldiers secured the hospital, the prisoners signed paroles and sat listening to the infantry battle raging at Gaines's Mill. Boos was eventually exchanged and returned to duty with the regiment that fall.[86]

That night, the exhausted Lancers slept on the battlefield. "Most of the men were wearied and exhausted by hard fighting and intense excitement for two days; many being entirely without food, threw themselves at their horses' feet, and sank to sleep." They got only a little rest. About 2 a.m., the regiment formed up and moved out. "It was with great difficulty the men could be aroused from their deep sleep." The Lancers crossed the Chickahominy and then helped to destroy Woodbury's Bridge, the bridge they had used to cross the river. On June 28, Capt. Henry C. Whelan's squadron, Companies C and H, reported to Maj. Gen. Philip Kearny for headquarters duty. The various companies of the regiment had been scattered across McClellan's army. The Lancers would not serve together again as a cohesive command for some time. The practice of scattering companies of cavalry meant that no unit cohesion would develop, served as a misuse of mounted resources, and also meant that the Confederate cavalry would continue to dominate its Union counterpart for the foreseeable future.[87]

The right wing of the Army of the Potomac fell back to a position along White Oak Swamp while the Confederates attacked the Union left. On June 29, the Confederates crashed into the Army of the Potomac at Savage's Station. Capt. Robert Milligan's Company F reported to Maj. Gen. Edwin V. Sumner that day, and this small force of Lancers spent two days under severe Confederate fire. As the Confederates retreated in the face of Union pressure, "Rush's Lancers now charged them as they retreated," observed a New York infantryman, "leaving all their ground in front covered with their dead and dying. And many a poor Rebel was speared in the back before reaching the woods. There the Lancers encountered a terrible fire from the Rebel masses, and soon returned in some disorder, with their red pennons half stripped from their lances, and many spear heads broken off and lost."[88]

After several hours of severe combat, McClellan crossed White Oak Swamp and assumed a position between the swamp, Malvern Hill, and the James River. Lee unleashed a furious assault on McClellan's line at Glendale and drove McClellan back to Malvern Hill, where the Army of the Potomac could shelter under the protection of Union gunboats anchored in the James River. Companies C and H of the Lancers covered the Army of the Potomac's retreat to Malvern Hill, helping to drive stragglers along to keep up with the balance of the army as it moved across the Chickahominy.[89]

On July 1, Lee pitched into McClellan's strong position on Malvern Hill. With most of the Army of the Potomac's artillery crammed onto the slope of the hill, the Union position was nearly impregnable. McClellan repulsed attack after attack by the Confederate infantry for most of the afternoon until Lee finally broke off the engagement and withdrew. However, Lee accomplished his goal—his aggressive counter punching drove McClellan from the gates of Richmond and forced Little Mac to go on the defensive with his back against the James River. Once again, the Lancers covered the Army of the Potomac's retreat, spurring on the stragglers. An Irish infantryman had picked up a lance somewhere along the line, carrying it with him as some sort of an odd trophy. Spotting the man, a member of the 6th Pennsylvania spurred up and demanded the return of the lance. The Hibernian refused, prompting an exchange of "uncomplimentary epithets." The Irishman's companions watched in amusement, which soon turned to annoyance with the delay. One of the infantryman's German comrades, who had grown tired of waiting, finally called out, "Och, give the man his stick and come on." As a consequence, the Pennsylvanians acquired yet another derisive nickname. "After this they were called the stick, or broomstick regiment," recalled a Regular artillerist.[90]

Robert E. Lee had scored a decisive victory in the Seven Days battles. McClellan and his grand army had been repulsed from the very gates of Richmond with heavy losses. McClellan retired to Harrison's Landing to lick his wounds. John P. Kepner of Company I, who was promoted to quartermaster sergeant, recounted his hardships during the recent campaign, although he remained optimistic about the prospects of the war ending that summer. "Soldiering is quite hard enough for a private on a march and just a little more than I can possibly stand as Q.M.S," he complained. "I have killed up three horses already (horseflesh is of no account) but I have a good one now. . . . I have ridden my horse in skirmishes until he was ready to drop from exhaustion have ridden over plains and marshes from the horrid stench arising from decomposing bodies . . . have stood by my horse's head from sundown till daybreak. . . . Have starved for three days at a time and still I am not tired of soldering."

On July 6, while McClellan planned his next moves, the Lancers received a different assignment. Special Orders No. 195, issued by McClellan, provided in part, "The 6th Pennsylvania Cavalry will be organized as a corps of guides, and will by frequent reconnaissances and scouts, be kept fully instructed as to the roads and character of the county. In case of a movement, General Stoneman will send detachments from this regiment to guide the different divisions."[91] This order marked a definite change in the mission of the Lancers and was important duty for an inexperienced regiment. Two days later, Stoneman issued his own orders. "Col. Rush will see that his Regt., both officers & men, becomes thoroughly acquainted with all the country in the vicinity of this army & detail an officer and 20 men to report daily at the HdQrs of each army corps to act as guides in that corps," instructed the division commander.[92] Although their comrades still ribbed them mercilessly, the Lancers were slowly but surely gaining respect in the eyes of the army's high command.

The regiment remained in camp at Harrison's Landing on the James River until July 24, performing daily guide and scout duty. Chaplain Gracey noted, "With this exception, our stay here was devoid of all service, and the monotony of camp life in midsummer uninterrupted."[93] The men endured extreme heat and humidity and poor drinking water. The combination meant that swarms of mosquitoes descended upon their camp and plagued the Lancers for the rest of their stay on the Peninsula. The combination of the insects and the stench of their camps tormented men and animals so much that the Lancers looked forward to doing picket duty, since it got them away from the source of their suffering for a while.[94] The poor drinking water supply also caused typhoid fever to develop. Malaria, called "Chickahominy Fever" by the men, also quickly broke out across the ranks of the Army of the Potomac. A member of the Lancers noted, "Notwithstanding all our discomfort, fever, and dysentery, but few deaths occurred in the regiment, owing to the untiring efforts of the surgeons, who were unceasing in their attentions, and called to their assistance all the aid to be derived from the Sanitary and Christian Commissions." As the Lancers suffered with the mosquitoes, they daily provided five detachments of men for scouting and escort duty, breaking up the monotony of the camp routines.[95]

The saga of Pvt. William S. Riddell provides a good example of the ravages of Chickahominy Fever. Twenty-one-year-old Riddell, of Company D, stood five feet, seven inches tall. A farmer in Lycoming County by avocation, he had enlisted in Philadelphia in the fall of 1861. He fell ill the following June, and was captured when the Confederate cavalry overran the field hospital at Cold Harbor on June 28. The Confederates paroled the ill trooper, and he was taken to an army hospital at New Bridge, Virginia. Riddell suffered in the army hospital until November 24, when he finally received a discharge for disability, which indicated that he suffered from "chronic hepatitis and lumbago." Years later, long after the end of the Civil War, Riddell applied for a pension resulting from "disability of Liver and Kidney, which was contracted in front of Richmond at the Peninsula sometime in May 1862." Riddell was just one of many Lancers whose health was shattered by the ravages of the tropical diseases that afflicted them on the Peninsula that hot, steamy spring and summer.[96]

The combination of the oppressive heat, the mosquitoes, and the poor drinking water also took a terrible toll on the regiment's horses. Lt. Frank Furness of Company I had paid $360 for his two mounts in the fall of 1861. One was killed in battle, and the other, a beautiful bay mare, died in the stifling heat.[97] The War Department, which had to deal with the logistics of maintaining a huge mounted force in the field, found its resources strained to the limit as the quartermaster's office struggled to find adequate remounts to keep the cavalry in the field. These hard lessons on the importance of logistics paid dividends during 1863 and 1864, when the travails of hard campaigning took an even greater toll.

On July 15, Brig. Gen. David Birney took a squadron of the 6th Pennsylvania Cavalry on a scouting and foraging mission. With twenty "fine milk cows" in tow, the column returned to camp and settled down for several quiet weeks of rest and relaxation, broken up only by the daily detachments for scouting and escort duty. The cows were turned over to the various field hospitals for the benefit of the sick and wounded.[98] The men had a pleasant respite, with (mainly) decent food. "I see it stated in the Papers that the Soldiers, sinse they have been here get Fresh Beef 4 times per week, that they are served with Cabbage Tomattos Potatoes and other vegatables and that they get Bread instead of crackers. Now sinse we have been here, we have had fresh Beef 4 times and one time it was so stinking when we got it, that we dug a hole and burried it right away," reported Smith. "As for Vegetables, the only thing of the kind we have had sinse we were here is Potatoes and only 5 Rations of them 3 Potatoes to a Ration. Bread we have never received a loaf. Some of the Sutlers have put up ovens, and got to baking bread, they bake it into 7 oz Loves and sell it at 15 cts per Loaf."[99]

The Lancers spent their days quietly, doing routine duty. "My time has been very busily occupied since my arrival here in straightening out the company records and papers which have been severely neglected," wrote Capt. Charles E. Cadwalader on July 19. "I have just squared them and gotten them in perfect order." Cadwalader also spent his days rounding up missing men to return to his company, which had the smallest duty roster in the regiment. "The men are of the very best stuff; a plucky lot; and of work if work is to be done, go at it at the jump." Cadwalader was justifiably proud of his company, which, although small, was becoming one of the best in the regiment. The other company commanders engaged in similar activities, making sure that their commands remained combat-ready at all times.[100]

The rigors of the campaign took a toll on Colonel Rush, whose health was somewhat precarious. Rush still suffered the effects of some tropical disease contracted during the Mexican War, and arduous duty on the Virginia Peninsula played on his health. "Col. Richard Rush, of the Sixth Pennsylvania Cavalry, arrived in the city yesterday from the seat of the war," declared the *Philadelphia Inquirer* on July 17, 1862. "He will remain for a few days to recruit his health, which has become very much shattered during the terrible ordeal through which he in common with his regiment, has passed lately." The same article noted that the Lancers had suffered six men killed, six men wounded, including Maj. Morris, and one officer and sixty-three enlisted men captured, for total losses of seventy-six, during the Seven Days battles of June 27-July 2.[101]

The James River, which separated Lee and McClellan, provided the Lancers' best source of entertainment. "There all the time you can see thousands bathing and ridding themselves of a load of graybacks," reported a disgusted Sgt. Hamilton S. Ballentine, describing the inevitable infestation of lice that accompanied contemporary armies in the field. "We leave them high and dry on the sandy banks of the James River. There you could not set your foot for large piles of them and the maggots which breed in the filth.

I heard yesterday that the lice had collected around a sutler's boat and undertook to haul it to shore. Did not hear the results," he concluded wryly.[102]

As Sgt. Thomas W. Smith stood guard duty on the night of July 31, the Confederates shattered the quiet. "Abought midnight the Rebbels on the other side of the River commensed throwing shell over at us verry Rappidly," he recounted. The first shells, resembling sky rockets, whistled over the Lancers' camp, but the Rebel gunners soon got the range and shells started dropping in the camp. The muzzle flashes of the Confederate guns gave away their positions in the inky darkness. The best Yankee artillerists zeroed in on the Confederate battery and quickly chased them off into the night, at a loss of three men killed, a shattered caisson, and a lost battle flag. "We had a little fun here too last Thursday night, playing balls with the rebels across the James River," reported Sgt. Christian Geisel, "but which is rather a dangerous play."[103] The shelling of the Lancers' camp killed Pvt. John Booth of Company C. He was found lying dead in a clear space in the middle of the camp, "without the slightest apparent wound or mark upon his person." A spent artillery round lay by the body.[104]

A few days later, McClellan pushed some of his cavalry forward to try to clear his front. They drove the Confederates back for several miles, and the men of the Army of the Potomac believed that they were about to begin another general advance on Richmond. "I do not know how long we will stay here yet," observed Geisel, "but I expect we will make a forward movement before long."[105] However, McClellan had other plans. On July 30, he reported to general-in-chief Henry W. Halleck, "The Cavalry scouts are daily extending their beats & meet with less resistance." He continued, "I am very weak in Cavalry. . . . I feel the want of it very much."[106] Instead of pressing on aggressively, the Army of the Potomac would withdraw down the Peninsula in anticipation of a return to the defenses of Washington. Maj. Gen. John Pope's Army of Virginia had been operating in central Virginia, threatening Lee's left flank. Lee began shifting forces west to counter the threat. With Jackson's Corps now threatening Pope, the War Department decided to recall McClellan's army in order to protect the capital.

On the morning of August 4, the Lancers marched back to Harrison's Landing, where they camped for three days. On the 7th, leaving some behind as rear guard, the regiment embarked on ships and departed. The last remaining squadron of Lancers arrived at Fortress Monroe on August 18. By the 20th, the entire army had pulled back to the vicinity of Yorktown and Fortress Monroe. "The armey is laying verry quiet at pressent, and there is no excitement of any kind," reported Smith, "except a little Cannonading on the River now and then, or an occasional Skirmish between the Cavelry Pickets and Scouting parties."[107]

McClellan had been defeated primarily due to his own caution and unwillingness to commit his entire army to a decisive battle. On August 12, Maj. Gen. Samuel P. Heintzelman expressed the frustration felt by the Army of the Potomac. "I think the withdrawal of this army of 90,000 men a most suicidal act. As soon as the Rebels learn we are retreating, they will reinforce Jackson and he can overwhelm Pope before we can aid him," he predicted. "We could easily advance to within ten miles of their capital and 120,000 men is too large an army to be so near without a large army to oppose it." Two days later, Heintzelman continued, "I don't know when I felt so badly as at the thought of this retrograde movement. . . . When will we quit falling back after each slight advance?"[108]

McClellan had "saved" his command from the perceived threat and protected his base of operations along the James River. The entire campaign, however, could only be considered a strategic defeat since McClellan was driven back from the gates of the Confederate capital by Lee's newly christened Army of Northern Virginia. The withdrawal mystified the men. "It is my oppinion and the oppinion of all with whom I have conversed on the subject that McClellen has been Defeated and Gained a victory both at the same time," wrote Smith.

> That is he was Defeated before Richmond before the fighting commensed, and he knew it. He knew several days before the fighting commensed, from the moovements of the Enemey that they intended to attack him with an overwelming forse, and he knew that if he attempted to hold his position that his armey would overpowered by numbers and annihilated. Therefore he determined to change his position (which he commensed two days before the fighting began by Removing his stores at the White House and also his heavy siege trains) to the James River, and with the assistence of the gun boats hold his position here untill reinforsed, and there is where he gained a great victory by saving his armey from a complete rout.

Smith claimed that the men of the Army of the Potomac "fairley idollise him and are more eager to be led into battle by him than ever whenever he makes an appearance among the soldiers he is greated by cheres on every Hand."[109]

About August 15, the balance of the 6th Pennsylvania Cavalry pulled out of the area around Hampton. They remained at Fortress Monroe for more than two weeks before finally embarking and sailing to Washington. On August 29, one of the army's quartermasters reported, "Rush's regiment is still here waiting to embark. I have no transports for him. The steamers and light schooners do not return rapidly from the Potomac. Everything has been loaded as fast as it arrived here, and no time shall be lost in shipping the cavalry after the vessels arrive."[110] While the Lancers languished at Fortress Monroe, Jackson and Pope fought a bloody but indecisive battle at Cedar Mountain on August 9. Jackson then marched through Thoroughfare Gap and assumed a position along an unfinished railroad cut near the old Bull Run battlefield, inviting Pope to attack. The rest of Lee's Army of Northern Virginia was operating in the central part of the state, looking for an opportunity to destroy Pope's army. That opportunity finally presented itself at the

Second Battle of Bull Run on August 29 and 30, where Lee thrashed Pope in a brutal two-day battle that sent the defeated Federals reeling back toward the defenses of Washington.

In the interim, the Lancers ended their role in the Peninsula Campaign quietly, finally embarking on transports, sailing up the Potomac River, and joining the garrison defending Washington, D.C. They spent their days scouting and picketing, waiting for more interesting duty to come along.

The Lancers finally saw action during the Peninsula Campaign, performing well in the various missions assigned them. They participated in the combined arms expedition to Hanover Court House and in the great mounted charge of the Federal cavalry at Gaines's Mill. They suffered their first casualties in the field, and felt the pain of seeing their brother horse soldiers die on the battlefield. They also faced significant physical obstacles during the campaign. The Peninsula offered difficult cavalry terrain—the narrow and sandy finger of land turned into impenetrable mud when wet. Thick forests and wide rivers split the peninsula, hemming in the mounted forces of McClellan's army. Add the stifling humidity and heat of the Virginia summer, not to mention the swarms of malarial mosquitoes, and the burden grew even heavier. "These conditions made cavalry operations in this region affairs of squadrons," observed Col. William Woods Averell of the 3rd Pennsylvania Cavalry.[111]

No longer green, the Lancers stood poised to play a significant role in the developing mounted arm of the Army of the Potomac, and they would not have long to wait. However, they needed a leader with a better understanding of the role of volunteer cavalry to take command of the army and make more effective use of their unique talents. In the wake of Pope's defeat at Second Manassas, the emboldened Confederates took the war to the North. Within a few days, Robert E. Lee's first great invasion of the North was under way. Charged with defending Washington from capture, the remnants of Pope's shattered army and McClellan's Army of the Potomac streamed into the defenses of Washington. Lee's army moved off into central Maryland, and McClellan, commanding the Federal forces assigned to the defense of the Federal capital, cautiously followed.

Chapter Four

THE MARYLAND AND FREDERICKSBURG CAMPAIGNS OF 1862

A FTER HIS STUNNING VICTORY OVER Pope's Army of Virginia at Second Bull Run, Robert E. Lee led his Army of Northern Virginia into the North. Panic spread as Pope's demoralized and beaten army limped and straggled into the defenses of Washington, D.C., after suffering three major defeats at the hands of the Confederates in just over thirty days. The Lancers came north from Hampton and rejoined the Army of the Potomac in the outskirts of Washington, D.C., where they awaited the chance to see action once again. The battered remnants of the Army of Virginia had to be integrated into the structure of the Army of the Potomac, and it had to happen quickly—Lee's Army of Northern Virginia was on the move toward the Potomac River.

While the Lancers rested, they took up a position on the familiar grounds of Meridian Hill. "Troops are arriving here all day yesterday and today. Burnsides troops are all here and Popes have been coming all day, and still they come," reported Sgt. Thomas W. Smith. "I dont know what it means, but I do wish that Little Mac was commander in chief. I believe that Popes armey are completely Demoralised, that Break and Run in every Battle they get into."[1] Smith got his wish. George McClellan took command of all Union forces assigned to the defense of the nation's capital. "Today we are now within a few miles of the Rebel Army where we will have a lovely fight unless the Rebs retreat," declared Sgt. Hamilton Ballentine of Company K on September 5. "I hope they will not until we get a fair shake at them."[2]

On September 7, two companies of the 6th Pennsylvania Cavalry, B and G, went to serve as headquarters guard for Maj. Gen. William B. Franklin's infantry corps. Company I joined them a few days later. The balance of the regiment reported to the defenses of the capital and was brigaded with the 4th Pennsylvania Cavalry. "We have got back to our old starting place," observed a member of Company C. "I think that we will soon get home for the rebles are striking for Penna as fast as they can but I guess they will meet with a warm reception before they get in old Penna."[3] Commanded by Colonel Rush, the small Third Brigade joined the Army of the Potomac's newly formed cavalry division, commanded by Brig. Gen. Alfred Pleasonton.[4] The regimental historian of the Lancers later observed that during this period, "Washington City was never in such a whirl of excitement."[5] By September 5, the Young Napoleon knew that the Confederates were advancing into Maryland. On the 6th, McClellan's pursuit began.

The Army of the Potomac followed Lee into western Maryland. "Last Sunday Evening at 6 o'clock, while in Camp on 7th St near Washington, we got orders to march with 4 days Rationes in our Haversacks and to leave all Sick and Sickly men behind, who were not able to stand an active and hard Campaign," recounted Smith. "Well we were soon on the Road, and by 11 o'clock we encamped haveing made 12 miles. On Monday morning we started again at Daylight and marched to Rockville and there encamped."[6]

When the Lancers broke camp, they left their esteemed regimental surgeon, Dr. William Moss, with the sick and dismounted recruits, tending to their needs. On October 4, Moss was appointed Assistant Surgeon, United States Volunteers, and resigned his commission with the Lancers. In December, he was promoted to Surgeon, United States Volunteers, and was assigned as Assistant Curator of the United States Army Medical Museum in Washington, D.C. He became a permanent member of a board for the examination of candidates for Assistant United States Surgeon and United States Surgeon, an important duty that he continued until the end of the war.[7] Dr. John B. Coover replaced Moss as the regimental surgeon of the Lancers.[8]

The Army of the Potomac moved out from the ring of forts surrounding Washington and marched into Maryland, cautiously feeling for Lee's Army of Northern Virginia. Pleasonton's cavalry had a couple of minor skirmishes on September 9 and 10 as the opposing horsemen jousted for position, each trying to keep the other from discovering the location of their respective armies. The Lancers did not participate in either of those skirmishes; instead, they accompanied the main army's northern advance.

Arriving near Frederick, McClellan profited from a remarkable stroke of good fortune. On September 13, two soldiers of the 27th Indiana Infantry spotted a small bundle lying in the grass. Inside, they found an official-looking document that turned out to be a copy of Robert E. Lee's Special Orders 191, which spelled out the disposition of the entire Army of Northern Virginia. It was inauspiciously wrapped around two cigars. The document was passed up the chain of command to McClellan, who after reading it proclaimed, "Here is a paper with which if I cannot whip Bobbie Lee, I will be willing to go home." The next day, Little Mac set the Army of the Potomac into motion, moving across Maryland toward Harpers Ferry and a date with destiny.[9]

As the army advanced, Pleasonton realized that he needed good intelligence on the Confederate movements. On September 12, he detached seven companies of Lancers and sent them to scout Jefferson Gap through the Catoctin Mountains. With Colonel Rush in command of a demi-brigade, Lt. Col. C. Ross Smith commanded the expedition, which returned to Frederick without finding the enemy. The next day, Col. Rush led the regiment on a second reconnaissance. A detachment of three companies of Lancers, commanded by eighteen-year-old Lt. Charles L. Leiper, drove off a large force of dismounted Confederate cavalry near Frederick. However, the enemy's rear guard, a contingent of the 2nd Virginia Cavalry, turned and charged the Lancers, temporarily blunting their pursuit.[10] Chaplain Gracey noted, "Although largely outnumbering his small force, [Rush] drove them in confusion, and made some prisoners. The enemy were armed with carbines, and though our men had only the lance and their pistols, by one determined charge, they succeeded in dislodging the enemy, who fled in dismay."[11]

Pursuing, the Lancers ran into a stronger force of Confederate cavalry and Capt. Roger P. Chew's battery of horse artillery, which opened on the advancing Federal horse soldiers. The Pennsylvanians quickly realized that their lances were no match for Southern carbines and cannons, prompting Rush to send for reinforcements from Col. Harrison S. Fairchild's Ninth Corps infantry brigade. Fairchild sent the 9th New York Infantry, known as Hawkins's Zouaves, to Rush's aid. As the Zouaves approached, they saw "in the fields confronting the edge of the woods that crowned the ridge, the scattered line of Rush's Lancers, their bright red pennons fluttering gaily from their spear heads."[12] The New Yorkers deployed in line of battle, reinforcing the Lancers. Munford's outnumbered Confederates pulled back into the gap, contesting the advance. Rush rode up to Colonel Fairchild and asked him to commit additional troops. Fairchild called up two companies of the 103rd New York Infantry, who took a flanking position and cleared the gap. Four additional companies of the 103rd New York then reinforced the Lancers. Munford's horsemen and Chew's gunners retreated toward Middletown.[13]

Capt. James Hazeltine's squadron of Lancers chased Chew's cannoneers and some of Munford's troopers.[14] The Lancers pursued aggressively, driving Munford's Virginians back across Catoctin Creek and Broad Run. Munford dispatched a handful of troopers of the 2nd Virginia Cavalry, commanded by Capt. Thomas B. Holland, to contest the pursuit. Company F of the Lancers briefly skirmished with the Virginians near Burkittsville. Munford deployed Chew's guns in the streets of the town, covering Holland's subsequent retreat in the face of the Lancers.

Far from their base of operations, uncertain of the strength of the force in front of them, and with no prospect of reinforcement, Rush called off the pursuit, and the Lancers headed back toward Jefferson. They had done exceptionally well against Munford's veterans and made a lasting impression on the Confederates.[15] The Yankee cavalry "is getting bold, adventurous, mighty, and numerous in these latter days," commented one of Chew's artillerists in his diary that night.[16]

The following day, September 14, the Army of the Potomac pushed its way through Crampton's, Fox's, and Turner's Gaps in South Mountain, opening the route to Harpers Ferry and Hagerstown. The three companies of Lancers attached to Maj. Gen. William B. Franklin's Sixth Corps headquarters scouted while the fighting for Crampton's Gap raged, and they were the only members of the 6th Pennsylvania Cavalry to engage during the Battle of South Mountain. The rest of the Lancers watched the battle unfold in front of them. Enemy artillery shells fell on their lines while they waited for orders to join the fray.[17] "We passed on through Middletown, and saw evidences of the enemy's hatred in the destruction of the property of Union citizens," observed Chaplain Gracey.[18] The Army of the Potomac surged through the South Mountain gaps toward a meeting with Lee's army along the banks of the Antietam Creek near the small town of Sharpsburg.

In the meantime, the Lancers beheld the cost of war when they marched over the South Mountain battlefield the day after the bloody struggle for the critical passes. Capt. Robert Milligan declared: "This was the first time I had ever seen a battlefield the day after the fight: it was a horrible, disgusting sight to look upon."[19] Finally alerted to the peril in front of him, Robert E. Lee began pulling the scattered elements of his army together near Sharpsburg. By September 16, McClellan had his army poised to attack Lee, and did so at daybreak the next morning. The great battle of Antietam raged on September 17, the bloodiest day of the American Civil War. McClellan's army launched a series of disjointed and largely unsuccessful attacks against Lee's vastly outnumbered forces, pinned between the Antietam Creek and the Potomac River. Three stone bridges over Antietam Creek played prominent roles in the battle.

Franklin's Sixth Corps supported attacks in the East Woods. The corps was not heavily engaged in the fighting, but as the regimental historian of the Lancers noted, "Companies 'B,' 'G,' and 'I' of our regiment, were with General Franklin on this part of the field, and were greatly exposed during all the afternoon."[20] The balance of the regiment spent most of the day supporting four batteries of Federal horse artillery assigned to the Fifth Corps. The batteries had been pushed forward to a vulnerable position on the west shore of Antietam Creek, exposing the gunners and the Lancers to a heavy fire. "Our whole Corps was here assembled, at least the enormous number of troops appeared to indicate it," recalled an officer of the Fifth Corps. "The sight was certainly a martial one, as massed on the slopes of the hill sides, Fitz John Porter's magnificent Corps . . . lay all day long ready to be called into battle. Back of this mass, Rush's Lancers, with their long spears and red pennants, added picturesqueness to the scene."[21]

Capt. John C. Tidball, commander of the Federal horse artillery, was critical of such tactics. "The employment of these batteries alone with cavalry is a dangerous experiment and will most probably lead sooner or later to the loss of guns, but cavalry is not armed properly for the support of batteries, which without support are of themselves helpless," he wrote. Instead of being supported by troopers armed with lances, Tidball recommended that the horse soldiers instead be properly armed with rifles and carbines, and that they fight as infantry, using their horses only for locomotion.[22] Tidball, who had a long and successful career in the Regular Army, went on to command all of the Army of the Potomac's horse artillery in 1863.

Regardless, McClellan should have sent his mounted forces to guard the Army of the Potomac's flanks. Had McClellan used the cavalry to picket the approaches to the battlefield at Antietam, his horse soldiers might have detected the approach of Hill's Light Division, and might have delayed them long enough to permit Burnside to shatter the Confederate right. The principal mission of cavalry was scouting and screening, not sup-

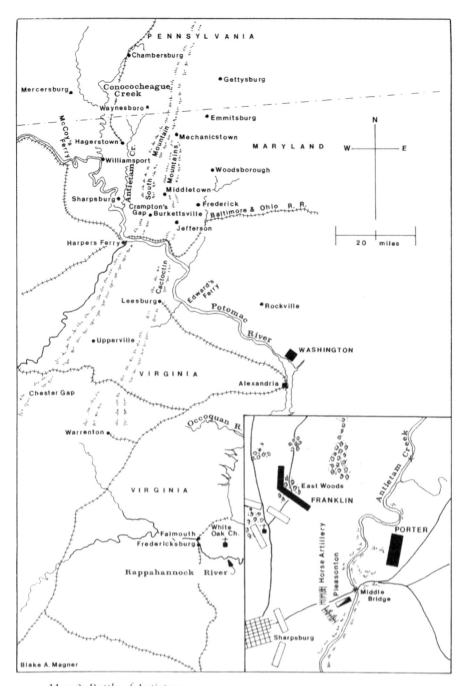

Map 2. Battle of Antietam.

porting batteries, and, once again, McClellan had made poor use of his mounted forces. Those poor dispositions probably kept the Army of the Potomac from scoring a decisive victory at Antietam, a victory that could have ended the war.

The Lancers also participated in a brigade-sized charge that took the Middle Bridge over the Antietam. "We made a rather desperate charge across the Antietam Bridge," recalled an officer of the 6th Pennsylvania a few days after the battle.[23] Under heavy fire from Confederate artillery, the Lancers "dashed across at full gallop through a terrible fire…and drove the rebel batteries from their position."[24] Col. James H. Childs, of the 4th Pennsylvania Cavalry, was killed during the action by a solid artillery shot that all but eviscerated him. Capt. Robert Milligan observed that the Lancers "made a handsome charge with three other Cavalry Regiments across the stone bridge on the left centre of our position, to support our advanced batteries, and were under a heavy artillery fire for 7 hours."[25]

Capt. Charles Francis Adams, Jr., of the 1st Massachusetts Cavalry, who also charged across the Middle Bridge, found the situation distressing as Confederate artillery shells fell on the exposed Federal cavalrymen and artillerists. So relentless was the crash of artillery fire that it soon grew monotonous. "I was very tired," remembered Adams, "the noise was deadening; gradually it had on me a lulling effect; and so I dropped quietly asleep—asleep in the height of battle and between the contending armies!"[26] Once again, the Federal cavalry had not been well-used that morning. After instructing Pleasonton not to expose the horse artillery batteries unnecessarily any longer, McClellan then asked the cavalryman, "Can you do any good by a cavalry charge?" Wisely, Pleasonton deflected the question and asked for additional infantry to support the guns, because he would not be able to support them properly if the cavalry made another charge. McClellan did not suggest any more rash action on the part of his cavalry, instead holding them out of the battle altogether.[27]

The Lancers suffered a few casualties in the morning charge on the bridge and lost several horses. They then assumed a position on the west bank of Antietam Creek, under the shelter of a hill, a stone barn, and a mill that overlooked the bridge. The Lancers spent most of the rest of the day in reserve guarding the bridge. That afternoon, when it looked like the Army of the Potomac might carry the day, Confederate Maj. Gen. A. P. Hill's Light Division completed a seventeen-mile-long forced march from Harpers Ferry just in the nick of time. Hill's division used an unpicketed road and had crashed into Burnside's flank, driving his Ninth Corps back from the streets of Sharpsburg. The Army of the Potomac did not detect the approach of the Light Division, and did nothing to protect Burnside's exposed flank. The day's fighting sputtered out not long after Burnside's repulse, and the exhausted Lancers camped near their bridge for the night. The men marveled at the sights they had seen that day. "From the minute I got on the field every minute was engaged until nearly 12 o'clock at night and by the time I got there again everything of any consequence had been carried off," complained Sgt. Hamilton S.

Ballentine of Company K, whose horse was killed in the charge on Middle Bridge. "I do not even want to think of that bloody battle."[28] Although McClellan had not used his cavalry well that day, his army still carried the bloodiest single day of the war.

The two armies spent September 18 licking their wounds and staring at each other, each waiting for the other to launch an attack that never came. Finally, on the 19th, Lee pulled his battered army back across the Potomac to the safety of Virginia. Two days later, the Sixth Corps marched to the important river crossing at Williamsport, Maryland, where it joined Maj. Gen. Darius N. Couch's division. Company I of the Lancers stayed with Couch's command. The Army of the Potomac established its camp near the Antietam battlefield and did not follow Lee's army into Virginia. McClellan's army remained inactive until pressure from Washington finally forced him to act. However, the cavalry remained diligent, scouting the countryside. "I have been 5 days out of every 7 in my saddle from 8 to 10 hours a day," reported Captain Milligan on October 7.[29]

In the interim, new recruits joined the regiment, and sick and wounded men, such as Pvt. Henry I. Cowan of Company K, who had been ill since before the Seven Days, returned to duty, thereby bolstering the strength of the unit before it took the field again. The regiment's size was to be increased from ten companies to the standard twelve companies of 101 men each. In the meantime, the Lancers were performing provost duty at Hagerstown, Maryland, with Major Morris in command.[30]

After his army withdrew into Virginia, Robert E. Lee knew that he lacked solid intelligence about the dispositions of the Army of the Potomac, as well as McClellan's intentions. After consulting with Stonewall Jackson, Lee decided to send Stuart off on another ride around McClellan. He instructed Stuart to make a deep penetration into Pennsylvania to study and disrupt Union lines of communications. North of Chambersburg, a strategic railroad crossed a branch of the Conococheague Creek. This railroad was one of McClellan's critical lines of supply for his railhead at Hagerstown, Maryland, and the destruction of this bridge would force McClellan to rely exclusively upon the severely taxed Baltimore & Ohio Railroad, perhaps crippling the Union war effort in the east. Stuart's objectives would be the demolition of the bridge, to strip south-central Pennsylvania of horses for the use of the Army of Northern Virginia, pin down McClellan's precise troop dispositions, and divine McClellan's intentions.[31]

Stuart and eighteen hundred select Confederate cavalry set off on their second ride around McClellan's army on October 10. "They went right through the enemy's lines a distance of 125 miles or so, and back again to someplace in close proximity to large bodies of their forces, [then] recrossed the river in open day without the loss of a single man," marveled an officer of the 2nd South Carolina Cavalry. "They made the longest of marches on record in one day. They traveled 94 miles. The brought back about 1,500 or 2,000 horses taken in Pa. and also pistols, clothing, etc. and destroyed perhaps $300,000 or $400,000 worth stores."[32]

The grayclad horsemen crossed the Potomac River at McCoy's Ferry, captured the pickets, and pushed into Maryland. Word of the raid did not reach McClellan for several hours, meaning that Stuart's force got a significant head start. McClellan gathered a scratch force of about one thousand Federal cavalrymen and a battery of horse artillery to pursue Stuart. Colonel Rush commanded this force, consisting of the 6th Pennsylvania Cavalry, the 1st Maine Cavalry, the 1st Regiment of Potomac Home Brigade Cavalry (a Maryland unit), the 5th Connecticut Infantry, the 29th Ohio Infantry, and a battery of New York artillery. The second ride around McClellan proved almost as embarrassing to the Federals as the first ride on the Peninsula.

When Stuart moved out on October 10, the Lancers were camped near Frederick. By the time word reached Colonel Rush of the gray cavalier's movement, the Confederates had already passed through Mercersburg and were marching on to Chambersburg, Pennsylvania. Stuart's troopers' efforts to destroy the iron bridge across the Conococheague failed, but they had wreaked havoc in the town, taking horses and emptying the coffers of the local bank.[33] Brig. Gen. John Buford, the Army of the Potomac's chief of cavalry, instructed Colonel Rush to patrol all roads to the north of Frederick. A company of twenty-five Lancers, under the command of Capt. Charles Cadwalader, indeed located the Confederate force. But as they watched them ride by, Cadwalader and Sgt. Archer Maris observed only that they were wearing blue uniforms. Believing that they were Union troopers, Cadwalader asked what regiment they were. "Stuart's cavalry," was the unexpected response. The captain quickly realized that his little force faced a good chance of making a trip to Richmond as prisoners of war unless he did something clever very quickly. Mustering a careless tone, Cadwalader replied, "I know, but what regiment are you?"

The grayclad trooper answered, but the captain's question raised his suspicions. He carefully eyed Cadwalader in the gathering darkness. As a relieved Cadwalader was about to move on, the Southerner cried out, "Hallo! You're a Yankee soldier, aren't you?"

Cadwalader snapped, "What in hell are you talking about? Don't you know the difference between a Yankee and a Confederate soldier?" Rattled, the Southerner gave his company and regiment and returned to his place in line. Cadwalader spurred off to report his findings to headquarters. "Only darkness & good luck got them out of the scrape," recorded an observer.[34]

With Cadwalader's intelligence in hand, Colonel Rush set out to try to intercept Stuart with less than three hundred troopers. He dispatched four companies of Lancers, numbering about one hundred forty additional troopers, off toward Emmitsburg and Gettysburg. They found no sign of the Confederate cavalry until reaching Emmitsburg, just south of the Mason-Dixon Line.[35]

On October 11, Rush's horse soldiers briefly engaged Stuart's horsemen near Gettysburg, and a large contingent of the regiment was nearly captured. Had Rush's small command arrived a few minutes later, the Confederates probably would have bagged them all.[36] Stuart's advance guard chased off the earlier arrivals as the main Confederate column entered the town.[37] As the Lancers advanced toward Gettysburg,

Cpl. John Anders of Company D dismounted and entered the town of Woodsborough alone and on foot. In disguise, he watched the Confederate column march past, gathering information from his observations and from discussions with the passing Southerners. The Confederates found Anders's conduct suspicious and briefly detained him. Anders fortuitously escaped, made his way back to Colonel Rush, and reported his findings. Rush praised Anders's performance, as well as that of Pvt. John Dougherty of Company D, who had boldly dashed through Emmitsburg while the Confederates occupied the town, carrying a message through to one of the Federal columns near Gettysburg.[38]

Soon after dark, an officer of the 1st Virginia Cavalry captured a courier carrying messages from Rush to the Lancers. Stuart was considering a dash into Frederick, but this intelligence caused Stuart to change his plans. "From him and his papers Stuart learned that the enemy was still unaware of his locality, although using every means to intercept him," recalled one of Stuart's staff officers, "and that General Pleasonton, with eight hundred men, was rapidly approaching Mechanicstown, only four miles from his line of march." Stuart altered his route to the east, but not before one of the vigilant scouting parties of the Lancers spotted the grayclad column near Waynesboro, Pennsylvania.[39] "We came up with Gen. Stuart's rear guard they numbering about 3000," recounted Pvt. Henry Cowan. "We were obliged to fall back until we were joined by Gen. Pleasonton with a brigade of cavalry and several pieces of artillery." After a skirmish between Pleasonton's command and the Southern raiders, the Confederates made it back to safety near Leesburg, Virginia, after marching nearly eighty miles through hostile territory in just over twenty-seven hours. Once again, Stuart had humiliated and demoralized the Federal cavalry by riding around the Union army. Cowan complained, "I hope that the next time they cross the river they will come in force enough to make a stand and give us some chance to try them in battle."[40] Cowan, of course, had no way of knowing it, but he would get his wish just nine months later.

The Lancers captured only one prisoner on the expedition, Pvt. John Scott of the 1st Virginia Cavalry, but that prisoner provided Colonel Rush with good intelligence regarding the size and disposition of Stuart's raiders. Scott, "a very intelligent young man," disclosed to Rush the make-up of Stuart's force, and reported that the Confederates were to cross back into Virginia via Edward's Ferry, near Leesburg. Rush then turned the prisoner over to the provost marshal in Frederick.[41] On October 11, about 150 of the Lancers, marching north toward Gettysburg, passed through Emmitsburg just an hour before the main body of Stuart's force, narrowly escaping being gobbled up by the Confederate raiders en masse. The information carried by the captured courier provided Stuart with positive intelligence that Rush's detachment in Gettysburg did not know the precise whereabouts of the Confederate forces and that the Federals were doing everything in their power to prevent him from reaching and crossing the Potomac. Rush's efforts failed, and Stuart's column slipped back across to the safety of Virginia on October 12.[42]

"I regret very much that this second raid has been so successfully accomplished by Stuart's cavalry," wrote Rush, "but, with the small and crippled force at my disposal near [Frederick] (but seven companies, of about 275 men), it has been impossible for me to do more than I have done to check this unfortunate raid." He suffered no casualties in his pursuit of Stuart's bold raiders.[43] In spite of the failure to block Stuart's route of march, Buford praised Rush's effort, noting that "you are doing admirably."[44]

The Lancers returned to their camp in Frederick on the night of October 13. The pursuit had taken its toll on the regiment's horses. The regiment required refitting, both of horses and equipment. "We have very good clothes and there are plenty here for us to draw," wrote Sergeant Ballentine. "I have not drawn any clothes except for some shirts and socks. I have plenty of everything. My clothing bill is now $20 more than the government allows which will be taken out of my next month's pay."[45] While their efforts to refit continued, the Lancers performed daily scouting and picketing duty in the vicinity of Frederick for almost two weeks until McClellan finally crossed the Potomac River on October 26. "Nothing has been seen of the of the Rebels in this neighborhood since I wrote last," reported Private Cowan, "although the inhabitants do not feel quite safe."[46]

When the 6th Pennsylvania Cavalry marched from Camp Meigs in the fall of 1861, it consisted of ten companies. The following fall, the War Department directed that all regiments of cavalry should have twelve companies rather than ten. On October 14, 1862, nineteen-year-old Lt. Charles L. Leiper of Chester, along with several other officers and noncommissioned officers, returned to Philadelphia to recruit two more companies to fill the regiment's ranks. Leiper opened a recruiting office at the corner of Eighth and Chestnut Streets, and quickly raised Companies L and M. Leiper was promoted to captain and took command of Company L. Lt. J. Hinckley Clark was also promoted and assumed command of Company M.[47] Lt. Charles Brinton Coxe, a mere nineteen years old, was assigned to Company M. Coxe was a cousin of General McClellan and came from one of Philadelphia's wealthiest families. He soon proved his mettle on the field of battle and advanced rapidly. The new squadron joined the regiment in time to move out with the rest of the Army of the Potomac.

By November 2, the Lancers reached Upperville, Virginia. That day, as they marched, Companies B, G, and I were relieved of duty at General Franklin's headquarters and returned to the regiment. Maj. Hazeltine's squadron, Companies E and F, and Capt. Frederic C. Newhall's Company K took their place as the Sixth Corps headquarters escort.[48] By November 5, the Army of the Potomac's cavalry was fanned out across the Loudoun Valley near Chester Gap. Two days later, the entire army concentrated around Warrenton.

Maj. Gen. George G. Meade of Philadelphia commanded the Army of the Potomac's Pennsylvania Reserve Division. When Hooker was wounded at Antietam, Meade temporarily assumed command of the First Corps. General Meade's young son George wanted to join the cavalry, much to his mother's consternation. General Meade tried to

calm her fears, writing, "He will have a comparatively pleasant time." The general quoted a captured letter that suggested that the cavalry was
the way to go, as there would be little chance of a
young man being killed in action. "We have not
lost over a dozen cavalry officers since the war
began," concluded the general.[49] This reasoning
prevailed, and young George received a commission in the Lancers as a lieutenant, and then
joined the regiment in the field.

A few weeks later, George visited his father.
"The more I see of the regiment, the better satisfied I am with George's being in it," reported the
general to his worried wife. "The officers, as a
body, are very much superior to any others
(except the regulars), and there is a tone, altogether, which is very marked and gratifying."

Lt. George Meade. (USAMHI)

General Meade pointed out that the regiment had been detailed to serve with the Sixth
Corps, and noted, "This they do not like, because it cuts them off in a measure from
chances of distinction."[50]

By then, the Army of the Potomac had a new commander, Maj. Gen. Ambrose E.
Burnside, who had replaced McClellan on November 8. "I suppose there was a great
deal of excitement about Gen McClellan's removal," wrote Capt. Emlen Carpenter, "it
was pending for a long time and was so much talked about that the idea became familiar,
and when it came, surprised the majority of us less than one might have supposed."[51]
The men remained loyal to McClellan. "I suppose you have heard of Gen. McClelland's
being relieved of his command. That was the worst thing they could do," declared
Ballentine. "Just when the Army was pushing on to Richmond with good progress. Now
we are at a standstill when by this time we might be at our journey's end. If my doubts
prove true this will be means of breaking up the Army." Ballentine observed that the
army's morale was low, and that the men were upset at the relief of their beloved army
commander. "I would rather suffer such privations if only we were pushing on. I think
there are as many abolitionists and politicians at home trying to have the war prolonged
until they have accomplished their own ends as there are poor soldiers in the field suffering every kind of hardship, breaking down their constitutions trying to preserve the
Old Constitution which gives peace and protection to all."[52]

Burnside, an affable West Pointer from Rhode Island, reorganized the army into
three Grand Divisions of two corps each. The new army commander decided to assault
Richmond by way of Fredericksburg, and the entire Army of the Potomac shifted its base
of operations there. The army's advance was largely uncontested, but Burnside found no

equipment for bridging the Rappahannock River at Fredericksburg, forcing him to wait for the needed pontoons. In the meantime, the Rappahannock rose and grew too swollen to ford. The delay permitted the Army of Northern Virginia to assume a formidable defensive position along high ground to the south and west of the town. The Lancers did not accompany the Army of the Potomac on its advance. "We are now almost in the rear of our army and hardly know what is going on in front," reported Cpl. Christian Geisel.[53] They did little of note as they waited. A typical day included two scouting parties to guard against guerrillas.[54] As late as December 3, the regiment languished back in Frederick, awaiting its next assignment.[55]

While Burnside waited for his pontoons to arrive, Companies A, C, D, H, and I of the Lancers, commanded by Lt. Col. C. Ross Smith, finally received orders to march from Frederick to join the army at Fredericksburg. After an eight-day journey that carried them through the defenses of Washington, these five companies arrived at Maj. Gen. William B. Franklin's headquarters at Falmouth on December 7. They joined the men of Company K, who were already there serving as Franklin's bodyguard and carrying dispatches up and down the line.[56] Sergeant Ballentine of Company K found the orderly duty dull. "My duty is not hard but it is confining. I cannot leave [Franklin's] quarters for 10 minutes night or day," he wrote to his brother on November 24, "I have to [look] after the men and horses, draw their feed and rations and keep some of them saddled up all the time. I have to get up 5 or 6 times some nights but all is nothing but a play."[57]

The men knew that a major battle loomed. "Tomorrow we march to battle, and it will be the last march for many of us," wrote Lt. Albert P. Morrow of Company C to his sweetheart a couple of days later. "If I fall (and I've a strange presentiment that I shall), think kindly of me, forget my faults I know that I have many." The men recognized that the long delay favored the enemy, who used the opportunity to build an almost impregnable defensive position on the heights overlooking the city. "I'm afraid our army will be whipped," continued Morrow, "I've no confidence at all in our leaders."[58] Sergeant Ballentine echoed a similar note. "I think this campaign is going to kill more men than were killed in the battle of Antietam," he wrote on December 8. "Yesterday I heard that about 150 men had frozen to death the night before last in this corps. I do believe that it is impossible to keep up a moving campaign this winter if this news is true. It will be inhuman. We cannot go farther now without having a fight."[59]

On the 11th, Franklin sent Company A, under command of Lt. Thomas W. Neill, out to picket the Rappahannock. They held this post until infantry relieved them at midnight on the 12th. Neill's little command returned to camp about 2 a.m., and got only a couple of hours of sleep. That day, the long-overdue pontoons were finally put in place, as the engineers dodged heavy Confederate sharpshooter fire and completed their task, and the bridges were ready to be used. By 4:30 that morning, the regiment was in the saddle, and the entire Army of the Potomac was on the move, finally ready to cross the Rappahannock. The Lancers escorted the Left Grand Division to the lower bridge across

View of Fredericksburg at the time of the battle. (Library of Congress)

the river, about two miles below Fredericksburg. The entire regiment dismounted and stood to horse in a skirmish line until 5:00 that afternoon, when they bivouacked for the night.[60]

Franklin's Left Grand Division crossed the river at daylight and assaulted the strong Confederate positions on the heights overlooking the Rappahannock. The Lancers crossed about 9 o'clock. The regiment spent the day guarding the bridge, acting as provost guard, and herding prisoners of war. They also had a prime view of the carnage playing out in the fields in front of them. "Before long the field was covered with the dead and wounded until night did our men stand at the mouth of the enemy's cannon he being almost entirely under cover of woods," recounted Henry Cowan.[61] The Lancers did not join Burnside's massive assault although they were exposed to artillery fire the entire day.[62] General Meade noted that George's "regiment was over here nearly all the time, as there was no use for cavalry."[63] After a day of uncoordinated, fruitless, bloody frontal infantry assaults, night finally brought a close to the day's fighting.

At least one of the Lancers, however, participated in the combat. Lt. Albert Morrow was in the thick of the fight that day. "I was acting aide-de-camp to Genl Franklin and was sent out to the front to Genl Mead just as the ball opened," he reported. "An intimate friend of mine on his staff was killed while I was talking to him, and I was foolish enough to wish to share his fate." Brig. Gen. George D. Bayard, the dashing and talented commander of the Union horsemen, was at Franklin's headquarters when a shell exploded nearby, tearing into the cavalryman's hip. Lieutenant Morrow was standing only a foot away when the shell exploded, and he barely escaped injury. His shoulder was badly bruised, though, when his horse fell on top of him while he tried to rally some panicked troops nearby.[64] Bayard died the next day, and with him died some of the spirit of the

Army of the Potomac's cavalry. The Army of the Potomac suffered more than 12,000 casualties at Fredericksburg, but only eight in the mounted arm.[65]

The Lancers spent the night on the battlefield huddling for warmth amidst falling sleet. Burnside spent the 14th demonstrating along the line, and pulled back across the Rappahannock under the cover of darkness on the night of December 15. The Lancers spent those two days burying the dead and carrying off the wounded, a thoroughly unpleasant task that took an emotional toll on the cavalrymen.[66] The exhausted and demoralized regiment then settled into its winter camp near Falmouth. "We are suffering very much with cold and hunger. The roads are in such a wretched condition that we can't transport supplies and we can't buy a single article in this miserable poverty-stricken country," complained Morrow.[67] The Lancers expected to establish their winter camp in Alexandria, but were disappointed to learn that they would instead remain at Falmouth, three miles outside of Fredericksburg, for the winter.

Colonel Rush asked Lt. Frank H. Furness of Company I to apply his ample talents to design and construct a comfortable winter camp for the regiment. Furness subsequently laid out a large, spacious camp in a dense stand of woods, "fitted up in the most beautiful camp style. The company streets were each a hundred feet in width, with officers' quarters at the head of each, and about thirty feet from the first company quarters. Huts were built of hewn logs, the roof being formed of shelter tents. They were very comfortable and attractive in appearance. . . . This camp was facetiously called by some, the 'Camp of Magnificent Distances.'"[68]

Their stay in this comfortable camp was short lived. On December 18, part of Company A went to serve with General Franklin's chief engineer. Another company stood picket duty along the river, with a corporal's picket post located in every house below Falmouth for four miles. A squadron, consisting of Companies E and I, went to serve as Burnside's escort at the Army of the Potomac's headquarters. Another squadron escorted Maj. Gen. John F. Reynolds, a company was assigned to Maj. Gen. John Newton, three companies remained with Franklin, and the balance of the regiment settled into its winter doldrums near White Oak Church.[69]

A week later, Lieutenant Colonel Smith received permission to use the Lancers on provost duty, and all companies but those assigned to General Franklin were relieved of headquarters duty. On the 24th, Colonel Rush arrived with Companies B and G, which had remained in Frederick on detached duty. Their march proved eventful. On December 18, Brig. Gen. Wade Hampton's Confederate cavalry captured a train of army wagons and a boat on the Occoquan River. The next day, the Rebels destroyed part of the boat but did not move the wagon train out. On the morning of the 19th, Colonel Rush, whose two companies were escorting a new regiment, the 17th Pennsylvania Cavalry, on its way to join the Army of the Potomac, came under fire when his column approached Occoquan. While staring intently at a map, Rush located a ford two and a half miles upstream from the Confederate pickets. He left the 17th Pennsylvania there

The 6th Pennsylvania Cavalry as sketched by Winslow Homer. (Battles and Leaders of the Civil War)

to occupy the enemy, and then rode off to find the ford with his squadron of Lancers, intending to circle around the rear of the enemy before pitching into them.

Arriving at the ford, Rush found 140 enemy cavalrymen dismounted and waiting in line of battle on the opposite bank of the creek. Supported by the rookies of the 17th Pennsylvania, who had come up once Rush found the enemy waiting for him, the Lancers splashed across the Occoquan and opened fire on Hampton's pickets. A brisk skirmish ensued. After a few minutes of severe fire, the Confederates dropped their weapons and fled, leaving behind two of their wounded, who were quickly captured by the Lancers. Pursuing the fleeing enemy, the Lancers recaptured twelve of the wagons lost the day before. Rush sent out scouting parties in all directions, some of who pressed the enemy so closely that the Rebels set the remaining wagons on fire and escaped. Rush then led his victorious squadron of Lancers and the 17th Pennsylvania into the Army of the Potomac's camp at Falmouth.[70]

The war's second Christmas came. Once again, the men grew melancholy thinking about their loved ones at home. "I got a tremendous fit of the blues," complained Lieutenant Morrow. "I could have cried from sheer vexation and a case of lonelyness." Part of their torpor resulted from their unhappy surroundings at Falmouth. "We are evidently going into winter quarters in this miserable place, and if we do I might reconcile myself to staying here all winter although it is hard," continued Morrow. In spite of the wretched surroundings, the Lancers resolved to make the best of their situation and to persevere. It would be a long cold winter, the winter of the Army of the Potomac's discontent.[71]

The year 1862 ended quietly. It began with much promise and ended with Robert E. Lee's victorious army glowering across the Rappahannock at the defeated and sullen

Army of the Potomac. In three major campaigns—on the Peninsula, at Second Bull Run, and at Fredericksburg—Lee soundly defeated the Union army. Antietam, while a victory for the Army of the Potomac, was the bloodiest single day of the entire Civil War. McClellan had not made good use of his horse soldiers, and Burnside proved to be even worse at managing cavalry. If 1862 marked the nadir for the Lancers, 1863 would be the apex of their service with the Army of the Potomac.

Chapter Five

THE STONEMAN RAID

THE ARMY OF THE POTOMAC'S morale sank in the wake of the debacle at Fredericksburg. One officer on furlough for the holidays complained, "I need not tell you I appreciated the short time I spent in Philadelphia and would liked to have staid at least three weeks."[1] Rumors abounded, including one rumor that anticipated a transfer of the Lancers to South Carolina. However, on January 9, 1863, Capt. Emlen N. Carpenter noted, "There is no truth in it. However, I am confident and I merely repeat it to show you what absurd rumors get afloat."[2] Two days later, Companies A and D received orders to report to Maj. Gen. John F. Reynolds for provost duty. Capt. Robert Milligan, the commander of Company F, resigned his commission due to ill health and returned to Philadelphia after turning over command of his troop to the newly promoted Capt. Charles B. Davis. Capt. William P. C. Treichel was appointed provost marshal of Reynolds' First Corps.[3]

In January 1863, hoping to redeem himself, Maj. Gen. Ambrose E. Burnside attempted a second campaign in the winter mud. "As sure as we recross that river we will be whipped worse than we were the last time," observed Lt. Albert P. Morrow the day before the new campaign began, "The army is not in a fighting condition by any means."[4] Despite the Army of the Potomac's poor state, Burnside's latest assault quickly bogged down in terrible weather and became known as the Mud March. "We passed through the town of Falmouth about dark and continued along the river road about 5 miles—there we found the Infantry, the artillery, and the pontoon train," recounted Pvt. Henry Cowan. "We halted in a piece of woods close to the river. We unsaddled and had had just 'retired' when the sky darkened and poured forth upon us a torrent of rain and continued so until day light, and in fact, until we were well settled in our old camp." The expedition was a miserable failure.[5]

"The movement so long talked of is over and resulted in nothing. The day we started a storm set in and in a short time the roads became almost impassable," complained a bitter Captain Carpenter. "Wagons, ammunition, trains, artillery carriages got stuck fast in the mud. In many case men sank down from sheer exhaustion. Suffering was very great. The pontoons stuck fast—multitudes of horses died. The march seemed what Napoleon's retreat from Moscow might have been."[6]

"And yet on, plodding on, through mud knee deep, came the brave and worn soldiers of this great army," noted a newspaper correspondent traveling with the army. "About noon we were pleased to see our friends of Rush's Lancers come plodding through the mud, and as they passed on to the right we judged, from the difficult which they experienced in moving at even a walk, that a charge even by this veteran regiment of the volunteer service would not be desired." Before long, the order to return to camp arrived, and the demoralized army slogged back to its starting point, the aborted campaign a miserable failure.[7]

"After lying out in the rain with muddy clothes for 3 days and nights the hateful return had to be commenced," complained a bitter Sergeant Ballentine. "I could not begin to describe the condition of the men but the roads were mud to the horses' bellies. In fact it was enough to make men curse their country and die." Once back in camp, Ballentine spent an entire day trying to feel clean. "I had to wash every stitch of clothes as well as the horse and equipment. It is wet as usual and everything is mud. I cannot give you any idea of how things are here but little good is to be gained until little Mac gets command." It was a desperate but futile hope—McClellan's days of commanding troops in the field were over for good.[8]

Burnside recognized that he was not up to the job at hand and asked that he be relieved of command of the Army of the Potomac in late January, a request President Lincoln quickly approved. On January 26, 1863, Maj. Gen. Joseph Hooker, known as "Fighting Joe," took command of the demoralized army, which went back into its winter camp on the hills to the north of Fredericksburg. There, the two armies lay scowling at each other.[9] "They have got fighting Joe for a leader now and maby he will try to do something," wrote twenty-two year-old Pvt. Clement Hoffman of Company E.[10] Hooker's appointment was controversial. Hooker made his dissatisfaction with Burnside clearly known, and Burnside had not appreciated it. Burnside tried, unsuccessfully, to remove Hooker, and then was forced to deal with an unhappy subordinate. The scheming Hooker prevailed, and he now possessed the prize he had long coveted—command of the Army of the Potomac. Only time would tell how he would fare under this heavy burden. Maj. Gen. George G. Meade, whose son served with the Lancers, correctly observed, "Hooker is a very good soldier and a capital officer to command an army corps, but I should doubt his qualifications to command a large army."[11]

Hooker immediately set about reforming the army, which was terribly demoralized after its two debacles under Burnside. Adopting a recommendation made by Pleasonton, Hooker organized all of the army's cavalry into a single corps of about 12,000 men, commanded by Colonel Rush's West Point classmate Maj. Gen. George Stoneman.[12] "From the day of its organization under Hooker, the cavalry of the Army of the Potomac commenced a new life," commented a Federal officer.[13] Stoneman established three divisions as well as a Reserve Brigade consisting of the army's Regular cavalry units. The Lancers were assigned to independent duty at army headquarters, and on March 1,

1863, Companies E and I became Hooker's escort contingent.[14] "This will give them a much better chance of seeing service than when attached to Headquarters, which is a lazy, loafing sort of duty," reported General Meade after visiting his son George.[15] The regiment established a pleasant camp in a stand of pine trees at Belle Plain Landing on the Rappahannock River, awaiting an assignment.[16] At the beginning of March, Companies L and M, the newly recruited squadron raised in the fall of 1862, escorted by Major Morris, joined the regiment. Its complement was now full.[17]

Once Stoneman took command of his newly formed corps, he had to fill out his staff. Rush's second ranking officer, Lt. Col. C. Ross Smith, was appointed provost marshal of the Cavalry Corps. Although Smith remained a member of the Lancers for the rest of his term of service in the Army of the Potomac, he never served with the regiment again. Instead, he filled various staff billets at Cavalry Corps headquarters.[18]

The regiment's roster of officers had changed. Some of the original complement of officers had left the army, and others were promoted. The following sets forth the regiment's roster of officers after Companies L and M joined the Lancers:

Colonel Richard H. Rush

Lieutenant Colonel C. Ross Smith

Majors Robert Morris, Jr., Henry C. Whelan, J. Henry Hazeltine

Adjutant Rudolph Ellis

Quartermaster Theodore Sage

Surgeons John B. Coover Thomas S. Morrison

Chaplain Samuel L. Gracey

Captains Frederick C. Newhall, William P. C. Treichel, Charles E. Cadwalader, William W. Frazier, Jr., Charles L. Leiper, Charles B. Davis, J. Newton Dickson, J. Hinckley Clark, James Starr, Henry Winsor, Jr.

1st Lieutenants R. Walsh Mitchell, Frank Furness, Thomas W. Neill, Albert P. Morrow, John Riddle, Edward L. Tevis, G. Irvine Whitehead, Samuel Smith, Eugene P. Bertrand, John Hendricks, Abraham D. Price

2nd Lieutenants Osgood Welsh, William White, Charles B. Coxe, George G. Meade, Jr., Thompson Lenning, Thomas J. Gregg, Samuel R. Colladay, Richard M. Sheppard, Archer Maris, Edward Whiteford, Phillip H. Ellis, Bernard H. Herkness.

The reforms implemented by Hooker paid immediate dividends. Many in the Army of the Potomac sank into the depths of despair after the Fredericksburg debacle, and many entertained thoughts of desertion. Hooker implemented a system of furloughs to allow the men a few days to go home and visit their families. He also improved the army's logistics, making certain that supplies were plentiful. "Hard tack is played out and fresh bread substituted," noted a Lancer. "Hooker feeds well."[19] The officers of the 6th Pennsylvania received invitations to participate in a steeplechase and to attend a grand ball at Brig. Gen. David Birney's headquarters in March, and they gleefully joined in the fun.[20] Gradually, the army's morale, which had sunk to an unprecedented low, came back, and soon the men had developed great confidence in Hooker.

Changes were in store for the Lancers, too. Colonel Rush's men impressed Stoneman, who complimented them publicly, declaring the 6th Pennsylvania Cavalry to be the best regiment in the service.[21] The new cavalry chief had big plans for the regiment. In early March, one squadron traded its trademark lances for carbines. "12 carbines (or Sharp's Rifle with short barrel) have been issued to 'light men mounted on good horses' to seek the enemy in the woods or in the saddle or in other words to be used by skirmishers," noted a member of Company K.[22] Not all missed the lances. "It is generally expected that in a short time the whole regiment will be thus equipped," reported General Meade, "and the *turkey driving implement* abandoned."[23] More widespread changes lay ahead.

In addition, the Lancers joined Buford's Reserve Brigade. "Originally organized with care, by Colonel Rush, containing excellent material in its ranks, and officered by the elite of the Quaker City, it may easily be imagined that the new-comers were heartily welcomed," noted an officer of the 2nd U.S. Cavalry. "When it is added that the term 'officer and gentleman,' in this connection, was not a stereotyped expression, but could be taken at its full significance when applied to nearly all of the 'Sixth' who wore 'straps,' and in part to many in its ranks we have given some idea of the worth of the acquisition."[24]

By the beginning of March, all but one company of the Lancers had come together at Belle Plain. "We have a very fine camp now but we had hard work making it so. The colonel paid a visit to our company ground and gave the sergeants great praise for having everything arranged in such fine order," reported Sergeant Ballentine on March 5. "He tells all the companies to pattern after Company K. It is really beautiful."[25]

Hooker had great expectations for his newly powerful mounted arm. Brig. Gen. Fitzhugh Lee's Confederate cavalry dashed across the Rappahannock River near Hartwood Church on February 24, 1863, surprising the Federal pickets and creating quite a bit of consternation. The grayclad horsemen then retired across the Rappahannock with 150 Union prisoners in tow. Lee left a taunting note for his old friend and West Point classmate, Brig. Gen. William Woods Averell. "We *ought* to be invincible, and by God sir, we *shall* be," proclaimed a furious Hooker to Stoneman. "You have got to stop these disgraceful cavalry 'surprises.' I'll have no more of them. I give you full power over your officers, to arrest, cashier, shoot—whatever you will—only you must stop these 'surprises'." Hooker concluded by threatening to relieve all of the officers of the cavalry corps and taking command of the mounted arm himself.[26] The bar was set quite high.

On March 17, 1863, Averell's cavalry squared off with its Southern counterpart at the Battle of Kelly's Ford, near Culpeper Court House, Virginia, fighting Fitz Lee's horsemen to a draw. However, that outcome raised the morale of the Cavalry Corps exponentially. Henry Cowan of Company K decided that he would not take the ten-day furlough he was entitled to until the Union cavalry had defeated Stuart's men on the field of battle. "I suppose you heard of the success of Gen. Averell's scout. Well, whenever you hear of the 'Rush Lancers' fighting Stuart and whipping him, then you may look for Henry taking his furlough," Cowan declared with great braggadocio. "Stuart may make his brags of capturing Brigadiers &c. in the night but when our cavalry cross the river engage their forces and drive them into their own camp then they may stop until they do something to retrieve it." He concluded, "As likely as not Stuart or some of his cavalry Generals are preparing for a raid but let them come and with a minute's notice we would be in line to receive him."[27]

In the meantime, the Lancers continued drilling, preparing to take the field again. A typical day looked like this:

6:00 a.m.—Reveille and roll call, followed by stable call, when horses were fed and groomed

7:00 a.m.—Surgeon's call. Sick men were to report to the surgeon

7:30 a.m.—Breakfast call, typically coffee and hard tack

9:30 a.m.—Water call for the horses, followed by time to police stables and company streets

10:00 a.m.—Morning drill until noon.

Noon—Lunch call, followed by water call again.

1:00 p.m.—Guard mounting, when the pickets are relieved and new ones sent out, followed by afternoon stable call to feed and groom

4:00 p.m.—Evening roll call.

6:00 p.m.—Dinner

7:00 p.m.—Free time

9:00 p.m.—Taps and lights out[28]

By the middle of March, this routine of intensive drilling had paid dividends. The regiment was in its fighting prime. The men had worked hard on their marksmanship, and the regiment had been furnished with twelve bar ribbons for the best marksmanship. "Really the regiment looks warlike and hopes to improve its fighting capacity," reported Sergeant Ballentine on March 17. "Undoubtedly Philadelphians would be proud of the brave Rush's Lancers."[29] They would get their chance soon enough.

Detachments and staff assignments had dramatically altered the regimental command structure by the end of March. Capt. Frederic C. Newhall was serving as inspector general of the Cavalry Corps. Lt. Col. C. Ross Smith was the Cavalry Corps provost marshal. Colonel Rush was absent, serving as the Army of the Potomac's Inspector of Artillery. These assignments left Major Robert Morris, Jr., in command of the regiment. The officer corps of the Lancers had undergone a dramatic shake-up, and it remained to be seen how this rearrangement would play out.[30]

On April 6, President and Mrs. Lincoln visited Falmouth to review the entire Army of the Potomac. These reviews worked wonders to restore sagging morale in the ranks of the army, which shook off the lingering effects of the hardships of the winter encampment. Brig. Gen. John Buford, a thirty-seven-year-old career dragoon, requested that he be put in command of the Reserve Brigade, and the Lancers often rode with the Regulars. The men of the regiment liked the no-nonsense Buford, who led the Cavalry Corps in the grand review before President Lincoln. It took more than three hours for the entire mounted force to parade past the president. One member of the 8th Illinois Cavalry noted in his journal, "Grand review of the Cavalry. Mud knee deep, but we marched the best we could. Lincoln and his wife were here. The President looks tired but he is as handsome as ever."[31]

Bringing up the rear of Buford's Reserve Brigade, the Lancers trotted by the reviewing stand with their polished lances glinting in the dim spring afternoon sunlight. "Rush's Lancers are presenting a perfect picture like effect in beautiful order," reported Col. Biddle to his wife, Julia. "They side wheeled into line, forming as they came up on the left of the preceding company at a gallop—it was with the Artillery, the most brilliant part of the whole affair."[32] Pvt. George Perkins of the 6th New York Independent Battery wrote to his hometown newspaper, "Over the vast plain as far as the eye could reach were stretched long lines of cavalry, while directly in rear of [the 6th New York Independent Battery], their red pennons fluttering in the breeze, were drawn up the only lancers in the service, the 6th Pennsylvania Cavalry. They were a fine sight, and their subsequent movements proved them to be as finely drilled."[33] The *Philadelphia Inquirer* reported that

> One of the most beautiful movements of the whole day was that near the close of the review, when the Sixth Pennsylvania Cavalry, familiarly known as Rush's Lancers, were brought around the house into the field at a full gallop, with company fronts, and at that gait executed most perfectly one of the most difficult cavalry movements, that of wheeling by companies into regimental line, facing the immense company of military authorities there gathered, and forming a most perfectly dressed line on the instant, every horse steady, just in his right place, the men looking neat and proud that they were able to accomplish so easily this most difficult maneuver while at full gallop, the distance between the several squadrons being most accurately preserved. I have really heard more

Sketch of Lancers escorting Mrs. Lincoln's carriage. (Author's Collection)

praise given to this one regiment and in this single movement than of any other occurrence of the day. It certainly exhibited the great proficiency in drill that has been attained by one of the best of Philadelphia regiments.[34]

The correspondent concluded that the grand review was "the finest cavalry display ever witnessed in the United States, was that of the review of cavalry to-day by the President. Every regiment turned out in its largest possible numbers, and the display was most imposing."[35] As a result of the reforms and the morale boost created by the reviews, the Federal troopers, for the first time, began to believe that they were the equal of the Confederate cavalry.

The grand review also signaled the arrival of the spring campaigning season. Hooker developed a plan to sneak a march around Lee's flank near a crossroads called Chancellorsville, located in a tangled, dense forest of undergrowth known as the Wilderness. If the plan worked, Hooker would get around Lee's flank undetected. To create a diversion, Hooker sent the Cavalry Corps, save for one small brigade, on a far-ranging raid on Richmond, leaving his army's advance largely unscreened. The cavalry would cut Lee's lines of communications with Richmond, and destroy, to the extent possible, the Aquia and Richmond Railroad.

On April 11, Hooker summoned Stoneman to his headquarters to instruct the cavalry commander on his role in coming campaign.[36] Hooker ordered Stoneman to march the next morning "for the purpose of turning the enemy's position on his left, and of throwing your command between him and Richmond and isolating him from his supplies, checking his retreat, and inflicting on him every possible injury which will tend to his discomfiture and defeat."[37] That night, Stoneman sent for his commanders, explained the objects of the expedition to them, and then assigned each his allotted tasks and duties. "The commanders had hardly left my Headquarters when…the sky suddenly became overcast, the darkness almost subterranean, and the rain began to fall," recounted Stoneman after the raid, "and, of course, our bright hopes and high expectations, than to which no command ever started with brighter or higher, began to be dimmed and lowered."[38]

The men knew something was afoot, too. "Today, there is every prospect of a move to be made by the army soon," reported Henry Cowan of Company K on April 11. "Today we done nothing but clean up our equipments, &c." At long last, they were nearly ready to employ the skills they had spent the winter honing. Time would tell how they would stack up against the Confederate horsemen.[39]

The Cavalry Corps moved out on April 13, 1863.[40] Colonel Rush led the Lancers out of their winter camp. During the expedition the men of the 6th Pennsylvania were assigned to special duty, which they intended to perform to the best of their ability. "After crossing the Rappahannock with the main command, we were to proceed rapidly to the vicinity of Richmond, destroy railroads, canals, telegraph lines, and by forced march, to join our forces either at Suffolk or Fortress Monroe," recorded Chaplain Gracey. "With minds stirred at the responsibility and honor of this selection, we were wakeful, and sat around our camp fires until after midnight, discussing the important work before us, its dangers and rewards."[41]

Buford and his Regulars, with the Lancers in tow, marched to Kelly's Ford, where they were to distract the Confederates and allow the rest of the Cavalry Corps to cross the Rappahannock at other fords upriver. On the 15th, Buford moved from Kelly's Ford to the railroad bridge at Rappahannock Station, and prepared to fight his way across the river. Col. Benjamin F. "Grimes" Davis's brigade crossed at Kelly's Ford and immediately encountered stout resistance from dismounted Confederate cavalry holding rifle pits. His advance quickly bogged down. Davis's men were driven back across the Rappahannock, and by the next morning, Buford could not cross the badly swollen river. The entire Cavalry Corps was stranded on the north bank of the Rappahannock River, stuck in the thick Virginia mud. Of course, the aborted attempts at crossing meant that the Federals had lost the element of surprise. Now, they would have to wait for the river to fall while the Confederates made preparations to entertain them on the other side of the Rappahannock.[42]

About 2:00 a.m., "one of the very worst storms of the season" began, raising the level of Rappahannock nearly seven feet in just a few hours, and "converting mere rivulets into torrents making the roads quite impassable."[43] The next morning, the men awoke and found themselves wrapped up in rainwater and their poor horses standing in mud to their bellies.[44] The flooding prevented Stoneman's men from crossing the Rappahannock and hopelessly bogged down the Northern cavalry. They made the best of their soggy surroundings and tried to remain active and vigilant.

Company K was sent out in pursuit of Confederate guerrillas on April 16. The Lancers caught sight of them near Warrenton Junction, but night came early, and the men stood to horse all night. The next morning, the company divided into three squads and set off on different roads that would converge later. Two squads failed to find the enemy, but one squad spotted them, chasing them for nearly six miles through the mud. "We gave them a hard chase and closed up on them considerably," noted a sergeant of Company K. "The sons of bitches hollered so loud that you could hear them for miles. Their numbers increased the farther they went until they had about 900 men. Our horses were pretty

Maj. Gen. George Stoneman.
(Library of Congress)

well played out and we thought that for our own safety we had gone far enough so we returned."[45]

On April 20, Captain Treichel led Company A on a reconnaissance to Warrenton. Treichel's small command dashed into the town, expecting to find it occupied by the enemy. Finding no Confederates, Treichel stationed pickets on the roads approaching the town and occupied it until the morning of April 22, when his company rejoined the regiment as it passed through on its way to Warrenton Junction on the Orange and Alexandria Railroad.[46]

The horrible weather frustrated the men to no end. "I think that when we started out we were going to make a raid in the rear of the rebels to cut off their supplies and destroy the bridges in their rear and go on to Richmond," correctly concluded Sergeant Ballentine. "The rain prevented us from crossing the river before the Rebels should get wind of it but they kept all their cavalry and two divisions of infantry opposite us. I think now that all our army will move in this direction in a few days." His prediction was remarkably accurate.[47]

On April 28, the men received five days' rations and three days' forage for their horses, as well as orders to be ready to move out at a moment's notice. The men struck their tents, loaded their wagons, saddled their horses, and waited. Near midnight, a hard rain resumed, drenching men and beasts as they stood, waiting for orders to move out.[48] The great raid finally began the next day, when the level of the river briefly dropped low enough to permit a crossing by his command.[49] "On Tuesday night it commensed to Rain and Poured down Incessently all night all Day yesterday and all night Last night," complained Sgt. Thomas W. Smith. "Today it has been clear, but it is now beginning to Rain again and it Looks as though it would continue for some time. The boys are afraid that there will another mud Skedaddle, but I think that the Troops will stay whare they are untill the weather is cleared off again."[50]

Because the rain had removed the element of secrecy from the expedition, Hooker altered his plans for Stoneman's expedition. On April 22, Hooker instructed the cavalry commander to divide his command and send its elements dashing off in different directions. "These detachments can dash off to the right and to the left and inflict a great deal of mischief and at the same time bewilder the enemy as to the course and intention of the main body," instructed the army commander.[51] The water did not recede enough for Stoneman's horse soldiers to cross the Rappahannock until April 27. In the meantime, the Lancers waited, wondering what would become of them. "We have undoubtedly some pretty hot work before us," recounted Sgt. Christian Geisel, "where we are going is not publicly known, but the general opinion is here that we are to get into the rear of the rebel army of the Rappahannock and cut off their communication from Richmond, while General Hooker will attack them with the Infantry."[52]

Richard Rush's tenure as a regimental commander also ended quietly. Rush took sick leave on April 25 while his regiment remained stuck in the mud, waiting to set off on the great raid. "The Boys are all disgusted with Colonel Rush," reported Capt. Walter S. Newhall of the 3rd Pennsylvania Cavalry, who served as one of Stoneman's staff officers, and whose brother Fred was the Lancers' regimental adjutant, "who has another sick leave of twenty days."[53] The colonel's days with the regiment were numbered. On April 25, he wrote, "I am mortified that . . . I have not the physical endurance to retain my health under the vicissitudes of our cavalry campaign."[54]

At regimental dress parade on the evening of April 27, Colonel Rush addressed his men, "deeming it very doubtful that he should be able to rejoin the command this campaign. He expressed great regret at being compelled to leave just at this juncture, but the severe exposure of the last three weeks had revived a chronic disease contracted while serving in Mexico." With that, Richard Rush took leave of the regiment that proudly bore his name and went to Washington. "The honorable position attained by the regiment in its later campaigns, is doubtless due to the military skill and knowledge, and the superior qualities of Colonel Rush as an organizer and disciplinarian," lamented Chaplain Gracey.[55] Major Morris, the ranking officer still serving with the regiment, assumed command, as Lt. Col. C. Ross Smith was serving on Stoneman's staff at Cavalry Corps headquarters.

While Stoneman waited for the wretched weather to break, Hooker continued planning his campaign. He intended to move his gigantic army of 133,000 men on April 27, even as the torrential rains continued unabated. The move began as scheduled, and the men were excited about their prospects for the spring campaign. The bulk of the Army of the Potomac crossed the Rappahannock at Kelly's Ford while two corps crossed at

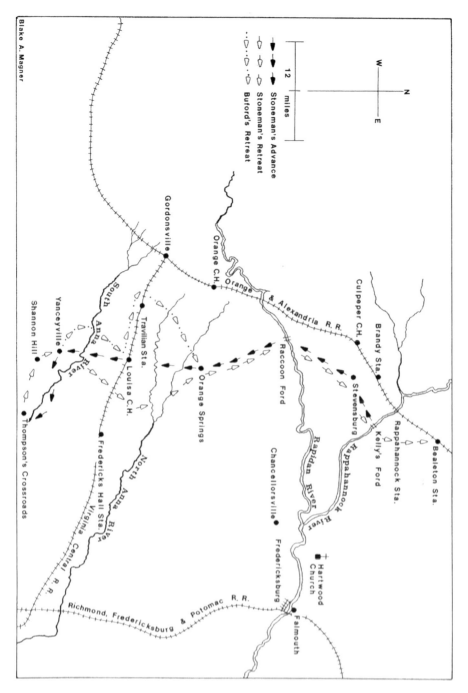

Map 3. The Stoneman Raid.

Fredericksburg. Their mission was to capture Marye's Heights, above the town, and to keep the Confederate forces there pinned down and prevent them from being shifted to meet the threat created by Hooker's main force. Pontoon bridges were pushed across the river, and the Union infantry poured into the already devastated town of Fredericksburg.

Having finally crossed the Rappahannock, Stoneman detached Averell's division, along with an additional brigade and some horse artillery, to march by way of Brandy Station and Culpeper, where they would engage Brig. Gen. W.H.F. "Rooney" Lee's Confederate cavalry brigade. Gregg's division and Buford's Reserve Brigade, with Stoneman at the head, would go to Stevensburg, where the disparate elements of the command would then sortie off in different directions. Although outnumbered by Averell's men, Lee's Virginians soon tied up Averell's advance and pinned down his command near Brandy Station.

After crossing the Rappahannock at Kelly's Ford, the Lancers enjoyed the contents of Granville Kelly's storehouse, emptying it of ham, pork shoulders, bacon, sugar, tobacco, and other sumptuous treats.[56] The column then halted for the night in a freshly plowed farm field, "and without fire, or shelter from a cold merciless storm, we spent the night," recalled Chaplain Gracey. "It was dark and dreary in the extreme; no bugle calls were sounded, and strict silence was observed, as we were supposed to be in proximity to the rebels. The vivid flashes of lightning alone illuminated the scene." The misery of the Lancers increased during the night when straggling bands of Confederate cavalry charged their pickets. In addition to being in hostile territory, they did not know what their mission or destination was. The uncertainty made the horse soldiers even more uneasy.[57]

Dr. John B. Coover, the regimental surgeon, recalled that morning as "the most disagreeable one I have ever seen."[58] That day, the blueclad horse soldiers fanned out across the countryside. Foraging parties emptied corncribs and barns, and the Yankee horsemen helped themselves to the rich bounties of the area. "Every smokehouse and farmyard near the line of march was made to contribute to our comfort," noted Chaplain Gracey, "Chickens, ducks, and hams, in great numbers, were secured."[59]

Stoneman's objective was the important transportation center of Louisa Court House. The Virginia Central Railroad passed through Louisa, and several major arteries also passed through or near the town. The advance of Buford's column reached Raccoon Ford on the Rapidan about noon on April 30. Capt. Charles L. Leiper led a reconnaissance and encountered a rebel force not far from the ford. Leiper scattered the enemy with a lance charge, returning with eleven prisoners, but losing Lt. Thompson Lenning, of Company M, captured by the Confederates. With these prisoners in tow, Buford learned the condition of the surrounding country and hurried his command across the Rapidan. After crossing and joining the rest of the column, the Lancers set up a miserable bivouac. "Hungry, wet, and fatigued, we were illy prepared to spend a night standing to horse, but such were our orders," remembered Chaplain Gracey. "Without unsaddling, the regiment was drawn up in close column of companies, the men dismounted, and ordered to stand at their horses' heads all night. No fires could be kindled, and as a dense fog settled down in the valley during the night, it became very cold, and our clothing being wet, we suffered greatly before morning." With reins fastened to their wrists, many exhausted Lancers sank to the ground at their horses' heads and got a few hours' sleep in spite of the miserable conditions.[60]

Gregg's division, along with the Lancers and Buford's Regulars, marched southwest through Orange Court House and then on to Louisa Court House. With no rations, columns of foragers fanned out across the countryside, slowing the pace of march as hungry men sought rations and fodder for their mounts. The Federals tore up five miles of railroad track, all the way to an obscure stop to the west called Trevilian Station. The Yankee horsemen also destroyed a water tank, commissary stores, and damaged public buildings. These men would visit the same ground a year later with much more deadly results.[61]

Rooney Lee disengaged from Averell and set off to chase after Stoneman's raiders. The Virginians caught up to the Federals at Trevilian Station, and a brief firefight took place. Rooney Lee reported that he "sent the Ninth Virginia in that direction; their videttes were driven in by the enemy; they charged and drove them three miles, killing and wounding a number, and took thirty-two prisoners, one lieutenant; my loss was three or four wounded; four prisoners taken represented three different regiments." Lee dispatched the 13th Virginia and two pieces of horse artillery to support the 9th Virginia, and then waited for Stoneman to attack. When he did not, Lee "learned that General Stoneman with his whole corps was at Louisa Court House, moving towards James River." Lee correctly surmised that Stoneman intended to tear up the railroad, and waited for the Yankees to approach. When the blueclad troopers did not come, Rooney Lee withdrew. Because his men and horses were "worried out by four days' fighting and marching, [I] left out my pickets and withdrew to Gordonsville."[62]

Not knowing how large an enemy force lay near Gordonsville, and not wanting to take unnecessary chances, Stoneman instead withdrew to the east, destroying the railroad as far east as Fredericks Hall Station. The main column proceeded on to Yanceyville, crossed the South Anna River, and marched on to Thompson's Crossroads, arriving late in the day on May 2. Buford's column captured a train of twenty-six wagons with four mule teams assigned to each wagon, and this prize slowed down the column's advance. "We were now in the very heart of the enemy's country," recalled Chaplain Gracey, "and what was to be done must be done quickly, as the enemy were known to be concentrating all the force they could get together to prevent the accomplishment of our designs."[63] The men traded their played-out horses for the horses of the wagon train and then shot their broken-down mounts to prevent them from falling into enemy hands. Some of the Lancers ended up riding mules as a result.[64]

Stoneman called a counsel of war. "At this point, the James and South Anna Rivers are less than 12 miles apart, and here I determined to make the most of my 3500 men in carrying out my previously conceived plan of operations," wrote Stoneman. "I called together my regimental commanders, showed and explained to them the maps, and gave them an idea of what I wished done. I gave them to understand that we had dropped in that region of the country like a shell, and that I intended to burst it in every direction, expecting each piece or fragment would do as much harm and create nearly as much terror as would result from sending in the whole shell, and thus magnify our small force into overwhelming numbers and the results of this plan satisfied my most sanguine expectations."[65]

This plan, while clever, deviated from Hooker's carefully drawn strategic raid. Instead of operating against Lee's lines of supply and communications, Stoneman intended to scatter his horsemen across the countryside, where they would spread terror and destruction. The cavalry chief also had no way of knowing what was occurring on the battlefield at Chancellorsville. Hooker originally intended for his horsemen to interdict Lee's line of retreat. However, the results of the battle meant that there would be no retreat. There was nothing for Stoneman to interdict. Thus, the die was cast.

On April 30, an optimistic Hooker issued a General Order to the army that proved hollow. "It is with heartfelt satisfaction the commanding general announces to the army that the operations of the last three days have determined that our enemy must ingloriously fly," he boasted, "or come out from behind his defenses and give us battle on our own ground, where certain destruction awaits him."[66] Only the part about the Confederates coming out from behind their defenses would come to pass.

The Battle of Chancellorsville was fought on May 1-4, 1863. Although he had stolen a march on Lee, and despite his great numerical advantage, Hooker lost the fight badly. After a day of fighting on May 1, Hooker pulled back and assumed a defensive posture. He announced to Maj. Gen. Darius N. Couch, commander of the Second Corps, that he had "Lee just where I want him; he must fight me on my own ground." Couch later wrote, "The retrograde movement had prepared me for something of the kind, but to hear from his own lips that the advantages gained by the successful marches of his lieutenants were to culminate in fighting a defensive battle in that nest of thickets was too much, and I retired from his presence with the belief that my commanding general was a whipped man."[67]

On the morning of May 2, Confederate cavalry chieftain Stuart discovered that the Federal flank was "in the air," meaning that it was entirely unprotected; the withdrawal of the Federal cavalry for the great raid left inadequate mounted support to screen Hooker's flanks. Capitalizing on the opportunity, Robert E. Lee ordered Lt. Gen. Thomas J. "Stonewall" Jackson to make a flank march around Hooker's right flank, find the exposed flank, and strike the Union right. Jackson succeeded in surprising the Union 11th Corps while its men were cooking their dinners in the late afternoon of May 2. A rout ensued, and only a spirited stand by Couch's Second Corps near Chancellorsville saved Hooker's army from complete destruction.

The men of Companies E and I, Hooker's headquarters escort, saw hazardous duty during the battle. Carrying messages back and forth between army headquarters and various subordinate commanders often exposed these men to great danger. "I was all through the late fighting and where the very warmist fighting was going on and met with narrow escapes," reported Clement Hoffman, "but it pleased the Lord to bring me out safe and I suppose always will until my turn comes for me to fall on the battlefield and when I do fall I shall bare it with all the patience and courage that lays in my power."[68] Sgt. Thomas W. Smith of Company I had carried a message to Couch, and was just delivering it when a savage Confederate attack crashed into Couch's lines. Couch was standing on his breastworks composing an answer when the Rebels attacked, "yelling like Hyeneas." Things looked desperate, but Couch had chosen his position wisely. Artillery hidden in the tree line opened on the Confederates and slowed them. A volley by the Yankee infantry stopped them and drove them back, "their yell ceases, they waver, break and Run, Then our Boys gave three times three cheers." Smith was relieved. "All this took plase in a good deal less time than it takes me to write it."[69] Even though the men of Capt. James H. Starr's squadron did not take part in the great raid, they nevertheless performed an important duty on the battlefield at Chancellorsville, giving a good account of themselves in the line of fire.

The crushing defeat had the expected result on the Army of the Potomac. "I think that Hooker will cross again in a short time. And if he does this Armey will get wipped so damn bad that they wont know themselves," wrote Smith, an astute observer, a few days after the battle. "I never seen the Armey so much demorralised as it is at the Present time. However the men do not blame Hooker for he done all that was in the power of man to do. I think that the Enemey have lost two men to our one in killed and wounded, for they were the attacking party. But they have taken a great many more Prissoners than we have."[70]

However, the victory at Chancellorsville cost Robert E. Lee the services of Stonewall Jackson. His own men mortally wounded Jackson in a confused sequence of events that occurred at night while he was out scouting for an opportunity to attack Hooker. He died a few days later. Despite Jackson's loss, Chancellorsville, as Smith pointed out, was a huge victory for the Confederates. Although he outnumbered Lee by a margin of more than two to one, Hooker nevertheless suffered a crushing defeat in a long and bloody battle. The Federals sustained more than 17,000 casualties in the battle, and the Confederates nearly 13,000.[71]

In the meantime, Stoneman's men continued their operations. Departing from Thompson's Crossroads on May 4, elements of the Cavalry Corps fanned out across the countryside, foraging vigorously as they went. "The next three days are long to be remembered," observed Dr. Coover, "for we were in the enemy's country far enough away from reinforcements & our command considerably cut up by separation for various expeditions."[72]

Edgar B. Strang, saddler for Company E of the Lancers, went out foraging with a few of his comrades. They rode up to a farm and were greeted at the gate by the owner. Rubbing his hands and smiling, the farmer said "he was glad to be able to look in the face of Union men again," but indicated that he had no food to spare. Suspicious, Strang and his fellow Lancers forced the man to open his smokehouse, where "there were huge hams like apples on a tree." The hungry Lancers quickly confiscated their prize and rode off, with cries of "You Yankee thieves!" echoing behind them. Unfortunately for Strang and his comrades, their expedition soon came to nought, as they were captured near the North Anna River and marched off to Richmond's notorious Libby Prison.[73]

Elements of the Cavalry Corps, under command of Col. Judson Kilpatrick of the 2nd New York Cavalry, approached the defenses of Richmond, while other contingents went off toward Ashland to destroy the railroad bridges of the Richmond, Fredericksburg and Potomac Railroad and the Virginia Central. Gregg would lead another party along the banks of the South Anna River, where they would destroy all of the road bridges and, if possible, the two railroad bridges that crossed the river. Col. Sir Percy Wyndham, a foppish English knight and commander of the 1st New Jersey Cavalry, led another expedition toward Columbia, where his men destroyed more than fifteen miles of the track of the Virginia Central and terrorized the local civilians. These expeditions did a lot of damage, and Kilpatrick's column brushed against the defenses of the Confederate capital, raising a hue and cry and forcing the Confederate government to call out the home guard. Kilpatrick veered to the east and headed for safety at Yorktown. Having accomplished his objectives, Stoneman realized that he would have to pull his far-flung columns back together and make his way back to the Army of the Potomac.

Rooney Lee and 900 troopers of the 9th Virginia Cavalry pursued Wyndham's men, and the race was on. After a chase of nearly sixty miles, Lee and his men fell upon a small force of Regulars commanded by Capt. James Harrison of the 5th U.S. Searching for Wyndham, the 9th Virginia pitched into Harrison's little column of 119 troopers and scattered them. Many of the Regulars, including John Buford's nephew, Lt. Temple Buford, were captured. After interrogating these prisoners, Lee learned that Stoneman's main column was nearby. Severely outnumbered, with his men and horses at the limits of their endurance, Rooney Lee broke off the engagement and withdrew to Gordonsville.[74]

Stoneman also heard rumors of a catastrophic defeat at Chancellorsville from runaway slaves and local citizens. This information, along with Harrison's defeat, decided the issue. Stoneman pulled back to Shannon Hill on May 4. The next day, he moved to Yanceyville and began working on a plan to make his way back to the Army of the Potomac and safety. On May 5, he sent Buford, with 646 hand-picked men from the Reserve Brigade and the Lancers (including the squadrons of Capts. W. W. Frazer and Henry Winsor), to try to deceive the enemy cavalry, and to oppose any force that might be operating in the area of Gordonsville. Buford left Flemming's Crossroads, crossed the

Yanceyville Bridge, and tried to go across country to Gordonsville. However, the dense woods and poor ground prohibited him from doing so.

The march was not pleasant. The rain began again, increasing in intensity as the day wore on. The men were in unfamiliar country, trying to navigate increasingly poor roads. Horses became hopelessly mired in the thick muck. Their riders often left them foundering in the mud, while the dismounted trooper, his saddle slung across his back, tried to make better progress on foot. If he was unable to find another mount, he often collapsed from sheer exhaustion and "would wrap himself in his horse blanket and sleep by the roadside until morning. Many of our men thus dropping out by the way, were captured by the enemy," reported one Lancer.[75]

Buford now headed for Louisa Court House. The second Federal visit in a week found telegraph service restored, so the Yankee troopers again put the telegraph out of commission and seized the post office. Buford then moved to Trevilian Station, hoping to find out whether Confederate cavalry held Gordonsville, eight miles away. There, his horse soldiers destroyed water tanks, rails, pumps, handcars, arms, ammunition, and a large supply of subsistence stores. His weary troopers then moved out toward Gordonsville. A local woman spotted the advancing Federals and came out of her house, clapping her hands and begging the Northern horse soldiers not to go any further because the woods on both sides of the road were full of soldiers with twelve guns waiting for them to come that way.[76] Two miles from the town, the intrepid Kentuckian encountered infantry and artillery and turned north. Buford reached the North Anna River and forded it just in time—its waters were rising from the constant rain. His rear guard crossed on rafts.[77]

By now, the Lancers had nearly reached the limits of their endurance. "The mud was deep, and worked into a very soft condition. From the unceasing splash of liquid mud, one would suppose we were marching in a stream of water to our horses' knees," recalled Gracey. "Our clothing being thoroughly saturated for more than two days, and a keen wind and cold driving rain in our faces, rendered this night's ride anything but pleasant." Exhausted men slept on their horse's necks as the faithful mounts struggled along with the rest of the column. Occasionally, "a weary rider and jaded beast were passed on the roadside, having marched to the point of possible endurance for that night." Relying on the good instincts of their horses in the cold darkness, men pushed beyond their limits could only hope to keep up with the column, trusting their steeds to bring them to safety.[78]

"That night I will never forget," declared Ballentine. "It was so dark that you could see the man at my side and we were fatigued and sleepy. Every now and then I would hear a voice holler, 'Sergeant Ballentine, I think one of the prisoners is drowning in the mud.' However, I lost two and one I had to stretch out on the road. Whether he died or not I cannot say." Ballentine shuddering when he remembered that "I shivered until morning like a dog in a wet sack."[79]

Buford had orders to join Stoneman at Orange Springs the next day. Buford waited for several hours for the rest of the corps to arrive, and was just about to give up and ride for Raccoon Ford when Stoneman and the rest of the column arrived at midnight on May 7. The men took advantage of the wait to try to rest a bit. Sergeant Ballentine found a board and made a crude bed of it. He was about to tie his reins around his ankles and lay down when Maj. Henry Hazeltine grabbed the board. Ballentine told him to put it down. Hazeltine asked if the sergeant knew whom he was talking to, as he was a major. Ballentine informed the major that he "didn't give a damn who he was." Ballentine and Hazeltine scuffled, and the major pulled a pistol and threatened to shoot the sergeant. "Shoot and be damned," declared the angry Irishman. Instead of shooting, Hazeltine went away, saying that he would have Ballentine reduced and tied up the next day. Ballentine lay down and stretched out on his board and was just falling asleep when Ballentine's Company K got orders to go to the rear to support a battery. Hazeltine never did press charges against the feisty sergeant.[80]

In a pelting rain, the soggy Federal troopers began the long march back to the Army of the Potomac. "The night was very dark, and much of the way led us through dense woods, intensifying the darkness," recalled Chaplain Gracey. "For several hours it was utterly impossible for one to see the person riding immediately in advance, or even the head of the animal upon which he was himself mounted."[81] Moving on through an extremely dark night, and having to navigate swamps, impenetrable woods, and cow paths, the blue-clad troopers tried to avoid the main roads. The cold, soggy, and exhausted horse soldiers struggled to stay awake.

During the night, Capt. William P. C. Treichel's squadron became separated from the rest of the column. Treichel marched several miles on a side road and, expecting to encounter great difficulty in crossing swollen streams, halted for the night and waited for daylight in their cold, wet bivouac. Fortunately, no Confederates were operating in the area, and the Lancers spent a miserable but largely unmolested night. They moved out early the next morning. By hard marching in awful conditions, Treichel and his men caught up to the main column the next afternoon.[82]

On May 7, they received permission to halt for breakfast and a rest. Stoneman confirmed that Hooker had suffered a crushing defeat at Chancellorsville, meaning that further raiding would serve no purpose. He would have to withdraw across the Rapidan and Rappahannock Rivers to reach safety. Stoneman dashed off a letter to Hooker. "We shall move on today, as fast as the nature of the roads and the broken down, worn out condition of the men and animals will permit, towards Germanna, from which point I am in hopes of to communicate directly with Headquarters." He closed by pleading for rations for horses and men, stating, "We can meet them at any point on the Rapphannock as far up as Bealeton Station, but not beyond."[83] After feeding and watering their horses, the column pushed on to Orange Court House and crossed the Rapidan at Raccoon Ford.[84]

Lancers, first row: Abraham Price*, Dr. Gustav Prieson*, Theodore Sage†; second row: Richard Sheppard*, C. Ross Smith*, James Starr*; third row: William P. C. Treichel*, Osgood Welsh*, Henry Whelan*. (*USAMHI, †Author)

That night, the weary troopers, who had spent two nights in the saddle and were cold, tired, and hungry, still had to make their way across the Rappahannock at Kelly's Ford. They unsaddled, built fires, and rested. They cooked and ate whatever they had and then moved down to try to cross the swollen river, arriving about 9 p.m. on May 7. They waited until morning, and found that they could only cross the river by swimming part way. "Our horses, being thoroughly exhausted, were scarcely able to stem the swift current of the stream, and in several cases both horse and rider were carried down the river," recalled a Federal.[85] After most of the command made it to safety on the north bank of the Rappahannock (one man and six horses drowned), they then went to Bealeton Station on the Orange and Alexandria Railroad, where they found supplies and a safe place to halt.[86] As one of Buford's Regulars put it, "We had gained experience and earned the right to sleep in a tent for a day or two."[87] The long ordeal of the Yankee troopers had ended.

Elements of the Cavalry Corps were scattered all over Virginia, and it would take time for the entire command to rejoin the Army of the Potomac. Stoneman's weary troopers finally made their way back on May 16 after two grueling weeks in the saddle. During the long raid, the men of the 6th saw difficult service and earned the respect of their hard-bitten brigade commander. In his after-action report of the raid, Buford noted, "The 6th Pennsylvania Cavalry, under Major Morris, had its equal share of trials and exposure, and has been more than equal to any task imposed on it."[88] Sgt. Christian Geisel of Company H noted that "From the 29th of April to the 9th of May we only had our horses unsaddled about three hours, after the provisions had run out we carried along we lived on ham and corncakes of which we found a large quantity stored away in some places."[89]

Ballentine summed up the plight of all of the Lancers quite well with his vivid description of his condition at the end of the ordeal of the Stoneman Raid. "We had a hard time of it all through," he reported. "We had had no rations for 8 days but what we could hunt up. Some lived high and others and nothing. I washed my face only once from the time I left camp until now. My clothes are stiff with mud and dirt. I am as hard a looking case as is made nowadays. Not a red cent in my pocket, no prospects, and not a towel to wipe my face on. When I do wipe it it has to be on my shirt tail. In fact I am miserable."[90]

During the raid, Lt. George Meade of the Lancers contracted measles, perhaps as a consequence of his exposure to the elements during the long ordeal of the cavalry during the Stoneman Raid. Meade took medical leave and went back to Philadelphia to recuperate. He never returned to the Lancers. By the time he recovered, his father, who would soon succeed Hooker in command of the Army of the Potomac, had arranged for a promotion and an appointment to his own staff. Capt. Charles Cadwalader, young Meade's friend, soon followed and also joined General Meade's staff.[91]

Lt. William Sproule of Company F likewise took sick on the third or fourth day of the raid, but continued on with the regiment until it returned to Kelly's Ford on May 9. Sproule was taken to the Cavalry Corps hospital on Acquia Creek Landing, but it was too late. He died on May 19. "He was greatly beloved by his comrades," recalled Gracey, "and possessed many admirable qualities." His company commander, Capt. Charles B. Davis, escorted Sproule's remains home to Philadelphia, where he was buried with full military honors.[92]

The raiders had destroyed a number of important railroad bridges, depriving the Confederacy of vital supply lines. When he penned his report of the expedition on May

13, Stoneman claimed, "Not one of the least valuable among other results of this expedition is the influence it has had upon the cavalry arm of the service, both in showing us what we are able to accomplish if we but have the opportunity and in convincing the country that it has not spent its men and money in vain in our organization."[93] However, Hooker's defeat at Chancellorsville rendered those efforts moot. "Unfortunately, our withdrawal across the Rappahannock will prevent advantage being taken of the cavalry success," wrote General Meade, "as they will now have time to repair damages before we can get at them again."[94] After its fine performance during Stoneman's Raid, the 6th Pennsylvania Cavalry permanently joined the Reserve Brigade, although Companies E and I remained attached to army headquarters.

Their participation in the raid became a matter of great pride to the men who endured its hardships. "We had a short but successful campaign as far as cavalry is concerned from April 29th to the 9th of May. It lasted but a short time, much shorter then I expected when we started," commented Sergeant Geisel to his sister, "but long enough for us to be going night and day getting but little rest or sleep and to do a great deal of destruction in rebeldom." He continued, "I would not have believed that we could have gone as near to Richmond as we did without encountering and being opposed by some portion of the rebel army. I have no doubt that Jeff Davis himself was alarmed about his safety in Richmond." Geisel came through his ordeal safely, although he lost his horse and two caps in the process. Fortunately, he found both a new mount and replacement headgear along the way.[95]

Dr. Coover proudly reported, "We captured an immense number of Horses, ate an awful quantity of the Confederacy's Hams and bacon, consumed all the corn and fodder we could find, and rendered ourselves generally agreeable. We also captured a large number of prisoners, burnt a great many bridge, R.R. stations, etc., and I am not altogether certain that some few chickens, ducks, & such other small fowl, were also captured." The surgeon and his horse had both tolerated the hardships of the raid well, and he recalled it fondly as "decidedly the biggest thing I have ever seen." He concluded, "We had thousand funny incidents that cannot be told on paper, lots of hard work & plenty of fun, and above all the majority got back safely."[96]

A Maine trooper summed up the feelings of the Cavalry Corps quite simply. "It was ever after a matter of pride with the boys that they were on 'Stoneman's Raid'," he wrote.[97] A New Jersey trooper echoed a similar sentiment. "For the first time the cavalry found themselves made useful," he wrote, "and treated as something better than military watchmen for the army. They saw that the long desired time had come when they would be permitted to gain honor and reputation, and when they would cease to be tied to the slow moving divisions of infantry without liberty to strike a blow for the cause of the nation. . . . It gave our troopers self-respect, and obliged the enemy to respect them."[98] Most of the weary Lancers shared this sentiment. However, not all saw it that way. "Raids are grand humbugs," complained Lt. Charles B. Coxe.[99] Of all of the Federal cavalry units assigned to the Army of the Potomac, they had suffered the most from misuse. The change was quite welcome.

The long raid took a devastating toll on the Cavalry Corps' mounts. Buford's brigade alone abandoned 365 horses during the expedition, and Brig. Gen. Alfred Pleasonton, then in temporary command of the Cavalry Corps, claimed that 6,000 horses were lost during the raid. On May 27, Pleasonton reported that only 4,677 horses were serviceable. The March return for the Cavalry Corps showed an effective strength of more than 12,000 men and horses. "It is now one-third of that strength, and, so far as I can ascertain, is not fitted to take the field," he wrote.[100] As a result of all the time spent slogging through the gooey Virginia mud, the horses developed a condition known as "mud fever" that disabled many. Many others had sore backs as a consequence of not being unsaddled for a week at a time. The Stoneman Raid left much of the Cavalry Corps *hors de combat* for a time, and it was unserviceable just when the Army of the Potomac needed it most. "I shall use every exertion to bring it to a state of efficiency at the earliest possible moment, but the responsibility of its present state, it is proper the major-general commanding should know, does not belong to me."[101] Pleasonton would not have much of an opportunity to prepare his command for further service in the field.

In losing the Battle of Chancellorsville, Hooker conceded the initiative to Robert E. Lee. Pvt. Clement Hoffman of Company E, which was serving headquarters escort duty, wrote home to his mother after the Chancellorsville debacle, "Gen'l Hooker is a bold and fighting Gen'l, but not one to plan out maneuvering of a large Army."[102] Hooker decided that Stoneman was the cause of the debacle and made him the scapegoat. On May 10, he told Secretary of War Edwin M. Stanton that "the raid does not appear to have amounted much." As time passed, Hooker became even more convinced that Stoneman had caused the defeat at Chancellorsville. In a letter to historian Samuel P. Bates, Hooker claimed, "I consider Stoneman as justly answerable for my failure at Chancellorsville as Howard."[103]

Throughout the raid, Stoneman suffered terribly with hemorrhoids, a condition that made every minute spent in the saddle sheer agony. On May 20, the embattled cavalry chieftain took medical leave to try to recuperate. "Stoneman is off on leave, and I don't think will return here again," reported General Meade. "He does not want to, and Hooker does not want him back."[104] During his absence, Hooker appointed Alfred Pleasonton to take temporary command of the Cavalry Corps. Stoneman never again commanded cavalry in the field as part of the Army of the Potomac, and Pleasonton's appointment to temporary command became permanent later that summer when Stoneman was assigned to head a new bureau being formed to provide for the logistics of the Federal government's large mounted force.[105]

The three members of the West Point class of 1846 who had so affected the development of the 6th Pennsylvania Cavalry were now gone. George B. McClellan, who armed the regiment with its trademark lances, languished in New Jersey, awaiting a

Mathew Brady's classic photograph of Company I, 6th Pennsylvania Cavalry, "Rush's Lancers." It may be the only photograph showing the weapon from which the unit derived its name. (USAMHI)

recall to duty that never came. Stoneman was on medical leave and would not return to the Army of the Potomac. Rush assumed command of the army's Invalid Corps and faded into obscurity. Col. Alexander Biddle of the 121st Pennsylvania Volunteer Infantry, husband of Rush's cousin Julia, wrote home, "Richard Rush is looked upon as almost not of the Army. He has a desk in the War Department, as Chief of the Invalid Corps and will probably never rejoin his regiment. I think he has ruined his military career."[106] However, the regiment he formed was forever known as Rush's Lancers.

In early June, Mathew Brady's photographic wagon pulled into Falmouth. One of Brady's photographers gathered the men of Company I for a photograph. Alfred Waud, the famous Civil War sketch artist, happened to be in camp and joined the Lancers in the photograph. Capt. James Starr sat on his camp stool, staring straight ahead. Lt. Frank Furness reclined on the ground, a pot of hot coffee at his side. The enlisted men of the company surrounded their officers. One soldier looked wistfully at the National colors, planted firmly in the ground beside a stack of lances. "We had an artist here the other Day, who took a Photograph of our Company first mounted and then dismounted," noted Sergeant Smith in a letter to his brother, "Perhaps you will see them in Philadelphia, if you let me know if you can Recognize me on them."[107]

Two days later, the last two companies of the 6th Pennsylvania Cavalry traded in their lances for carbines. The 6th Pennsylvania was no longer Richard Rush's regiment, and it no longer carried the hated lances. Few of the men were sorry to see the lances go. "The red pennant on the lance-pole had been a veritable target for the enemy when a lance was out on picket," complained Sgt. Joseph Blaschek of Company M, "besides, they had been a decided nuisance in a wooded country."[108] At least one officer decried the decision to get rid of the lances. Turning in the lances meant that the 6th Pennsylvania Cavalry lost "its individuality as a regiment," observed Lieutenant Coxe.[109] The loss of the lances necessitated a name change for the regiment. "We have always been known by the name of Rushes Lancers, but we are knowen now to be the 6th Pa Cavalry for we have turned in our Lances," reported Clement Hoffman to his mother. "We have carried them going on two years and have never had a chance to make a charge with them to any advantage, and so they were turned in and carbines given out to the regiment instead."[110]

Brig. Gen. Montgomery Meigs, the army's chief quartermaster, was also sorry to see them go. "I do not believe that any two rebel regiments, either foot or mounted, in an open field, would resist or await a charge of the 6th Pennsylvania, armed with the lance," wrote Meigs, in an effort to retain the weapon in service. "A regiment of lancers, with the protection of the bullet-proof steel vest, would have great advantages."[111] Meigs's pleas fell on deaf ears. The lances vanished forever, replaced with model 1863 Sharps single-shot breech-loading carbines, a weapon that could pump out more than six shots per minute in the hands of a proficient trooper. All of those hours spent mastering the lance drill came to nought.

Meigs was not the only one to lament the passage of the lances. In an article about lancers and dragoons in the fall of 1863, the *Army and Navy Journal* wryly observed, "Of lancers, we have in the regular service made not a single experiment, and but a single one, that of Colonel Rush's regiment, among the volunteers. The fate of that is well known; the steeds are not dust, but 'the lances are rust,' 'turned in to the quartermaster,' and unlikely to see the light again." The commentator noted that while the theory of using the lance was admirable, it was unwieldy an awkward in practice, and no use at all in a close melee. "While granting that the weapon has not had a fair trial in America, we are inclined to think it better for show—a forest of spears and pennons—than for use," dismissively concluded the article.[112]

Now relieved of their lances, the men of the 6th Pennsylvania Cavalry spent the next several weeks picketing and scouting the north bank of the Rappahannock River. On May 9, Lt. Theodore Sage, the regimental quartermaster, arrived at Bealeton Station with the unit's wagons, and the men enjoyed the simple luxuries of tents, blankets, a change of clothing, and plenty to eat. On May 10, the regiment moved to Hartwood Church, near Falmouth, where it enjoyed some much needed rest, with the men's leisure interrupted only by their regular tours of picket duty and the occasional scout for guerrillas. "The only trouble we have here is with Guerrillas," declared Cowan. "They are not of much account except to attack unarmed men when straggling from camp, and the like."[113] On May 13, Lt. Albert P. Morrow rode out toward Morrisville to check on his picket posts and was captured by men of Maj. John S. Mosby's 43rd Battalion Virginia Cavalry. He was then sent to Libby Prison for the second time in twelve months.

Fortunately, his stay lasted less than two weeks this time. He was exchanged at City Point, near Petersburg, on May 25, and reported to the parole camp on June 4. Morrow received orders to report to his regiment on June 6, and rejoined the Lancers on June 8, just in time to participate in the great Battle of Brandy Station, fought the next day.[114]

On May 24, the regiment moved to Dumfries, where it spent five pleasant days picketing and refitting from the hardships of the raid. On May 29, the Lancers moved to Warrenton and on to Bealeton and Catlett's Station, where they bivouacked for the night. The next morning, they received orders to prepare permanent camps. With Furness's help, they selected fine ground on the edge of a wood near Cedar Run, which provided an excellent source of water. They remained there until June 8, scouting and picketing toward the mountains and the Rappahannock, spreading as far as Warrenton. On May 30, Companies A and D marched to White Ridge, where they spent the next several days carrying messages back and forth between Pleasonton's and Buford's headquarters, located not far from Beverly's Ford on the Rappahannock.[115]

As Hooker regrouped his defeated army, Robert E. Lee and the Confederate high command decided to invade the North. Preparations began, and the Rebel army began massing in the area near Culpeper Court House. All the Confederate cavalry concentrated there while it prepared to cover Lee's invasion. The Army of the Potomac's Cavalry Corps was poised to cross the Rappahannock River at Beverly's and Kelly's Fords, where it would fall upon the Confederate cavalry. This cavalry fight, known as the Battle of Brandy Station, involved nearly 21,000 mounted troopers on both sides and was the largest cavalry engagement ever fought in North America. It also marked the opening of the second Confederate invasion of the North, the Gettysburg Campaign.

Chapter Six

THE BATTLE OF
BRANDY STATION

Following his dramatic victory at Chancellorsville, Robert E. Lee decided that the time was right for another invasion of the North. After a series of meetings held in Richmond, the Confederate leadership approved the audacious plan, which would serve a variety of purposes: First, it held the potential of relieving Federal pressure on the beleaguered Southern garrison at Vicksburg. Second, it provided the people of Virginia with an opportunity to recover from "the ravages of war and a chance to harvest their crops free from interruption by military operation." Third, it would draw Hooker's army away from its base at Falmouth, giving Lee an opportunity to defeat it in the open field. Finally, Lee wanted to spend the summer in Pennsylvania, living off the rich farms there, and giving the war-weary farmers of Virginia a break.

Following the decision to invade the North, Lee shifted troops west for a strike up the Shenandoah Valley, set to kick off on June 3. Rumors of this activity trickled into Union headquarters almost immediately. On May 27, Col. George H. Sharpe, of the Provost Marshal General's office and chief of intelligence for the Army of the Potomac, reported, "There are three brigades of cavalry 3 miles from Culpeper County Court House, toward Kelly's Ford . . . These are Fitz. Lee's, William H. Fitzhugh Lee's, and Wade Hampton's brigades. . . . The Confederate army is under marching orders, and an order from General Lee was very lately read to the troops, announcing a campaign of long marches and hard fighting."[1] Sharpe's report provided the impetus for Hooker, who decided to "send all my cavalry against" the assembling mass of Confederate horse, in an attempt "to break . . . up [the offensive] in its incipiency."[2] In accordance with this strategy, Pleasonton ordered Buford to reconnoiter the area around Bealeton in an effort to determine the true object of the Confederate movement.

On the 28th, Pleasonton received a report from Gregg that a large force of Confederate cavalry occupied the vicinity of Culpeper Court House. The report indicated that the cavalry brigades of Fitzhugh Lee, W.H.F. Lee, Hampton, and Charles Field had gathered there. Pleasonton asked Hooker for permission to send Buford's Reserve Brigade and a battery to reinforce Gregg at Bealeton. Since Buford had previously reported bad grazing for his horses at Dumfries, Pleasonton recommended the transfer, since the new position would provide better lines of supply.[3]

Hooker wasted no time in approving the request. He also ordered Buford to assume command of all cavalry forces operating in the area. Further, Hooker gave an important order: "if he should find himself with sufficient force, to drive the enemy out of his camp near Culpeper and across the Rapidan, destroying the bridge at that point." Hooker correctly guessed that the Southern cavalry had concentrated there to mask a Confederate advance up the Shenandoah Valley. Buford received explicit orders to spare no effort to find out the objective of the enemy movement, stating that "at all events, they have no business on this side of the river."[4]

On June 2, Buford learned that three brigades of J.E.B. Stuart's cavalry had gone into the Shenandoah Valley for unknown purposes. Pleasonton instructed Buford to "aid in the fixing the locality and numbers of the enemy's cavalry especially, with a view to our future movements. Send us by telegraph all the news obtained, and have scouting parties active. The capture of prisoners, contrabands, etc., may give much information."[5] Uncertain of the enemy's whereabouts or plans, Hooker had every reason to be worried. Knowing the value of good cavalry scouting, the Army commander wanted the ever-diligent Buford to find the enemy and ascertain the Rebels' intent.

On June 5, Buford sent a remarkably accurate dispatch to Army headquarters. He reported:

> I have just received information, which I consider reliable, that all of the available cavalry of the Confederacy is in Culpeper County. Stuart, the two Lees, Robertson, Jenkins, and Jones are all there. Robertson came from North Carolina, Jenkins from Kanawha, and Jones from the Valley. Jones arrived at Culpeper on the 3d, after the others. Since the Chancellorsville fight, their cavalry has been very much increased from the infantry; 800 Texans from Hood's command have been recently mounted upon horses from Richmond. My informant—a refugee from Madison County—says Stuart has 20,000; can't tell his instructions, but thinks he is going to make a raid.[6]

While Buford overestimated the number of Confederate cavalry by nearly two times, he still provided Army headquarters with excellent intelligence of the enemy's whereabouts and dispositions.

On June 6, Buford reported to Pleasonton: "The information sent yesterday has been partly corroborated; none of it denied. Yesterday cannon firing was heard toward Culpeper. I suppose it was a salute, as I was told Stuart was to have had that day an inspection of his whole force." Buford noted that Confederate Maj. Gen. John Bell Hood's infantry division was camped on the Rapidan at Raccoon Ford, but that he could not determine whether any Confederate infantry occupied the area north of the Rapidan. Buford offered his belief that "there is a very heavy cavalry force on the grazing grounds in Culpeper County."[7]

Buford's information about Stuart's "inspection" was correct. In fact, Stuart had staged his second grand review of his cavalry in a two-week period on the June 5. The first grand review of the Confederate cavalry occurred on May 22, with much gaudiness and swagger, Stuart being especially fond of pageantry. Confederate Secretary of War James A. Seddon and a large entourage of local ladies attended the second review. As Stuart's adjutant, Maj. Henry B. McClellan, described it, "Eight thousand cavalry passed under the eye of their commander, in column of squadrons, first at a walk, and then at the charge, while the guns of the artillery battalion, on the hill opposite the stand, gave forth fire and smoke, and seemed almost to convert the pageant into real warfare. It was a brilliant day, and the thirst for the 'pomp and circumstance' of war was fully satisfied."[8] That night, Stuart and his dashing cavaliers romanced the local belles at a grand ball.

Not all the Confederate troopers appreciated the spectacle of the grand review as much as Major McClellan. The brigade commanded by Brig. Gen. William E. "Grumble" Jones had only arrived at Brandy Station on June 3 and 4, after completing a long and taxing raid in western Virginia. Jones and his men were tired and tattered. "Many . . . grumbled about the useless waste of energy, especially that of the horses; and when it was announced a few days afterward that there was to be another grand review on the 8th, the grumblers were even more numerous and outspoken." Nearly all the complaining ceased, however, when Jones announced that Robert E. Lee had ordered another inspection for June 8, and that the general planned to attend in person.[9] The Confederate troopers set about preparing their equipment and horses. Their attention distracted, the Southerners seemed unaware of Buford's presence in the area.

Union cavalry continued probing at Stuart's pickets, attempting to ascertain the precise whereabouts and intentions of the Rebel cavalry. Buford sent Col. Alfred Duffié's division into northern Culpeper County. Duffié came within four and a half miles of Culpeper. He took no casualties, and reported that the Confederates seemed to be avoiding a fight. At 3 a.m. on June 7, Buford forwarded this intelligence to Pleasonton, who was on his way to Warrenton Junction to assume field command of the Cavalry Corps.[10]

Upon arriving at Warrenton Junction, Pleasonton knew only of the great concentration of enemy cavalry near Culpeper. He did not know whether Confederate infantry was also camped there. Neither Pleasonton nor Hooker was aware that Stuart's cavalry had been sent to Brandy Station to cover the northward movement of Richard S. Ewell's and James Longstreet's Corps or that Lee had ordered the march north to resume on June 10.[11] In case the cavalry encountered enemy foot soldiers, Pleasonton requested infantry support for his cavalry. Hooker informed Pleasonton that a brigade of 1,500 picked infantry under the command of Brig. Gen. David A. Russell would be ordered to report to Pleasonton at Kelly's Ford, and that a similarly sized infantry force under Brig. Gen. Adelbert Ames would also join them there.

That afternoon, Hooker issued critical orders to Pleasonton. "From the most reliable information at these headquarters, it is recommended that you cross the Rappahannock at Beverly and Kelly's Fords, and march directly on Culpeper," directed Hooker. "For this you will divide your cavalry force as you think proper, to carry into execution the object in view, which is to disperse and destroy the rebel cavalry force assembled in the vicinity of Culpeper, and to destroy his trains and supplies of all description to the utmost of your ability." Hooker further told Pleasonton to keep his infantry forces together, and to use the woods and terrain to mask their movement as much as possible in order to maintain the element of surprise. If the strike succeeded and the Confederates were routed, Hooker wanted Pleasonton to pursue the Southern cavalry vigorously, and to use all available means to destroy Stuart's corps once and for all.[12]

Brig. Gen. Alfred Pleasonton.
(Library of Congress)

The gently rolling terrain around Brandy Station was mostly fields and woods, but its well-defined road network lent itself to rapid movement by large bodies of mounted troopers. Several fords on the Rappahannock, including Beverly's and Kelly's Fords, allowed for easy passage. Beverly Ford Road, which crossed the river near St. James Church, was a major artery for commerce. Fleetwood Hill rises above the railroad station that gave the settlement its name. One officer of the 6th Virginia Cavalry observed, "Fleetwood Heights is a beautiful location. Being an elevated ridge . . . it commands the country and roads leading north and south from Brandy Station."[13] Stuart's headquarters crowned this prominence overlooking the area around Brandy Station. One of Stuart's staff officers described the area: "The country is open for miles—almost level without fences or ditches and the finest country for cavalry fighting I ever saw."[14] This ground had already witnessed several cavalry engagements.

Early on the morning of June 9, Col. Alfred N. Duffié marched his division to Kelly's Ford, where he joined Gregg's command for the crossing. The night before, Buford's division and Ames's brigade of infantry took position at Beverly's Ford, four miles upriver from Kelly's Ford. Five companies of the Lancers rode with Buford. The other five companies were doing picket duty along the Orange and Alexandria Railroad at Bealeton and Warrenton Junction. These five companies would not arrive on the battlefield until later in the afternoon on June 9.[15] Thus, the forces fell into place for the great cavalry battle at Brandy Station, where 12,000 Union and 10,000 Confederate cavalrymen would meet in intense and prolonged combat.

While the Union troopers prepared to attack them, Stuart's unsuspecting troopers held another inspection for Robert E. Lee. This was a businesslike affair, the spectators being all soldiers. A straight furrow was plowed into the adjacent farmland, and the twenty-two regiments of Confederate cavalry were arrayed along both sides. Stuart's famed Horse Artillery deployed four fine batteries of sixteen guns atop nearby Fleetwood Hill. "It was a splendid military parade; Stuart's eyes gleamed with peculiar brightness as he glanced along this line of cavalry in battle array, with men and horses groomed their best," noted one Confederate, "and the command arrayed with military precision, with colors flying, bugles sounding, bands playing, and with regimental and brigade officers in proper positions."[16] Lee watched from atop a low rise near the railroad bed.

Lee's artillery chief, Gen. William Pendleton, recalled that Lee and Stuart and their staff officers "had a ride of it, some six miles at full run for our horses, down the line and up again, and then had to sit our horses in the dust half the day for the squadrons to march in display backward and forward near us."[17] In an effort to conserve ammunition, Lee ordered that no artillery rounds be fired in this review.[18] Stuart's magnificent display lasted several exhausting hours.

Grumble Jones felt that the great show was a waste of resources. "No doubt," muttered Jones, "the Yankees, who have two divisions of cavalry on the other side of the river, have witnessed from their signal stations, this show in which Stuart has exposed to view his strength and aroused their curiosity. They will want to know what is going on and if I am not mistaken, will be over early in the morning to investigate."[19] Jones proved right on target in his estimate of the Yankee intentions.

Pleasonton developed a plan for his attempt to destroy Stuart's force. Buford would command the right wing of the operation, including the First Division and a brigade of selected infantry regiments to be commanded by Brig. Gen. Adelbert Ames. Brig. Gen. David Russell would command a second brigade of select infantry regiments. These regiments came from all the corps of the Army of the Potomac, and included some of the best fighting regiments of the army. The men considered their selection for this assignment a great honor. In addition, several batteries of Federal horse artillery would also accompany the columns, adding firepower to the already potent Union force. Brig. Gen. David McM. Gregg would command the left wing.

Under Pleasonton's plan, Buford's men were to cross the Rappahannock at Beverly's Ford and ride to Brandy Station, where they would meet Gregg's Third Division. Gregg's division would cross the Rappahannock at Kelly's Ford several miles to the south. Duffie's small division was to cross at Kelly's Ford, and then proceed to the small town of Stevensburg, several miles south of where they would link up with Gregg's column. The united columns of Federal troopers would then push for Culpeper, where they would fall upon Stuart's unsuspecting forces and destroy them. The infantry would support these attacks, in case Confederate infantry showed up. Careful timing would be required to pull off the attack as planned.[20]

Pleasonton's plan assumed that the Confederate cavalry was concentrated at Culpeper, five miles from Brandy Station. A rude surprise awaited the Federals the next day, when they discovered that the Rebel cavalry lay just across the Rappahannock. This critical flaw in Pleasonton's plan had major consequences for the coming battle.

On the night of June 8, Buford's men camped on the north side of the Rappahannock in Fauquier County, just across from Beverly's Ford. One of his troopers later recalled, "we marched that night to within a mile or two of the fords, and awaited the approach of dawn."[21] Chaplain Gracey described the eve of the great battle. "Late in the night we arrive behind the wood nearest the river, and bivouac for the night. No fires are allowed, and we make our supper of cold ham and hard tack, spread our saddle-blankets on the ground, and with saddles for pillows, prepare for a night's rest," he wrote. "Our minds are full of the coming battle on the morrow, and various speculations are indulged in regard to our prospects of success. We understand that the cavalry forces of the two armies are to meet at early dawn in what will doubtless prove the greatest cavalry engagement of the war. Our men are confident of success, and eager for the fray. A group of officers are eating their cold supper, perhaps the last they shall all take together. The morrow will soon break upon us, full of danger and death. Messages are committed to friends to be transmitted to distant loved ones, 'in case anything should occur.' And after solemn and earnest prayer we are all sleeping soundly."[22]

At two in the morning, the Federal troopers awakened to hushed orders; the command "to horse" was whispered, instead of being blared by the Division's buglers. Buford's troopers quietly mounted up and moved stealthily toward Beverly's Ford, arriving at 4:30.[23] That night, a thick fog settled across the river, and a ghostly haze covered the approach of the Union troopers, making it difficult to discern shapes across the river in the cool and pleasant dawn. The water at Beverly Ford was three and a half feet deep, with narrow openings atop the steep river banks, forcing the Union troopers to cross the river in columns of four.

Col. Benjamin F. "Grimes" Davis commanded Buford's First Brigade. One of Davis's staff officers sat mounted at the Ford, and as each company commander came through the Ford, he received the whispered order, "Draw sabers!" Davis's command splashed across the Rappahannock, his 8th New York in the lead, followed by the 8th Illinois and the 3rd Indiana.[24] Once across the river, Buford ordered Davis to push any enemy videttes back from the Ford a mile or so.[25]

In fact, Buford's old nemesis, Grumble Jones's Brigade, lay just across the river, standing picket duty after the inspection by General Lee. Unbeknownst to the Federals, Jones's men had built a sturdy barricade of rails along the edge of a wood near the ford.[26] A company of the 6th Virginia picketed the area. Davis's sudden appearance in their front shocked these Virginians. Many of them were either still asleep or cooking their breakfasts when Davis's onslaught caught them. As Buford's men closed in on their camps, Confederate officers turned out their commands and ordered them "to horse."

Company A of the 6th Virginia, commanded by Captain Bruce Gibson, vigorously resisted the Union approach. Gibson fell back slowly, his retreat protected by ditches in the low ground on either side of Beverly Ford Road, thereby preventing the Union troopers from flanking the Virginians, and limiting their attack to the 6th Virginia's front.[27]

Gibson's delaying action permitted Maj. C. E. Flournoy, the regimental commander, to scrape together a force of 150 men with which to blunt the Union onslaught. The sleepy troopers sprang to horse after they were awakened by the crack of gunfire coming from the vicinity of the Ford. Flournoy led a hasty countercharge, many of his men pitching in without their coats or saddles.[28]

The two forces collided in the road, and a brief but savage saber fight occurred. Flournoy yielded to the sheer weight of numbers. However, Lt. Robert Owen Allen, of Company D of the 6th Virginia, riding in the rear of Flournoy's retreating column, spotted Grimes Davis, alone and approximately seventy-five yards ahead of the rest of his column. Seeing an opportunity, Allen rode up to Davis, who was facing his men, urging them on. Davis's last words were, "Stand firm, Eighth New York!" Even as he yelled this, Davis evidently sensed danger and turned upon Allen with a swing of his saber. Allen avoided this blow by throwing himself on the side of his horse and fired his pistol. Davis fell from the saddle, killed instantly. Sgt. John Stone of Company D of the 6th Virginia rode forward to Allen's assistance. Enraged by the loss of their commander, the Union troopers charged Stone, and mistaking him for Davis's killer, attacked him ferociously. A saber blow split Stone's skull "midway between eyes and chin," killing him on the spot.[29]

At the same time, the 7th Virginia Cavalry, under command of Lt. Col. Thomas Marshall, grandson of the great Chief Justice of the Supreme Court, John Marshall, arrived and joined the 6th Virginia's counterattack. The 8th New York, confused and demoralized by Davis's death, lost its way in the woods and pulled back to regroup. Command of the brigade devolved on Maj. William S. McClure of the 3rd Indiana. The 8th Illinois, next in the Union column, held off the Confederate counterattack, permitting the rest of the column to regroup and prepare to resume the charge. The loss of Davis hit the Union troopers hard. "When the sad news of Davis's fall reached me, I crossed and pushed to the front to examine the country and to find out how matters stood," wrote Buford. "I then threw the 1st Division on the left of the road leading to Brandy Station with its left extending toward the R[ail] Road." Buford also brought up Ames's infantry brigade and posted the Reserve Brigade on the right, all connecting from right to left.[30]

As Buford's troopers formed lines of battle, the aroused Confederate cavalry and horse artillery pressed them hard. The surprise of the original Union assault had nearly bagged four batteries of Confederate horse artillery, but quick thinking by Capt. James F. Hart of the Washington (South Carolina) Artillery saved the guns. Seeing the approaching Union onslaught, Hart unlimbered one of his guns in the Beverly Ford Road to cover the retreat of the Confederate troopers and the other batteries of horse artillery. This action slowed

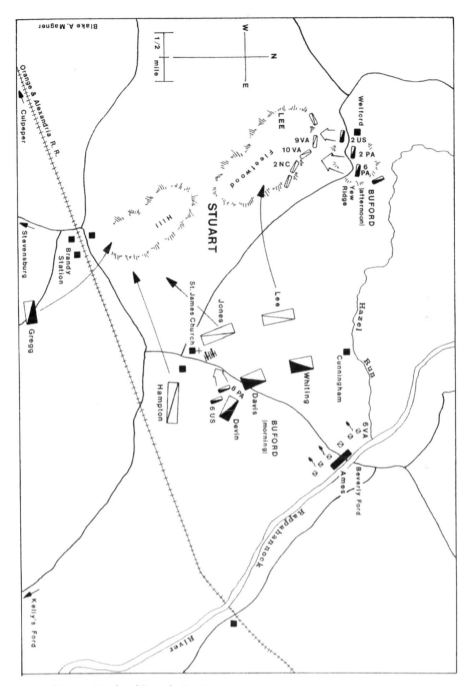

Map 4. Battle of Brandy Station.

the Yankee approach long enough for Grumble Jones to deploy his brigade in line of battle to protect the guns from the Union attack. Once safely out of range of the stalled Yankees, Stuart's batteries unlimbered again just east of St. James Church, approximately a mile and a half from Beverly Ford, defending a ridge that they held for much of the morning's fight. These Confederate batteries maintained a steady and accurate fire, helping to repulse repeated Union attacks on the St. James Church position.

Seeing the approaching Union troopers and recognizing the danger facing his lone brigade, Grumble Jones committed the last of his reserves to the fight. In an effort to secure his flanks and rear, he sped the 11th and 12th Virginia regiments, along with the 35th Virginia Battalion, to reinforce his battle line at St. James Church.[31] Before the 35th could even form line of battle, Jones ordered it to countercharge the Yankee approach while the Union troopers charged the 12th Virginia. A member of the 12th Virginia remembered the charging Yankees "as thick as angry bees from a hive."[32]

The 35th Battalion of Virginia Cavalry struck the lead elements of the Federal charge and blunted it. After a brief melee, the Virginians drove the Union troopers back into the woods. Rallying, the Union troopers again charged and drove the 35th back into the woods from which it came. In the meantime, the 12th Virginia became heavily engaged. A member of the 12th Virginia recalled, "For hours this seesawing was kept up. Finally, after we had driven them the fourth or fifth time to their rallying point [the nearby woods], they showed no disposition to charge again, and we fell back to the hill."[33]

In the meantime, Buford, along with the five regiments of the Reserve Brigade, including the 6th Pennsylvania Cavalry, crossed the Rappahannock and headed toward the sound of the firing. Advancing, the Regulars met little resistance for the first mile of their approach. They were finally stopped by the Confederate line of battle and massed artillery near the Churchyard. Several batteries of Stuart's famous horse artillery were deployed along the ridge in front of a tree line, arranged to the right of the wood-framed church. Their barrels frowned down at the Union horsemen below. Buford did not know the strength of the force guarding the Confederate guns at St. James Church. These cannons presented a very tempting target: if Buford could take them, Stuart would be deprived of his vaunted horse artillery.

Buford deployed the guns of Lt. Samuel S. Elder's battery of horse artillery and ordered the Lancers to charge the Confederate cannon and capture them. This was unusual for Buford, who was not in the habit of ordering rash, blind charges. However, he had a great deal of respect for and trust in the abilities of the Reserve Brigade, and for the Lancers, and he ordered the charge in spite of the associated risk. The Lancers faced a stiff challenge: any charge would have to cross an open field, criss-crossed by ditches, charging uphill into the teeth of a Confederate force of unknown strength and multiple guns manned by veteran artillerists. Five companies of the 6th Pennsylvania— Companies A, D, F, K, and L—made a "dash of conspicuous gallantry" across a field and into the teeth of the Confederate artillery at St. James Church.[34]

Following Major Morris, who drew his saber and led them away, the five companies of Lancers "charged the enemy home, riding almost up to the mouths of his cannon," reported Buford, nearly capturing two of the Confederate guns.[35] "We charged with drawn sabers," recounted a sergeant of Company K.[36] As the column of Lancers emerged from the shelter of the woods, the Confederate artillerists "rained shell into us, and as we approached nearer, driving them like sheep before us, they threw two rounds of grape and canister, killing as many of their men as ours," recalled Capt. Ulric Dahlgren of Philadelphia, a fearless twenty-one-year-old staff officer who joined the charge. The Confederates advanced their carbineers, who opened fire on the flank of the Lancers as they ran by. "All this time we were dashing through them, killing and being killed," recalled Dahlgren, "some were trampled to death in trying to jump the ditches which intervened, and falling in, were crushed by others who did not get over." Dahlgren's horse was shot in three places, and the young man was thrown. He managed to remount the badly injured horse and rallied the Lancers on the colors before escaping, but not before receiving a bruising saber lick from a pursuing Confederate.[37]

"We dashed at them, squadron front with drawn sabres, and as we flew along—our men yelling like demons—grape and cannister were poured into our left flank and a storm of rifle bullets on our front," recalled Maj. Henry C. Whelan.

> We had to leap three wide deep ditches, and many of our horses and men piled up in a writhing mass in those ditches and were ridden over. It was here that Maj. Morris's horse fell badly with him, and broke away from him when he got up, thus leaving him dismounted and bruised by the fall. I didn't know that Morris was not with us, and we dashed on, driving the Rebels into and through the woods, our men fighting with the sabre alone, whilst they used principally pistols. Our brave fellows cut them out of the saddle and fought like tigers, until I discovered they were on both flanks, pouring a cross fire of carbines and pistols on us, and then tried to rally my men and make them return the fire with their carbines.[38]

Pvt. Henry I. Cowan of Company K made the charge. "Taking them by surprise we drove their centre and continued on without pulling up until we arrived in front of their battery where they opened grape and canister which cut us terribly," he wrote. "It was at this point that the rebel brigade closed in on us from the right and left when the fighting was terrific." Cowan had a very close call. "In the engagement I saw a Rebel making a cut at me, not being fully prepared to receive it I wheeled my horse when he struck him on the head and staggered him but a load from my carbine sent him to his long home."[49]

Many of the Confederates mistook the well-disciplined Lancers for their Regular Army comrades. Confederate artillerist Capt. James F. Hart believed that Regulars charged his guns. He remembered that "never rode troopers more gallantly than those steady Regulars, as under a fire of shell and shrapnel, and finally of canister, they dashed up to the very muzzles, then through and beyond our guns, passing between Hampton's left and Jones's right."[40] At the muzzles of the guns, the Confederate artillery opened up, raking the Union line.

"What an awful fire! So close that we are almost in the smoke of the battery. Many of our saddles are emptied, and the horses, freed from the restraint of their riders, dash wildly away; and at the same moment, hundreds of carbines send their charges of death into our never-wavering ranks," recalled Gracey. "Our color sergeant reels, and falls from his horse; another sergeant catches the colors before they reach the ground; and on through the storm of death our weakened lines advance until they meet the enemy, and hand to hand the conflict rages. Though we are outnumbered two to one, we break their ranks, and pursue them into the woods. Now the enemy on our right begin to close upon us: our commander has fallen. Major Whelan assuming command, attempts to withdraw us from our terrible position. But how are we to retreat? The enemy have completely surrounded us—all is lost!"[41] Capt. Charles L. Leiper, the commander of Company L, received a severe saber cut to his head during the melee for the guns. Leiper needed fifteen days of medical leave to recuperate from this slash.[42]

Although Chaplain Gracey indicated that the colors were recovered before hitting the ground, it does not appear to be the case. The men of Jones's Brigade, who defended the guns, captured six flags or guidons during the fighting that day. The 12th Virginia claimed two, while the 35th Battalion Virginia Cavalry claimed four stands of colors.[43] The Lancers' regimental guidon was recovered in Richmond at the end of the war, and this episode is the single known instance where the regiment lost a color bearer. It appears, therefore, that the regimental guidon was lost in the melee for the guns.[44]

"There seemed to be no hope of our escape. I saw our orderly sergeant and some of our officers give up their arms. A large number of them were lying on the ground. Some beckoned me not to run over them," recounted Sgt. Hamilton Ballentine. "I was struck on the bridle hand with a saber and one of my fingers was badly cut. I then dropped my saber to quiet my horse. I was rushed upon by 8 or 9 with pistols. One of the men put his pistol up to my mouth. I don't think any of the pistols had ammunition for some of the rebels turned and galloped away."

Seeing an opportunity, Ballentine emptied three saddles with his pistol. However, when he fired his third shot, he horse broke its bridle chain and galloped away. Ballentine lost his saber and his pistol as his runaway horse ran deeper into the Confederate lines. Grayclad troopers clutched at Ballentine as he dashed by them on the out of control horse. "I then bore all of my strength on my left side line which I thought would either throw me or turn him to the road by which we had come in. I accomplished the latter and he turned and passing in front of the rebel battery never stopped until he and I fell in a piece of woods near the river." Ballentine was safe for the moment, but he was eager to get back into the fray.[45]

Troopers who lost their mounts to the ditches and artillery fire opened with their carbines and laid down a steady, deadly fire. Seeing the predicament facing the 6th Pennsylvania, Buford ordered four squadrons of the 6th U.S. to charge in support of the gallant Pennsylvanians.[46]

Dr. John B. Coover, the Lancers' regimental surgeon, followed along behind the charge. He stopped to tend to an injured man, but took shelter behind the trunk of a tree as he ministered to the man. "As I reached out my hand to take the man's arm a shell came *whizzing* through the trees taking off the top of a smaller one just by my side," recounted the doctor. Coover quickly pulled back and retreated to the woods. "The ride back through the woods I think was the most unpleasant ride I ever made," he recalled. "I know not how many balls and shells *escaped* me but they were sufficient in number to render the trip simply terrible." Dr. Coover stayed in the relative safety of the woods for the rest of the long day.[47]

Maj. Robert Morris, Jr. (USAMHI)

Just as the Confederates prepared to fall upon the bloodied Pennsylvanians, the 6th U.S. arrived on the scene, distracting the Rebels. The blue and gray troopers merged in a wild melee among the guns. "The warlike scene was fascinatingly grand beyond description, and such as can be produced and acted only by an actual and real combat. Hundreds of glittering sabres instantly leaped from their scabbards, gleamed and flashed in the morning sun, then clashed with metallic ring, searching for human blood, while hundreds of little puffs of white smoke gracefully rose through the balmy June air from discharging firearms all over the field in front of our batteries," recalled a Confederate artillerist. "The artillerymen stood in silent awe gazing on the struggling mass in our immediate front."[48] The line of battle swayed back and forth from the woods in front, toward the church, now advancing, now receding.

In the confusion created by the melee for the guns, the Yankees, realizing that they were not strong enough to hold the position, retreated across the same fields toward the main Union line, all the while taking heavy Confederate artillery fire, sometimes from a range as short as fifty yards. With the air whistling with the sounds of shrapnel and minie balls, the beleaguered Federal troopers desperately clung to the necks of their horses as they dashed across the fields toward friendly lines in the woods. "Oh! What a fearful ride, full two miles of ground covered with dead and wounded men and horses, wide ditches, which my dear sorrel cleared like an antelope, and [all] the time pursued and fired at by those grey blood hounds, who kept yelling for me to surrender," described Major Whelan of his escape. His sorrel "Lancer" cleared a five-foot high stone wall and carried the major to safety, shots ringing in his ears.[49]

Their gallant charge took a fearful toll on the five companies of Lancers. Sgt. Hamilton Ballentine, who barely escaped capture in the melee for the guns, was stunned by the carnage. "Up until 12 o'clock I had found 15 of our company hunting for the company but there was no company to be found," declared Ballentine the next day. "Our only lieutenant and Sergeant [Michael J.] Golden with the remainder of the company had been killed or wounded. I then reported to Captain Davis who had gathered up the balance of other companies who with our 15 numbered about 50 in all. We then formed a company and counted off. We were commanded by Captain Davis and [Lieutenant] Lening."[50]

As the Lancers played out their drama among the guns strung along the ridge, the rest of Buford's division got into the action. Col. Thomas C. Devin's small brigade crossed the Rappahannock and prepared to join the fray. McClure's brigade also rallied and began re-forming to get back into the fighting. Before long, Buford would have three brigades to bring to bear. However, for now, the Lancers, with just the 6th U.S. Cavalry to support them, would have to go it alone for just a bit longer until the other two brigades got into position to support them.

Recognizing that he was about to be overrun and desperately hoping that Stuart would arrive with reinforcements, Jones sent the 35th Battalion and the 11th Virginia charging into the midst of the Federal attackers. Their determined charge blunted the advance of the bluecoats, and McClure's troopers fell back through the woods onto the oncoming columns of Devin's Second Brigade, coming up to join the fighting. McClure's men eventually retired all the way to the Rappahannock before rallying and regrouping. The 35th Battalion also drove Devin's supporting troopers back into the woods nearly one hundred yards.[51]

Devin's brigade rallied and formed a dismounted line of battle in the woods. Charging the Virginians on foot, Devin's men shoved the gray cavalry back toward St. James Church in a severe engagement that became hand-to-hand in many places. The 35th Battalion captured and sent more than twenty-five Union officers and enlisted men to the rear. The fight had turned out to be much tougher than any of the Union officers had anticipated, and Buford was surprised to learn that Brig. Gen. Wade Hampton's command had now arrived on the field.

Hearing the crash of gunfire while drinking his morning coffee at 8:30 a.m., Jeb Stuart hurried off toward the sound of the firing. Along the way he had to dodge the panicked teamsters of the Confederate wagon trains hurrying away from the fighting: "The wagon trains came first and went thundering to the rear mid clouds of dust—then came the cavalry regiments at a trot with here and there a battery of artillery,—all hurrying to the front with the greatest possible speed."[52] Stuart reached St. James Church and took personal command of the fight.

While Stuart tried to bring order to the chaos at St. James Church, Brig. Gen. W.H.F. "Rooney" Lee's brigade also came up from its camp at the nearby estate known as Welford, rushing to the sound of the guns. Thus, Jones's hard-pressed command received reinforcements at a critical moment. Seeing the fierce combat raging around Beckham's guns, Stuart ordered Hampton's men to form line of battle, to the right of Jones, facing north. To flush the Federal cavalry from the woods, Hampton ordered some of his horse soldiers to dismount, and sent them forward as skirmishers. Before long, several hundred of Hampton's command fought dismounted against Devin's brigade. They attempted to outflank Devin's position, shifting steadily to his right. Thus stymied, Devin remained in position along the Union right for much of the afternoon, anchoring the flank.[53]

Rooney Lee's command fell into line to the left of Jones, extending to the north. A stone wall that offered a strong defensive position ran parallel to Lee's line. The line itself was L-shaped, with both wings almost at right angles to each other. Lee posted his dismounted troopers along the wall and others along a ridge directly behind and above it. These defensive positions offered excellent fields of fire at advancing Federals and afforded Lee's men an opportunity to enfilade the flank and rear of the Union position. The Confederates awaited the next attack with determination, with some of their best troops on line, and with their chieftain in personal command.[54]

Lee's men fended off a number of uncoordinated, piecemeal attacks by Buford's cavalry. When an attack by the 5th U.S. enjoyed limited success, Buford decided to commit the entire Reserve Brigade to the assault. He ordered the Regulars forward, supported by Elder's battery and Ames's infantry brigade. Buford deployed the dismounted Regulars into line of battle alongside McClure's and Devin's Brigades, with the infantry regiments deployed along either flank. While the fresh troops were being organized, Buford called up his artillery.

Buford's troopers had been fighting constantly for nearly six hours. Although Gregg's attack was supposed to have been coordinated with Buford's, Buford had stood alone for the entire morning. Nobody expected a battle of such magnitude, but neither side was willing to quit. Both Stuart and Pleasonton used the lull to redeploy and to take the opportunity to recover dead and wounded comrades. At that moment, as Stuart prepared to launch a full-scale counterattack, the unmistakable sound of fighting to his rear shifted his attention away from Buford. Finally, around 11:30, as one member of the 8th New York recorded in his diary, Buford's men "heard the booming of distant cannon which told us that Gen. Graig had arrived from Kelly's Ford and was engaging the enemy."[55]

Gregg's Third Division passed around behind Stuart to the southwest of St. James Church before being spotted near Fleetwood Hill. A protracted and desperate fight broke out along Gregg's front. Hearing the sound of Gregg's guns, Buford "resolved to go to him if possible." With that goal in mind, Buford took all of his force, except for the 5th U.S., which had been left to support Graham's Battery, to anchor the right, "swung around under a tremendous artillery fire and gained the crest overlooking Brandy Station, then came the infantry."[56]

In order to counter Gregg's threat, Stuart detached Jones and Hampton from Buford's front and ordered them to the defense of Fleetwood Hill, leaving only Rooney Lee's Brigade in Buford's front. Pleasonton had ordered Buford to hold his position, so the Kentuckian did not move directly around Lee's flank to Fleetwood Hill. Instead, he remained in a defensive position along a ridge on the Cunningham farm. Perhaps Lee's strong defensive position behind the stone wall also deterred Buford.

Buford took advantage of the withdrawal of the two Confederate brigades to extend his lines in an effort to outflank Lee's position along the stone wall. Eventually, he worked his dismounted troopers into a position that threatened to envelop Lee's lines.[57] The waist-high wall provided a natural breastwork and complicated the task faced by the Yankee horsemen. Also, Confederate artillery covered the entire area. In short, Rooney Lee held a formidable defensive position. A successful attack by Buford would have placed him in the rear of Stuart's position, poised to roll up the Confederate flank from the side and rear. However, at 4:00 p.m., Rooney Lee attacked first, pushing forward his own skirmishers in an attempt to flank Buford's position and to sever his lines of communication and retreat across Beverly's Ford.

In response, Buford called up some of his infantry support and parried Lee's thrust. Emboldened by the success of the infantry, Buford ordered Maj. Henry C. Whelan, now in command of the Lancers, to launch a mounted charge against the Confederate position. Once again, the Pennsylvanians thundered across an open field of nearly six hundred yards, passing "through a perfect tempest of shell, grape, canister, solid shot and rifle bullets." Supported by Capt. Wesley Merritt's 2nd U.S., the Pennsylvanians dashed toward the 10th Virginia through a storm of small arms and artillery fire. Capt. Charles B. Davis and two enlisted men were killed before they reached the wall, leaving Lt. Frank Furness to take command of Davis's company. The Confederate canister belching from the top of the ridge dismounted fully one-third of the men. Eight officers lost their mounts.[58] Major Whelan later described this second charge as "decidedly the hottest place I was ever in. A man could not show his head or a finger without a hundred rifle shots whistling about. . . . The air [was] almost solid with lead."[59] Spearheaded by the impetuous charge of the Lancers, Buford's Federals pressed forward until they collided headfirst into a countercharge by the 9th Virginia.

The 9th Virginia, with sabers drawn, crashed into the charging Pennsylvanians, and casting "them into confusion and forcing them back, not along the line of their retreat,

Pleasonton's cavalry operating as skirmishers. (Library of Congress)

but directly on the stone fence through which there was but a narrow opening; and dealing them some heavy blows during the necessary delay in forcing their way through it. They were followed by men of the Ninth at a gallop through the field beyond the fence to the edge of the woods, where a Federal battery was in position. A good many of the prisoners which the Federals had taken were released by this charge."[60]

Outnumbered three-to-one, the 6th Pennsylvania had no choice but to fall back. "We then being so hard pressed we had to fall back," shuddered Sergeant Ballentine. "There we lost heavily."[61] Major Whelan's beloved horse Lancer was shot out from under him, prompting his master to write, "although in that hail storm of iron and lead I could have sat down and cried. I own that my eyes filled with tears as I walked slowly away." Fortunately, Whelan's orderly gave up his mount, and the major made it to safety. Only then did Whelan realize that the bullet that had killed Lancer had also bloodied his wrist.[62]

Henry Cowan made his second hell-for-leather charge of the day, and also had his second close call of the day. "After the charge the remnants of the 5 companies in command of Capt. Davis were ordered to advance as skirmishers to a stone wall and fence where we dismounted. Capt. Davis was killed before we reached the stone wall here the dismounted Rebels charged us but we repulsed them," he wrote. "When they charged us my horse became excited—reared and jumped, and broke loose from me—when our ammunition was exhausted they charged us again when we were obliged to retreat. Here I got a gray horse his rider being killed. I had hardly mounted him when he was shot in the fore shoulder but he managed to carry me safe while I found my own—I am safe."[63]

The Confederate success was short-lived. No sooner had they driven the 6th Pennsylvania from the hill than the 2nd U.S. attacked. The 2nd U.S. had spent much of the day supporting one of the Federal batteries and eagerly joined the fray. Merritt later wrote, "At last an order—which we all had hoped and all but asked for, and which General Buford told me he was anxious to give, but had not the authority, but which no doubt he carried—finally came."[64] In addition, Buford ordered Lt. Albert O. Vincent's battery of horse artillery to unlimber within 400 yards of the enemy and to open fire in conjunction with the Regulars' attack.[65]

Following the line of the 6th Pennsylvania's attack, and supported by the fire of Vincent's battery, the 2nd U.S. pitched into the flank of the 9th Virginia, driving it back. In his after-action report, Buford described the charge of the Regulars. "Out flew the sabres, and most handsomely they were used," he declared.[66] Capt. Wesley Merritt led the charge of the 2nd U.S., which, in "its impetuosity, carried everything before it. It bore up the hill, across the plateau, and to the crest on the other side." The Regulars repulsed more than twice their numbers in their savage attack.[67]

However, a vicious counterattack by the 2nd North Carolina and the 10th Virginia reached the hill, crashed into the Regulars, blunted their attack, and pushed them back toward the Union starting point, although Col. Solomon Williams, the commander of the 2nd North Carolina, fell mortally wounded by a pistol ball.[68] The Confederates eventually rallied and drove the Regulars back. Rooney Lee was badly wounded in the leg during this melee.

When Buford prepared his report of the battle, he wrote that his men had "gained the crest overlooking Brandy Station," but that they could not hold it. He further noted that "The enemy, although vastly superior in numbers, was fought hand to hand and was not allowed to gain an inch of ground once occupied."[69] The fight for Yew Ridge was savage and bloody, with hundreds of sabers flashing in the afternoon sun. One Union trooper recalled, "At one time the dust was so thick we could not tell friend from foe."[70] Had Buford and Gregg coordinated their efforts and linked forces, they may very well have driven the Confederates from the field. However, they failed to do so, and a golden opportunity slipped away. Buford must have been frustrated by the nearness of total victory.

Earlier in the afternoon, Hooker had given Pleasonton discretionary orders allowing him to withdraw if he felt it was necessary to do so. By 5 p.m., Pleasonton's command was fought out, and the Cavalry Corps commander exercised that discretion when he learned that Confederate infantry was reaching the battlefield. In fact, Robert E. Lee himself came to investigate after he received a dispatch from Stuart describing the attack. Lee wrote back that two divisions of Confederate infantry were nearby, and that Stuart was "not to expose his men too much, but to do the enemy damage when possible. As the whole thing seems to be a reconnaissance to determine our force and position, he wishes these concealed as much as possible, and the infantry not to be seen, if it is possible to avoid it."[71] Lee wanted to avoid tipping his hand regarding the proximity of his infantry.

As the day dragged on and the fighting grew more desperate, however, the Confederate commander finally ordered Confederate infantry to come to Stuart's support.

Concluding that his men had done enough for one day, Pleasonton sent one of his staff officers, Capt. Frederic C. Newhall of the 6th Pennsylvania, to ride to Buford with orders to withdraw from the field. Newhall found Buford "entirely isolated from the rest of the command under Pleasonton . . . but paying no attention and fighting straight on."[72] Buford later wrote that once the firing ceased on Gregg's front along Fleetwood Hill, "I was ordered to withdraw. Abundance of means was sent to aid me, and we came off the field in fine shape and at our convenience. Capt. [Richard S. C.] Lord with the 1st U.S. came up fresh comparatively with plenty of ammunition and entirely relieved my much exhausted but undaunted command in a most commendable style. The engagement lasted near 14 hours."[73]

Covered by the fresh men of the 1st U.S., which was kept in reserve to support the artillery for most of the day, and the men of Ames's infantry brigade, Buford's division splashed across Beverly's Ford at a leisurely pace. Newhall, who communicated the order to retreat to Buford while he watched the charge of the 2nd U.S., recalled that Buford himself "came along serenely at a moderate walk." Buford then climbed the knoll above the river and joined Pleasonton and a large group of officers to observe the final act of the day's drama as the sun dipped below the horizon.[74] Pleasonton later noted, "General Buford withdrew his command in beautiful style to this side, the enemy not daring to follow, but showing his chagrin and mortification by an angry and sharp cannonading."[75] That night, the Lancers occupied the same bivouac as the night before.[76]

The 6th Pennsylvania used up all its ammunition in the day's heavy fighting, and suffered the largest Federal loss at Brandy Station—108 casualties, including eight officers.[77] "Our company, I might say, is no more," lamented Henry Cowan, who escaped unharmed. "Of the 5 companies that charged I don't think that they would make a full company—when we returned we left 32 men I believe laying on the field out of our company alone. Only 5 of our wounded, in our company, that we were able to bring off."[78]

"I think I have God's blessing or else some better Christian than I am is praying for me," declared Cowan's friend, Sergeant Ballentine. "The 9th of June will never leave my memory. I had two small wounds, one on the left hand with two fingers cut a little and a ball in my left thigh. It just scorched my pants and blackened my leg." The spent ball raised a large lump—probably a hematoma—that pained him for days after the battle at Brandy Station. It could have been much worse.[79]

Major Morris was taken prisoner and would die a lonely death in Richmond's notorious Libby Prison. Sgt. Lewis Miller of Company L lamented that the loss of Morris was "worse than one hundred men."[80] "He had lived in a narrow and proud circle at home," recalled Captain Newhall, "he was the great grandson and namesake of the famous Robert Morris of the Revolution, and had a fiery temper which at first he could not curb;

116 **Rush's Lancers**

but he was a born soldier, and after a little learned by the contact that other men were his equals, and from that time he was a model cavalry officer."[81]

Capt. Charles B. Davis was killed in action. Sgt. Hamilton Ballentine found the body and, with nine men of Company K, carried it to safety. Ballentine and his squad escorted the body to Bealeton Station.[82] Chaplain Gracey took Davis's remains to Washington to be embalmed and sent him home for burial. "He is a great loss to the regiment and is deeply mourned," noted Whelan.[83] Capt. Charles L. Leiper was severely wounded and was taken to the Cavalry Corps hospital. So was the regiment's adjutant, Lt. Rudulph Ellis. Lts. Thompson Lenning and Samuel R. Colladay were captured with Major Morris.[84] Leiper, in particular, accounted well for himself. "He fought like a Turk with pistol and sabre, and was surrounded and disarmed, but still stuck to his horse and striking with his fists finally broke away and escaped," praised Major Whelan.

Twice, Maj. James H. Hazeltine was struck by spent balls, one of which injured him rather badly but did not force him to leave the field. Hazeltine had a bad day. During the morning, he stood at his horse's head, engaged in conversation, when a Confederate ball "banged" his horse, shattering its spine. "The Major could not have looked sorrier had it struck him instead of the horse," observed Dr. Coover.[85]

Buford wrote, "The men and officers of the entire command without exception behaved with great gallantry." He had good reason to be proud of his Regulars that day—they had acquitted themselves well, and they had matched their foe blow for blow.[86]

Indeed, he said that the Lancers "had covered themselves with glory," and henceforth called them "my Seventh Regulars."[87] This was high praise indeed from the hard-bitten old horse soldier, who was not prone to excessive praise. His recognition of their sacrifices at Brandy Station provided a source of great pride for the men of the Lancers.[88] Many Confederates already considered the former Lancers a Regular unit—trooper George W. Watson of the 12th Virginia later remembered them as "the Seventh Pennsylvania Regulars."[89]

"The conduct of the officers and men of the regiment was so uniformly good that it is impossible to mention any for particular distinction," declared Major Whelan.[90] Maj. Charles J. Whiting, an old Regular, commanded the Reserve Brigade at Brandy Station. "No old regiment could have conducted itself better," he proclaimed.[91] "The handsomest charge of the day was by the 6th Penn (Rush's Lancers) but without their lances," declared Ulric Dahlgren, who would have known.[92] "Nothing more can be said against the Lancers as they at last have got into the thick of it," observed an officer of the 3rd Pennsylvania Cavalry.[93] The men of the regiment realized what they had been through. Trooper Thomas L. Yergey of Pottstown, who had served in Company D, said in an interview to his local newspaper years after the end of the war: "He thinks Beverly Ford [Brandy Station] was the hardest battle he was ever in," noted the reporter.[94] A sergeant of Company F quite correctly described the fight at Brandy Station as the "Red Letter Day in the History of our Regiment."[95]

Word of the stellar performance of the Lancers soon reached the highest echelons of the Army of the Potomac. General Meade, after hearing of the day's ordeal, wrote home, "The Lancers particularly distinguished themselves, though I am sorry to hear with considerable loss. . . . I am glad that the regiment has had a chance and so brilliantly availed themselves of it."[96] Brandy Station became the regiment's defining moment, its greatest accomplishment. After the end of the war, the veterans chose June 9 as the date for their annual reunion in tribute to their valor that day.

The Philadelphia newspapers noticed the heroic performance of the 6th Pennsylvania Cavalry at Brandy Station. "We have communications from witnesses of the great cavalry fight on the Rappahannock, which speak in terms of the highest commendation of the gallant conduct of the Sixth Pennsylvania Cavalry, formerly known as 'Rush's Lancers'," reported a correspondent. "This fine regiment, which, by the way, abandoned the lance as unsuited to the service . . . and is now armed with carbines and sabers, was in the extreme advance of General Buford's Division, and was on three distinct occasions during the day engaged in the most desperate hand to hand conflicts, in all of which it greatly distinguished itself by the most brilliant charges and the most determined fighting." He concluded, "It gives us great satisfaction to award to this splendid regiment the laurels it has so proudly won. Circumstances of various sorts have hitherto prevented the Sixth Pennsylvania from proving in the field of what manner of metal they were made; but none who knew anything of the quality of the officers and men comprising the regiment, are surprised at the record it has now made for itself."[97]

Pvt. Clement Hoffman of Company E, who was not present at Brandy Station, raised an interesting point in describing the fight. "Our regiment was the first to charge on the rebels and were pretty badly cut up when if they had had their lances when they charged they would not have been half so badly cut up," he observed.[98] Perhaps the lances might have made a difference on the plains in front of St. James Church. Perhaps General McClellan's theory would have been borne out. It was not to be. The Lancers' performance was all the more notable, considering that this was their first engagement without the lances. They employed tactics that were as unfamiliar as the lance drill was familiar, and they met the challenge in every way imaginable that long, hot day.

For the second time in the war, Federal cavalrymen had slugged it out with Stuart's men and fought them to a standoff. One trooper of the 8th New York wrote, "the Rebels were going to have a review of their cavalry that day, but our boys reviewed them."[99] The Confederates sustained 51 killed, 250 wounded, and 132 missing, while the Yankees suffered 484 killed and wounded and 372 taken prisoner. These casualties speak volumes for the severity of the fighting that day. "The once pertinent question 'Who ever saw a dead cavalryman' can no longer be asked with the same degree of quiet satire," keenly observed Surgeon Coover.[100]

Perhaps the greatest consequence of Brandy Station was its effect on the morale of the Federal cavalry. As Stuart's aide Henry McClellan later wrote, "This battle . . . made the Federal Cavalry. The fact is that up to June 9, 1863, the Confederate cavalry did have its own way . . . and the record of their success becomes almost monotonous. . . . But after that time we held our ground only by hard fighting."[101] Another Confederate, Trooper John N. Opie of the 6th Virginia, noted, "In this battle the Federal cavalry fought with great gallantry, and . . . they exhibited marked and wonderful improvement in skill, confidence, and tenacity."[102] The historian of the 10th New York Cavalry noted that the performance of the blue troopers that day "forever settled the question of superiority as between the gray and the blue cavalry in favor of the latter."[103]

On June 11, upon returning to Warrenton Junction two days after the brutal fight, Pleasonton reported to Hooker that he had "just reviewed [the] cavalry. They are in fine spirits and good condition for another fight."[104] However, in spite of the superb performance by his command, Pleasonton failed to disperse the concentration of Confederate cavalry in the area around Culpeper. He also failed, ultimately, to delay the departure of the Confederates on their march north—the great invasion started just one day later than originally planned. After Gettysburg, Pleasonton disingenuously claimed that he discovered the Confederate plan to invade the north at Brandy Station, but this argument has little merit. Pleasonton's subsequent actions and communications with army headquarters simply do not support this contention. Capt. Charles Francis Adams, Jr., of the 1st Massachusetts—never an admirer of Alfred Pleasonton's—grumbled, "I am sure a good cavalry officer would have whipped Stuart out of his boots, but Pleasonton is not and never will be that."[105] That was, perhaps, true.

Chapter Seven

THE GETTYSBURG CAMPAIGN

T HE GREAT CAVALRY BATTLE AT Brandy Station delayed the beginning of Lee's invasion by just one day. On June 10, Confederate infantry began moving north, with
the Union army following tentatively. As the army marched, Pleasonton reorganized his
staff as he settled into permanent command of the Cavalry Corps. On June 13, he made
his own staff appointments, superseding Stoneman's February appointments. Capt.
Frederic C. Newhall was appointed assistant inspector general of the Cavalry Corps, and
Lt. Col. C. Ross Smith was appointed chief ordnance officer for the corps, replacing
Capt. Wesley Merritt, who assumed command of his regiment, the 2nd U.S. Cavalry.[1]
Events were moving quickly now, and many changes were afoot.

By June 15, the Reserve Brigade had reached Thoroughfare Gap. Troopers of the 6th
Pennsylvania found Rebels picketing the entrance of nearby Manassas Gap, triggering
suspicion that the Southern army was concentrating in the Loudoun Valley of Virginia.[2]
Over the next week, a series of heavy engagements between the cavalry of both armies
ensued while Pleasonton's horsemen desperately searched for Lee's army and Stuart's
command struggled to prevent the Federals from discovering Lee's advance toward the
Potomac River. The opposing cavalries performed an elaborate dance that led to significant battles at Aldie, Middleburg, and Upperville on June 17, 19, and 21, respectively.
The battered Lancers sat out these fights, missing some of the toughest cavalry fighting
of the war. Instead, they stayed at Fairfax Station, licking their wounds and trying to
return to combat readiness after their mauling at Brandy Station.

The Army of the Potomac cautiously pursued Lee's advance. As the army inched its
way north, Hooker desperately sought information regarding the whereabouts of the
Confederate army, sending couriers all over the countryside to find the far-flung elements of the Army of Northern Virginia. Native Pennsylvanians like the Lancers grew
worried as Lee's army neared and eventually entered the Keystone State.

Company K had lost all of its commissioned officers, its orderly sergeant, and its
quartermaster sergeant in the charge at Brandy Station, meaning that command of the
company—and all of the accompanying administrative duty—fell upon the shoulders of
the ranking sergeant, Hamilton S. Ballentine. "I am really tired of my life," Ballentine

complained on June 23. "Since the 13th of this month we have had no rest. We had had heavy skirmishing every day since. Last night we had orders to go into camp. We had just got our horses unsaddled and I was in the act of changing my underclothes when 2 or 3 of Jeff's shells paid us a visit. Then came the scamper to get saddled and mounted. The enemy was soon repulsed and we had time to come back and gather up our trappings. We stood to horse all night." The Lancers did not get much of a rest while the invasion of Pennsylvania played out in front of them.[3]

The Lancers finally moved out on the afternoon of June 24, marching to Fairfax Court House. On June 26, they crossed the Potomac River on pontoon bridges at Edwards Ferry, and then onto Poolesville, Maryland. They eventually reached Frederick on the 27th. "I am perfectly satisfied being whare I am for we have a chance of seeing and knowing all of the movements which this Army makes," wrote Clement Hoffman of Company E, "I am well satisfied with the duty which we perform and could not wish for anything beter."[4]

Sgt. Thomas W. Smith agreed. "You must excuse me for not writing sooner, but the fact is for the last two weeks we have been kept so buissy," he wrote on June 27, "that it seems more like an indistinct Dream to me than anything else. We have been kept running Night and Day ever sinse we left the Rapahanock." He speculated about what might happen if the armies entered Pennsylvania. "If the Rebs are marching through the old Keystone State I think they will get into a Trap. For if the Militia are able to hold them in check at Harrisburgh, and Hookers Armey in their Rear which it is by this time or will be in a few Hours! We have got them Foul."[5]

On June 28, at his own request, Joseph Hooker was relieved as commander of the Army of the Potomac, and was replaced by a Philadelphian, Maj. Gen. George Gordon Meade, the commander of the Fifth Corps. "Gen Mead has command of the army now but I do not think he will have command long," declared saddler Dorastus McCord that night. "It is my belief that that Little Mac will take hold the rope again. I have been arguing so much for him since he has left the army that they call me Mac Altogether."[6] Meade's appointment to command prompted a Lancer to observe, "It is my opinion that the President had relieved [Hooker] for fear that he would get outgeneralled again as he was at Chancellorsville."[7] The Philadelphian quickly demonstrated that he was an able army commander who earned the respect of those serving under him. "Meade has the army under his thumb and his subordinates know that he cannot be trifled with," noted Capt. Charles Cadwalader of the Lancers, who was appointed to Meade's staff. "He is a thorough soldier and requires his orders to be thoroughly executed and everything is done on the jump."[8]

The Reserve Brigade also needed a new commander. Maj. Samuel H. Starr of the 6th U.S. Cavalry had commanded it since Brandy Station. However, Starr, an unpopular martinet, had not performed well at Upperville. Eager to rid himself of officers such as Starr, Pleasonton arranged for the promotion of three young staff officers, Wesley

Pleasonton giving chase to Stuart's cavalry during the Battle of Aldie. (Library of Congress)

Merritt, George A. Custer, and Elon J. Farnsworth, directly from captain to brigadier general of volunteers.[9]

Merritt assumed command of the Reserve Brigade. The twenty-nine-year-old New Yorker was very much John Buford's protégé. Talented and modest, Merritt was a professional soldier from the West Point class of 1860.[10] He rose quickly through the ranks and commanded the 2nd U.S. Cavalry at the Battle of Brandy Station. Bigger and better things awaited this young man—he was to have a forty-three-year career in the U.S. Army, retiring as a major general and the Army's second ranking officer after triumphantly accepting the surrender of Manila during the Spanish-American War. A staff officer recorded that he "had a constitution of iron, and underneath a rather passive demeanor concealed a fiery ambition. He was and is, I am glad to say a successful and very able soldier, and well deserves the high rank he now holds in the regular army of the United States."[11]

Merritt was "the embodiment of force." He was "one of those rare men whose faculties are sharpened and whose view is cleared on the battlefield. His decisions were delivered with the rapidity of thought and were as clear as if they had been studied for weeks. He always said that he never found that his first judgment gained by time and reflection," noted a Regular officer. "In him a fiery soul was held in thrall to will. Never disturbed by doubt, or moved by fear, neither circumspect nor rash, he never missed an opportunity or made a mistake."[12] An officer of a Michigan cavalry regiment had numerous opportunities to observe Merritt over the years. He noted, "Modesty, which fitted him like a garment, charming manners, the demeanor of a gentleman, cool but fearless bearing in action, were his distinguishing characteristics."[13] The new brigadier proved to be the right man to command the Reserve Brigade.

On June 29, Merritt's men moved to Middletown, Maryland, at the foot of South Mountain, and remained there until June 30. Then, over Buford's objections, the Reserve Brigade was detached and sent to Mechanicstown (Thurmont), Maryland, where it spent the next several days guarding wagon trains. Buford, who was most comfortable with his Regulars and the Lancers, wanted his largest and most reliable brigade for the difficult duty that awaited his command in Pennsylvania. His pleas for the return of the Regulars went unfulfilled, leaving him to enter Pennsylvania with only two brigades. He moved on to Gettysburg and took up position on the northern outskirts of town.

The Battle of Gettysburg opened with Buford's courageous defense of the "high ground" on McPherson's Ridge. Without his preferred brigade, Buford conducted a magnificent delaying action on the morning of July 1, holding off the better part of two divisions of Confederate infantry for several hours, long enough for a portion of the Army of the Potomac's infantry to come up and relieve the hard-pressed cavalry. The next day, Pleasonton ordered Buford's two brigades to march to Westminster, Maryland, where they spent the next day and a half guarding the Army of the Potomac's critical lines of supply and communication. Ten frustrated companies of the Lancers, sitting idle at Mechanicstown, could hear the great battle raging just a few miles north. They yearned to rejoin the rest of the army, but orders were orders, and they were stuck guarding the trains at Mechanicstown.

In the meantime, Capt. Emlen Carpenter's squadron, consisting of Companies E and I, was still serving as the army's headquarters escort. On July 1, they marched to Gettysburg, arriving there about 10 p.m. Meade established his headquarters in Lydia Leister's clapboard house, and his headquarters escort companies filled Mrs. Leister's yard. "At the Battle of Gettysburg Gen Mead had his Head Quarters at a White Frame House 50 yds in Rear of the Left Center.[14] The Staff Officers and Orderlies were all in the Garden around the House (a space of about 30 yds square)," recalled Sgt. Thomas W. Smith, who was a member of Company I. He had a good view of the day's action. "On July 2nd there was Heavy Skirmishing all Day with Artillery Firing on our side, which the Rebs did not answer untill 4? o'clock p.m. When the Engagement became general all along our lines," he recounted. "They pressed our Left verry hard untill 7? p.m. when we repulsed them. At mid day July 2nd our Lines were in the same position as in the Morning but our Skirmishers were some what advanced."[15]

Carpenter's squadron passed an uneventful morning on July 3, listening to the fighting raging on nearby Culp's Hill. However, at 1:00 that afternoon, the Army of Northern Virginia's artillery suddenly opened the largest barrage ever heard on the North American continent. Clement Hoffman, of Company E, found himself under heavy fire. "About noon the Rebels opened on our left & center with all of the artillery they had in the

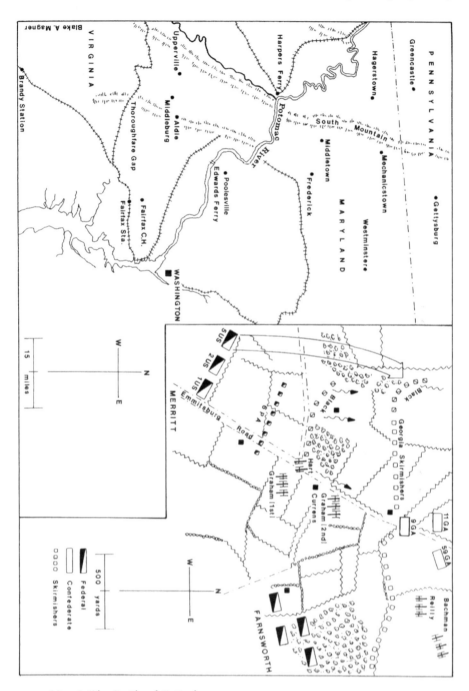

Map 5. The Battle of Gettysburg.

intention of breaking our lines, but they found it a mistake. . . . It was the hardest Artillery fighting that ever took place during this war," he reported. "I was at the front during all of the fight and came safe and sound altho both men and a wonderful sight of horses fell all around me. . . . Our captain had both of his horses shot dead and slightly wounded himself some half a dozen of our company had their horses shot but no one was killed."[16]

Sgt. Thomas Smith left a similar account. "At this point our Lines took a turn to the Right so that Head Quarters were under a terrable Cross Fire from the Rebble Artillery. There were 21 Horses killed outright in the Garden at Head Quarters. We Lost 11 Horses out of our Sqaddron, Capt Carpenter of Comp E lost two Horses," he wrote home. "Nearly every Horse at Head Quarters was wounded or scrached by pieces of Flying Shell, some of them so bad that they had to be Killed afterwards. There were several Officers and men killed, and some badly Wounded at Head Quarters, but strange to say. . . . I had not one man disabled, though several of them were struck by Pieces of Shell."[17]

Carpenter's troopers had a close-up view of Pickett's Charge, a grand spectacle few would ever forget. "At 1 o'clock p.m. the Rebs opened a terable fire on our Left and Center from 16 Batteries. They tried verry hard to break our left," recalled Smith. "Charging by whole Divisions but after a severe contest were hand somely repulsed."[18]

Having finally left the trains at Mechanicstown behind them, eight companies of Lancers saw heavy combat on the afternoon of July 3 when they, along with the 1st, 2nd, and 5th U.S. Cavalry, launched a dismounted attack upon Lee's thinly defended right flank after the repulse of Pickett's Charge. The Reserve Brigade marched to Gettysburg via the Emmitsburg Road, where it linked up with Farnsworth's Brigade operating on the Confederate far right, not far from Big Round Top. The Lancers led Merritt's advance, uncertain how large an enemy force lay in front of them. With two companies serving as Meade's headquarters escort, and another one hundred men detached for a special mission, only eight companies participated in the fighting at Gettysburg.

As they neared the battlefield, the Lancers were thrown forward as skirmishers. "The Sixth Pennsylvania, having the advance of our brigade, was the first of the cavalry engaged," recounted Chaplain Gracey. "The men were dismounted, led horses taken to the rear, when we pushed forward to meet the infantry line of the enemy."[19]

Col. John L. Black, of the 1st South Carolina Cavalry, was guarding the Confederate right flank. Black spotted the advancing Pennsylvanians, ordered his small detail of a hundred troopers and the "ragtag and bobtail" of the Army of Northern Virginia, mostly teamsters and ambulance drivers, to prepare to meet the attack of the Lancers. Believing that his "ragtag and bobtail" would prove to be little more than a nuisance, Black ordered "the part of my command I could rely on dismounted & deployed as skirmishers." After making his dispositions, Black rode off to Brig. Gen. Evander M. Law's headquarters to report the threat developing on the flank. Law, commanding Hood's Division after Hood suffered a severe wound on July 2, was responsible for this sector of the Confederate battle line.[20]

Law had only Black's ragged command, two pieces of horse artillery of Capt. James F. Hart's battery, and the batteries of Capts. William K. Bachmann and James Reilly in place to meet this threat. Brig. Gen. George T. "Tige" Anderson's brigade, consisting of the 7th, 8th, 9th, 11th, and 59th Georgia Infantry Regiments, held the Confederate far right flank. They were quickly mobilized. Anderson had been badly wounded on July 2, and his brigade had suffered heavy losses that afternoon. Although badly shot up, a substantial force of infantry and artillery nevertheless awaited Merritt's attack. An officer of the 6th Pennsylvania observed, "It is risking little to say that on the whole Confederate line at Gettysburg, there was hardly a point so well guarded by the enemy when Merritt's little cavalry brigade, lacking one whole regiment—the Sixth Regulars—and the others reduced by detachments, and fighting and marching of the last three weeks, came up this way from Emmitsburg."[21]

Eight companies of Lancers dismounted and drove Black's skirmishers, "the carbines and rifles rattling on both sides of the [Emmitsburg] Pike, till the enemy's line was met across the road from [Currens'] house," recounted Capt. Frederic C. Newhall. "It had that confident look of being there to stay, which soldiers appreciate, and either Merritt called a halt, or Law brought him to a stand, just as you may happen to fancy from the report of one or the other."[22] Although they took heavy fire, they held their position. "The 6th Pennsylvania was on the advance, and soon found line on either side of the road," noted Lt. Eugene Bertrand, who, although a member of the Lancers, served on Merritt's staff. "Driving in the enemy's outposts, [they] proceeded until within about a mile of Gettysburg where they met the enemy in full force, but still held their ground."[23]

The stone Currens farmhouse proved to be especially troubling to the Lancers—it was filled with enemy sharpshooters who took a toll on the advancing skirmishers.[24] Accurate fire by Capt. William M. Graham's battery of horse artillery provided much needed support. Graham's gunners took a position on the right side of the road on a small hill that "had splendid observation of the entire front."[25] The Lancers drove the Confederate skirmishers from the Currens house, drawing fire from an entire brigade of infantry and ten pieces of artillery. The Lancers sheltered behind a low stone wall that ran perpendicular to the Emmitsburg Road (at the site where the monument to the 6th Pennsylvania Cavalry stands today). They held a position about halfway across a large open field, which sloped from the woods down to a low point and then back up again toward the wood line held by the Confederates. "The Pa. Cav. were in an ordinary skirmish line," remembered trooper Samuel Crockett of the 1st U.S. Cavalry, who could see their position from Merritt's main line of battle.[26]

Merritt advanced troopers to support the Lancers. Two squadrons of the 1st U.S. came into line alongside the Pennsylvanians and added to their fire. Reinforced by a squadron of the 2nd U.S. and a squadron of the 5th U.S., these Regulars extended

Merritt's line in an attempt to outflank the Confederates. They assumed a position to the right of the Lancers, extending the line in front of Graham's battery.[27] Capt. Isaac R. Dunkelberger commanded Company E of the 1st U.S. Cavalry. "A portion of the 6th Pennsylvania Cavalry occupied a stone house in rear of me," recalled Dunkelberger, "the enemy shelled the house, the 6th Cavalry vacated it, and came up on my line. There was a cornfield in my immediate front. The enemy were discovered putting in a horse [Hart's] battery in position in my front. I ordered a charge on foot and we captured the battery before they could load but the enemy retook the battery with a regiment of infantry and in retreating I was struck by a spent ball on my left heel."[28]

The Regulars formed a heavy skirmish line and advanced, passing through the line of the 6th Pennsylvania, struck the Confederate line, and drove it back toward its artillery support. Colonel Black, now very worried about what appeared to be a determined Union attack, went searching for reinforcements. He found General Law and two regiments of infantry, marching along at a leisurely pace. Law ordered his command into line of battle and to open fire on the advancing dismounted Yankee horse soldiers.[29] Law detached the 11th and 59th Georgia, and sent them around to the right, personally placing the 11th Georgia in line of battle.[30]

Law ordered the Georgians to strike Merritt's line "on its end and double it up."[31] Supported by two and a half batteries of artillery, the Georgians filled the air with lead, driving the Regulars and the Pennsylvanians back. "We drove them clean away & Law took his Regiments and went back saying he hoped I could hold the ground," recalled Black.[32] With that, Law took most of his infantry and marched it off to rejoin the main Confederate line of battle in defending against a desperate but ill-advised mounted charge by Elon Farnsworth's brigade in the vicinity of Big Round Top.[33]

Merritt responded by bringing up Graham's guns, which "poured a stream of shot and shell into ranks" of the Confederates.[34] The intense Federal artillery fire forced the Southerners back, again forcing them to abandon their strong position at the Currens house.[35] A spirited contest for possession of Hart's two guns broke out, and after the Federal horsemen failed to take the guns, a lull fell across the battlefield. It did not last long. Soon, Merritt ordered the 5th U.S. Cavalry to make a mounted charge on the Confederate position. The Regulars briefly gained the enemy rear, forcing Law to double-quick his Georgia infantry back across the open fields in the hope of blunting the Federal thrust. Capt. George Hillyer's 9th Georgia Infantry, with Law in personal command, found that "the enemy was nearly at the battery. Passing through from behind the guns, with a yell, the Georgia regiment charged the Federals in the open field, scattering and chasing them away in a moment, killing and wounding a number and capturing several horses."[36] Two more Southern regiments reinforced the 9th Georgia, and the Federal momentum ground to a halt.

The Confederates then fell back to their original position, and after nearly four hours of hard fighting, the engagement on South Cavalry Field petered out. A heavy thunderstorm deluged the weary men of both sides. Soaked and exhausted, Merritt's brigade withdrew to a nearby farm, where they spent the night. The repulse of this attack ended the great Battle of Gettysburg.

Captain Dunkelberger correctly summarized the nature of the action on South Cavalry Field. "When we attacked on the right and left of the Emmitsburg Road, we then entered the enemy's right and rear, had we been successful, we could have occupied their line of retreat. But the real object of our attack was to force the enemy to draw troops from their main point of attack (Pickett's Charge) and repel us. In this we were successful as the Divisions of Hood and McLaws were held back to repel our attack."[37]

Years later, when the Lancers' handsome monument was dedicated on the Gettysburg battlefield, Capt. Frederic C. Newhall, who delivered the dedication speech, correctly observed, "In fact, the operations of Merritt's brigade just at this point were not, and in the nature of things could not be of a very aggressive character. No one familiar with the circumstances can fail to see that he had far too little force to do anything but create a diversion on this flank of Lee's army which was strongly and cautiously held." Newhall concluded, "A brigade of infantry, backed by an army in position, will stop, if it wishes to, a brigade of cavalry outside of the lines of its own army, devoid of any support, and simply moving against the enemy's flank."[38] A great opportunity was lost on the South Cavalry Field that afternoon. However, the Lancers performed admirably under adverse circumstances.

One hundred members of the 6th Pennsylvania Cavalry had a different adventure that day. Capt. Ulric Dahlgren, the aristocratic young daredevil who had helped rally the Lancers at the mouths of the guns at St. James Church, had led a scouting expedition to Greencastle, Pennsylvania, the day before. Along with several enlisted scouts, he had captured important dispatches from the Confederate high command in Richmond to Robert E. Lee.[39] The fearless twenty-year-old staff officer, described by one of the Lancers as "a noted scout," then undertook an even more daring mission, this time taking a hand-selected force of the 6th Pennsylvania Cavalry with him.[40]

Although he was exhausted from a late-night ride of nearly forty miles the previous day, Dahlgren awoke early on July 3, and headed down the Emmitsburg Road toward Mechanicsville, Maryland, looking for the Reserve Brigade, which had spent the first two days of the battle of Gettysburg guarding supply wagons. Dahlgren carried an order from Pleasonton, instructing Merritt to give the young captain some officers and one hundred handpicked troopers to go on a second raid toward Greencastle.[41]

Merritt detailed one hundred horse soldiers from Companies D, F, K, and L of the 6th Pennsylvania Cavalry, which were four of the five companies that made the charge at the guns near St. James Church at Brandy Station. Capt. Charles P. C. Treichel commanded the contingent, along with Lts. Albert P. Morrow, Edward Whiteford, Bernard H. Herkness, and Charles White. Mounting up and moving out, the small column set out toward Greencastle, reaching Waynesboro late on the afternoon of the 3rd. There, the column bivouacked, with the men standing to horse for part of the night. They had a comfortable camp with plenty of food, so the Pennsylvanians welcomed the respite.[42]

At 2 a.m., the horse soldiers again set out for Greencastle, which had been briefly occupied by Brig. Gen. John D. Imboden's Northwestern Brigade of Confederate cavalry on its way to Gettysburg. Captain Newhall complained bitterly. "Soon this fine detachment . . . bearing away to the left and crossing the Blue Ridge at Monterey Pass, was thrashing around in the enemy's rear, on the wrong side of the mountains for safety or comfort, or for any reasonable hope of accomplishing with such a small party, anything to compensate for the risk they ran," he said.[43] They arrived at Greencastle just as it became light.

Chaplain Gracey also left an account of this march. "The small force moved . . . along the roads in the rear of Lee's army over which his trains must pass. They were joined by a large number of civilians mounted and armed with shot-guns, while others carried axes to be used in the destruction of the wagons," he wrote. "On arriving near Greencastle they were informed that the enemy's cavalry held possession of the town. Our little band, led by Captain Treichel, charged through the streets, surprising the enemy and taking 84 prisoners. Lieutenant Morrow received a slight would while leading a portion of the force in this charge, while his horse was killed under him."[44] Lieutenant Whiteford captured a Rebel paymaster and the money he carried.[45] Dahlgren elaborated on their triumph in his diary. "Passed the 4th in Greencastle. The enemy's communications entirely destroyed. Remained in the town all day, feeling proud of our work. Citizens very uneasy about our being there."[46]

Lt. McHenry Howard, a Rebel staffer, recalled that when his small party of horse soldiers came within about a mile of the town, they "heard a shot and then met a mail carrier galloping down the road, who reported that he had been attacked while passing through the town." When Howard and his comrades rode into Greencastle that day, the town "seemed sullenly quiet, doors and windows closed and nobody on the street." When they reached the town square, the blazing carbines of the Pennsylvania horse soldiers met them. There, "about fifty of the Southern Cavalry came down South Carlisle Street, demanding to see the town authorities, but just before they reached the square, the Federal soldiers made a dash and drove them out in splendid style, capturing a considerable number. Though the shots whistled in close proximity to our ears, the citizens remained on the street to witness the result." Howard later commented, "So much for my twenty hours in Maryland and Pennsylvania and so much for my only cavalry experience. I had fired but one shot . . . and this was one of the only two shots I fired during the war. I should add that in this little campaign, we had three men captured—at Greencastle—and one wounded, who got off."[47]

The residents of the town were happy to see Union soldiers after being mostly occupied by the enemy for the better part of two weeks. Residents opened their doors and windows and showed the soldiers hospitality. "A very fine young lady helped me to some nice cakes and cherry pies, recalled Sergeant Ballentine. "She carried a basin of water to me to wash my face for the first time in some days. I was a hard looking case. At the same time I think she took a fancy to me. I know I did to the cherry pies." Ballentine barely had time to savor the sweet treats when Dahlgren sent him with three men to capture some Confederate troops rumored to be hiding in a nearby farmhouse. "Having the pleasant smile of that young lady I was ready for anything." Ballentine and his little detachment charged and captured a detail of twelve Southerners. As a reward, a local man offered Ballentine some whiskey, a gift gratefully accepted by the Irish sergeant. Unfortunately, Ballentine never got to meet his maiden fair again. "I was sorry to leave Greencastle so suddenly without bidding the girl there good-bye," he lamented. "I think that if I had stopped there a day longer I would not be an old bachelor today."[48]

Dahlgren and his Lancers spent the night camped to the south of the town. They got an early start again the next morning.

Confederate Brig. Gen. John D. Imboden faced a daunting task. Robert E. Lee had assigned him to command the Army of Northern Virginia's wagon train of wounded—a seventeen-mile-long traveling sea of misery which wound its way from Gettysburg through the Cashtown Gap south toward Greencastle, on to Hagerstown, and ultimately southwest to the Potomac River fords at Williamsport. Torrential rains and roving parties of Federal cavalry made the task all the more challenging. The 18th Virginia Cavalry, commanded by the general's brother, Col. George Imboden, led the train's advance.[49]

Marching toward Greencastle, Dahlgren found John Imboden's column, happening upon a train of six hundred wagons, accompanied by the 18th Virginia cavalry and a regiment of infantry, supported by a battery of artillery. After following the wagon train for several miles to size it up, the bold Dahlgren allowed the advance of the column to pass and then pitched into the wagons. "The command was moved near to the road and lay concealed until about 300 wagons had passed, when, the force being divided between Lieutenants Morrow and Herkness, they charged to the front and rear of the train at the same time," recounted Gracey. "With the assistance of citizens they destroyed 130 wagons and run the horses off to the woods, captured two iron guns, and 200 prisoners. The strong infantry guard of the train soon appeared in overwhelming numbers, and a severe fight ensued, in which we lost nearly all the prisoners we had previously taken, and a number of our own men captured. Lieutenant Herkness received a severe saber cut and was taken prisoner." Gracey concluded, "Our men fled to the woods and were scattered in small squads during the night. They rendezvoused at Waynesboro, Pa. On the following morning they succeeded in bringing to Waynesboro about thirty prisoners."[50]

During the fracas, Dahlgren's horse was shot out from under him, and "it was only by dispersing his men in different directions amid the deep forest, that he avoided close pursuit and contrived to reach the vicinity of Boonesboro [Maryland]."[51] Despite these tribulations, Dahlgren triumphantly noted in his diary, "Attacked and destroyed one hundred seventy-six wagons. Captured two hundred prisoners, and three hundred horses, and one piece of artillery, which was retaken. Made our way near Boonesboro."[52]

Captain Newhall described these events at the dedication of the Lancers' monument at Gettysburg in 1888. "Near Greencastle, after various adventures, they came upon a section of the enemy's supply-train, amply guarded by infantry and able to take care of itself; but Dahlgren ordered a charge, to which the party responded with all their might, and in a moment they were in the midst of the wagons banging away and trying to capture the train; but the infantry and cavalry escort was entirely too strong for them and they were obliged to beat a retreat, and finally to scatter to avoid the enemy's close pursuit," he said. "Lieutenant Herkness of our regiment was severely wounded and captured, with ten or more of the men, and the whole command was badly cut up, while before Treichel could get the remnant together again the country about him was swarming with rebels retreating now from their bitter defeat at Gettysburg."[53]

Gen. John Imboden also left a vivid account of this encounter. "After the advance—the 18th Virginia Cavalry—had passed perhaps a mile beyond the town, the citizens to the number of thirty or forty attacked the train with axes, cutting the spokes out of ten or a dozen wheels and dropping the wagons in the streets. The moment I heard of it I sent back a detachment of cavalry to capture every citizen who had been engaged in this type of work, and treat them as prisoners of war," recalled the general. "This stopped the trouble there, but the Union cavalry began to swarm down upon us from the fields and cross-roads, making their attacks in small bodies, and striking the column where there were few or no guards, and thus creating great confusion. I had a narrow escape from capture by one of these parties—of perhaps fifty men that I tried to drive off with canister from two of [Capt. J. H.] McClanahan's guns that were close at hand. They would perhaps have been too much for me, had not Colonel Imboden, hearing the firing turned back with his regiment at a gallop, and by the suddenness of his movement surrounded and caught the entire party."[54]

"The Federals had cut the train," noted a Virginian. "My company turned back and Company I came forward; we struck the Yankees in both flanks and drove them away, getting back all they had taken, together with some prisoners."[55] The intense fight took its toll on Dahlgren's little column. By the morning of July 6, only about eighty men remained with him. The young cavalryman's command was "greatly scattered, being secreted by loyal citizens." Lieutenant Whiteford, along with his squad of ten Lancers, hid in Hagerstown while Longstreet's infantry corps passed through the town two days later.[56] Despite the disorganization, Dahlgren learned that some of Jenkins' cavalry had demanded a ransom from the town of Waynesboro. Once again galloping off, he led his horse soldiers on another reckless head-long charge, surprising the Rebel troopers in the streets of the town and scattering them. After a pursuit of nearly six miles, Dahlgren finally gave up the chase, choosing to attack yet another wagon train. His men destroyed a large number of them, and took more prisoners along the way.[57]

On the morning of July 6, Dahlgren found the vanguard of Brig. Gen. Judson Kilpatrick's 3rd Cavalry Division advancing on Hagerstown. The dangerous and taxing raid was over. "On this expedition they destroyed over two hundred wagons, loaded with valuable supplies, that had been stolen from the farmers and merchants of Pennsylvania," noted Chaplain Gracey. "At one time they held more than double their number of prisoners, many of whom escaped during their several engagements, although they succeeded in bringing in to General Buford's headquarters between seventy and eighty of them."[58] The Lancers consistently distinguished themselves throughout the Gettysburg Campaign, enhancing the solid reputation that they had already established.

Brig. Gen. John D. Imboden (Library of Congress)

Back at Gettysburg, the two armies had begun the race to see who would get to the Potomac River first. If Lee's army won, it might be able to make it to safety in Virginia; if the Army of the Potomac got there first, the Federals would be able to bring Lee's army to battle on ground of its own choosing. Thus, the stakes were extraordinarily high as the Rebel retreat from Gettysburg began.

On July 4, soaked by torrential rains that continued unabated for several days, the armies waited in their lines for hostilities to resume. Other than a few limited probes, full-scale combat did not break out. Late that afternoon, the Army of Northern Virginia began retreating toward Virginia, with Imboden's seventeen-mile-long wagon train of wounded leading the way. Uncertain as to Lee's intentions, Meade did not set the Army of the Potomac into motion until July 7. However, Buford's cavalry division, which was rejoined by the Reserve Brigade on July 4, vigorously pursued the beaten Confederates.

After the Regulars joined Buford, the Kentuckian received unexpected orders to mount up and head south toward Frederick, Maryland, about five miles away.[59] As one officer of the 1st U.S. recalled, "The rain fell in torrents, men and horses hungry and worn out."[60] The Federals were in a bad humor as they slogged through the rain and mud. Along the way, they passed a large brick mill. Buford summoned the miller, who happened to be a Pennsylvania Dutchman. The general explained that his horses needed hay and corn and that his men needed flour. "Are you the general commanding these troops?" inquired the farmer.

"Yes," responded Buford.

"Many of my neighbors are rebels. They say the Union army is whipped and in full retreat. Some of my neighbors are Union men. They say the Rebel army is whipped and in full retreat. Will you tell me the truth?"

Without hesitation, Buford answered, "The Rebel army is whipped and in full retreat. We are trying to get to the Potomac ahead of them."

"Thank God," replied the relieved Dutchman, "I would rather have a country and nothing else, than everything my heart could wish and no country. I have about thirty ton of hay, several thousand bushels of corn not shelled, plenty of flour, wheat and buckwheat. Also plenty of corn meal."

Of this manna, the buckwheat flour was most in demand. "Soon hundreds of fires were kindled in the rain with fence rails and six thousand horses had all of the hay and corn they could eat. A ton of buckwheat cakes baked there that morning would be a small estimate," recalled Capt. Isaac R. Dunkelberger of the 1st U.S. The miller did not want to accept a quartermaster's voucher so that he could receive reimbursement for his goods, but Buford insisted. "I wonder if mortal man ever made six thousand men more happy and grateful than that Dutchman did," quipped Captain Dunkelberger. "I regret that I never met him afterwards to personally thank him."[61]

As the six companies of Lancers passed through Emmitsburg, Maryland, six miles south of Gettysburg, the men noticed that the town was in bad shape—a major fire two weeks earlier had destroyed nearly half of the town's best houses and stores, and the town hotel—so that there was no shelter and no place to rest in the howling storm. Chaplain Gracey and a correspondent for the *Philadelphia Inquirer* stopped at a roadside farmhouse and got a scanty meal. Their hostess informed them that the Confederates were only three miles off, and that they were running a small mill only five miles from Emmitsburg. Unfortunately, the weather prevented Merritt from pursuing this opportunity aggressively.[62]

Bogged down by the terrible weather, Buford's Division made it only as far as Frederick, where his troopers camped for the night about five miles west of the town. The rain continued falling in torrents, making the ride miserable for men and animals. "A horse would give out and its rider would dismount and lead or rather pull it along, for the poor animal had scarcely enough strength left to move its own carcass," noted the newspaper correspondent. "Horses dropped down in the road from sheer exhaustion, and were left with their saddles, blankets, and bridles, as there was no way to transport them. Men, whose horses were 'played out,' trudged along on foot, in the mud and wet, with nothing to eat and night coming apace, and no spot to lay down upon, except the wet ground. Truly half of what our officers and soldiers endure in this war has never been told, and yet they stand it all cheerfully, and look upon it as a matter of course."[63] Supplies awaited them in Frederick. Fresh horses were drawn, and the men rested for a short time, sprawling on the wet ground, too tired to care. Even Merritt slept on the soggy ground.

That night, an older man, about sixty years of age, came into Buford's camp. He was a familiar sight to the Union troopers—during the Antietam Campaign, he had been a regular visitor in the Union camps, peddling songbooks.[64] The civilian, who was also under suspicion for his propensity for asking questions of a military nature, found Buford sitting on a log, and began querying him. Shortly, Buford called to his provost marshal, Lt. John Mix, and said simply, "Arrest this man, he is a spy."[65]

The man, one William Richardson, was promptly taken into custody and searched. In his clothing were found detailed drawings of the Federal troop dispositions, passes from Lee and Longstreet, and large sums of both Federal and Confederate money. Based on this evidence, Buford sternly looked Richardson in the eye and said, "You have three minutes to pray." Field officers such as Buford had been given authority to carry out drumhead courts-martial, and to conduct executions by Congressional Act passed in March 1863, so Buford was within his rights to order Richardson's death.[66] After the three minutes were up, the General ordered that Richardson be hanged. Using the ropes from several tents, a heavy line was thrown over the branch of a nearby locust tree, and without further ado, the spy was strung up. A Regular noted, "Buford never got up from the log, nor stopped smoking his pipe, while the man was being executed."[67]

Brig. Gen. John D. Imboden had shepherded the Confederate wagon train of wounded to the Potomac River crossings at Williamsport, Maryland. However, when he arrived, he found that the torrential rains had so swollen the Potomac that it was impassable. Ordered to care for the wounded and protect the river crossings, Imboden prepared to defend the town with a small force consisting of his cavalry brigade, the army's walking wounded, a couple of regiments of infantry, and twenty-four guns.

Buford attacked with his whole division about 1:30 the afternoon of July 6. The Confederates tried to outflank Merritt's position with infantry, which, according to Buford's report, "was most admirably foiled by General Merritt." While no direct attacks were made on Merritt's front, the Confederates there "were so obstinate that General Merritt could not dislodge them without too much sacrifice."[68]

It was about 5:30 before Buford's division, then located four miles from Williamsport near St. James College, encountered one of Imboden's advanced detachments. As Buford's command advanced, it came under both artillery and small arms fire. The Confederate gunners briefly compelled Buford to fall back until Lt. John H. Calef's battery of horse artillery could be brought up. Calef unlimbered and engaged the Confederate artillerists in a counter-battery duel, which the Confederates won by briefly driving Calef's men from their guns, leaving them vulnerable to capture. In response, Buford supported Calef with William Gamble's brigade, and a sharp fight broke out along the Boonsboro Road. Gamble's dismounted troopers attempted to flank the enemy defenses in an effort to get between the Confederates and the river. Federal carbine fire drove the Confederates several miles back to Imboden's main line of defense at Williamsport.

The six available companies of the 6th Pennsylvania Cavalry held the center of Merritt's line, supported by the Regular battery of Capt. William K. Graham. There, the Lancers maintained their position under heavy fire for four hours, knowing that "more than one determined charge of the rebels would have broken our line but for the timely use of canister by Graham's guns."[69]

Devin's brigade massed in the woods to the rear of the Union position, awaiting further orders. At 7 p.m., they relieved Gamble's men on the left front, carrying instructions to disengage and fall back to the woods after dark. Meanwhile, Imboden received word from Fitz Lee that if he could hang on for another half hour, Lee's strong brigade would come to his aid. Resolved to hold his ground, Imboden gamely resisted until Lee's troopers reached the field. Thanks to these reinforcements, the Confederates began shoving back the Union forces.[70]

Devin held the woods until morning, allowing the rest of Buford's command to withdraw. The feisty New Yorker's troopers then conducted a fighting retreat, covering the main line with skirmishers as they retired. Devin heavily picketed the roads in his rear, as members of the 6th New York had detected approaching Confederate infantry and artillery seeking to cut off the Union troopers. Around midnight, the Confederates advanced skirmishers and encountered Devin's picket lines. After a brief firefight, the Rebels withdrew. Devin's brigade suffered significant casualties in this clash.[71]

At 7 p.m., the vanguard of Kilpatrick's division marched down Hagerstown Road, deployed, and opened fire. Hearing this, Buford sent word to Kilpatrick "to connect with my right for mutual support." The connection was made, Buford reported, "but was of no consequence to either one of us."[72] Unfortunately, Fitz Lee's brigade arrived about the same time, and supported by strong and effective artillery fire, drove off Kilpatrick's division. Buford noted, "Just before dark, Kilpatrick's troops gave way, passing to my rear by the right, and were closely followed by the enemy."[73] Fortunately for the Federals, the firing ended at about 8 p.m. The regimental historian of the 6th Pennsylvania observed, "Had the daylight lasted another hour, we would have suffered the most disastrous defeat."[74]

The exasperated and weary Federals drew off. After removing his wounded, Buford retired to a position along the Sharpsburg and Hagerstown Turnpike, and threw out strong picket lines. Properly protected, his cold, wet, and tired division bivouacked for the night. The torrential rains continued to fall, and the Yankee horse soldiers wallowed in a sea of mud.[75]

July 6 was not a good day for Buford. He had failed to drive off Imboden's scratch force, and was unable to capture the great prize at the ford at Williamsport. Brig. Gen. John Imboden did a masterful job of shifting his makeshift force to meet threats, and repulsed both Buford and Kilpatrick in sharp fighting. Imboden proudly wrote years later, "My whole force engaged, wagoners included, did not exceed three thousand men. The ruse practiced by showing a formidable line on the left, then withdrawing it to the right, together with our numerous artillery . . . led to the belief that our force was much greater. . . . A bold charge at any time before sunset would have broken our feeble lines, and then we should all have fallen an easy prey to the Federals."[76]

Safely out of harm's way, most of Buford's division rested on July 7.[77] However, the 6th U.S. Cavalry sortied out in the direction of Funkstown, where it encountered Grumble Jones and his brigade. The 7th Virginia Cavalry attacked and routed the Regulars, chasing them almost all the way back to Buford's main camp. Nearing those environs, the Confederates drew up and fired a volley, which was met by a counter-charge from the startled Yankee troopers. The 7th Virginia then withdrew at a gallop, with men of the 1st U.S. and the Lancers in hot pursuit. "As soon as the Confederate cavalry saw us coming they halted and then commenced to retreat, but their horses were so tired and winded that we soon caught up with them . . . a short running fight took place," recalled Capt. Isaac Dunkelberger of the 1st U.S.[78] When reinforcements of the 11th Virginia joined the 7th Virginia, Buford's troopers gave up the chase.[79]

On the night of July 7, some twenty hours after being hammered back from the eastern approaches to Williamsport, Buford's division bivouacked just north of Boonsboro. Because the Union cavalry command feared a night attack by Stuart's horse soldiers, most of the men stayed awake. The Lancers spent most of the night "dismounted in a ploughed field in line of battle, in a heavy storm of rain, without fires and with clothes thoroughly saturated . . . standing in mud to our knees, every horse remaining saddled and in position, and every man at his horse's head," remembered Chaplain Gracey. "This was one of the most wretched nights of all our experience in the cavalry service."[80] Most of the survivors of the hundred-man detachment sent with Dahlgren rejoined the main body of the regiment at Boonsboro. Their horses were played out, but there was still plenty of hard work remaining to be done.[81] It was the division's worst day of the campaign, and more heavy fighting lay ahead in the coming days.

General Buford, impressed by the toughness and performance of Lt. Albert P. Morrow, added the handsome young officer to his staff. Morrow, a transplanted Illinoisan, had risen through the ranks of the Lancers from sergeant to first lieutenant, and his derring-do during the recent Dahlgren raid impressed Buford.[82]

The next morning, July 8, Jeb Stuart sensed an opportunity to give battle and moved his command eastward along the National Road. Stuart came in force with the brigades of Fitzhugh Lee, Grumble Jones, John R. Chambliss, Jr. (Rooney Lee's brigade), and Laurence S. Baker (Hampton's Brigade) in tow. Pleasonton had been ordered to hold the South Mountain gaps open to enable Meade's infantry to cross the range and attack Lee's army before it could bridge the rain-swollen Potomac. The advance by the Rebel cavalry led Pleasonton to believe that Stuart intended to seize the South Mountain passes. But Stuart was feinting in an effort to keep the Federals on the defensive long enough for the rear of Lee's columns to clear Hagerstown and to reach their final defensive position along the Potomac.

Buford formed his command in an arc athwart the National Road, with Devin on the left, Merritt in the center, and Gamble on the right. Most of the division spent the night dismounted and was still deployed in line of battle. Buford held Kilpatrick's two brigades in reserve and threw out skirmishers on both flanks. At 5 a.m., Stuart opened the fight with an artillery barrage from a height commanding the Yankee line. Shells exploded in the streets of Boonsboro, terrifying the residents of the attractive and well-kept little town. Although Calef's men returned the fire, Confederate artillery enfiladed Gamble's troopers, forcing them to pull back to the south. Seeing Gamble retire, Stuart sent his dismounted skirmishers forward toward Buford's position. However, it was quickly determined that the sodden ground was too wet and muddy for a mounted charge, especially since it was raining again.[83]

While Buford contended with this movement, Stuart launched a flank attack with Jenkins' cavalry brigade, led since July 2 by Col. Milton Ferguson. The battle soon became widespread, and Buford's troopers were hard-pressed by the determined Confederate attacks. Devin's brigade in particular faced heavy fighting, and his troopers nearly exhausted their ammunition. Gamble and Merritt had held off the Confederate attacks for several hours, and were also running low on cartridges. To allow them to replenish ammunition, Kilpatrick's units briefly relieved them. They then reformed for a counterattack. Buford dismounted Gamble's brigade to repulse a flank attack, and, supported by mounted troopers from Kilpatrick, counterattacked with the entire brigade. Gamble's men quickly drove the Confederates from the woods under a heavy fire of artillery.[84]

Confronted by the Union counterattack and also worried about running short of ammunition, Stuart's command fell back toward Funkstown, a small village of about six hundred residents situated both on the National Road and the banks of Antietam Creek.[85] Gamble's dismounted troopers chased Stuart's command nearly three miles, with a badly winded John Buford leading the pursuit in person. The Confederates were driven back across Beaver Creek, where they took up a strong defensive position approximately four miles northwest of the day's battlefield. As pursuing Union troopers approached, Chew's battery opened fire on them and the pursuit ended with the Federals withdrawing to the previous night's campsite near Boonsboro. A member of the 8th Illinois wrote of his comrades in arms, "They are all bully boys, and they don't fear the Rebbs a bit. . . . Gen. Buford says . . . the only fault he finds with us is that he can't stop us when we once get the Rebbs to running."[86]

The men spent another night lying in their lines of battle, awaiting another counterattack by the Confederates.[87] The tired troopers relaxed for most of the day on July 9. Late in the afternoon orders to mount up arrived. At about 4 p.m., Buford sent Devin's command out to reconnoiter the Confederate dispositions west of Beaver Creek between Boonsboro and Funkstown. Devin found a detachment of cavalry and artillery left by Stuart on high ground near his main line, and engaged in a sharp skirmish. During the night of July 9, the first of Meade's infantry reached the scene. Part of the Vermont Brigade of Maj. Gen. John Sedgwick's Sixth Corps came up in preparation for an attack on Lee's lines guarding the Potomac bridgehead. Buford's cavalry was assigned the task of driving in Confederate outposts and clearing the roads for the advancing infantry.

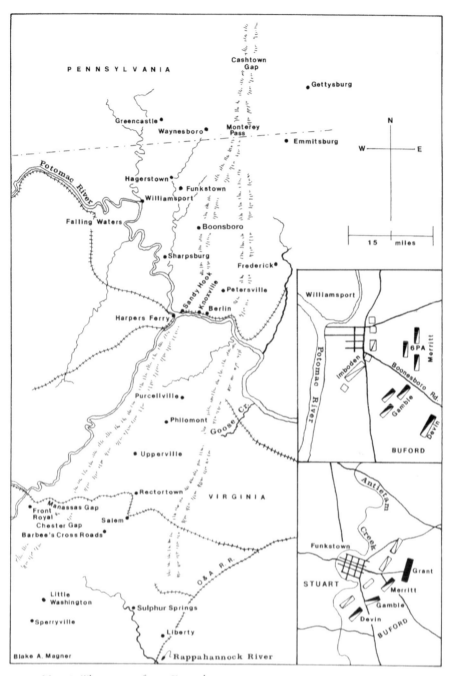

Map 6. The retreat from Gettysburg.

On the morning of the 10th, Buford dismounted his brigades, Gamble in the center, Merritt on the right, and Devin on the left, and sent them across Beaver Creek, where they lashed out at the Confederate videttes. Seeing the size of the force advancing upon them, Stuart's troopers fell back to Funkstown. Buford's men pursued the Rebel cavalry back onto their infantry supports on the banks of Antietam Creek. Jasper Cheney of the 8th New York Cavalry recorded in his diary, "Attacked the enemy about 8 am. and drove them almost to Funkstown, where we found the enemy strongly posted."[88] The Confederates had the advantage of numerous trees, rocks, and fences to use as cover as they fell back. Reinforced by infantry, Stuart made a stand. Fitz Lee placed the infantry of G. T. Anderson's Georgia Brigade across the creek and around Funkstown. The foot soldiers, supported by the Confederate horse artillery, eventually dislodged Buford's skirmishers from a low ridge outside the town.

In the interim, Federal infantry continued to arrive. Elements of the Sixth Corps came to Buford's aid just as his men began running out of ammunition. One member of the 8th Illinois recalled, "We were battering them when relieved by our infantry."[89] The arrival of the foot soldiers and their supporting artillery invigorated the tired Federal troopers. The regimental historian of the Lancers observed, "Great was the rejoicing of our exhausted cavalry force when they saw the infantry lines moving up to take their places in line of battle."[90] These reinforcements could not have come at a more opportune time for Buford's hard-pressed horse soldiers.

By late afternoon, the weight of two divisions of Federal cavalry, supported by infantry and artillery, drove the Confederates from Funkstown, clearing the roads for the advance of Meade's army to the Potomac River. The victory at Funkstown permitted Meade to march most of his army to within two miles of Lee's entrenchments near the Potomac. Lee's position extended from Hagerstown to Falling Waters and was impressively fortified. One Federal officer observed that Lee's "line of works . . . were by far the strongest I have seen yet, evidently laid out by engineers, and built as if they meant to stand a month's siege."[91] Most of the Confederate entrenchments sprawled atop a series of ridgelines along Marsh Run, a tributary of the Potomac. They held a commanding defensive position—concerted infantry attacks would likely have resulted in Union slaughter, very much like the debacle at Fredericksburg.

Buford's troopers, relieved by the arrival of the Federal infantry, withdrew from the front that night. They passed through Boonsboro, crossed over South Mountain, and camped near Middletown, along the Catoctin Creek. "We here had access to our wagons; put up our tents, and luxuriated in clean linen," recounted a Lancer, "and [with] an abundance of commissary supplies, enjoy[ed] positive rest for two days."[92] Most of the division spent the next two days picketing and watching the movements of the Confederates, who waited for the level of the Potomac to fall far enough to cross while anxiously expecting a Federal attack.

The inactivity frustrated the Federals, who recognized the opportunity for a decisive engagement. "There is two army corps on our right, while one division holds the ground

Brig. Gen. John Buford, left, and Brig. Gen. Wesley Merritt. (Library of Congress)

to the Potomac distant three miles. It seems to me that the whole rebel army must be over the river by this time, tho I suppose the commanding general knows better," wrote a Yankee trooper.[93] "We are expecting another battle now every hour," recounted a member of the 6th Pennsylvania. "We are all saddled up and expect the General to go to the front every moment."[94] They watched and waited. The three-day delay must have tried the patience of all.

Meade called a council of war on the night of July 12 to determine whether to attack Lee's formidable line of entrenchments. The Rebels had no escape route other than to fight their way out, as elements of the 14th Pennsylvania Cavalry had destroyed a pontoon bridge over the river on July 4. Meade chose not to attack on the 13th, giving his men another day's rest from their forced marches.

On July 14, Buford's and Kilpatrick's divisions were ordered to advance at 7 a.m. They soon discovered that, with the exception of Lee's rearguard, the Confederate army had finally escaped across the Potomac into Virginia. Buford believed that Pettigrew and Heth—the Confederate rearguard divisions—could be cut off from the river. As Buford planned his attack, Kilpatrick recklessly pitched into the Confederate infantry, engaging Pettigrew's division while Heth's troops crossed the river. While Kilpatrick waged his disjointed battle, Buford's division advanced about three miles, got around the Confederate flank and into their rear. Unfortunately, Buford's and Kilpatrick's attacks were not coordinated, and were not particularly effective. The Regulars did not join the fight, being held in reserve. Brig. Gen. James J. Pettigrew was mortally wounded; however, most of the Southerners escaped to the safety of Virginia. "As our troops neared the bridge," Buford recalled, "the enemy cut the Maryland side loose, and the bridge swung to the Virginia side."[95]

By July 15 the fighting had ended for the time being. The tired, hungry men of Buford's division marched through Sharpsburg, Harper's Ferry, Sandy Hook, and Knoxville and camped near Berlin. Merritt's brigade had marched and skirmished for several days without wagons, forage, or rations. Despite the lack of supplies, Merritt proudly claimed that his Regulars had destroyed nearly eight hundred wagons, captured three thousand horses, and nearly five thousand prisoners in the ten days since the end of the Battle of Gettysburg.[96] The men needed clothing, shoes, ammunition, food, and sleep. On July 16, Buford moved his camp to Petersville, where his men got two days of well-deserved rest. More rain fell on the 17th. "In the last fifteen days we had engaged the enemy in ten battles," proudly noted Chaplain Gracey, "had marched over two hundred miles, with but little sleep and on half rations, and in every engagement fighting against superior numbers of infantry."[97] In spite of the lost opportunity to bring an early end to the war, the Federals' morale remained good.

Finally, at about 2 p.m. on July 18, Buford's division crossed the Potomac at Berlin and encamped near Purcellville, Virginia. "On the 18th we wended our way back across the pontoon bridges to the territory from which we started, most of us duly appreciating Southern chivalry," noted a member of the 8th Illinois.[98] Buford's veterans had returned to familiar territory—their camp in the weeks subsequent to the Antietam Campaign. Buford's division headed south again at 4 a.m. on July 19, marching through Philomont, and bivouacking on familiar grounds along Goose Creek near Rector's Cross-Roads, about three miles from the Upperville battlefield. The next day they rode to Rectortown, where the division split up and marched in three different directions. Merritt's brigade rushed west to hold Manassas Gap; Gamble's brigade was assigned to guard Chester Gap; and Devin, with the division's trains, marched to Salem. While at Rectortown, the men received an issue of sorely needed clothing.[99]

Merritt encountered heavy enemy forces at Manassas Gap. The 1st U.S. was sent forward to the town of Front Royal in the Shenandoah Valley. "It was at once determined that the safest way to defend the passage of the Gap was to deceive the enemy as to the smallness of the force defending the Gap," noted Merritt, "and impress him with the belief that a large part of the Army of the Potomac was in occupation." Reinforced by the 2nd and 5th U.S., the 1st U.S. Regulars skirmished with enemy infantry at Wapping Heights, in the western approach to Manassas Gap. Merritt observed, "The command did its work nobly, and abundantly succeeded in impressing the enemy with the heavy work it would have in attempting to force a passage of the Gap."[100] The Regulars captured five officers and twenty-five enlisted men of the 17th Virginia Infantry and obtained intelligence that Longstreet's Corps occupied the area between Manassas Gap and Chester Gap. Merritt discovered that Montgomery Corse's brigade blocked his path, and that he would be unable to break through to Front Royal. He determined to resume his probing the next day.[101]

Merritt's men spent July 22 skirmishing with Confederate infantry. Although Merritt's troopers were greatly outnumbered, his artillery kept the Confederates from driving them from their position in the saddle of Manassas Gap.[102] Gamble joined in the fighting on July 22. At 8 a.m., his pickets reported the approach of Confederate skirmishers from Chester Gap via the road to Little Washington and Sperryville.

When the head of the Confederate column came into view, Gamble's men opened fire with artillery and carbines. Surprised, the Rebel column halted and fell back out of range but maintained contact with Gamble's skirmishers. Gamble's men held their positions until 6 p.m., when Longstreet sent five regiments of infantry through the woods with fixed bayonets. The Rebels assailed Gamble's left, drove in his skirmishers, and forced him to retreat several miles to Barbee's Cross-Roads. Due to defective ammunition, Gamble got little support from his artillery. "About one shell in twelve . . . explode, and then it would be prematurely, over the heads of our own men," he reported. Even so, Gamble slowed Longstreet's efforts to force the cavalry from their position at the vital intersection for most of the day, and it took a large force of Confederate infantry to finally drive off the dismounted Union troopers. In this skirmishing, Gamble suffered twenty-five casualties and assumed that Longstreet had sustained at least as many. He also captured a large herd of livestock on its way to Lee's commissary, meaning that these Yankees would eat well for a few days.[103]

Yet again, the Army of Northern Virginia slipped away. Merritt later expressed the opinion that had Meade been more aggressive, the Confederate army would never have reached its safe haven south of the Rappahannock.[104]

Finally, on July 26, the division moved to Liberty, where the weary horsemen spent the night. The division next rode to the Rappahannock, where it picketed the river from Warrenton (Sulphur Springs) to Kelly's Ford.[105] Buford's division had come full circle, returning to the same positions from which it began the campaign. Private Daniel Peck of the 9th New York wrote to his sister on July 30, "Things look like a forward movement. Our Brigade have not been engaged since we crossed the river into Va., but are getting anxious to have another chance at them and we probably will not wait long before we have the privilege."[106]

After fifty days of hard marching and fighting, the Gettysburg Campaign ended with Buford's war-weary troopers right back where they started, staring at their adversaries across the no-man's land of the Rappahannock River. During the course of the campaign, the division suffered 1,160 casualties, exceptionally heavy losses for the Yankee horsemen.[107] "For the last 27 days we have had 7 fights and rest of the time we have been marching and had 3 horses shot from under me and one ball went through my coat pants shirt and just fetched the blood but did not make me leave the field but I thought that I was gone—that was at Boonsborough," reported a member of the 2nd U.S. "Last night we came in from 2 days fighting at Mannassus Gap and have got to go again tonight. We are all saddled in our horses ready to go at any minute."[108] Another of Gamble's troopers observed, "I think I have not spoken of the dark and rainy nights we have had to crawl out of our tents and saddle up and march until the next day, nor have I mentioned hard tack and pork, and often we are without a paper for over a week at a time. But we do not complain; all we want is our ranks to be filled up."[109]

Not only did the men suffer during the long and brutal campaign, so did their horses. On July 28, Sergeant Ballentine reported that, in addition to the horse that he had played out during the expedition to Greencastle and the escape from the Confederate trap, he had worn out two more mounts in just eight days. That made three horses in two weeks for just one trooper. Extrapolate those losses out to the entire First Division, and the losses among Buford's horses must have been staggering.[110]

Sgt. Thomas W. Smith, whose Company I was part of Meade's headquarters escort, reported on the discontent caused by Lee's escape to the safety of Virginia. "Last night I overheard a conversation between two Officers high in Command of the Armey of the Potomac," he recounted on July 28. "And from their conversation I gathered, that Gen Mead has Received orders from Washington not to attack Lee's Forses nor to cut off their line of Retreat. In fact we are merely to Follow them up, but not molest them in any way untill further Orders," he wrote. "What in the Devel is the meaning of such Orders, coming at such atime. Surely it can not be that our Government can be so Foolish as to Grant the Rebs an armistice in their pressent Crippled Condition. If so, we might as well throw down our Arms and go Home."[111]

Nevertheless, during the Gettysburg Campaign, and especially during the Rebel retreat, the Northern horse soldiers had consistently fought the Confederates on even terms, and finally, as the campaign progressed, they had defeated them regularly. Their high level of confidence and the resulting improvement in morale marked John Buford's enduring legacy to the Army of the Potomac. The Lancers, in particular, had finally shed their image as soft prima donnas, and had earned the respect of their fellow horse soldiers as well as the Army of the Potomac's infantry.

Chapter Eight

IN THE FIELD AND IN
WINTER CAMP WITH THE
ARMY OF THE POTOMAC

A S AUGUST 1863 BEGAN, THE TWO FOES were once again stalemated on the banks of the Rappahannock River. A series of sharp cavalry engagements developed as the Federal cavalry probed the Confederate defenses to try to ascertain Robert E. Lee's intentions. On August 1, another Battle of Brandy Station was fought, again featuring John Buford's division and the valiant service of the 6th Pennsylvania Cavalry. His command saddled up at 2 o'clock that morning and waded across the Rappahannock, with the Lancers in the lead. Although he had started out on a reconnaissance in force to develop the Confederate dispositions around Culpeper, Buford soon found himself involved in a full-scale battle.

Buford's division launched a pincers attack, with the Lancers leading the advance on the extreme right. "Our cavalry swung their sabers with delightful freedom in one of the most murderous cavalry fights of the war, second only to that of Beverly Ford," reported one Philadelphia newspaper.[1] "I have to inform you that the first day of August was the hardest day's fighting we ever had," reported an exhausted Sergeant Ballentine.[2] The ferocious day-long fight raged over the hills and fields near Brandy Station, including the familiar battlefield of June 9. "Our Regiment got pretty Badly Cut up in that Fight at Culpepper the other Day," reported Sgt. Thomas W. Smith. That day, the Lancers were commanded by Maj. James H. Hazeltine. In spite of Hazeltine's poor leadership, the "men stood up bravely against the overwhelming fire of the enemy notwithstanding the disparity of numbers."[3]

Buford put his horse artillery into action. However, the Confederate horse artillery quickly found the range and replied. The Lancers were assigned to support the Federal batteries, but "the Rebels having such a fair range, every shot they fired told in our ranks," observed Ballentine. "One shell plowed into the ground about 2 yards ahead of our line, lay there about 2 or 3 minutes, then burst not hurting horse or man. That was the only one that did not damage."[4]

Reacting, Buford ordered Hazeltine to attack Capt. Roger P. Chew's fine battery of horse artillery. As the Lancers charged under heavy fire, Hazeltine gave the wrong command, and "the Consequense was a Panick." Buford saw the confusion, rode out to rally the demoralized Lancers, and called out, "6th Pennsylvania what is all this confusion, you are a Regiment I always depended uppon, I never expected to see you Run." Some of the Lancers, who were embarrassed by their performance that day, responded. "General tis not our Fault, tis not our fault!" they yelled. Lt. Edward Whiteford seized the colors, got Buford's attention, and cried out, "General the Sixth Pennsylvania never Runs when they have Proper Officers to lead them."

"No men I know it tis not your Fault," responded Buford, who then turned to Hazeltine and declared, "It's your fault you cowardly Son of a Bitch you consider yourself under Arrest Sir." Their morale restored, the troopers gave three cheers for Lieutenant Whiteford, rallied, and repulsed a determined Confederate charge. Buford sent the disgraced Major Hazeltine to Meade's headquarters under arrest.[5] The battle reached its climax late in the afternoon with multiple charges and countercharges, much like the fighting of June 9.

Sergeant Ballentine left an especially vivid description of the see-saw fighting. "We charged them driving them inside their line of infantry. We took several of them prisoners. They charged us forcing us back about 200 yards when we reared up and charged them again," he wrote. "Then they rallied and charged us again. At that time my horse fell over a man and a horse that were ahead of me." The grayclad cavalry charged over Ballentine's prostrate body before a countercharge led by Lt. Charles L. Leiper and Capt. William P. C. Treichel crashed into them and drove them back. "The day was very hot and I had nothing on but my pants and a very dirty gray shirt which I think saved me from being captured. Iwas very much bruised on the right shoulder and thigh though I did not feel them very much at the time," concluded Ballentine.[6] "I remember seeing Leiper lead a sabre charge at Culpeper on the 1st of August 1863 which was one of the most gallant I ever saw," observed Capt. William M. Graham, commander of the battery of Union horse artillery attached to the Reserve Brigade.[7]

"The charge became so disoriented that it was every man for himself. Neither side could be driven one yard. Several of our men were within saber cut of the Rebel battle flags," recalled Ballentine a few days later. "For about 10 minutes it was hand to hand contest and the two brigades' battle flags were within 15 or 20 yards of each other for over a quarter of an hour but finally Stuart and his dirty rags had to retire. I cannot say whether or not he was hurt but he got a salute of carbine shot."[8] When Confederate infantry came up to reinforce Stuart's cavalry, Buford was forced to fall back, stubbornly resisting every step of the way.

"Terrific charges were made upon the enemy's line when near Culpeper," recalled Chaplain Gracey, "in which we drove the cavalry in dismay back upon their supports of infantry, coming up in regular and solid line of battle with their long Enfield rifles, were too strong for our cavalry division, and we were withdrawn in perfect order to Brandy Station, our rearguard resisting the advance of the enemy."[9] Finally, about 7:45, Buford broke off the engagement and withdrew to Rappahannock Station, where Union infantry protected his division of horsemen. When Buford's men finally halted, it was nearly 10 o'clock that night, and they had been in the field, fighting almost constantly, for twenty hours. The Lancers lost more than sixty men in this engagement as a result of Hazeltine's bungle, including Capt. William P. C. Treichel, the commander of Company A, who received a hip wound during one of the numerous mounted charges that ranged across the fields that day.[10] Company K went into action with ten privates, three sergeants, and two corporals. It came out with three privates, two sergeants, and one corporal, although all but one corporal and three privates rejoined the company the next day. Company K also lost five horses in the brutal fighting.[11] After Hazeltine's relief from command, Capt. Benoni Lockwood, a Sunday school teacher, assumed command of the regiment.

Buford's reconnaissance was successful. He ascertained that at least a portion of Lee's infantry was encamped around Culpeper, and his men gave as well as they took in another desperate slugging match with the Confederate cavalry. The First Cavalry Division suffered 20 killed, 100 wounded, and 148 missing in action that day.[12] A furious Buford sent Major Hazeltine back to Philadelphia in disgrace. On August 8, he was reassigned to duty at Camp Cadwalader in Philadelphia. He never returned to the regiment.[13]

Buford rewarded Whiteford, the son of a British officer, who emigrated from Ireland in 1861 while waiting for a commission in the British army. Instead, he came to America in the hope of seeing action immediately. He originally enlisted in the 5th New York Cavalry and resigned his commission due to illness in November 1862. He briefly served as an aide to an infantry officer, but longed to rejoin the cavalry service. Maj. Gen. Winfield Scott Hancock endorsed his application for a commission in the Lancers, writing, "I have known Mr. Whiteford for some time. He was a faithful staff officer, a refined gentleman, and is a young man of excellent habits. I can recommend this young gentleman to you." However, Whiteford had a hard time obtaining a commission, so he acted as a commissioned officer in the Lancers even though he had been appointed as such. On August 3, Buford wrote, "He has been serving as a com. Officer for about 13 months, has not received any pay, has had several horses killed under him in action, has won a name as a gallant and enterprising officer and worthy of more consideration than he has received." Buford concluded, "I have confidence in him and hope he may be allowed to have a fair shake."[14]

A few days later, General Meade weighed in. "I desire to call your attention to the case of Mr. Whiteford, now serving in the 6th Reg. Pa. Cavalry, and an applicant for a commission in that regiment," he wrote to Governor Curtin. "Mr. Whiteford has been serving in the capacity of a commissioned officer, under the acting appointment of the Commander of the regiment, for several months, during which time he has not only evinced capacity but as I understand distinguished gallantry." Meade concluded, "Having been appealed to, on behalf of Mr. Whiteford, I feel bound to say, from the evidence placed before me, that I know of no case, where an appointment is more highly merited, or where the public interest could be better advanced by making it; and I therefore venture to express the hope that you will coincide with me and commission Mr. Whiteford accordingly."[15] That did the trick. Curtin commissioned Whiteford, who served out the remainder of the war with the Lancers. In 1865, he was promoted to captain and was the final commander of Company G.[16]

After a few days of rest, the Lancers took the field again, and fought another significant skirmish near Culpeper on August 5. As Buford prepared to advance his division, a Confederate artillery shell fell "immediately in front of the camp where the 6th Pennsylvania bivouacked," encouraging all to get ready to meet an attack. Boots and saddles sounded, and the Lancers scrambled for their horses. Buford quickly formed a line of battle, with two squadrons of the Lancers, led by Capt. Benoni Lockwood, holding the extreme right of Buford's position. Lockwood's advance drove the Confederate pickets, opening the battle.[17] Supported by the highly accurate fire of the Union horse artillery, the Reserve Brigade drove a brigade of Confederate cavalry several miles before the pursuit was called off. The Lancers lost one man killed and three wounded in this action.[18] The Federal cavalry then camped near Brandy Station for a well-deserved rest and some long-overdue pay.

"After coming in all our horses, arms and equipment were inspected and will be turned over today to equip the other cavalry," reported Ballentine on August 7. "We are to go to Alexandria to rest and to be fitted out again. I think it is time we had a rest. Since the 8th of June we have not had a day without fighting, marching, or skirmishing."[19] The long, hot summer had taken a severe toll on the weary Pennsylvanians.

On August 15, the regiment was relieved from duty and was sent to Washington to refit and recruit. "There was great rejoicing in the camp of the 6th Pennsylvania Cavalry . . . when they heard they were to go to Alexandria and be recruited," declared a Philadelphia newspaper correspondent. "The 6th Pennsylvania had 600 men last April; now Major Hazeltine tells me that there are but 150 left."[20] The entire Reserve Brigade was equally worn to a frazzle. As the regimental historian noted, "We were ordered to this point to recruit, refit, and reorganize, and after our long campaign, of unprecedented marching and fighting, greatly needed the rest thus secured to us."[21] Sgt. Christian Geisel of Company H wrote home to his sister, "Our whole bregade only numbered 763 men for duty, when we were relieved our Regt 163."[22] On August 17, Captain Lockwood applied to have nine officers, then serving on detached duty, returned to the regiment.[23]

Capt. James H. Starr, who commanded the squadron that consisted of Companies E and I, applied to have those two companies relieved from their headquarters escort duties and returned to rejoin the balance of the regiment.[24] "This makes the Fourth time that he has done so, and I hope that he will succeed no better this time than he has done heretofore," complained Sergeant Smith, who plainly enjoyed the soft job of headquarters escort. Since the army's commanding general rarely stayed in unpleasant or uncomfortable quarters, his escorts typically shared in the good fortune.[25] "We are still at

General Meades headquarters and are well satisfied here," noted a member of Company E. "All remains quiet through the Army just now."[26] Most of the men of this squadron believed that escort duty was an honor and a privilege. "No light and trifling duty was laid upon the troopers of troops E and I, then, but one of danger and ceaseless activity, requiring for its exercise dauntless courage, quick perception and a cool head," noted Capt. Irvine Whitehead years after the war.[27]

The Army of the Potomac had a brief period of inactivity while the high command planned the fall campaign. "The Armey of the Potomac—what is left of them—are mostley scattered along the line of the Rapahanock watching the Rebbles, but between you and I think that more than one half of the old armey have been shipped off to New York and Charleston," recounted Smith in September. "To be sure we have received and are receiving a great maney Conscripts, but I think that if Lees Armey should advance on us we should have to fall back on to the Defences of Washington without giving them Battle."[28] Things remained relatively quiet throughout the balance of September, as the two armies occupied opposite sides of the Rappahannock River. Several weeks later, Smith wrote again. "I should not be much surprised if the larger portion of this Army were sent away. And the remainder of it, fall back onto, the Defences of Washington and the line of the Potomac," he wrote.[29]

Most of the 6th Pennsylvania spent their time in Washington, D.C., drilling and refitting, while Companies E and I remained on headquarters duty. They spent four hours per day drilling in order to get their green horses ready to see action as quickly as possible. "I thought my duty would be decreased but it has increased as the man are harder to keep together," groused Ballentine on August 21. "In fact the men are worn out and drilling seems like an old song or like playing a fiddle to a dead dog."[30]

"There is some talk of our leaving for the front again," Henry Cowan reported on September 9. "We have drawn new belts and revolvers."[31] Their horses, arms, and all other public property were turned over to the divisional quartermaster, and the regiment set up its camp at the newly established remount depot at Giesboro Point. "Captain Lockwood commanded the regiment, which was now reduced to about two hundred men present for duty," noted Gracey.[32] The men resumed drilling twice a day, breaking in new horses, practicing charging, and jumping ditches and fences. "We will soon have them as same as the old stock," said one member of Company K.[33]

While the Lancers enjoyed their respite, the sad news of the death of Maj. Robert Morris, Jr., reached them. After being captured at Brandy Station, the major was sent to Richmond's Libby Prison, where the terrible conditions and poor food soon broke his health. He died on August 12 after a short illness, and was interred in nearby Oakwood Cemetery. Three of his pallbearers, Lts. Bernard Herkness, Samuel R. Colladay, and Thompson Lenning, were officers of the 6th Pennsylvania Cavalry, and the presiding chaplain was a member of the Reserve Brigade. "Major Morris was a brave and able commander, a thorough disciplinarian; of purest principles and noblest impulses; reliable as a friend, and a model soldier," lamented Chaplain Gracey. "He was loved by many, honored, and respected by all."[34]

Sgt. Lewis Miller of Company L had been asked to give a candid assessment of the state of the regiment. He did not pull any punches. "There was not two hundred men present when the regiment was relieved from duty, with the Army on the Rappahannock, a month since," he wrote. "We had but ten officers, including the Commanding officer, Quartermaster, Commissary, Adjutant, and Surgeon. We have had but one officer killed—Captain Davis—and two to die—Maj. Morris and 2nd Lieut. Sproul." He concluded, "The discipline of the regiment is not as good as when Maj. Morris had command of it. Our commanding officers have been changed so often of late, and every one had a different mode of conducting affairs, which has manifested itself in a perfect state of indifference in the men."[35] However, the men were eager to get back after the Rebels. "When we receive our share of conscripts we will go to face the Johnnys again," declared Cowan on September 9.[36]

While the Lancers refitted, a new unit, the 1st New York Dragoons, also known as the 19th New York Cavalry, replaced the 6th U.S. Cavalry, which was badly chopped up during the Gettysburg Campaign and was now serving as the Cavalry Corps headquarters escort contingent. Morale was low during this period, even though the Lancers were not serving on the front lines. "I regret very much [that General Meade] is not granting leaves of absence," complained Capt. Charles C. Cadwalader, who was serving on Meade's staff. "There is no good reason for the prohibition that I know of and I think it would have a highly salutary effect on the army and be politic for the General."[37]

An amusing incident occurred while the Lancers rested in the defenses of Washington. Secretary of War Edwin M. Stanton was visiting the camps of the Reserve Brigade one afternoon, riding in an open carriage, when he encountered Capt. William P. C. Treichel of the Lancers, riding back from Washington on horseback. Treichel, "who was well known and very popular in our brigade, though disposed to be rather wild in his habits," was personally unknown to Secretary Stanton. However, on meeting Stanton, Treichel thought he recognized the Secretary and mistakenly believed that they were not only acquainted, but that they were on bad terms. "It is probable that Captain T. had been dining rather freely," drolly noted an officer of the 1st U.S. Cavalry. Mistaking Stanton for his supposed friend, Treichel addressed the Secretary by the wrong name, and "on the Secretary resenting in his well known haughty manner the advance, hot words passed." The livid Stanton ordered Treichel to his quarters under arrest, informed the officer who he was, and demanded his name. "Capt. T. laughed in derision at the statement that he was the Secretary, and riding close to the carriage seized Mr. Stanton by the luxuriant beard that he wore at the time, and gave it a violent tug, and also slapped his face." Treichel then put spurs to horse and dashed off.

Instead of going straight to Reserve Brigade headquarters, Stanton returned to the War Department and sent an aide-de-camp to scour the camp, find the cheeky officer,

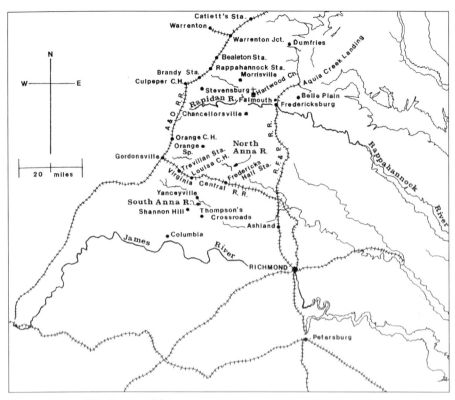

Map 7. The Virginia Theater.

and bring him to Stanton for inquisition. Long before the staff officer arrived, word of the incident spread throughout the Cavalry Corps, and Treichel "was hurried off at once on some manufactured piece of duty which took him out of sight for a day or two." The staff officer thoroughly inspected the Reserve Brigade, and, not surprisingly, failed to find an officer who fit the description given by Stanton among the Regular regiments. Stanton did not designate the Lancers as a possible billet for the offending officer, so the staff officer did not inspect them, meaning that the staff officer returned to Stanton with the report that no "gentleman at all answering the description could be found." Fortunately, the Lancers were about to return to duty in the field, and "the offending and badly-scared Captain was kept well out sight while we did remain," concluded the amused Regular.[48]

On October 9, Meade learned that the main body of Lee's Army of Northern Virginia had disappeared from his front along the Rapidan River. Responding, Pleasonton ordered the cavalry out to find out what Lee was up to. "The Cavalry had some pretty severe Fighting During Friday and Satturday," reported Sergeant Smith. "But they ascertained that Lee was making a Flank movement on our Right so on Sattturday Night our Army commenced to fall back to Rapahanock Station and on Sunday we crossed the

Rapahanock to the Station."[39] Although they had retreated in the face of Lee's advance, the men still retained a great deal of confidence in Meade's tenure in command of the Army of the Potomac. "Genl. Meade soon found out what was up and immediately put our Army on the backward move toward Washington and took up a position at Centreville to meet with Lee," recounted Clement Hoffman in an October 26 letter. "Lee did not care about attacking Genl. Meade for it was too near Washington for him, and so Genl. Lee fell back against the north of the Rappahannock for the purpose of drawing Genl. Meade after him, but I don't think he will make much of Meade for Meade is to cautious to be trapt like Hooker and Burnside."[40]

This movement abruptly ended the Lancers' stay at the remount camp. With Maj. Henry C. Whelan now in command, the Lancers, along with the rest of the Reserve Brigade, received orders for an immediate return to the front. "On Saturday the 10th after coming in off drill we had orders to clean up for inspection," reported Hamilton Ballentine. "After having done that near 5 o'clock we were ordered to pack up and be ready to march at a moment's notice."[41] They were hurriedly mounted, armed, and moved out on the morning of October 11. The brigade passed through Washington, D.C., crossed the Potomac River on the Long Bridge, and made it as far as Bailey's Crossroads. "We had just gone into camp for the night and unsaddled when a dispatch came ordering up our brigade to the front. We saddled up, mounted and started out."[42] On the 13th, they moved to Fairfax Court House, and finally rejoined the Army of the Potomac at Centreville on October 14. The Reserve Brigade had missed a number of actions during its respite, but its men were itching to get back into the fray.[43]

On October 11, while the Reserve Brigade was still marching back to rejoin the First Division, John Buford fought yet another battle of Brandy Station. The next day, Buford's division, supporting the advance of the Fifth and Sixth Corps, recrossed the Rappahannock and drove the enemy all the way back to Culpeper. However, the Confederates attacked Gregg's Second Division at Sulphur Springs and drove Gregg's horsemen back across the river, meaning that the center of the Federal line also fell back from Culpeper across the Rappahannock. A race for possession of Manassas Junction and the high ground at Centreville commenced, with the opposing armies advancing along parallel roads. It looked like there might be a third Battle of Bull Run. "I think that Mead has Out Generalled Lee and spoilt his plans," observed Sergeant Smith, "and if Mead Keeps on as he has begun, he will yet prove himself one of if not the best General that we have got."[44]

On October 14, Lt. Gen. A. P. Hill's Third Corps of the Army of Northern Virginia moved toward Bristoe Station, a stop on the Orange & Alexandria Railroad not far from Manassas Junction. Spotting Union infantry there, Hill deployed his infantry and attacked without first reconnoitering the enemy's position. Launching a hastily planned and ill-advised attack, Hill pitched in. They ran into Gouverneur K. Warren's defenses, and Warren's Second Corps repulsed Hill's infantry with heavy losses after several hours of intense fighting. Warren then retired. "I am convinced," declared Hill, "that I made the attack too hastily, and at the same that a delay of half an hour, and there would have been no enemy to attack. In that event I believe I should equally have blamed myself for not attacking at once."[45] The next day, Hill showed Robert E. Lee the battlefield, explaining all that had gone wrong. "Bury your dead," spoke a grim Lee, "and say nothing more about it."[46]

With the armies in motion once again, Captain Starr's long-held wish was finally granted. Companies E and I were relieved of their headquarters escort duties and were ordered to return to the regiment, which had taken the field again near the old Bull Run battlefield. The 6th Pennsylvania Cavalry was finally serving as a complete regiment for the first time since the 1862 Peninsula Campaign. On October 17th, Smith and his comrades from Companies E and I marched to the area around Warrenton and rejoined the regiment.[47]

The entire regiment went out on a reconnaissance that day, skirmishing vigorously with Confederate cavalry under bright starlight. "We crossed the Bull Run at 6 oclock and commensed skirmishing with the Rebs," reported Sergeant Smith, "we drove them all the way to the Junction without any trouble, but here they made a stand, and we had a pretty sharp skirmish, but we succeeded in driving them a half mile further, when we posted Pickets and fell back to the Junction, and stood to horse all night."[48] The next day, Merritt ordered the Lancers to head for Bristoe Station, where they would "draw the fire of the enemy."[49] "I advanced to Bristoe Station and found the enemy's cavalry in considerable force," reported Merritt. "They opened two batteries of artillery on my advance. They are in a strong position. I think they are still moving to our right."[50]

On October 18, the Reserve Brigade again met the Confederate cavalry. When the Confederates brought up horse artillery, the Lancers retreated and waited for reinforcements. The 5th U.S. Cavalry came up to support them, and the combined force then counterattacked. The Federals drove the enemy all the way to Bristoe Station before falling back out of range of the Southern horse artillery. "We then posted pickets, and our Regiment withdrew to the Junction and rejoined the Brigade," concluded Sergeant Smith. Even Chaplain Gracey got in on the action. During the skirmishing, Gracey captured a Rebel cavalryman, who was "evidently attempting to escape his own ranks."[51] The Lancers lost three men wounded, two horses killed, and five horses wounded in this action. One of the wounded men eventually died of his injuries.[52]

They went on another reconnaissance the next day and again engaged the enemy's pickets near Catlett's Station. "On the 19th we started again and got to Catlett's Station. We held that until yesterday when the infantry came up," reported Hamilton Ballentine on October 21. "Then we fell back to here to rest. We were played out and our horses had but little feed and not unsaddled since we started except for a few hours out of Washington."[53]

On the 20th, the Lancers were ordered to return to Bristoe Station, where they met Maj. Gen. Gouverneur K. Warren and his infantry corps marching to the front. The combined force then advanced to Catlett's Station, where they repaired the Orange & Alexandria Railroad, which was severely damaged by the retreating Confederates. While the railroad repairs were under way, the Lancers established their picket lines in front of Warren's foot soldiers.[54] This campaign proved to be a test for men who had just spent more than a month enjoying soft duty and comfortable quarters. "For five days we did not unsaddle nor wash nor eat, so to speak, nor sleep," reported Major Starr, who had learned to be careful about wishing for things. "This was my first experience after our soft life at headquarters, and was little severe."[55]

The Lancers remained in the field until October 23, when they camped near Manassas Junction for a few days. On the 27th, they moved to Germantown, Virginia, where they set up an "uncomfortable camp." That night, "while the officers were nearly all gathered around our large headquarters fire, orders were received to make preparation for immediate movement." Within a couple of hours, the regimental camp had been struck, the tents were packed, and the regiment was once again on the move. About midnight, they arrived at the abandoned campsite of the Federal Second Corps at Catlett's Station, rested for an hour or so, and then moved out again, finally halting at 4:30 near Germantown. "The night was stormy," remembered a Lancer, "and we suffered greatly from cold."[56]

Although the Lancers had enjoyed a month away from the front lines and had received fresh mounts, the Bristoe Station Campaign was nevertheless hard on men and horses. With the notable exception of the infantry battle at Bristoe Station, virtually all of the fighting during this campaign was done by the cavalry. On October 24, Buford reported that his division had only 2,000 men and horses fit for duty. "One-half of these, in my opinion, are not fit for arduous duty, being poor in flesh and leg-weary," he wrote. "It is impossible to ascertain the number of diseased horses, for the disease alone is on the increase daily, and to feed them here with grain alone is impossible with my present means of transportation." Buford reported that the Reserve Brigade numbered 1,488 men, but that only 850 of them were mounted and fit for duty.[57]

With Meade having repulsed Lee's flanking movement at Bristoe Station, President Lincoln, Secretary of War Stanton, and General-in-Chief Henry W. Halleck began prodding Meade to attack the Army of Northern Virginia. "I take this occasion to repeat that which I have before stated that if my course, based on my own judgment, does not meet with approval, I ought to be, and I desire to be, relieved," stated Meade.[58] Undaunted, Lincoln summoned Meade for a conference at the White House. Although the President praised Meade's conduct of the war, Lincoln continued agitating for another advance against Lee's army. He also declined to relieve the Philadelphian of command, saying, "What can I do with such generals as we have? Who among them is any better?"[59] On October 24, Halleck issued a peremptory order to the army commander. "The President desires that you will prepare to attack Lee's army," he wrote.[60] Thus, the die was cast for a late fall campaign. Obeying the order, Meade began planning a thrust across the Rapidan River at Germanna Ford.

On October 31st, the regiment moved to Elk Run, Virginia, where it bivouacked for several days. The Cavalry Corps waited for orders to fight that never came. "The rebels destroyed the railroad from Bristoe Station to the Rappahannock," reported Sergeant Geisel, "and our men are at work repairing it as speedily as possible, and as soon as supplies can be transported on it again, I think our army will advance again."[61] Instead, the Lancers picketed the line from Hartwood Church to Kelly's Ford.

On November 4, Maj. John S. Mosby's forces ambushed and killed the regimental quartermaster, Lt. Theodore Sage, near Elk River. Mosby's command, known as the 43rd Battalion of Virginia Cavalry, had become a force to reckon with. Using hit-and-run tactics, Mosby's Rangers wreaked havoc on the Union lines of command, control, communication, and supply. Their missions completed, the Rangers then melted back into their local communities, where they led normal lives until they were called upon to conduct their next mission. Sage, who was escorting a wagon on its way from Elkton to Gainesville, was killed instantly when the guerrillas burst from a thicket, charged him, and fired several shots into his body at point-blank range, any one of which would have been fatal.[62] Before long, and in part as a result of Sage's loss, the Federal high command had to devote significant resources to trying to run down Mosby and his Rangers. Most members of the regiment grieved his loss, as Sage was popular with the men.[63] Sage was just one of many Federal soldiers who died at the hands of Mosby's guerrillas.

On November 8, while two of the Army of the Potomac's infantry corps advanced on Rappahannock Station, the First Cavalry Division splashed across the Rappahannock River at Sulphur Springs, marched toward Culpeper, and passed through Jefferson to Rixey's Ford on the Hazel River. General John Buford, the tough, competent, and popular division commander, had fallen ill, and was unable to take the field, meaning that Wesley Merritt commanded the division in his absence. The advancing Federals drove a few squadrons of enemy horse soldiers from Sulphur Springs and continued on until they encountered the 10th Virginia Cavalry at Rixey's Ford. After dispersing the 10th Virginia, Merritt continued on until his division was within four miles of Culpeper, where he bivouacked for the night. The Lancers spent the night picketing in sight of the enemy.[64]

The next day, November 9, when the advance resumed, the Yankee horsemen found Maj. Gen. Cadmus Wilcox's Confederate infantry division blocking their way. Merritt formed two brigades, including the Reserve Brigade, and attacked dismounted. Responding, Wilcox advanced a heavy line of battle, supported by artillery. "The 3d Indiana, 8th Illinois, and 6th Pennsylvania received the greatest attention from the enemy," recalled Chaplain Gracey. "We were forced back a short distance, but after a sharp fight, lasting about one hour and a half and terminating at dark, the enemy retired from their advanced position." Merritt suffered more than fifty casualties in this heavy skirmish. The Lancers remained on the field, doing picket duty. The Confederates withdrew during the night, and on the morning of November 10, Merritt advanced and occupied Culpeper, setting up his picket line two miles from the town.[65]

On November 10, the Cavalry Corps established its camps along the northern bank of the Rappahannock River. The Northern horsemen continued to picket and scout as usual until the afternoon of the 25th.[66] "This morning we rec'd orders to be ready to move at a moment's notice," recounted Surgeon Coover. "Heavy firing was to be heard on our left, but soon subsided. I have been waiting for orders to march all day and am now of the opinion that we may not be called this night. At least I hope we may not."[67] Coover's suspicions proved correct.

During this period, Pvt. William Harbeson of Company G received a severe injury. His horse reared and fell over backward, crashing down on Harbeson's breastbone, causing him to "hurt all over." Harbeson spent twelve days in the regimental hospital before he could walk again. He suffered a severe lower back and spinal cord injury that left him totally disabled later in life. Harbeson was not only a tough customer, he was a dedicated soldier who nevertheless fulfilled his term of service and then reenlisted in April 1864. He served out the balance of the war before returning to his home in Reading. However, his career as a blacksmith was largely over owing to his back injury.[68]

On November 18, the *Philadelphia Inquirer* reported that Lt. Col. C. Ross Smith, the ranking officer in the regiment, had been promoted to colonel. Smith, who was still on detached duty at Cavalry Corps headquarters and had not served with the regiment since early in the war, was described as "an able and efficient officer, of considerable military experience." The newspaper concluded, "His promotion is well earned, and a fair subject of congratulations by his numerous friends."[69] However, these reports proved to be untrue. Smith was never promoted to colonel, although he received a brevet to colonel in 1868, in recognition of his service during the war. Smith's service records indicate that he was still a lieutenant colonel when he mustered out at the end of his term of service in September 1864.[70] The regiment, without a colonel since Rush's resignation in April, would not receive a new colonel until the war's final weeks in the winter of 1865.

The First Cavalry Division covered the right flank of the Army of the Potomac, and picketed from James City to the Robinson River. "There is no force of any account this side of the Rapidan so I expect we are in this position on the lookout for a flank movement on the part of Lee," declared Henry Cowan. However, Cowan recognized that a new campaign was afoot. "I think that before long Meade will cross the Rapidan and we will make things howl along the line of the railroad. The Regular Brigade is ready at any time to share alike the gains & losses."[71] Cowan would not have long to wait.

At the end of November, George Meade finally launched the campaign that Lincoln had prodded him into, known as the Mine Run Campaign.[72] On November 26, the Reserve Brigade left its camp near Culpeper and moved to Stevensburg, where it spent the night. "Our cavalry was not called for any duty other than to protect the regiment and the rear," recounted Sgt. Hamilton Ballentine. "We were all the time on the go either on picket duty or feeling out the enemy."[73] That night, word of Maj. Gen. Ulysses S. Grant's great victories at Lookout Mountain and Missionary Ridge at Chattanooga reached the Army of the Potomac. "The reports created great enthusiasm amongst our troops," declared Chaplain Gracey. "Long and loud cheers were given for Grant and the Army of the Cumberland."[74]

The next day, the Reserve Brigade moved out of its camps at Stevensburg, and marched about five miles, where it joined up with the wagon trains of the First and Sixth Corps. The horse soldiers escorted the wagons and acted as the Army of the Potomac's rear guard. Portions of the 6th Pennsylvania Cavalry spent the next few days picketing while the Army of the Potomac advanced toward Locust Grove, not far from the old Chancellorsville battlefield. However, Robert E. Lee had set a trap for the Army of the Potomac along the banks of the Rapidan River. Maj. Gen. Gouverneur K. Warren, whose Second Corps led the Union advance, spotted Lee's ambush and wisely declined to fall into it. Warren refused to attack, prompting an angry Meade to ride out to see what the problem was. When Meade arrived, he too spotted the Confederate trap, and agreed that Warren was correct in deciding not to attack. The result was an aborted campaign. "There is some talk of our going back to Warrenton Junction but do not believe it," reported Ballentine. "They must do something soon as this is fifth day for our horses to be without anything to eat and the men are not much better off. As for myself I could eat a horse at present. I never had such an unmerciful appetite and I have never had better health. Neither cold nor lack of sleep has any effect on me."[75]

After Meade withdrew from Mine Run, the Lancers returned to Stevensburg, where they reestablished their camp in the same place where they occupied prior to the aborted campaign, in almost the same position that they had held during the previous winter. However, more arduous duty lay ahead. "We have hard picket to do," declared Sergeant Ballentine. "We have to be out one day out of every four. If they keep up such a long line all winter most of the cavalry will be played out. Neither men nor horses can stand it."[76]

Ballentine defended both the Army of the Potomac and its commander from criticism of the aborted Mine Run Campaign. He demonstrated a remarkable depth of understanding of the circumstances and political considerations that hindered Meade's ability to operate freely. He wrote to his brother William on December 11:

> I am surprised to hear in your letter of the people finding so much fault with General Meade and the Army of the Potomac. I think that if they would come out and try themselves they would have so much to say. They must understand that Meade did not retreat; he merely fell back to his old position. Besides the Army of the Potomac is not like any other army. It has to fight and also protect the capitol. If it had not the latter to do it could move any way it had a mind to do. It could do battle on any ground and run the risk of being defeated. But if it gave battle and got defeated the fall of the capitol would be the result. But to satisfy these fault finders I hope that Father Abraham will make a draft this winter and bring

out every man of them. Then there will be more done and less said. Anyway I think the Rebs are about played out. They are coming into our lines every day and they say they are literally starving. They live on one pint of corn a day. This I saw myself.[77]

As Ballentine's letter plainly demonstrates, morale remained high in spite of the failed campaign.

Unfortunately, the tribulations of the long, difficult campaigning season, combined with his Brandy Station wound, proved to be too much for Maj. Henry C. Whelan. "The exposure of the campaign of 1863 proved too great for his constitution, which was never strong," lamented Chaplain Gracey, "and he was obliged to leave the field in the winter, soon after the Mine Run campaign." Whelan "was distinguished in the regiment for his soldierly qualities, his manly preference, and courteous manners; he was a strict disciplinarian in camp and a brave and judicious leader in the field, a man in whom the war developed great thoughtfulness of character and earnestness in purpose." Whelan went home to Philadelphia and never returned to the war. He died of pulmonary disease on March 2, 1864. "His death was sincerely and deeply felt throughout the regiment, where he had won the esteem and respect of all, and to which he left a conspicuous example of self-sacrifice and devotion to duty."[78] Maj. Benoni Lockwood briefly assumed command of the regiment until pressing private matters at home forced him to resign his commission not long after.[79]

During this period, the division underwent a major command shakeup. Buford's illness turned out to be typhoid fever. The Kentuckian left the division to go on medical leave on November 21; Merritt assumed command of the division as its senior brigadier. Command of the Reserve Brigade fell upon Col. Alfred Gibbs of the 19th New York Cavalry, described by one observer as "a very jolly Colonel."[80] Gibbs was a hard-living fellow. "He is a perfect epicure," observed an officer of the 19th New York. "Very few men live at home as well as he does in the field. His high living will kill him before long I fear."[81] This change in the divisional command structure became permanent after Buford succumbed to typhoid fever on December 16, dying in George Stoneman's rented house in Washington, D.C.

After the Mine Run affair, the Lancers spent several weeks preparing their permanent winter quarters near Mitchell's Station. Their camp was located about three miles in front of the most advanced infantry lines, and five miles behind the picket lines. The regiment continued to perform its share of picket duty in the winter cold. The division's picket lines extended from the Robertson River on the right by Cedar Mountain to Sommerville Ford, and then along the Rapidan to Raccoon, Morton's, and Mitchell's Fords. They had a lengthy front to cover, and the duty taxed the men of the First Cavalry Division. On December 8, Capt. Emlen N. Carpenter of Company E noted that "seven to ten men froze to death in the trenches—fifteen or twenty rebels were also found frozen to death. Poor fellows—that is worse almost than being shot. The wounded must have suffered horrible torture during those cold nights that we had."[82] The Army of the Potomac spent a long winter camped around Brandy Station. The Cavalry Corps did extended stints of picket duty that wore on both men and horses.

"Joe we have it Damn hard out here, just now," declared Sergeant Smith in a letter to his brother. "There being only 4 Regiments in our Bregade, for Picket Duty (The 2nd Regulars being on Provost Duty in Culpeper) which brings us on Picket every 4th Day. And as we are generally absent from camp from 32 to 34 hours, we have 2 Days and 3 nights in camp, and 2 days and 1 night on Picket. And I tell you what, setting still on ones Horse from 2 to 4 Hours, these sneaking cold, Frosty nights, ones Blood, Damn near freezes up in his vains. An Infantry man, on Picket, can walk his Post, and by that means keep his Blood in Circulation. But we cannot do so." Regular probes by Stuart's active cavalry meant that the Federal horsemen spent lengthy stints standing to horse, waiting for orders to move that never came.[83] While on picket, the men were vulnerable to enemy fire. Picket fire rang out regularly, making it dangerous for a man to ride along the banks of the Rapidan and Rappahannock Rivers.[84] These episodes wore on the Cavalry Corps and took a real toll that left many men without mounts.

Christmas Eve proved to be a sad day. The Lancers came in from the picket line that afternoon, in time for a brigade review. At the conclusion of the review, Colonel Gibbs announced the death of John Buford on December 16. "Our colors were all bound with crepe, our brigade flag which was his first command was in a crepe bag, next came the Division flag with a tassel of crepe on top. As they passed along the lines everything was silent and I tell you there were some tears shed for that cool old hero of a hundred battles," lamented a member of Company K.[85]

On December 25, the Lancers finally settled into their permanent winter quarters, which were "very substantial and comfortable," observed a visitor. "Log huts, shingled roofs. The Sibley tents affording the soldiers much better accommodations than they have ever heretofore possessed."[86] The men got a scare that day, when orders to mount up arrived. They marched about five miles before the orders were countermanded. It turned out to be a false alarm, and the Lancers passed a "pleasant evening" on the third Christmas of the war.[87] Approximately 170 of the Lancers reenlisted for the duration of the war, collected a $100 bounty, and received thirty-five-day veteran furloughs that permitted them to spend the holidays at home with their loved ones.[88] Some reenlisted for the bounty, and others for patriotic reasons, as noted by one trooper of Company H: "The reason why I enlisted was I made up my mind to see the thing through to the end for I believe that U.S. Grant will hurry up the cakes in short meter."[89]

Maj. James H. Starr enjoyed a ten-day furlough over the holidays. Although he spent the time with his family in Philadelphia, he also missed his old friends from Harvard. "I had only ten days, and what I could have spared to you would have been too little to satisfy me," he wrote. "Oh! for a good talk over the fire once more, and, God willing, we'll have that same next winter. I wish you would make us a visit; it would be a Christian charity to us. We have nothing to offer but a hearty welcome, muddy rides, and a view of the Rebs *trans* Rapidan."[90] Starr was now the second-ranking officer serving with the regiment, and he faced a trying year in 1864.

The year 1863 had been arduous for the regiment, marked by endless marching and fighting. It also marked the emergence of the Lancers as a force to be reckoned with, earning them the respect of John Buford and Wesley Merritt, and the proud title of the Seventh Regulars. 1863 was also a year of great change for the 6th Pennsylvania Cavalry: Colonel Rush resigned his commission due to failing health, Major Morris was captured at Brandy Station and died a lonely death in Richmond's notorious Libby Prison, Maj. George E. Clymer of Company E resigned his commission during the spring, and Major Whelan fell ill from the hardships of the Gettysburg Campaign and was forced to leave the regiment. Major Hazeltine was relieved of command for his bungle at Brandy Station on August 1, and a mere captain, William P. C. Treichel, commanded the regiment at year's end.[91] The hated lances were swapped for Sharps carbines, and the men learned to fight and scout with the best of the Federal cavalry. After such an eventful year, the Lancers took up their permanent winter quarters with an enviable record and with an optimistic eye toward the future.

By January 1864, things had taken a decided turn for the worst. The Lancers relocated their camp closer to the Rapidan River, meaning that they would have to build new quarters about five miles from the town of Culpeper Court House, near Mitchell's Station on the Orange & Alexandria Railroad. The regiment's resident architect, the newly promoted Capt. Frank Furness, helped to lay out the new camp. After several days of hard work, new huts were ready and the Lancers moved in. Chaplain Gracey recalled, "Very excellent log huts were erected, in regular streets and to uniform dimensions."[92] A heavy rain set in, turning the entire winter encampment into a sea of deep, thick mud. "We all fixed ourselves the best way we could until it stopped raining, then we commenced to build winter quarters again, and we are now beginning to get pretty comfortable fixed again in our log houses," reported a sergeant. "The fire in my chimney is roaring this evening as if it wanted to encourage me to write faster, but don't look very pleasant outside, it has commenced to snow again."[93]

Although their new accommodations were pleasant enough, those huts were poorly placed. "The Reserve Brigade is probably encamped on the worst ground within the lines of the army," reported Capt. Frederic C. Newhall who, although commissioned as an officer in the Lancers, was serving as an assistant inspector general at Cavalry Corps headquarters. "No amount of care or police will render the camps neat or healthy." In addition, the Reserve Brigade's horses were in terrible condition. "This brigade, in my opinion, needs an opportunity to rest and recuperate, that its well-known efficiency in the field may not be destroyed," concluded Newhall.[94]

Lancers, first row: unidentified*, William White†, Edward Whiteford†; second row: Irvine Whitehead†, Henry Winsor†, unidentified†. (*Author, †USAMHI)

The soldiers searched for ideas to keep themselves entertained. "The men would resort to different schemes to create a little amusement, chief among which was throwing cartridges in each other's chimneys," noted saddler Edgar Strang of Company M. "Many a pot of coffee or mess pan of bean soup was sent flying across the tent just as their owner would be counting on a good supper. But as nearly all of the men were given to those kind of tricks there was not much excuse for one getting angry when he lost his supper in that way." These simple pranks eventually led to increasingly complex stunts that required more and more planning in order to pull them off.[95] They helped the men to pass the time while they waited for their interminable turns at picket duty to come around again.

When not on the picket lines, the men wrote letters, visited with friends from other regiments, drilled, and waited for spring to come. Occasionally, they rode down to the picket line along the Rapidan, where they had a clear view of the Confederate camps across the way. "There we looked down on the gray backs and could discern their movements, their signal station on Clark's Mountain, and a number of encampments," noted a visitor to the Lancers' winter quarters. "Some days they are seen playing baseball."[96]

Days went slowly, and so did the cold nights. Although spring would inevitably bring more fighting, the men were eager for the arrival of warmer weather.

The Lancers stood picket duty one full day out of every four, and then spent three days in camp, drilling, resting, tending to their horses, and being bored. The Reserve Brigade covered an eight-mile-long front, as well as a signal station on Cedar Mountain.[97] Sometimes, the pickets fraternized with their counterparts on the other side; at one point, Confederate Lt. Gen. Richard S. Ewell sent across a note under a flag of truce, asking that the Federal pickets be pulled back far enough to prevent fraternizing.[98] The Lancers regularly drew new items of clothing, and occasionally drew new mounts. Periodically, they performed different missions, thereby relieving the tedium of their regular routine. As an example, on January 29, Lt. Albert P. Morrow, now commanding Company C, led a detachment of one hundred Lancers to guard the nearby signal station on Slaughter Mountain.[99]

The officers of the regiment enjoyed a special luxury that winter—thanks to the talented Captain Furness, they had their own clubhouse. "A Sibley tent, mounted on a stockade, and supported from the exterior, furnished a very beautiful and attractive club tent for the use of the officers," noted an observer. Furness, who designed the clubhouse, used a novel combination of exterior posts and cables, not interior tent poles, to support the clubhouse, meaning that there was an uninterrupted interior span. The wildly innovative Furness used the officer's clubhouse as a prototype for future building designs.[100]

A determined effort to obtain the reenlistments of the men of the Lancers got under way in earnest that winter. Most of the unit's enlisted men were scheduled to muster out in September and October 1864, and veteran cavalrymen would be needed. Those who reenlisted received a bounty of $502, along with a thirty-five-day furlough to go home. "A great many are taking up with this offer and have reinlisted," reported Clement Hoffman of Company E, "but I have not and haven't any inclination to. I have made up my mind to serve my three years time through which will be up the 20th of next September, and then if I feel inclined to soldier any longer there will be just as good inducements for me to inlist as thare is now."[101] About 140 men reenlisted that winter and enjoyed the bounty and their veteran furloughs.

Meade decided to probe the Confederate pickets, looking for weaknesses and signs of activity on Lee's part. On February 5, the regiment drew five days' worth of rations and was relieved from the monotony of picket duty. The next morning, they marched, crossing the eastern spur of Thoroughfare Mountain and then crossed the Robertson River at Smoot's Ford, where they drove in the enemy's cavalry pickets. However, "owing to the heavy roads and obstructions which had to be cleared away for the passage of the artillery, the Reserve Brigade and battery did not get up in time to do anything on the 6th."[102]

On the 7th, Merritt's division resumed the attack, meeting Confederate horsemen again near Barnett's Ford on the Rapidan River, where a brisk artillery and small arms skirmish raged until about midday. "The enemy did not show much infantry till a movement was made by us to cross the ford, when a brigade, which a deserter reported five regiments strong, moved down to the ford to support the skirmishers occupying the defenses on the south bank," recounted Merritt. The Federals maintained their fire until Merritt received orders to return to camp.[103] The Lancers, who were sent off to the right to guard against a potential enemy flank attack, suffered one man wounded in this action.[104] After two days of hard marching and fighting, they returned to camp, cold, tired, and happy for the comforts of their warm, dry huts.[105] On February 13, Merritt reviewed the First Division, and two days later, Pleasonton reviewed the entire Cavalry Corps, which was pronounced to be in good fighting trim.[106] They would need to be ready—they were about to undertake a mission in support of a cavalry raid.

On February 27, a select force of 550 men, made up of 110 men from each of the five regiments of the Reserve Brigade, participated in a raid on the Virginia Central Railroad near Charlottesville. Brig. Gen. George A. Custer, who normally commanded the Michigan Brigade of the Third Division, led this expedition.[107] This mission was intended to distract Confederate attention from the thrust toward Richmond by part of Kilpatrick's Third Division, intended to liberate Union prisoners of war held at Belle Isle and Libby Prison. Kilpatrick commanded the main column, while Col. Ulric Dahlgren, the same young man whose fate was already closely tied to that of the 6th Pennsylvania Cavalry, would lead a second column, giving this expedition its name: the Kilpatrick-Dahlgren Raid. Maj. Gen. Wade Hampton's Confederate cavalry division repulsed Kilpatrick at Atlee's Station, and a scratch force consisting of elements of the 9th Virginia Cavalry and Confederate home guard units ambushed Dahlgren's column in King & Queen County, northeast of Richmond. Dahlgren was killed, and incriminating documents suggesting that the true mission of the expedition was the kidnaping and murder of Confederate President Jefferson Davis and his cabinet were found on the body. The failed expedition proved to be a gross embarrassment to the Union high command, and ultimately cost Kilpatrick and Pleasonton their positions with the Army of the Potomac.[108]

Custer's diversionary raid commenced at 1 a.m. on the morning of February 29. Custer's makeshift force had several violent skirmishes along the way and was nearly destroyed by a Confederate ambush, only to be saved from destruction by quick thinking and action by Custer.[109] On the 29th, they burned an enemy artillery camp, and fought Confederate troops at Rio Hill, a few miles north of Charlottesville. After another day of skirmishing near Madison Court House, Custer's expedition returned to the Army of the Potomac's winter encampment at Brandy Station.[110]

Sgt. Thomas W. Smith of Company I was one of the 110 Lancers selected for Custer's excursion. He left an extremely detailed description of the travails of Custer's command that may be the best surviving account.

> On the 26th of Febuary we heard that our Infantry were on the moove,
> and we got orders to be ready to moove at a moments notice. On the

evening of the 27th of Feb (at 6 O'clock P.M.) there was a detail of 12 men, from each Company, from each Regt of our Bregade, Ordered to Saddle up with 3 Days Forrage and Rations. Major Trickle[111] took command of the whole,[112] and marched us to Pony Mountain, where we Bivauocked for the night. On the 28th we left Pony Mountain at 11 O'clock A.M. and marched to within one mile of Madison Court House, which we reached at 7 O'clock P.M. We halted here, Fed & cleaned our Horses, got our suppers, and Rested untill midnight (we were joined here by a detail, of the same number of men as our own, from General Custers Bregade, of Kilpatricks Division, we were now told that we were going on a Raid to Charlottsville to try and destroy a large lot of Rebel supplies which the Rebs had stored at this place). Custer now took command of the whole affair. At midnight we saddled up and mooved forward, our Regt on the advance, with orders to Halt for nothing, but if we met pickets and they fired into us, to Charge on them, and drive them before us. We marched forward at a fast gait untill 4 O'clock P.M. on the morning of the 29th, when we had got within about 3 miles of the ford where we intended to cross the Rapidan. Here we met the Rebs Pickets, they Fired into us, we charged them so hard that they did not get annother chance to fire on us untill we got to the ford where we had a pretty sharp skirmish with them. But we drove them and captured two, 6 Horse Waggons loaded with Flour, we now took the Road to Green[113] County Court House driving the Rebs pickets where ever we met them which was quite frequently untill after daylight when they left us aloone.

At 8 O'clock A.M. we reached Green Court House,[114] charged the Town with a yell that served as a morning Revellee for a small Boddy of Rebble Cavalry that were quartered there. They skedaddled in every direction some on Horse Back, but the Largest number of them taking to the Woods on foot. At this Place we captured a Rebel mail, and Destroyed a large number of Saddles, Saddle Trees, Horses, &c.

We now mooved forward at a rappid rate for the next Three or Four Hours without anything of interest occurring. Then we commensed to meet the Rebel Pickets again. They would fire on us and fall Back, and we would drive on after them, without returning their shots. We kept on at this for 3 miles further, when, our Horses being completed fagged out we were releived by the first Regulars,[115] who took the advance, and we fell in the rear of Bregade.

Two miles further and we came to the Ravenna River,[116] there was a Cavalry camp on this side of the River, but we never Halted. We charged right through their camp, and they fled to the Woods in every direction leaveing their Horses, Arms, and Acccoutrements of every description scattered promiscuously around camp, which prooved that they were taken completely by supprise and that they never drempt that there were any Yanks within 60 Miles of them.

It was now 2 O'clock P.M. We had been in the saddle 14 Hours, and had Rode over 60 Miles without Halting. But still the Command was Forward. After Watering our Horses in the Ravenna, we crossed the Bridge, and pushed on for about 2 miles further when the commensed shelling us from some 8 or 10 peices of Artillery, this checked our advance, and even compelled us to fall back a little out of Range. We now discovered that they were receiving Reenforsements of Infantry, by Rail, (supposed to have come eather from Orange Court House, or Gordonsville). It was now decided by our Officers, to divide our small forse into two collumms and do them as much dammage as possible, before we were compelled to fall back for good. Capt Ash[117] of the 5th Regulars took a By Road to the Left through a Woods, with about two Hundred men, and the Rest of us mooved forward on the Road that we were on. We had not gone more than a quarter of a mile, when we heard a devil of an explosion on our Left. Our collumn Halted and Gen Custer went up on a small Hill to Reconnoiter, he discovered Capt Ash's command on the Back Track, and also discovered the Rebel infantry marching in three collumns on our Left to get posession of the Bridge in our Rear, and thus cut off our retreat. So we weeled about and made for the Bridge as fast as our tired out Horses could carry us. We now recrossed the Bridge and then set fire to it. We also Burnt a Large mill, full of Flour and Grain at this point. (When Capt Ash took the Road to the Left, the first that he knew, he was right into a Rebbel Artillery Camp. He blew up 7 caisons, when he found that the Reb Infantry were closing in on him. He then Rallied his men and cut his way out, In this Fight he Lost one man Killed, and 4 men wounded, all of the 5th Cavalry. The whole affair did not Last scarsely 5 minuts).

It was now 5 O'clock P.M. and the weather was verry Disagreable, and it was commensing to Rain. So we took the Back track, our Regiment acting as rear Guard. Some Rebel Cavalry followed us up, but when ever they would come too close, we would weel about and charge them, when they would always show us their Heals. At 8 O'clock P.M. it was Raining verry Hard, and Dark as the Devil. About this time we lost our Road in a thick and tangled Woods and after wandering about for about two Hours we found it would be impossible for us to get our Artillery through so we come to the conclusion to dismount and stand to Horse where we were untill Day Light, it continued to Rain verry hard all night.

The next morning at Day Light (March 1st) having found the Right Road, we mounted and mooved on again. We were now Fired upon by small Bodies of Rebel Cavalry (as we advanced) from every cover. We had made about 3 miles, and were passing through a thick Woods when our Company being the extreme Rear Guard, we were attacked by a Boddy of Rebel Cavalry.[118] We succeeded in Holding them in check untill the ballance of our Regiment came back to our assistance, when we charged them and drove them off.

In this Skirmish Sergt Wright[119] (My Butty) received a severe Pistol shot Wound in the Hip. When we came to Green Court House we destroyed a Large quantity of Wheat, and Burnt annother Flour mill. We then went on untill we came to a cross Roads, going to two different Fords on the Rapidan. The one on the left going to Banks Ford where we crossed before, was held by a Boddy of Rebel Cavalry. So we took the Road to the right which went to Berthels Ford.[120] We had marched about 5 miles on this Road, and had got pretty near to the Ford, when we dis-covered that it was held by Cavalry, Artillery, and Infantry. General Custer said that we could cut our way through at Banks Ford, easier than we could at this, so we wheeled about again, and started for Banks Ford which we crossed without opposition (the Rebel Cavalry having taken the River Road to Bertels Ford when they Discovered that we had gone to that Place). We Burnt another Large Mill at this place, and then mooved on to Madison Court House which we Reached at dark. We then went about 3 miles further crossing the Robison River,[121] where we watered our jaded Horses.

We then halted for two hours, to Feed our Horses and get something to eat for ourselves. At 10? O'Clock we mounted again, and marched to Camp which we reached at 3 O'clock A.M. on the morning of the 2nd, soaked with Rain, Covered with mud, and completely tired out.

We brought in with us, some 30 prissoners, about 50 Contrabands,[122] and between Three and Four Hundred Fine Horses. Besides this every man had his Saddle Loaded with chickens, Turkeys, Ducks, Geese, Hams, &c.

We could have taken Hundreds of Prissoners if we had been so mind-ed. But that was not out object, we did not want to be encumbered with them. So we took no more than what actually fell into our hands.[123]

Of the feint that got the entire column safely across the river, General Custer reported, "The enemy discovered the change in my movements, but too late to profit thereby. A force of 500 cavalry, which had been hurried up from Burton's Ford to intercept us, only arrived in time to see my rearguard safely across the river."[124] One Lancer noted that Companies I and M "skirmished with the enemy all day."[125] Custer crowed:

> My command returned to its camp without having suffered the loss of a man. While on this expedition it marched upwards of 150 miles, destroyed the bridge over the Rivanna River, burned 3 large flouring mills filled with grain and flour, captured 6 caissons and 2 forges, with harnesses complete; captured 1 standard bearing the arms of Virginia, over 50 prisoners, and about 500 horses, besides bringing away over 100 contrabands. A large camp of the enemy was also captured and destroyed near Charlottesville. The conduct of the officers and men of my command was all that I could desire.[126]

Capt. Theodore S. Garnett, one of J.E.B. Stuart's aides-de-camp, also left an account of this fight.

> After traveling less than a mile from our "ambush," met a squadron of Custer's brigade coming toward them. Gen. Stuart at once ordered a "Charge," and in another moment the Yankees were retreating at full speed, and orders were sent to the 2nd [Virginia Cavalry] Regiment . . . to come up at a gallop.
>
> In less than five minutes, Co. K [of the 1st Virginia Cavalry] was seen hurrying back closely followed by a charging squadron of Yankees, which was only induced to draw rein at sight of our advancing column. But now the range of hills in our front was literally swarming with Yankee cavalry, which deployed right and left on either side of the road, and pushed forward a heavy line of skirmishers. . . . The Yankees were now getting ready to dash upon us, and in another moment they commenced a charge . . . [they] came within easy pistol shot of Gen. Stuart . . . to whom they gave chase. The General seeing that they could not get at him over the fence, cantered along down the lane rather too leisurely, turning every now and then to his ordnance officer and saying, "Shoot that fellow, Grattan! Shoot him!" pointing to a Yankee who was plugging away at both of them.[127]

Maj. Gen. Alfred Pleasonton, commanding the Cavalry Corps, informed Custer of "his entire satisfaction at the result of your expedition, and the gratitude he has felt at the prompt manner in which the duties assigned you have been performed."[128] While Custer's expedition was a success, the main raid turned out to be a disastrous failure that had far-reaching implications for the Federal mounted arm.

After the conclusion of Custer's raid, the 6th Pennsylvania returned to its camp, where it spent a quiet month of March picketing a front of about eight miles and guarding a signal station atop Cedar Mountain.[129] "We do not have much time to ourselves that is we do not have much time to write and for ourselves hardly time enough to wash our cloaths and keep ourselves decent, but this is not always the case with us, it has only been the case during this winter," reported a member of Company E on March 6. "The reasons that we have been kept so busy is that we have had a great deal of picket duty to perform. We have had done more picket duty this winter than we ever done befor in all put together, but picket duty is not all that have kept us so buisy for we have been all winter (while not on picket) at work on our quarters."[130]

It was arduous duty. "I respectfully call attention of the major-general commanding to the immense amount of duty now being performed by the men and horses of this division," complained Wesley Merritt on March 4. "If it continues much longer there will scarcely be a man or horse fit for duty in the division." He proceeded to explain the plight of the Reserve Brigade. "In the Reserve Brigade the available command is on picket duty and guarding the signal station at Cedar Mountain each alternate day. It occupies nearly the entire day to relieve the line, and thus the horses are saddled a greater part of the time." He concluded by pointing out that the combination of constant picketing and the toll taken by the protracted marches of the two recent raids had "greatly reduced the horses of the command." Pleasonton forwarded Merritt's letter to army headquarters with the suggestion that infantry be used to guard the signal station, and not the cavalry of the Reserve Brigade.[131]

In the meantime, the Army of the Potomac was reorganized into fewer, larger infantry corps, and the Federal forces received a new general-in-chief, Lt. Gen. Ulysses S. Grant, formerly commander of all of the Federal forces in the Western Theatre. This grim and unbending westerner was a fierce warrior, bent on winning the war at all costs. He set about planning his strategy for doing so with a steely determination. Brig. Gen. Rufus Ingalls, the chief quartermaster of the Army of the Potomac, met Grant for the first time and keenly observed to General Meade, "I tell you, Meade, Grant means business."[132]

Grant planned for a coordinated simultaneous assault by all of the Federal armies, designed to prevent the Confederacy from shifting forces to meet threats. In an effort to grind down Southern resistance, Grant intended to put relentless pressure on the Confederate armies on all fronts. The plan included a spring campaign for the Army of the Potomac in the east, a combined move on Atlanta by the Armies of the Tennessee, Cumberland, and Ohio, and an advance up the Shenandoah Valley by a force commanded by Maj. Gen. David Hunter.

The Army of the Potomac was always a rumor mill. The winter of 1863-1864 was certainly no exception, and the bored soldiers had little to divert their attention from the spreading of rumors. That winter, a rumor surfaced that Pleasonton would supplant Maj. Gen. George G. Meade in command of the Army. That unhappy prospect left most of the Cavalry Corps's officer cadre "in a great stew." Lt. Charles B. Coxe of the Lancers proclaimed the idea "absurd," announcing that Pleasonton was "not fit to command a regt in active service," let alone an army.[133] While Meade would retain command of the Army of the Potomac, one part of that rumor was correct—big changes were in store.

In the wake of the failed raid on Richmond, blizzards of bad press swirled around the headquarters of the Army of the Potomac. "Although the service now possesses a considerable number of more than respectable leaders of horse, we have no one of such preeminent distinction . . . [as to be] the fit head of all the cavalry of so great an army as that of the Potomac," opined the *New York Times*. "John Buford came the nearest to it," continued the editorial, "if he did not actually snatch the laurels." It concluded that Pleasonton lacked "the qualities, mental and physical, that go into the composition of a first class cavalry leader."[134] On March 25, at Grant's behest, General Meade relieved Pleasonton of command of the Cavalry Corps.[135] Although Meade had long protected Pleasonton from his many critics, the cavalryman testified against Meade's conduct of the Battle of Gettysburg before the Committee on the Conduct of the War, enraging the ill-tempered Meade, who rightfully felt betrayed.[136]

One cavalry officer noted that "Even [Pleasonton's] success and the proofs he had given of the value of the cavalry, when properly used and led, were not sufficient to overcome the force of traditions and customs, and among higher authorities the idea still prevailed that the mounted force was secondary to, and should be used for the protection, convenience and relief of the infantry." He continued, "Serious difference of opinion on these questions between Generals Meade and Pleasonton had from time to time occurred, and at last had gone so far that the latter . . . could no longer retain his command."[137] Pleasonton was exiled to Missouri under the command of Maj. Gen. William S. Rosecrans, where Pleasonton brought Gen. Sterling Price's 1864 Missouri Raid to bay.

On April 5, Grant appointed his protégé Maj. Gen. Philip H. Sheridan to take Pleasonton's position as Cavalry Corps commander, even though Sheridan had almost no experience commanding horse soldiers.[138] Sheridan's appointment marked a major change in both leadership style and philosophy for the Cavalry Corps. The First Division also got a new commander, Brig. Gen. Alfred T. A. Torbert, another veteran infantry officer who had never commanded horse soldiers during his eight-year career in the Army. One of Merritt's Regulars astutely observed that Torbert was "a handsome dashing fellow, at this time, a beautiful horseman, and as brave as a lion; but his abilities were hardly equal to such large commands."[139] Merritt reverted to command of the Reserve Brigade.

As spring approached, the Lancers enjoyed warm days that made picket duty less miserable. "I am getting fat as a pig again," reported Pvt. John W. Wells of Company B contentedly. He continued, "Mother, I have not the nerve to tell you but I think we will be on the march before long for a summer campaign."[140] From their picket posts on the Rapidan, they could see the Confederate camps near Clark's Mountain. They occasionally bartered and bantered with them.[141] "In the morning we went down to exchange papers but the river was too high to throw them across on account of the rains," Henry Cowan wrote on April 17. "The Rebels sang the 'Bonny Blue Flag' and one of our men sang a song. The rebels did not say much but showed no displeasure."[142]

"The whole army has undergone a reorganization and believe that General Grant will have the Army put in motion against General Lee as soon as the weather will admit," noted Clement Hoffman on April 16. "I judge that we will be on the move about the first of next month."[143] His prediction proved accurate.

The new Cavalry Corps commander, Sheridan, reviewed Torbert's division on April 21. The appearance of the First Division pleased the little Irishman, who praised them, even though a large contingent had no horses and paraded past him dismounted. The men knew that a major campaign was afoot. "I cannot say much about things here at present but it is my opinion that we will soon have an attack from Lee who is getting reinforcements," observed Hamilton Ballentine on April 21. "Every day we go out we can see a new camp on the opposite side of the river. Still the boys are anxious to get a slap at them. They all feel so good after their 35 days of freedom." They would get their chance soon enough.[144]

On April 24, Cowan got a pass. He rode out of camp, around the foot of Pony Mountain and on to Stevensburg. After taking a look at the main camp of the Army of the Potomac, he then rode to take another look at the Brandy Station battlefield, "where we used to quarrel with the rebels in June & August of last summer," he wrote. "Graves and bones of dead horses mark the places where the Regulars and 6th Penna. charged from Brandy Station." After touring the battlefield, he rode along the tracks of the Orange & Alexandria Railroad, by Sheridan's headquarters, and then returned to camp. It was an enjoyable day. It was the last one he would have for a very long time.[145]

After his disgrace at Buford's hand, Major Hazeltine resigned his commission on November 12, 1863.[146] As they prepared to take the field, the Lancers had a new commander—William P. C. Treichel, formerly commander of Company A, returned to duty in September after recovering from his August wound. However, Treichel took ill in December and went on medical leave in Philadelphia. When he returned, he was promoted to major on January 11, 1864, becoming the highest-ranking officer still serving with the regiment.[147] As the long, cold winter wound down, the men enjoyed pleasant respites while they awaited the spring campaigning season.

Chapter Nine

1864: Campaigning with Grant and Sheridan

THE NEW COMMANDER OF THE Army of the Potomac's Cavalry Corps, Maj. Gen. Philip Henry Sheridan, was largely unknown to his men. Col. Charles Wainwright, a pithy artillerist, reflected in his diary, "I know nothing . . . of . . . [Sheridan], but a change I think was needed; neither Pleasonton nor [Maj. Gen. George] Stoneman proved themselves equal to the position."[1] Brig. Gen. Henry E. Davies, who commanded a Second Division cavalry brigade, wrote, "It was not known that he had ever served with or in command of cavalry, and the prejudice . . . among mounted troops against being placed under the orders of an officer whose experiences from which the Army of the Potomac had previously suffered had not induced the belief that the West was the point of the compass from which the advent of wise men bringing rich gifts of victory and success was to confidently expected."[2]

Sheridan was not, at first blush, the best choice to command the Cavalry Corps. Born on March 6, 1831, the diminutive Irishman ranked in the bottom third of his West Point class of 1853. He served as a second lieutenant in the 4th Infantry and, after service as a staff officer in the early days of the war, was appointed colonel of the 2nd Michigan Cavalry, a command he held for only three months. He then was promoted to brigadier general and assumed command of an infantry division. Sheridan performed well in leading his foot soldiers in many of the Western Theater's primary battles. His bravery and aggressiveness in assaulting the strong Confederate position at Chattanooga in November 1863 caught Grant's eye, and the commanding general marked the young man for advancement.[3]

Col. Horace Porter, one of Grant's staff officers, wrote that the new cavalry chief "had been worn down almost to a shadow by hard work and exposure . . . he looked anything but formidable as a candidate for a cavalry leader."[4] Maj. James H. Kidd, commander of the 6th Michigan Cavalry, recorded his observations:

> [Sheridan] was square of shoulder and there was plenty of room for the display of a major general's buttons on his broad chest. His face was strong, with a firm jaw, a keen eye, and extraordinary firmness in every lineament. In his manner there was an alertness, evinced rather in look

than in movement. Nothing escaped his eye, which was brilliant and searching and at the same time emitted flashes of kindly good nature. When riding past or among his troopers, he had a way of casting quick, comprehensive glances to the right and left and in all directions. He overlooked nothing. One had a feeling that he was under close and critical observation, that Sheridan had his eye on him, was mentally taking his measure and would remember and recognize him the next time. No introduction was needed.[5]

Sheridan did not make a good first impression on Lincoln, who commented that he was "a brown, chunky little chap, with a long body, short legs, not enough neck to hang him, and such long arms that if his ankles itch he can scratch them without stooping." Grant quickly replied, "You will find him big enough for the purpose before we get through with him."[6]

Sheridan set about reorganizing and inspecting his command, meaning, according to the Lancers's historian, that "nothing of special interest occurred in our army during the month of April."[7] The respite gave the Federal horse soldiers an opportunity to familiarize themselves with their new weapons. Most of the Army of the Potomac's Cavalry Corps had been given new seven-shot, breechloading Spencer carbines. One Regular officer noted of the Spencers: "The workmanship of this gun was indifferent, but it did, notwithstanding, excellent service and gave an immense advantage to the troops armed with it. [They] could throw in a tremendous fire when necessary, with great effect upon the enemy, who was naturally very often deceived in his estimate of the force opposed to him, judging by the unintermitting, incessant rattle along the line that he was contending with at least a division" when only a brigade was involved.[8] A South Carolinian, Edward Laight Wells of Charleston, later observed that troops armed with Spencers "ought to have been equal to at least double their number carrying only muzzle-loaders."[9] Compared with the single-shot muzzle-loaders carried by most grayclad horse soldiers, the Yankee troopers now enjoyed a significant advantage in firepower.

The Federal mounted arm was in a poor state after the long winter of difficult picket duty. "I do not think that there will be much cavalry Fighting in the coming campaign. As our cavalry was never in such poor condition as it is at Pressent. Our Horses are the most miserable looking Kanks, that you ever laid eyes on, and only Half of the men mounted at that. Our Regiment has only two Hundred and twenty five men mounted. The Rebel Cavalry, are reported to be in splendid condition, they having been Laying back and recruiting their Horses, While we have been on out Post duty, Raiding and Reconnoitering, all Winter," noted a sergeant of the 6th Pennsylvania Cavalry a few days before the beginning of the spring campaign.[10]

Appalled by the state of his command and by the wretched condition of its mounts, Sheridan blamed excessive winter picketing for the toll taken on men and beasts.

Sheridan observed, "shortly after my taking command, much of the picketing was done away with, and we had two weeks of leisure time to nurse the horses, on which so much depended."[11] As the horses rested, Sheridan developed a new approach for his troopers.

Sheridan later alleged that he had faced stiff resistance to his new plan from Meade. According to Sheridan, he laid out his "idea as to what the cavalry should do, the main purport of which was that it ought to be concentrated to fight the enemy's cavalry. Heretofore, the commander of the Cavalry Corps had been, virtually, but an adjunct at army headquarters—a sort of chief of cavalry—and my proposition seemed to stagger General Meade not a little." Little Phil continued, "I knew that it would be difficult to overcome the recognized custom of using the cavalry for the protection of trains and the establishment of cordons around the infantry corps, and so far as subordinating its oper-ations to the movements of the main army that in name only was it a corps at all, but I still thought it my duty to try."[12] Meade's reluctance to accept to this paradigm shift set the army commander and the cavalry chieftain into conflict.

In spite of it, the men were itching to get back into the game. "The time coming shortly for the commencement of the summer campaign," reported Pvt. Henry Cowan of Company K. "The men are all anxious for the start. I only hope that we whip them in the first general engagement. It will dishearten them and encourage our army. I am [sure] if the ground will allow a fair sweep the cavalry will either make or break things." He was, of course, correct. The question was whether things would play out that way in practice.[13]

When the Army of the Potomac's Cavalry Corps set out for its spring campaign in the first days of May 1864, it was one of the largest and most powerful fighting cavalry commands the world had ever seen. With a well-equipped, well-led, and reasonably well-mounted force of more than 10,000 horsemen, Sheridan champed at the bit to pitch into the Confederate cavalry. Little Phil finally received orders to prepare to move on April 22, and his troopers were issued 150 rounds each as well as subsistence rations.[14] "We mooved out of our Winter Quarters about two weeks ago, and mooved back to within a mile of Culpeper where we are now encamped," reported Sergeant Smith of Company I. "We are under marching orders, and are expecting the Army to moove every Hour. For the last two weeks we have drawn nothing but the marching Ration, which consists of Coffee, Sugar, Pork and Hard Tack."[15] On April 29, the Cavalry Corps' dismounted men were consolidated into a single regiment until new mounts could be located, a sure sign that the rest of the command was nearly ready to move.[16]

As Sgt. Christian Geisel of Company H wrote just before the march began, "All the way from our camp back to Brandy Station the country is covered with camps as far as the eye can reach, and the troops all in fine condition and good spirits."[17] Sgt. Hamilton Ballentine of Company K made the following prediction on April 30, "We have now started our summer campaign and I think it will wind up the war."[18] John T. Baynes, another member of Company H, noted, "We will go down and give *'Old Lee'* a hell of a *thrashing* for we are just the boys to do it."[19] Maj. James H. Starr had command of the regiment as the Lancers prepared to move out of their comfortable winter camps. Starr was a Harvard-trained lawyer who had served in the First City Troop. He had recruited Company I, and was promoted to major after Maj. Henry C. Whelan's death, and Maj. Benoni Lockwood's resignation in March 1864. Starr now commanded the regiment as a result of Maj. William P. C. Treichel's ongoing health problems.[20]

As the army prepared to move, Sergeant Valentine rode the Union picket line. A Confederate major who commanded the Southern picket line hailed him from across the Rapidan River. Ballentine rode over, and the major gave him a Southern newspaper and observed that the Army of the Potomac was up at dawn, marching toward Early's Ford on the Rapidan. "That was the first I knew of the move," commented Ballentine, who then shared a "sociable drink" out of the major's flask. They bid each other goodbye in the hope of meeting each other the next day in the crash of battle. As Ballentine approached the river, the major crossed to the north bank, and before doing so, ordered the company of Southern infantry that held the ford to lay down their arms and not pick them up again until Ballentine had gone. The Southerners obeyed.[21]

Ten days later the Cavalry Corps scouted the major fords over the Rapidan River. At midnight on the night of May 3, the Cavalry Corps began crossing the Rapidan as the Army of the Potomac moved into the Wilderness.[22] Grant's campaign took the army over the same ground where it suffered a disastrous defeat under Hooker at the Battle of Chancellorsville exactly a year earlier. Sergeant Geisel wrote home to his sister Louisa, "Gen. Grant is in no hurry about moving, but I think when he starts once there will be some warm work to be done."[23] Geisel did not realize how right he was.

The last of the Army of the Potomac moved out of its winter camps before midnight on May 3. On the morning of May 4, Pvt. John P. Kepner of Company I noted in his diary, "The inspiring music of our Hd Qrs Band rang loud and clear on the morning air at 2 A.M. calling the warriors from sweet repose to pack up for the campaign just opening."[24] The Army of the Potomac plunged into the Virginia countryside and collided with the Army of Northern Virginia. The Battle of the Wilderness raged in the snarled undergrowth of the Virginia bottomland for two days, with both armies suffering huge casualties in a blind, close fight. The Lancers played no role in the main battle; they spent May 6 supporting an attack by Custer's Brigade of the First Cavalry Division.

As the fighting in the Wilderness wound down, Grant decided to move the Army of the Potomac around Lee's flank by way of the important crossroads town of Spotsylvania Court House. The Cavalry Corps had the critical task of clearing the roads for the Union infantry. Merritt commanded the First Division as Torbert was on medical leave. His horsemen led the advance to a ramshackle hotel called Todd's Tavern that stood at the strategic intersection of the Brock and Catharpin Roads. There it ran into heavy resistance from Gray cavalry, which dug in its heels around the tavern. "We went out to feel, our squadron in the advance we found Stuart's cavalry about a mile from Todd's Tavern," recounted Cowan. "We attacked them and fought stubbornly until after dark."[25] Much was at stake. If the Federal troopers could push their way through, they could win the race for Spotsylvania Court House and force Lee to attack the Army of the Potomac on ground of Grant's choosing.[26]

Maj. Gen. Philip H. Sheridan. (*Library of Congress*)

The men of the Reserve Brigade were guarding the Cavalry Corps wagon trains when fighting broke out. However, Merritt sent for them once the fighting grew heavy, and placed them in line immediately upon their arrival. The Lancers saw a great deal of combat at Todd's Tavern on May 7. The Lancers and the 1st New York Dragoons led the initial Union attacks, the Lancers on the right side of the road, while the Dragoons took the left side, and a fierce battle immediately followed.[27] One participant remembered that the "air seemed filled with leaden missiles from either side. For a while the issue is doubtful, for support comes up tardily; but still the desperate but unequal conflict is kept up with unabated fury."[28] Fitz Lee recorded, "A severe combat raged until dark."[29] "The rebels holding a strong position in the woods we then took it on foot," reported Cowan. "Sent the horses to the rear charged them and drove them from the wood. Here we lost many wounded, few killed and prisoners."[30] Reserve Brigade commander Col. Alfred Gibbs had his horse shot out from under him, and the Lancers took heavy casualties, including the killing of the regimental adjutant and the serious wounding of Maj. James H. Starr, who was hit in the face by a pistol ball.[31] The regiment's most senior uninjured captain, Charles L. Leiper, of Company C, assumed command.

The officer corps of the Lancers took a battering that day. Capt. Emlen N. Carpenter, the commander of Company E, was captured. After being held as a prisoner of war in South Carolina, Carpenter escaped and made his way back to Federal lines. He eventually rejoined the regiment after his arduous experience and was brevetted to major and lieutenant colonel for gallant and meritorious service.[32] Lt. William Kirk, the regimental commissary, was mortally wounded at Todd's Tavern. Lt. Charles B. Coxe, of Company K, was severely wounded in the left shoulder.[33] Two corporals were killed, and four sergeants and a number of privates were wounded in the severe fighting.[34] The handsome gray horse that Capt. Frank Furness had ridden since the beginning of the war was shot out from under him. Furness tumbled to the ground uninjured.[35] "In this one ingagement our regiment lost more than we have lost altogether in all our skirmishes," noted Clement Hoffman. "In Company E, the Company to which I belong, we had two killed five wounded with our Captain and three others taken prisoner. Here I must mention that this is the heavyest loss our Company has met with yet."[36]

Reinforced by infantry of the Fifth Corps, the Federal cavalry finally drove the Confederates from their strong defensive positions near the tavern. The *Philadelphia Inquirer* reported, "General Merritt had the right, where the fire was the hottest. The Reserve Brigade suffered the most, as it was most hardly pressed, and most nobly did they meet the desperate onslaught. Our cavalry were all dismounted, for the contest occurred mostly in thick woods, where horses could not be used to advantage."[37] Complicating matters further, Meade and Sheridan had both issued orders to Gregg, confusing the division commander, and infuriating the mercurial Sheridan. Ultimately, Sheridan's failure to act promptly after receiving orders for May 8 prevented the road to Spotsylvania Court House from being cleared. While Todd's Tavern was a tactical victory for the Federal troopers, the delay it created permitted Robert E. Lee to shift his infantry to Spotsylvania Court House, where it took up an imposing defensive position. Instead of forcing Lee to attack him, Grant would now have to attack Lee, or find a way to flank him out of his strong position. Characteristically, Grant attacked.[38] Because Meade had failed to beat Lee to Spotsylvania Court House, the two armies fell into a brutal and bloody stalemate, slugging it out there for nearly two weeks.

Annoyed by the cavalry's failure, Meade summoned Sheridan to his headquarters. Sheridan, in turn, was furious that Meade had issued direct orders to one of his subordinates outside the chain of command. There, according to Grant's chief of staff, "a very acrimonious dispute took place between the two generals." Meade told Sheridan in no uncertain terms that he was unhappy with the performance of his cavalry, and an extended argument took place.[39] Sheridan later recounted telling Meade that he "had broken up my combinations, exposed Wilson's division and kept Gregg unnecessarily idle, and . . . such disjointed operations as he had been requiring of the cavalry . . . would render the corps inefficient and useless."

According to Little Phil, the discussion took on a loud and ominous tone. "One word brought on another until, finally I told him that I could whip Stuart if he (Meade) would only let me, but since he insisted on giving the cavalry directions without consulting or even notifying me, he could thenceforth command the Cavalry Corps himself—that I would not give it another order."[40] Sheridan stomped out of the meeting in a rage. Meade, perhaps wanting to relieve the Irishman of command for insubordination, went directly to Grant's nearby tent and recounted what had occurred. When Grant heard Sheridan's remarks about whipping Stuart, he responded, "Did Sheridan say that? Well, he generally knows what he is talking about. Let him start right out and do it."[41]

An elated Little Phil summoned his subordinates on the night of May 8. "We are going out to fight Stuart's cavalry in consequence of a suggestion from me," he said. "We will give him a fair, square fight; we are strong, and I know we can beat him, and in view of my recent representations to General Meade I shall expect nothing but success." The enemy cavalry was to be the primary target. "Our move," he ordered, "would be a challenge to Stuart for a cavalry duel behind Lee's lines, and in his own country."[42] With his entire corps in tow, Sheridan set out to whip J.E.B. Stuart and his vaunted cavalry.

On May 9, after a hard, forced march, the Federal horsemen, with the Lancers in the lead, reached Beaver Dam Station, where they burned two engines and trains carrying two days' worth of rations for Lee's army and tore up the tracks of the Virginia Central Railroad.[43] Encountering a force of enemy horsemen there, the Federals pushed through their thin ranks. Their charge captured a train of ambulance and freed nearly four hundred Union prisoners, including a colonel, two lieutenant colonels, and a number of other officers captured during the Battle of the Wilderness. "The poor fellows were overjoyed at their unlooked for good fortune and expressed their gratitude in unmeasured terms." Left with no alternative, and deep behind enemy lines, these freed prisoners joined Sheridan's burgeoning column.[44] After tearing up the railroad tracks, Sheridan was ready to move on. As they marched, Confederate cavalry harassed the Federal rearguard, but did little to delay the column's progress. "Keep moving boys," roared Little Phil, "We're going on through. There isn't cavalry enough in the Southern Confederacy to stop us."[45] The Lancers suffered one man wounded and six captured or missing in the fighting at Beaver Dam Station.[46]

On the night of May 10, elements of the 5th U.S. Cavalry, supported by a small detachment of Lancers led by Sgt. Lewis Miller, Company L, destroyed Davenport's Bridge over the South Anna River. The Lancers felled trees in their rear to block the pursuit route, and then bivouacked near Ground Squirrel Bridge.[47] The next morning, Wickham's brigade attacked the Federals at Davenport's Bridge, costing two officers and fifty enlisted men as casualties. As they withdrew, the Federals burned Ground Squirrel Bridge and then spent the night near the smoldering remains of the bridge. On the morning of May 11, Confederate cavalry renewed their attack as the Federals were forming up to move out, but held their position until the rest of the command had marched. They crossed the railroad at Glen Allen Station, tore up the tracks, burned the railroad ties, and destroyed the telegraph wires and some culverts before advancing toward an important crossroads called Yellow Tavern.[48]

When word of Sheridan's departure reached Stuart, the Confederate cavalry chief rallied his command for a forced march. Driving his command mercilessly, Stuart kept his men pushing until they finally intercepted Sheridan's line of advance at Yellow Tavern, the intersection of the Valley and Telegraph Roads, a few miles north of Richmond. Stuart had only Fitz Lee's division with which to try to stop Sheridan's entire Cavalry Corps. "As we moved in the direction of Richmond, we could see occasionally through openings in the woods the long columns of their cavalry evidently straining every nerve to get ahead of us in the race and take up some position of defense in our front," remembered one of Torbert's staff officers.[49]

On the 11th, with the Lancers leading the way, the Federals found Stuart's horsemen massed in front of them at the Y-shaped intersection of Mountain and Telegraph Roads, near the small Yellow Tavern Hotel, where Brig. Gen. Williams C. Wickham's brigade of Virginia horsemen awaited the arrival of the Federals. Wickham had selected a good position. In his front were fields fringed with dense woods, and a natural choke point where the two roads came together. Brig. Gen. Lunsford L. Lomax's brigade took up a position alongside Wickham's Virginians on the Telegraph Road. "We thought we had [Sheridan] penned and would surely capture his while command," recalled one of Stuart's men. "With this expectation we closed in on him."[50]

About noon that day, while the Northern cavalry tore up the tracks of the Richmond, Fredericksburg & Potomac Railroad, one-half of the Lancers picketed the road in both directions, while the other half of the regiment, under command of Capt. Charles L. Leiper, deployed along the turnpike as skirmishers. "A long line of flankers on each flank connected with the advance, the whole of the Reserve Brigade thus acting as the advance-guard of the cavalry corps," Chaplain Gracey recorded in his diary. The skirmishers were spread across country, moving straight ahead in spite of barns, fences, woods, or other obstacles. One of the Lancers spotted one of Stuart's officers—who had surreptitiously visited his home—trying to escape. The officer ran for the safety of the woods, and "a bright-eyed youth of the Sixth happening to direct his glance that way, he was ordered to withdraw from his undignified and unwarlike position. A more sullen, uncommunicative rebel was never gobbled."[51]

Seeing an opportunity, Wickham ordered his troopers to attack. They formed line of battle and advanced toward the approaching Yankees. Some of the diligent Pennsylvania videttes spotted the advance of the 6th Virginia Cavalry, the van of Wickham's column, and reported it to Gibbs, who quickly sent the rest of the Reserve Brigade to support the Lancers, thereby bringing on a great battle that had implications far beyond what anyone could have realized at the time.[52]

Gibbs immediately deployed skirmishers and ordered his men into line of battle. Stuart opened the ball by shelling the Federal column. "The sound of the first gun had scarcely reached us before the whole column broke into a gallop, and within ten minutes we wheeled into line of battle," recalled another member of the 1st New York Dragoons.[53] "The battle of Yellow Tavern is scarcely known in history," observed an officer of the 1st New York Dragoons years later, "yet, considering the numbers engaged, it was the greatest cavalry encounter of the war. For hours, eighteen thousand horsemen, the flower of both armies, engaged in fierce combat."[54]

Before long, the fighting had become general, spreading along a wide front. The two sides fought both mounted and dismounted. Merritt's aggressive dismounted charges drove the Confederates beyond Yellow Tavern and got possession of the direct road to Richmond—the Brook Turnpike—but severe and accurate fire by Stuart's horse artillery made the area around the tavern a decidedly hot place. "The enemy fought with much

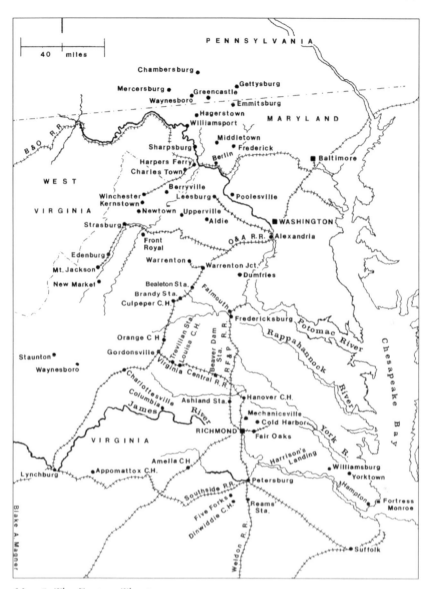

Map 8. The Eastern Theater.

desperation," reported an admiring Merritt, "employing seriously every available man of the Reserve Brigade and two regiments of the Second Brigade, but finally his line was cut and a charge made mounted by one regiment of First Brigade (the Fifth Michigan) and a regiment of [Brig. Gen. George] Chapman's brigade, Third Division (the First Vermont), headed by the intrepid commander of the First Brigade (General Custer), and drove the enemy discomfited off the field."[55] Hamilton Ballentine reported, "while our brigade was driving them in front Custer charged with his brigade in the rear taking 2 pieces of artillery and several prisoners."[56] The battle lasted until dark, "when the thoroughly whipped seceshers abandoned the field, leaving us complete victors," as one Federal crowed in a letter home.[57]

After a huge melee, in which J.E.B. Stuart was mortally wounded by one of Custer's Wolverines, the Federals brushed the Confederates out of their way. His column cut in two, Fitz Lee, now commanding the Southern horsemen, broke off and withdrew toward Richmond. An officer of the 1st New York Dragoons noted, "General Stuart, the Rebel Cavalry leader is killed, which is worth a victory to us."[58] Col. Alfred Gibbs, temporarily commanding the Reserve Brigade, observed, "The enemy was badly punished and driven off. Our loss that day was but small."[59] Wickham lost nearly one hundred troopers that day, and Lomax twice as many. However, none of those losses matched the magnitude of the loss of Stuart, who was, in many ways, irreplaceable. The victorious Yankees bivouacked on the battlefield as the skies opened and rains fell on the tired troopers. The Lancers suffered only four men wounded in the long day's fighting at Yellow Tavern.[60]

The road to Richmond now lay open, and Sheridan knew it. Capt. George B. Sanford, of Torbert's staff, noted that their bivouac was short. "The camp, however, turned out to be scarcely more than a rest, for we had a cup of coffee, when orders came to mount, and by eleven o'clock at night we were in on our way toward Richmond again."[61] Sergeant Geisel wrote, "What a moment of excitement, in the cold, damp hours of a May morning to see ten thousand strong men halted, and waiting in breathless suspense."[62] The victorious Federals continued on toward Richmond, stopping within three miles of the city. "You could hear the joy bells of Richmond calling out the Home Guard to arms and the roar of locomotives rolling up troops from Lynchburg," recounted Ballentine.[63] "The general impression was that we were going *in*," recalled Captain Sanford of the 1st U.S. Cavalry, "and indeed there would probably have been little difficulty in doing so. How we would have got out is another story, and I suspect a doubtful one."[64]

The Northern horse soldiers faced another trying note on the march. "The night was very wet and dark, the road choked with the column, and march slow and painful," recalled Chaplain Gracey. "Suddenly we heard three explosions to the front, and supposed that the artillery of the Richmond fortifications had opened upon the advance; but it turned out that the rebels had planted torpedoes in the road, with wires ingeniously attached, for the horses to trip over." Three of these primitive landmines had exploded, killing several horses of Sheridan's staff, and narrowly missing the cavalry chief himself.[65]

Facing the fortifications around Richmond, Sheridan realized that the Rebel capital's defenses were too strong to be broken by a cavalry raid, and he turned his column away from the Confederate capital.[66] "The night was very dark, and I remember hearing two explosions on the road during night," recalled Cpl. Edgar H. Klemroth of Company A. "After the last one, there was a halt for a while, and sounds of a scrap off on the right." When the sun rose on May 12, he realized that the Cavalry Corps was inside the outer ring of defenses of Richmond, on high ground overlooking Meadow Bridge.[67] "On the

12th we made a dash on Richmond but we soon learned that there was enough rebels left in its fortifications to keep us out of it," noted another Pennsylvanian.[68]

However, the Southern cavalry had laid a trap for Sheridan at Meadow Bridge, an crossing over the Chickahominy River, not far from the defenses of Richmond. By May 12, Sheridan's men were nearly out of food, forage, and ammunition, and the grayclad horse soldiers had hemmed them in. One New Yorker called it "the tightest place in which the corps ever found itself," and another Federal recalled it as "the most foreboding experience of my army life."[69] With Wilson's division in the lead, Sheridan began pushing toward Meadow Bridge, "fighting all the way," as a trooper of Company C noted.[70] The initial Confederate line, manned largely by clerks from Richmond, broke. As the Yankee horsemen moved east toward Meadow Bridge, the resistance stiffened. "The swamp was full of Rebs masked in the underbrush with 2 pieces of artillery," said Hamilton Ballentine. "Things had changed since I was there before for then we held the Rebels works and they held McClellan's."[71] Elements of Custer's Michigan Brigade moved out, cleared the causeway, and established a fragile bridgehead over the Chickahominy.

Sheridan recognized that he held a tenuous position, and was greatly worried about his predicament. Maj. Gen. Fitzhugh Lee's Confederate cavalry division had joined the fray, as had infantry from the defenses of Richmond. Custer's Wolverines managed to keep the Confederate horsemen at bay long enough for Federal pioneers to repair the railroad span over the Chickahominy that had been destroyed earlier by Lee's cavalry. "We got over by single file, on the stringpieces of the bridge, as, for some unaccountable reason, his determination to stop us did not seem strong enough to induce him to break cover, and the range was rather long for his armament," recounted an officer of the 2nd U.S. Cavalry.[72] With a severe thunderstorm raging, Northern horsemen streamed across the bridge. Led by the Reserve Brigade, they launched a desperate attack that shattered Lee's line and cleared the way for Little Phil's escape. "Our regiment charged them with the sabre and routed their left capturing many prisoners," recounted Cowan. "We used the revolver freely."[73] Sgt. Christian Geisel described this action as "our desperate struggle in getting possession of the little bridge across the Chickahominy. . . . We were completely surrounded, and only cut our way through by the greatest dash and daring of the War."[74] The Confederates made a stand at Mechanicsville, where the Reserve Brigade had another three-hour fight. The Lancers suffered one man killed and nine men wounded in the desperate fighting at Meadow Bridge.[75]

Repulsed from Richmond, Sheridan veered down the Peninsula, skirmishing and reconnoitering the whole way, revisiting ground that his horsemen had covered extensively two years earlier. "On the morning of the 13th we marched to Dispatch Station. We crossed the Chickahominy at Bottom's Bridge," reported Ballentine. "The Rebs were still following up our rear. We got here last night and were met by 3 large shells from our gun boats who had mistaken us for Rebs." The men continued pressing on.[76]

On May 20, Clement Hoffman of Company E reported, "We retired down the James river and reached Malvern Hill on the 14th inst. whare we lade a few days and whare I commenced this letter, but as I have stated we are now on the banks of the Pamunkey or York River. How long we have to lay here or where we will go from here I cannot yet tell."[77] The Cavalry Corps ended up near Yorktown, effectively out of the war for a couple of weeks. However, the long raid took a toll on the Federal horsemen. "I was on the Raid, and with the Regiment ever sinse the Campane opened. 21 Days out of 29 we have been in Fight," reported Sergeant Smith. "Our Regiment have lost 97 men, all told, including 7 Officers. Sergt Pennington[78] and Sergt Reinhart[79] have both been wounded. I am the only Sergt left in the Company with the exception of Quartermaster & Commissary Sergt. But they do not go into fight."[80]

The mortally wounded Stuart died in Richmond on May 12 while the Army of Northern Virginia slugged it out at the Bloody Angle at the Battle of Spotsylvania Court House. Stuart's death created problems within the command hierarchy of the Army of Northern Virginia's cavalry that had far-reaching implications. It also meant that Robert E. Lee was left without his good right arm—he reportedly wept upon hearing the news of his cavalry chieftain's death, lamenting, "He never brought me a piece of false information."[81] William L. Wilson of the 12th Virginia Cavalry of the Laurel Brigade lamented the dashing cavalier's passing: "The Cavalry corps has lost its great leader the unequalled Stuart. We miss him much. Hampton is a good officer but Stuart's equal does not exist."[82]

As a result of Stuart's death, Lee now faced a difficult situation. There was a smoldering rivalry and growing hostility between his nephew Fitz and Hampton. One of Fitz Lee's troopers staked his hero's claim: "The mantle of Stuart finally came to Fitzhugh Lee," he asserted. "This was but natural. Stuart and Fitz Lee had fought side by side, and planned cavalry campaigns together, and Fitz was Stuart's trusted officer to carry out the boldest maneuvers. The cavalry of the Army of Northern Virginia wanted no other leader than Fitz Lee after Stuart's death."[83]

However, Hampton was senior in rank to Fitz Lee. "Hampton's seniority in rank was based upon his commission as brigadier two months ahead of Fitz, and the listing of his name immediately above Fitz's in the recommendations for promotion to major-general," Hampton's biographer commented. "This was a margin so narrow as perhaps to seem no margin at all to Fitz and his friends."[84] Because of this conflict and tension, General Lee elected not to appoint a new corps commander, and instead maintained the three divisions as independent commands, with each division commander reporting directly to him.[85] While this was probably a good move politically, it created its own problems, as there was no clear chain of command in the field.

Although Sheridan won the fight at Yellow Tavern and earned a reputation with the Confederates as a "vicious" cavalry leader, his raid failed to achieve its objectives. His grand excursion covered nearly three hundred miles, and took a heavy toll on men and horses.[86] Because Sheridan and his horsemen did not rejoin the main body of the Army of the Potomac until May 25, for more than two weeks Meade had only one small brigade of cavalry available. The lack of a cavalry screen to lead the way nearly caused the Army of the Potomac to fall into a trap set by Robert E. Lee along the banks of the North Anna River, leaving Grant to grope blindly for his adversary.

The unusually hot spring of 1864 severely damaged Sheridan's horses during the lengthy May raid. Additional refitting was required before another major raid could be attempted. Despite a leisurely pace of march, worn-out beasts dropped by the score. Rather than allowing broken-down horses to fall into Confederate hands, where they could be nursed back to health and put back into service, the Richmond raid marked a new and harsher turn to the war. As horses broke down they were shot by the Yankee troopers, who then trudged off, saddles and equipment slung over their shoulders.[87] Despite the fearful toll taken on the horses by the long and grueling raid, the Cavalry Bureau still provided sufficient remounts and reinforcements to maintain a large and effective force in the field. With no similar mechanism for providing remounts, Robert E. Lee's mounted arm was slowly worn down by attrition.

The morale of the Lancers remained high, in spite of their tribulations. Sgt. Hamilton Ballentine declared at the end of the raid, "I must say it was the best conducted expedition ever known and all the confidence in the world is placed in our little commander Sheridan."[88] "I suppose there is a great deal of excitement at home, about Grant's fighting so hard," recounted Sgt. Christian Geisel on May 22. "We have lost a great many men but are steadily going ahead. And I think Grant is the man to bring this thing to a close," he concluded. Unfortunately, Geisel received a mortal wound a few days later at Haw's Shop, and did not live to find out whether his prediction was accurate.[89] Like the grim warrior that now led them, the Lancers remained determined to see the thing through.

On May 28, Sheridan faced Hampton's grayclad cavalry force at the bloody battle of Haw's Shop, remembered by some veterans as the most severe cavalry fighting of the war. It was a long and brutal day of fighting primarily involving David Gregg's veterans. The Lancers participated in the fight, operating on the Confederate left flank for much of the afternoon. "As we advanced and pressed close upon their lines, they opened upon us with canister from two guns, which checked us," recorded Chaplain Gracey. "About 5 o'clock we were joined by the 19th New York Cavalry, when we again charged dismounted, and drove the enemy back about a mile and a half."[90] Brig. Gen. Matthew C. Butler's newly arrived brigade of South Carolina mounted infantrymen carried the burden of the fighting for the Confederates. Haw's Shop inflicted more heavy losses on Sheridan's command, prompting him to break contact for some much-needed rest and refitting. Thus, Haw's Shop effectively removed three brigades of Sheridan's Cavalry Corps from the war for two days.

Warren's Fifth Corps crossed Totopotomoy Creek on May 29, but a want of cavalry support cost Meade the opportunity to crush Lee's vulnerable right flank the next day. Nevertheless, a few days after Haw's Shop, a Federal staff officer noted, "Our cavalry is full of confidence and does wonders."[91] This new confidence, bordering on arrogance, was Phil Sheridan's major contribution to the Army of the Potomac's Cavalry Corps.

By the end of May, the Army of the Potomac was working its way toward the James River. On May 30, Torbert's First Division fought the Confederate cavalry near Old Church. Merritt and the Reserve Brigade led the attack, and heavy fighting lasted until after dark. The Lancers charged the enemy flank and engaged it in hand-to-hand combat, "in which our brave boys fought with desperation, though losing heavily." After being reinforced by Custer's Wolverines, a general charge by the dismounted Federal cavalry finally drove the Southern horsemen from the field.[92] "The Sixth Pennsylvania Cavalry was also distinguished for its conduct in this battle," declared Merritt. "It had been held in reserve with a view to acting mounted, but upon advancing for that purpose found the country impracticable, and dismounting dealt the enemy some heavy blows in the right place."[93]

Capt. Charles L. Leiper was badly wounded in the right foot "while with his usual intrepidity he was leading his regiment into action," reported Merritt, leaving Capt. J. Hinckley Clark of Company M in command of the regiment.[94] Lt. S. H. Martin, the regimental adjutant, was killed. "He was a severe loss to the regiment and the service at large," lamented Merritt, "having brought himself by important services on a former occasion to the especial notice and commendation of the division and corps commanders."[95] Pvt. Richard J. Gibbs of Company E was shot through the throat and neck, through the left arm near the shoulder, and again through the right arm near the elbow.[96] Pvts. Charles Horner and Thomas Whalley were killed, and the Lancers took a total of twenty-five casualties.[97] That night, the regiment camped on the same ground where it had spent a night in 1862, using the same picket posts that they had manned during the Peninsula Campaign.[98]

On May 31, the Cavalry Corps was on the move by 5 a.m., pushing forward until the horsemen encountered strong entrenchments. The Federals dismounted and prepared to fight on foot.[99] This resulted in a sharp engagement for Merritt with the Confederate cavalry near the old Mechanicsville battlefield of the Peninsula Campaign. "Here was accomplished a work of which every one connected with the brigade is justly proud," declared Wesley Merritt, "a success by cavalry which has no parallel in this war—a single brigade contending with and taking from an enemy, at least three times its numbers, one-third infantry, a naturally strong position, made doubly strong by artificial means."[100] Merritt's attack drove the Confederate infantry and cavalry almost a mile before he called off the pursuit.[101] "As we were ordered to hold this position, our fight was even more desperate the next day," recalled a Lancer. "We held our own until darkness closed upon a disputed field." Lt. Arthur E. Murphy was killed in action while encouraging the regiment's skirmishers to hold their position against a determined Confederate attack, "making [him] the third of the adjutants of this brave regiment who have fallen at the post of honor."[102]

By June 1, the two armies faced each other across an elaborate network of trenches at Cold Harbor. A stalemate developed, with the Confederate infantry launching desperate attacks against Merritt's strong line of dismounted troopers. That day, during a bayonet charge, a Rebel infantryman fell wounded in front of the Federal works, shot in the thigh and bleeding badly. Capt. Robert W. Mitchell of the Lancers spotted the man, and pointed him out to his friend, Capt. Frank Furness, saying, "My God, look at that one."

The man would quickly bleed to death if steps were not taken to save him. Proclaiming, "I can't see him suffer," Furness climbed over the barricade and went to assist the wounded man. "What moved my pity more than in the countless other cases in which we almost daily witnessed was that when the poor fellow was struck, believing himself near death, he tried to struggle to his knees and clasped his upright hands in prayer," recalled Furness. "What man with memories of bedtime and his mother's gentle hand would see that sight unmoved?"

Furness made his way to the wounded man, noticing that his blood-soaked pants resembled "a dark alligator hide," and realized that the Confederate required an immediate tourniquet if he was to survive. Furness asked whether the soldier had a handkerchief and was told "inside pocket." Furness tightly wrapped the makeshift tourniquet and made the man as comfortable as possible. He gave the Southerner his canteen and wished him luck. As he crawled back, the Rebel called out, "You may be a Yankee, but, by Gad, you are a gentleman."

After returning safely, Furness realized that the Confederates had held their fire while he tended to the wounded man. "Captain Mitchell, I don't believe those gentlemen fired a single shot in my direction while I was out there," he said. Furness never found out what happened to his patient—not long after, the Federal horsemen were relieved by the Army of the Potomac's infantry and moved out. This episode haunted Furness for the rest of his life.[103]

The next day, June 2, the Federal cavalry reached Bottom's Bridge over the Chickahominy River, not far from Cold Harbor and the old battlefields of McClellan's 1862 campaign. The Northern horsemen threw up entrenchments, heavily picketed the river, and spent the night there, drawn up in line of battle. On June 3, Meade ordered a massive assault that failed miserably, costing his army heavy casualties in a matter of minutes in exchange for only light Confederate losses.[104] Years later, Grant candidly admitted: "I have always regretted that the last frontal assault at Cold Harbor was ever made . . . no advantage whatever was gained to compensate for the heavy loss we sustained. Indeed, the advantages, other than those of relative losses, were on the Confederate side."[105]

The recent fighting had left the regiment fearfully short of commissioned officers. On June 4, infantry relieved Sheridan's cavalry at Cold Harbor, as another raid loomed. Additional officers would be required in order for the regiment to be able to field its full complement. That day, word came through that two sergeants—Theodore J. Wint and Andrew Lanigan—had been commissioned as second lieutenants. In addition, several new recruits from Philadelphia arrived and joined the regiment. They were about to have quite a baptism of fire.[106]

As part of his grand strategy, Grant sent an army under command of Maj. Gen. Franz Sigel up the Shenandoah Valley, with the intent of depriving Lee of his primary source of rations and provender. When a scratch Confederate force defeated Sigel at New Market on May 15, Grant replaced him with Maj. Gen. David "Black Dave" Hunter, a man derisively described by Confederate cavalry general John D. Imboden as "a human hyena."[107] Hunter consolidated his command and then advanced up the Valley toward Staunton, intending to destroy the railroad depot there. Doing so would sever a critical supply link to Richmond. Once he completed his mission at Staunton, he would then advance on Charlottesville.[108]

Finally realizing that the terrain around Richmond left little room for maneuver, and aware that the rebel works at Cold Harbor were too strong to be broken, Grant revised his strategy entirely. He decided to cross the James River and advance on Petersburg, twenty-five miles south of Richmond. Petersburg had great strategic significance as the junction of the major southern railroads supplying the Confederate capital. If Grant could capture Petersburg and Hunter obtained Staunton, Lee's army would be entirely cut off from its lines of supply and would have to come out and fight, surrender, or attempt to flee. Grant realized that the move south of the James had to be hidden from Robert E. Lee's vigilant cavalry if he was to maintain the element of surprise. With Federal armies on both sides of the James River, Grant knew that the safety of the Confederate capital would be "a matter of the first consideration with executive, legislative and judicial branches of the so-called Confederate government, if it was not with the military commanders. But I took all the precaution I knew of to guard against all dangers."[109]

While commanding in the West, Grant had learned and exploited the importance of the strategic cavalry raid as an effective means of distracting the enemy's attention from his movements. In order to screen his crossing of the Mississippi below the bluffs at Vicksburg, Grant ordered Col. Benjamin Grierson to lead a daring cavalry raid deep into the heart of Mississippi, with the assigned task of destroying railroad lines and telegraph wires and creating havoc in the enemy's rear. Spectacularly successful, Grierson drew away much of the enemy's attention and badly distracted Rebel Lt. Gen. John C. Pemberton, commander of Vicksburg's defenses. This diversion permitted Grant to make a nearly uncontested crossing of the river, prompting William T. Sherman to proclaim the exploit "the most brilliant expedition of the war."[110] Sheridan's May Richmond Raid diverted enemy attention and drew off a large portion of Lee's cavalry, thereby clearing the way for Meade's advance toward Spotsylvania.

Having used this tactic so successfully in the past, Grant decided to try it again. On June 6, Hunter defeated a small Confederate army commanded by Brig. Gen. William E. "Grumble" Jones at Piedmont. Jones was killed in the fighting, and his force withdrew.[111] After hearing of Hunter's victory at Piedmont, Grant ordered Sheridan to lead another strategic cavalry raid designed to distract the enemy. Sheridan was to take Torbert's and Gregg's divisions, march along the course of the North Anna River, fall upon the important rail junction Gordonsville, and then march to Charlottesville, where they would destroy the railroad junction. The horsemen would then join Hunter's army near Charlottesville. The combined force would march east to join the main body of the Army of the Potomac, which Grant hoped would be safely across the James River and moving on Petersburg.[112] Grant ordered the destruction of the railroad at Charlottesville, Lynchburg, and Gordonsville as the raid's primary mission. On the return trip, Sheridan was to remain on the course of the railroads until "every rail on the road destroyed should be so bent and twisted as to make it impossible to repair the road without supplying new rails," or until "driven off by a superior force."[113] Accordingly, Sheridan recounted, "in view of what was anticipated, it would be well to break up the railroad as possible on my way westward."[114]

When he penned his report of the 1864 campaigns after the war, Sheridan commented, "There also appeared to be another object, viz., to remove the enemy's cavalry from the south side of the Chickahominy, as, in case we attempted to cross to the James River, this large cavalry force could make such resistance at the difficult crossings as to give the enemy time to transfer his force to oppose the movement."[115] While this statement appears to be the product of hindsight, it nevertheless raises a valid point; drawing off the attention of the Confederate cavalry is wholly consistent with Grant's vision for his strategic cavalry raid. Brig. Gen. James H. Wilson's Third Division would remain with the main body of the army so that some cavalry could screen the move across the James. Further, Sheridan directed all of his dismounted men, a significant contingent of his command, to report to Wilson to strengthen his force.

Hunter was instructed that the destruction of both the railroad and the canal were of the highest importance to the Federal high command. Hunter was to advance to Lynchburg and then turn east, hopefully taking Lynchburg and its critical supply depot in a single day. Grant's order suggested that Lynchburg had "so much importance to the enemy, that in attempting to get it such resistance may be met as to defeat your getting onto the road or canal at all." If Hunter did not receive his instructions until his army was already in the valley between Staunton and Lynchburg, he was to turn east by the most practicable road until he struck the Lynchburg branch of the Virginia Central Railroad. Having done that, Hunter was to move eastward along the line of the railroad, destroying it completely and thoroughly, until his command joined Sheridan's. The orders concluded, "After the work laid out for General Sheridan and yourself is thoroughly done, proceed to join the Army of the Potomac by the route laid out in General Sheridan's instructions."[116]

After studying the lay of the land, Sheridan decided to pursue a course along the north bank of the North Anna River, marching westward nearly sixty miles from Richmond. He would cross the river at Carpenter's Ford and strike the Virginia Central at an obscure stop located at Trevilian Station, six miles west of Louisa Court House, and approximately six miles east of Gordonsville. He intended to destroy the railroad between Trevilian Station and Louisa, bypass Gordonsville, strike the railroad again at Cobham's Station, and then destroy it from there to Charlottesville, where he would link up with Hunter's advancing army. The march west would cover nearly one hundred miles.[117]

Sheridan wanted to travel light. He ordered his command to carry only three days' rations, intended to last five days, two days' grain for the horses, and only one hundred rounds of ammunition, forty of which would be carried in the soldiers' cartridge boxes. Finally, he would take a pontoon train, only one medical wagon, eight ambulances, and one supply wagon each for division and brigade headquarters, for a total of approximately 125 wagons.[118] The force was to march early on the morning of June 7.

Word of the impending raid spread quickly among the Federal horse soldiers. Regimental officers received orders to relieve themselves and their men of all unnecessary encumbrances, and all were warned not to expect to find themselves near any supply depot or other resting place for up to twelve days.[119] The two divisions concentrated at New Castle Ferry on the Pamunkey River, the jumping-off point for the expedition. A few stray Confederate shells fell on the assembling Yankee troopers, annoying them, but causing no harm.[120]

On June 6, Sheridan left Old Church Tavern and proceeded to New Castle Ferry. On the way, he was joined by soldiers of the 50th New York Engineers, with their bridge train in tow. The Engineers promptly laid their bridge across the river in preparation for the coming expedition. After being relieved by Wilson's men, Gregg's division came up from its position near Bottom's Bridge on the Chickahominy. Nathaniel Davidson, a correspondent of the *New York Herald* who was traveling with Sheridan's command, noted, "Every one knew now that something was up—another raid probably—and nothing pleases a cavalryman so much as the idea of a raid, if it only be through a country where supplies may be obtained."[121] One Pennsylvanian wrote, "The principal duties which Gen. Sheridan's cavalry are called upon to perform are to make raids into the enemy's country, destroy communications, and harass and annoy the enemy as much as possible."[122]

"We were in the saddle at 3:00 A.M. and in line of march for a four days' march. It was very hot and dusty and the horses had not had any feed for some time before," remembered Ballentine. "On this march we had to shoot 125 horses. Every day we had to shoot some and these men could not be mounted. They marched with the column like the bravest of men. Their comrades let them ride in turn. Some of them were much fatigued and one who could not keep up any longer pulled out his pistol and blew out his brains rather than fall into the hands of bushwackers."[123] It was a long, brutal march that took a heavy toll on men and animals.

Sheridan's second expedition culminated in the Battle of Trevilian Station, wherein the Confederate and Federal mounted corps spent two days, June 11 and 12, in heavy fighting at close quarters. The Reserve Brigade opened the action and spent the first day of the battle in a brutal dismounted slugging match with Hampton's cavalry. Without dashing saber charges, the battle more resembled an infantry fight than the traditional image of mounted combat. During the first day's fighting, George Custer's small brigade was trapped and nearly destroyed before it cut its way out. The Lancers were heavily engaged in the dismounted fighting against Maj. Gen. Matthew C. Butler's division the whole day on June 11, suffering at least forty-three casualties.[124]

Capt. Frank Furness of Company F was awarded the Medal of Honor for his heroics at Trevilian on June 12. As the fighting raged that afternoon, the Lancers held the far right end of Merritt's line, anchored in some woods among farm buildings. Furness and Capt. Robert Walsh Mitchell learned from a noncommissioned officer that an outpost of their Pennsylvanians located among the farm outbuildings was nearly out of ammunition, leaving this detachment in jeopardy of being captured. An open grass field separated the house and the outbuildings. The sergeant crawled on his hands and knees through high grass to carry this message to Furness. Reacting quickly, Furness took two boxes of ammunition from his already scanty supply, and placing one atop his head, asked for another officer to volunteer to help carry the ammunition out to the isolated detachment. Mitchell volunteered, and the two men ran across the killing field between the isolated detachment of Lancers and the main battle line. They deposited the fresh supply of ammunition, which permitted the Pennsylvanians to hold their ground and the Reserve Brigade's exposed flank until the day's fighting finally ended.

Their return trip was even more dangerous. The Confederates sent swarms of lead buzzing by their heads like so many angry bees. Mitchell remarked to Furness, "For God's sake, run zig-zag so they can't draw a bead on you!" No sooner did Mitchell speak these words than one bullet passed through the top of his cap and another through the skirt of his coat. The two officers made it back to the main line, and held their position until near morning, when Sheridan withdrew. For this feat, and with the endorsement of Merritt, Furness received the Medal of Honor in 1899. Furness was the only member of the Lancers to earn a Medal of Honor during the Civil War, and he is also the only American architect of note to earn that distinction.[125]

During the course of the fighting on June 12, the Reserve Brigade launched seven unsuccessful dismounted attacks against stout Confederate rifle pits, with the Lancers losing another thirty-six men in this fight, which "raged furiously."[126] Pvt. John T. Baynes of Company H received his second combat wound during one of these assaults. Baynes, with his tongue planted firmly in his cheek, wrote to his sister, "I have been lucky enough to get wounded again at Trevilian Station, near Gordonsville on the 12th of this month. The rebels seem to have a great spite for my legs as the other time I was wounded it was in the right leg this time was in the left, but shall not grumble if they do not hit me in the head."[127]

Sgt. Abraham Geissinger of Company B was killed in action on June 12. "He fell while in the front doing his duty nobly and manfully," recounted Captain Mitchell. "His loss is deeply regretted in the Company and Regiment. His qualities were those of a good Soldier. He was promoted for his ability, and I mourn, as my company does his loss, feeling that a better and truer man never served a Government." In the circumstances, Geissinger's body was left on the battlefield when Sheridan broke off and withdrew. "The Company would have risked their lives to have had the chance to bury so good a man and so true a comrade. We were obliged to fall back under a very heavy fire & were finally ordered back, leaving a well-contested field, and Sergt. Geissinger's body in the hand of the enemy."[128] The Lancers had suffered six killed, twenty-six wounded, and four men captured on June 12, prompting Chaplain Gracey to proclaim, "the fighting on the 12th was, if possible, more desperate than that of the day previous."[129] For the two days of severe fighting at Trevilian Station, the battered Lancers reported six enlisted men killed, one officer and fifty-five enlisted men wounded, and five enlisted men captured or missing for total losses of sixty-seven.[130]

Sheridan finally realized that further attacks were futile and withdrew; according to the Confederates, "The enemy are driven back in confusion until night and the thickness of the country prevents further pursuit. Enemy appears to be retiring in disorder."[131] In his after-action report, Torbert praised Merritt's men: "During the engagement the Reserve Brigade fought with more than their usual desperation, driving the enemy before them."[132] A member of the 1st New York Dragoons put a different face on the fighting at Trevilian Station. "At dark our force was withdrawn without having accomplished anything," he noted, quite accurately.[133]

After several days of hard marching, the Federal Cavalry passed through the Spotsylvania Court House battlefield, where "the debris of the battle strewed the ground; large trees were seen cut nearly in two; scarred and shattered by solid shot, shell, and musket balls, while heavy lines of earthworks marked where the severest charges were made and resisted. The graves of those who fell on this terrible field were on every hand."[134] By the 19th, the Lancers had reached Dunkirk on the Mattapony River.

On the 21st, the Reserve Brigade went into camp for a brief rest. "Here some of us are said to have bathed and changed our clothes for the first time in two weeks, the latter part of which seems more credible than the first, for, ever since June 7th, when we started on the Trevillian raid, we had marched daily at 5 o'clock p.m., not reaching camp often until after dark, after such days of heat and dust as choke one to look back upon," noted Chaplain Gracey. "All our wardrobe was on our backs, so that our camp here, where our wagons rejoined us, was an oasis."[135] These men were ragged and frayed. "We are expecting to draw Cloathing soon, and I hope it will not be long a comming, for I was never so Ragged in my Life as I at Pressent," complained Sgt. Thomas W. Smith of Company I.[136]

On June 21, Maj. William P. C. Treichel rejoined the regiment after a lengthy recuperation from malarial fever, relieving Capt. J. Hinckley Clark of command.

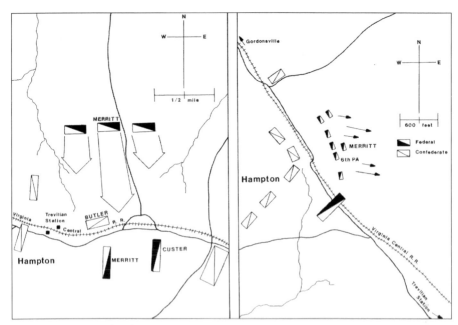

Map 9. Battle of Trevilian Station.

Unfortunately, the malarial fever had shattered Treichel's health, and he was able to retain command for only about three weeks. On July 12, Surgeon John B. Coover issued Treichel a certificate of disability, and Treichel returned to Philadelphia to recuperate. On July 14, Treichel resigned his commission, his military career over.[137] Maj. James H. Starr, who had recovered from the disfiguring wound he suffered at Todd's Tavern, returned to duty and assumed command of the regiment.

The Lancers spent several restful days there, before moving on to a new camp near Charles City Court House on the June 25. "The rest was very acceptable to us as it was the first we may say for 2 months," observed Ballentine. "Being pretty well played out of clothes not having had time to wash our duds that we wore for that time you may judge the picture we made." The rest gave the men an opportunity to clean up themselves and their horses.[148]

Sheridan's exhausting expedition failed to achieve any of its objectives, and Hampton thrashed Sheridan's Federals in two different battles. "Altogether I think this last raid was something of a failure," reported regimental Surgeon John B. Coover.[149] That night, after spending several hours standing to horse in the blazing summer sun, the Lancers marched to Wilson's Wharf on the James River, where they stayed until the 28th. Sergeant Smith reported on the status of the regiment. "On the 25th we succeeded in getting our waggon trains all safe through to this point. We have now got them all across the river and the cavalry are comming to cross to join Grant," he wrote. "We have to cross every thing in ferry Boats which is a verry tedious operation. I suppose by the time we get across, we will be considered sufficiently recuperated for annother Desperate expedition of some kind. Sinse the Campain opened our Regiment have lost, in Killed, Wounded and Missing Ten (10) Commissioned Officers and One Hundred and Sixty Six (166) Enlisted Men."[140]

Clement Hoffman stated the plight of Sheridan's command on June 23. "All of our Cavalry of this Army have done more hard fighting this summer than it ever did before altogether since the Army has been organized," he declared. "We have lost more men on this rade than we did on [the May Richmond Raid], and especially horses, nearly one 4th of our horses played out and a great many of our men were dismounted. I had two horses play out but I am still mounted. We are all pretty well tired out and will gladly except a rest to fix and get ourselves cleaned up once more, if Grant does not hunt up another long jurney for us to perform."[141] Although Hoffman could not know it, another mission for Sheridan's command that directly resulted from Sheridan's defeat at Trevilian Station loomed. The respite so strongly desired by Hoffman and his comrades in arms would be short.

While the Trevilian Raid wound down, Grant launched a second mounted expedition, this time by Brig. Gen. James H. Wilson's 3rd Cavalry Division, and the small cavalry division assigned to the Army of the James, commanded by Brig. Gen. August V. Kautz. This sortie was intended to cut the Weldon and South Side Railroads, Petersburg's direct rail links to the Deep South. Its success depended upon Sheridan keeping Hampton's cavalry occupied. Wilson and Kautz departed on June 21, just as Sheridan was arriving at the White House Landing.

On June 23, two days into the Wilson-Kautz Raid, Col. George Chapman's Federal brigade unexpectedly encountered enemy infantry at Nottoway Court House. After Chapman's men enjoyed some initial success, Brig. Gen. Rufus Barringer's brigade of North Carolina cavalry arrived and reinforced the infantry. The infantry and dismounted cavalry drove off the Yankee raiders, forcing Wilson to withdraw, to his embarrassment.

Finally, on June 29, the entire Confederate cavalry force—three divisions strong—pounced upon Wilson and Kautz at Reams Station. Soon, Kautz's entire force was completely encircled, and the raiders had to cut their way out, narrowly avoiding total destruction. "I have to report that my division and a portion of General Wilson's division have just arrived here. Our expedition was very successful until this afternoon, when we were surrounded and overpowered and had to abandon our transportation, wounded and prisoners," reported a clearly relieved Kautz upon his arrival at Petersburg. "I escaped with my division by taking it through the woods and charging across the railroad."[142]

Wilson lost all of his artillery and his wagon trains. The surviving raiders finally reached the safety of the Federal lines around Petersburg on July 2. Wilson and Kautz had set out with approximately 4,500 men, and lost about a third of them along the way. When it became obvious that Wilson and Kautz were in trouble, Meade had ordered

Sheridan to reinforce them. "The moment I received orders from General Meade to go to the relief of Wilson," claimed Sheridan, "I hastened with Torbert and Gregg by way of Prince George Court House and Lee's Mills to Ream's Station . . . but I was too late to render any material assistance, Wilson having already disappeared, followed by the enemy."[143]

On June 29, the 6th Pennsylvania Cavalry, along with the rest of the Reserve Brigade, was ferried across the James River, marched east, and went to try to assist Wilson and Kautz. "Gen. Wilson with his and Kautz's Div. are said to be in trouble," ominously observed an officer of the 1st New York Dragoons in his diary.[144] "In the afternoon the bugle sounded to Horse, we saddled up and Started, Marching all that night, and all next day, when we arrived at Reams Station, on the Weldon Rail Road," recounted Sergeant Smith. "We now found that Wilsons Cavalry, which had been on a Raid and were Returning had got themselves into a bad fix and we were sent out to help them through." The First Cavalry Division spent a couple of long, hot, exhausting days skirmishing and maneuvering until Wilson's men finally made contact on July 2.[145] "We visited the Norfolk & Petersburg R. R., Petersburg & Weldon R. R. and the destruction being complete we returned," noted a Lancer. "Wilson & Kautz attended to the Danville & Richmond R. R. & Petersburg & Lynchburg R. R. Every tie was burned and every reail heated and bent."[146]

Capt. Frank Furness. (Michael J. Lewis)

Sheridan's weary horsemen finally got a well-deserved rest at Lighthouse Point on the James River on July 3. While Lighthouse Point was a pleasant enough place in the spring, it was hot and humid during the summer months, and "one would hardly choose it for a July residence," noted Capt. George B. Sanford of the 1st U.S. Cavalry. "Still to us it was *luxury*. For the first few days no one cared to do anything but lie under the shade of the trees, and rest and smoke." Although work remained to be done, such as shoeing and grooming horses, the Federal horse soldiers were happy for the respite, which included new clothing for the first time since they left their winter encampment.[147]

"This is the first time sinse the 4th Day of May (when this Campane opened) that we have been in any one Camp for 20 hours at a time," observed Smith on July 6.[148] The long and brutal campaign took a heavy toll on the 6th Pennsylvania Cavalry. "Sunday morning, July 3rd, we went into camp after a month's absence from the old Army of the

Potomac," observed saddler Edgar Strang of Company M, "and that night forty-three of our men who answered roll call on the morning of June 4th failed to do so then, some of them were sleeping their last sleep, while others were lying in hospitals suffering from wounds."[149] Henry Cowan noted that after a few days' rest, the regiment's horses looked fresh again, which was a good thing after the ordeal they had been through.[150]

Despite the terrible heat, the Lancers enjoyed their respite for nearly a month, although they led an uneventful reconnaissance toward Charles City Court House on July 13-14.[151] "The 3rd of July found us located in a beautiful camp on the James River, where we were permitted to enjoy the long promised rest, which men and horses so much need-ed after sixty days hard marching, and much severe fighting since crossing the Rappahannock," observed Strang.[152] The many men who had lost their mounts during the two long, grueling raids rejoined their units on new horses, infusing renewed strength into the Reserve Brigade.[153] During this period, Major Starr asked that the Lancers be sent home to Pennsylvania to recruit, but General Meade rejected this request, meaning that the unit "was but a skeleton of a regiment for the rest of the war."[154]

Sheridan reviewed the Reserve Brigade on July 22. "Our brigade looked well but it is very small," reported Ballentine. "There are many rumors around. Some have it that the Regular Brigade is going to Washington. Some that the 6th Penna. Cavalry is going to Phila. to reorganize and get filled up; others have us going on a raid. Now I do believe that we are willing to do anything that Sheridan orders." Another raid was in the offing, but the regiment was in a bad way. With the impending discharge of most of the regi-ment, there would be sufficient men to fill only four companies instead of the requisite twelve. Just ten officers remained with the regiment. Of the 32 veterans in Company K, 15 were waiting to receive their discharges, meaning that Company K, which started out with 101 men, would have only 17 left.[155]

On July 23, Grant ordered all detachments of the Lancers in the Washington area to return to the regiment, "having but a short period to serve."[156] This decision meant that instead of being permitted to recruit replacements, the ranks of the Lancers would dwin-dle. When the terms of service of most of the regiment expired during the fall of 1864, there would be only a handful of men remaining.

Although the distraction caused by the Trevilian Raid permitted the Army of the Potomac to steal a march across the James River, Grant's movement on Petersburg bogged down as a result of poor execution by his subordinates, a valiant defense by Gen. P. G. T. Beauregard, and unforeseen circumstances. The Army of the Potomac faltered in front of the trenches around Petersburg, and the war rapidly devolved into a tedious siege. With little to do, the Federal cavalry went into camp, doing little more than picket duty for three weeks. Torbert inspected his division on July 22, always a sure sign that they would be taking the field again soon.[157]

There would be one more major test for the Cavalry Corps during this campaign. On July 25, after several days of heavy skirmishing, and responding to Lt. Gen. Jubal A.

Early's invasion of Maryland and Pennsylvania, Grant decided to make a foray north of the James River, in part to detract Confederate attention from a large-scale attack that would be launched along the lines at Petersburg when a mine dug under the Confederate lines would be exploded. If all went according to plan, the massive explosion would tear a hole in the Southern line that could be exploited in an infantry attack by the Army of the Potomac. Grant ordered Maj. Gen. Winfield Scott Hancock's Second Corps, nearly 25,000 men strong, Brig. Gen. August V. Kautz's cavalry division of the Army of the James, and two divisions of Sheridan's Cavalry Corps to advance from Petersburg to Deep Bottom, move northwest toward Richmond, and threaten the enemy garrison at Chaffin's Bluff. Sheridan would cross the Chickahominy, proceed to destroy the Virginia Central Railroad north of Richmond, and then return to the Army of the Potomac. If the opportunity presented itself, Sheridan might even make a dash into Richmond.[158] It was an ambitious but flawed plan.

The infantry, commanded by Hancock, would make the primary thrust, and the plan depended good execution. Hancock's Corps moved out on July 27 and was stymied by Gary's small brigade of cavalry, less than 1,000 men strong, who made one of the bravest stands of the Civil War. Torbert's and Gregg's divisions also moved out, but made little progress that first day. Merritt's Regulars engaged Gary's men near Fussell's Mill on Curle's Neck, and finally drove them off after a stout resistance. "The men sprang forward to the crest and poured in volley after volley from their breech-loading carbines," noted a staff officer. "The Rebels faltered, then halted, and then turned and ran like good fellows for the woods. As our trumpets sounded the charge, the men sprang forward in pursuit and drove them clear across the valley and through the woods."[159]

A reconnaissance determined that Confederate infantry blocked Sheridan's route of march, and that the flank could not be turned. Instead of pressing the attack, Torbert bivouacked for the night; one of his staff officers claimed, "on our side there was no desire to push forward, as the object of the movement had been accomplished. The purpose was to draw as large a force of Lee's troops as possible, from the South to the North side of the James River."[160] The Lancers spent a long, uncomfortable night standing to horse, waiting to resume the action.[161] "General Lee had anticipated the movement around his left flank by transferring to the north side of the James a large portion of his infantry and W.H.F. Lee's division of cavalry," claimed Sheridan in rationalizing the cavalry's failure.[162]

On the 28th, Gregg and Kautz would try to turn the Confederate flank while Torbert's brigades held the enemy in place by demonstrating in their front. "Our turn comes next," declared an officer of the Lancers as he prepared his men to pitch into the fray.[163] The Lancers were soon engaged, and an unidentified member of the 6th Pennsylvania Cavalry captured a Confederate battle flag during the day's fighting.[164] "We had a hard fight dismounted with a portion of A. P. Hill's Corps," recounted Cowan. "Our division had a splendid position and repulsed the rebel charge and charged in return capturing three Battle-Flags, one of which was captured by our Regiment."[165]

Hancock's cautious advance impeded the cavalry, and the attack by the horsemen quickly bogged down when it encountered Confederate infantry. When Torbert's attack on the left drove back the enemy line, Hancock failed to support the cavalry's advance, and the opportunity slipped away. "Skirmish commensed and kept up all the morning until noon when the Rebbel Infantry Charged our Lines, we being in line of Battle, Dismounted," recounted Sergeant Smith. "We Left them come up to within fifty yards of us when we gave them a volley with our carbines and then Drew our Pistols and with a yell we Charged them fireing our Pistols as Rapidly as possible, they broke and Run, we following them up across an open field for a half a mile, Capturing a good many prisoners, and our Bregad alone captured three Stand of Colours."[166]

Lt. Andrew L. Lanigan, the 6th Pennsylvania's latest regimental adjutant, was badly wounded in the thigh during this fight, making Lanigan the fourth adjutant to fall since the Lancers broke their winter camp at the end of April.[167] In addition, six enlisted men were wounded, including one mortally. The arrival of Confederate reinforcements caused Torbert to withdraw toward the James River. The Northern cavalry formed line of battle and waited for an attack that never came.[168] Chaplain Gracey made an especially cogent observation about the employment of the Union cavalry during the fighting on July 28. "There is one thing that a cavalryman very naturally protests against, and that is, being transformed into an infantry soldier; fighting on foot he objects to,—but he can often see the necessity of it, but he cannot be made to understand that it may perchance be his duty to leave his horse and turn tramper," he wrote. "This is what our division was called upon to do this hot July day. The Mine, so far as we knew, was not exploded yet, but part of the Second Corp had left us, while the necessity still remained of showing a force on the north side of the James." They finally recrossed about 11 that night, reclaimed their horses, and rejoined the rest of the Federal task force.[169]

Finally, Meade called off the attack on the 29th, and the battle ended. A principal reason for the failure was Sheridan's unwillingness to exercise command over his troopers, again leaving his subordinate commanders to fend for themselves. One historian noted, "None of the Union commanders did well at First Deep Bottom. Hancock and Sheridan delivered a dismal performance . . . Sheridan seems to have . . . genuinely feared an attack by overwhelming Confederate numbers."[170] Sheridan later claimed that he did not push the attack because the presence of the Confederate infantry "rendered useless any further effort on Hancock's part or mine to carry out the plan of the expedition," but these rationalizations ring hollow.[171]

The Lancers recrossed on July 30 and marched to Petersburg, arriving at daylight on July 31, just in time to witness the explosion at the Crater and the sacrifice of the African-American troops who bore the brunt of the fighting there. "If they had been properly supported Petersburg would have been ours," observed Sergeant Ballentine. The Lancers then took up a position on the Army of the Potomac's left flank on the Weldon Railroad.[172]

Sheridan also claimed that the twin failures of Hancock's attack and the infantry attack at the Crater in Petersburg had caused Meade to cancel the cavalry's expedition along the Virginia Central.[173] The cavalry then went into camp, and its role in Grant's grand campaign ended with a whimper and not with a bang. On July 31, the Lancers drew three days' rations, prompting the men to believe that they were getting ready to commence another raid.[174] However, the high command had other plans for the Cavalry Corps. "The 1st Div's. Cavalry has been ordered to Washington," reported Dr. Coover. "Our Brigade is now arriving. We are all very glad to get back to the Potomac line. I think we may possibly have some hard work up here—we march in a day or two out after the enemy just as soon as we can collect ourselves together and get our horses in condition to travel. I imagine we will interfere somewhat with rebel raiders."[175]

On August 8, 1864, Grant ordered Sheridan to take two divisions of the Cavalry Corps to the Shenandoah Valley, where Little Phil would assume temporary command of the Middle Military Division. The Lancers went with him. For many of them, the trip to Shenandoah Valley would be their last expedition as members of the Army of the Potomac's Cavalry Corps.

Chapter Ten

THE LANCERS GO TO THE SHENANDOAH VALLEY

D ESPERATE TO BREAK GRANT'S hammerlock at Petersburg, Robert E. Lee gambled. Remembering that Lt. Gen. Thomas J. "Stonewall" Jackson's Army of the Valley drew Federal forces away from Richmond in the summer of 1862, Lee decided to try the same ploy in the hope that the tactic would succeed a second time. He sent Lt. Gen. Jubal A. Early's Second Army Corps away from the lines at Petersburg. Early's command marched overland to Charlottesville, where he put his force on trains of the Virginia Central Railroad and transported it to Lynchburg. There, it joined forces with the small command of Maj. Gen. John C. Breckinridge. The joint forces then repulsed the advance of Maj. Gen. David Hunter's army, moving up the Shenandoah Valley.[1] This combined force then advanced down the Valley toward the Potomac River and Maryland.

Early crossed the Potomac, defeated a scratch force of Union troops under Maj. Gen. Lew Wallace at Monocacy Junction, Maryland, and then marched on Washington, D.C. Responding belatedly, Grant detached the Sixth Corps from his lines at Petersburg, boarded it on trains, and sent it to the defense of the national capital. The Sixth Corps arrived just in time to repulse Early at Fort Stevens, in Silver Spring, Maryland.[2] Early then retreated across the Potomac. On July 24, Early defeated Brig. Gen. George Crook's Army of West Virginia at Kernstown, just south of Winchester, Virginia. On July 30, Early sent a cavalry force under command of Brig. Gen. John McCausland into Pennsylvania. McCausland's troopers burned the town of Chambersburg and then rejoined Early in the Shenandoah Valley. The sacking of Chambersburg triggered a tidal wave of protest throughout the North, making the destruction of Early's army a political priority for the Lincoln Administration. With a force of less than 20,000 men, Early waited for the Yankee army to come after him.

Grant had originally wanted to send Meade to the Valley to deal with Early, but he ultimately decided not to for fear it would appear as if Meade had been relieved of command of the Army of the Potomac after the debacle at the Crater. Grant's next idea was to make Maj. Gen. William B. Franklin department commander, with Sheridan as tactical commander. When the War Department rejected Franklin, Grant proposed Hunter as department commander, but Hunter was unsuccessful as a combat commander, so Grant wanted to place Sheridan in command of the troops in the field. On August 1, Grant wrote Halleck, "I want Sheridan put in command of all the troops in the field, with instructions to put himself south of the enemy and follow him to the death. Wherever the enemy goes let our troops go also."[3] Secretary of War Edwin M. Stanton opposed the appointment, believing Sheridan too young for such a high level of command. He eventually agreed, provided that the appointment was a temporary one.[4] Hunter suggested that if Halleck mistrusted him to command troops in the field, the best thing for the service would be for him to decline the appointment. Thus, Sheridan ended up in overall command of the Middle Military District in spite of Stanton's objections.[5]

The next day, Sheridan reported to Grant at Monocacy Junction, where he took command of the Sixth Corps and two divisions of the Nineteenth Army Corps, Crook's Army of West Virginia, and all available cavalry forces. He had good subordinate commanders—the steady Maj. Gen. Horatio G. Wright commanded the Sixth Corps, Maj. Gen. William H. Emory commanded the Nineteenth Corps detachment, which had served along the Gulf of Mexico, and Sheridan's former roommate Crook commanded the Army of West Virginia. Crook, a fine tactician, possessed a first-rate mind.

As the men of the 6th Pennsylvania Cavalry marched for the Shenandoah Valley, the majority of them had between thirty and ninety days remaining on their terms of service. Less than 20 percent of the regiment's original strength had reenlisted for the duration of the war, meaning that the rest were about to go home. Most of the officers would be discharged. A new slate of officers would have to be promoted, even though a mere handful of men would remain with the Lancers; even a shell of a regiment required a full complement of officers. Those who were about to leave the army were understandably reluctant to face danger again, and they did not relish the idea of chasing Early's dangerous little army. Capt. Charles L. Leiper, fully recovered from his May combat wound, rejoined the regiment and received a promotion to major.[6]

After consulting with Grant at Monocacy Junction on August 6, Sheridan traveled to Harpers Ferry and assumed command. Grant had issued explicit orders. "In pushing up the Shenandoah Valley, as it is expected you will have to go, first or last, it is desirable that nothing should be left to invite the enemy to return. Take all provisions, forage, and stock wanted for the use of your command; such as cannot be consumed, destroy," wrote the lieutenant general. "It is not desirable that the buildings should be destroyed; they should rather be protected; but the people should be informed that so long as an army can subsist among them recurrences of these raids must be expected, and we are determined to stop them at all hazards. Bear in mind the object is to drive the enemy south, and to do this you want to keep him always in sight. Be guided in your course by the course he takes." He concluded with decisive and important instructions: "Give the enemy no rest, and if it is possible to follow to the Virginia Central Railroad, follow that far. Do all the damage to railroads and crops you can. Carry off stock of all descriptions, and negroes, so as to prevent further planting. If the war is to last another year, we want the Shenandoah Valley to remain a barren waste."[7]

Sheridan had his work cut out for him. "My object was to destroy, to the best of my ability, that which was truly the Confederacy—its armies. . . . Every officer and man was made to understand that when a victory was gained," noted Sheridan in his report of the campaign. "It was not more than their duty, nor less than their country expected from her gallant sons."[8] His consolidated force of nearly 45,000 men, dubbed the Army of the Shenandoah, was responsible for the defense of the Middle Military Division, consisting of Maryland and the Shenandoah Valley.

Grant also gave Sheridan authority to choose his own cavalry commander. As the senior division commander, Brig. Gen. William Woods Averell was entitled to the command.[9] Averell's force, which had been an independent command, merged with the veteran units from the Army of the Potomac, including the First Cavalry Division and the Reserve Brigade. However, Sheridan exercised the discretion given him by Grant and appointed Torbert chief of cavalry for the newly formed army. Merritt took command of the First Division, Averell commanded the Second Division, and Wilson led the Third Division. Col. Alfred Gibbs of the 1st New York Dragoons assumed command of the Reserve Brigade. In all, Sheridan's Army of the Shenandoah would generally outnumber Early's little army by about three-to-one as the campaign wore on.

Sheridan took a few days to consolidate his new army and put his infrastructure into place. He knew that Early was camped near Little North Mountain, northwest of Winchester, about twelve miles from Harpers Ferry. He planned an advance that would flank Early out of his strong positions and place his army to the south of Early's, as Grant had ordered, which would induce the Confederate commander to come out and fight. On August 10, Sheridan began his advance down the Valley. The Northern army moved to Berryville by way of Charles Town. The Lancers led Sheridan's way, but the Federals encountered little organized resistance, causing them to grow overconfident. "About 4 p.m., met the enemy's pickets," reported Colonel Gibbs, "when the Sixth Pennsylvania Cavalry and First New York Dragoons were thrown out as skirmishers, dismounted, and handsomely drove back the enemy through a thick wood and upon the road leading toward Newtown."[10] Capt. Abraham D. Price of Company I captured a prisoner, a threshing machine, and a couple of wagons.[11] After a brief cavalry skirmish, Early retreated toward Winchester, and for two days the armies moved down the Valley. On August 11, Sheridan intended to cross the Opequon Creek and attack Early.

The Lancers were the army's rear guard on August 11. The Federal cavalry drove the Southern horsemen back on their infantry supports, and the attack bogged down. "General Merritt at once engaged them, and, though contesting stubbornly every foot of the ground, drove them across the pike and several miles towards Newtown."[12] The Confederates repulsed regiment after regiment of Federal cavalry. "We had a very severe fight," recalled Capt. George B. Sanford of the 1st U.S. Cavalry.[13] Finally, the Lancers got their chance. One squadron was detached and sent off to the left under command of Capt. Joseph H. Clark of Company M, while Major Starr led the other squadrons in a dismounted attack. "Not a man flinched, and the line moved forward steadily, without firing a shot, to a fence about a hundred yards from the woods," proudly recalled Chaplain Gracey. The Lancers joined elements of the 1st and 2nd U.S. Cavalry at the fence line, but found the enemy fire too hot, and withdrew. They turned a nearby ditch into a rifle-pit. Receiving artillery support, they remained in place until they were relieved after dark. The Lancers then learned they had been fighting Maj. Gen. John B. Gordon's entire infantry division, which was covering Early's retreat.[14] When Grant heard rumors that Longstreet's infantry corps was also on its way to the Valley to join Early, he realized Sheridan's force was not strong enough to defeat two corps, and instructed Sheridan to go on the defensive. Sheridan promptly obeyed this order, ceding the initiative to Early.

In fact, Maj. Gen. Joseph Kershaw's division from Longstreet's Corps reinforced Early. Grant, however, instructed Sheridan to go on the defensive. The cavalry leader had to obey the order. Sheridan consulted the maps to find a suitable defensive position and then withdrew past Winchester to Halltown and, with the exception of cavalry missions, declined to give battle for nearly a month.

When the Lancers returned to their camps, their sutler greeted them. While his arrival usually boded well, it did not this time. He carried the unwelcome news that Col. John S. Mosby's irrepressible guerrillas had attacked and destroyed the Reserve Brigade's wagon train, meaning that all the regimental baggage and personal effects were gone. The Union horsemen lost whatever of life's little luxuries they had, and they swore revenge.[15]

On August 14, Major Starr led the regiment on a reconnaissance toward Strasburg. They encountered Southern pickets and realized that they had run into the bulk of Early's army, which was strongly positioned on high ground, supported by artillery in place. Starr then reported to Merritt, and the Lancers, now reinforced by Sixth Corps infantry, attacked and drove Early's infantry back through Strasburg. Having completed their mission, the Reserve Brigade retired and returned to its camps. The Lancers spent the next two days doing picket duty.[16]

On August 24, the bulk of Company A, which served as Torbert's headquarters escort, was mustered out, its term of service completed. Those members of Company A who reenlisted, or whose terms of service were not complete, rejoined the rest of the regiment. The others headed for home. Company B mustered out four days later. The departure of these veteran troopers signaled the beginning of the end for the Lancers—their combat strength quickly drained away as the majority of the regiment left for home.[17] On August 25, the regiment broke its camp and marched through Shepherdstown, where a portion of it met Early's army near the Baltimore & Ohio Railroad. The grayclad infantry drove the dismounted Federals back through Halltown.[18]

Sheridan did not have an encouraging start to his tenure as an army commander. On August 26, correspondent James E. Taylor noted, "After an auspicious opening, in which he had penetrated to the upper valley within 20 days, he was back and bottled up in the works he left, which he honestly expected he would not again reoccupy while an armed grayback was in the valley. . . . That the general felt keenly this humiliating termination of his first essay in his new field, goes for the saying, and that it was looked upon with alarm by the Federal authorities in Washington cannot be questioned. Was history about to repeat itself in the valley, and was another military grave being dug?"[19] A few days later, Col. Rutherford B. Hayes, future president and commander of one of Crook's brigades, noted in a letter, "General Sheridan's splendid cavalry do a great share of the work; we look on and rest."[20]

On August 28, the Army of the Shenandoah began a new advance. Passing through Leetown, the 2nd U.S. Cavalry, which was leading the way, encountered enemy cavalry. Realizing the enemy force was too large for a single regiment to handle, the commander of the 2nd U.S. asked Merritt to send reinforcements. Merritt sent Major Starr and his Lancers up to support the Regulars. Starr dispatched Capt. Albert P. Morrow and a mounted squadron across country to try to get into the rear of the Confederates while the remaining Lancers and the Regulars attacked dismounted. The enemy did not wait for this attack, but instead retreated up the Valley Pike, with the victorious Federals in pursuit. Merritt then deployed his entire division, which advanced toward Smithfield, where the bulk of the Confederates were deployed in line of battle. The 5th U.S. made a saber charge that broke Early's line. The Confederates withdrew to the hills between Smithfield and the Opequon, leaving their skirmishers in the town, Early's gunners swept the road with their artillery. Custer's Michigan Brigade launched a flanking attack that drove the enemy cavalry back upon its infantry supports, drawing Early's infantry into the fight.

The grayclad infantry crossed the Opequon and attacked the 1st New York Dragoons and the Lancers. "They were too strong for us, and driving us from the ford, crossed in large force, endeavoring to turn our left," recalled a member of the 6th Pennsylvania. This brought on a severe engagement that lasted nearly the entire day. "Inch by inch we disputed the advance, taking advantage of every tree, fence, or elevation to make a stand, but we could not hold them in check," he continued. As the men of the Reserve Brigade ran low on ammunition, they were forced back into Smithfield. The unfortunate and untimely withdrawal of a Union cavalry brigade left a hole in the Federal line, which the Southern infantry exploited immediately, driving the Federals from the town.

Realizing the danger, Merritt dashed over to Major Starr. "Is this your regiment?"

"Yes, sir," replied Starr. "My men are out of ammunition and well-nigh exhausted; our left is completely exposed; you can see the rebels closing in on us through that cornfield."

"Turn about," ordered the undaunted Merritt. "You must make a stand; use your pistols, if you have no carbine ammunition." The Lancers sent up a rousing cheer, faced

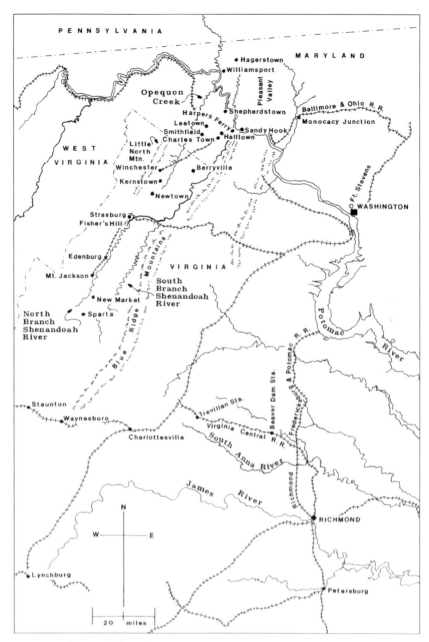

Map 10. Shenandoah Valley.

about, and moved forward to a stone fence.[21] "The Sixth Pennsylvania Cavalry, Major Starr commanding, came up in a few minutes, and the [1st New York Dragoons] in column, over fences and through a creek, charged the enemy, breaking their line and driving them beyond Leetown, on the Smithfield pike," recalled an admiring officer of the 2nd U.S. Cavalry.[22] However, the Lancers could not hold their position, and a severe firefight broke out in which Sgt. Tyson Stanley of Company M was killed in action. Sgt. John Wagner of Company K, a German immigrant whom Captain Leiper praised as being "noted for his good conduct, attention to duty, and whole courage," lost the thumb and the index finger of his right hand to a Confederate bullet.[23] As things grew desperate, the advanced elements of Sheridan's Sixth Corps infantry arrived and relieved the weary and hard-pressed horse soldiers, who redeployed to the right flank of the Union infantry.

The Reserve Brigade counterattacked through the woods, driving the enemy infantry in their wake. Confederate cavalry tried to make a stand near Smithfield, but a determined saber charge by the 2nd U.S. Cavalry drove them across the Opequon, ending the day's fighting. The Reserve Brigade then retired and camped near Charles Town, with the Lancers standing to horse all night in the hope of being relieved by one of the other cavalry brigades.[24] The Lancers lost two men killed and another sixteen wounded that day, including twenty-one-year-old Pvt. John P. Rausenberger.[25] "This day is one of the most memorable in our history," noted Chaplain Gracey, "for it was the last time that the original regiment met and fought the enemy."[26]

The next day, August 29, Early threw a large force of infantry across the Opequon, driving in Merritt's pickets. "So rapid and determined was their advance that the division was driven back a mile before we recovered our equilibrium and could make the necessary dispositions to check the enemy," noted an officer of the 2nd U.S. Cavalry. Dr. John B. Coover called this day's fighting "about as heavy & severe a fight as I have ever witnessed."[27] Dr. Coover was kept busy—both sides suffered heavy casualties in the day's fighting.

The Lancers supported the Federal horse artillery. "The Sixth Pennsylvania Cavalry constructed a barricade of rails in front of the battery, which was occupied by one of its squadrons, under Captain Morrow," reported Gibbs. The rest of the Reserve Brigade, including the balance of the 6th Pennsylvania, dismounted and deployed in the woods on a ridge overlooking the Opequon. At about 11:30 that morning, Southern artillery opened "furiously" from two batteries, "and made good practice, many case-shot and shells exploding in and about the [Union] battery and led horses," causing casualties among the Lancers. "We held our own until the afternoon when they got around on our left and flanked us," recounted a sergeant of Company K.[28] The Federal cavalry fell back in the face of the determined Confederate attack, "contesting sharply every foot of ground, retiring without confusion and leisurely for about three miles, which took about four hours and a half."[29]

Capt. Frank Furness of Company F, whose term of service was about to expire, commanded a squadron that day. "Fighting bravely at great disadvantage, the enemy pressing them in front and on their left flank, they were in great danger of capture before reaching their horses." Colonel Gibbs ordered a mounted charge by the 2nd U.S., wherein they were to throw themselves in front of the Lancers in an effort to extricate them from their

Sheridan's march into the Shenandoah Valley. (Library of Congress)

impending capture. "We turned and drove them back faster than they had done us," observed a Lancer.[30] The Regulars made two unsuccessful attempts to do so before succeeding on the third try. "As we charged the third time, in the face of a heavy musketry fire, we placed ourselves directly in front of the line of the Sixth Pennsylvania, which they instantly took advantage of, falling back in good order, and reaching their horses," noted a Regular. After saving the Lancers, Merritt ordered the Reserve Brigade to fall back upon the Sixth Corps infantry supports, which ended the pursuit. The Confederates then retired. Captain Furness and his men had escaped harm, and the relieved troopers were ready to get their discharges and head for home.[31]

A member of Company H reported that his company lost three men out of fifteen engaged. "Our regiment was so small that we were ordered to the rear to recruit, we have 200 men in our regiment of 12 companies of them 50 time is out," he reported. "We have about 200 wounded in the hospitals in the north beside our wounded in Richmond and the Southern States."[32] The same man also noted, "All together our regt has lost more in killed and wounded than most infantry regiments since we commenced in the Wilderness."[33] Trooper Charles H. Coller of Company C was killed in action during that day's fighting, just a few days prior to the expiration of his term of service.[34]

As the fighting ended and the Confederates withdrew, the Federals marched back over the same ground that had been the subject of the day's slugging match. As the Lancers marched, they passed the bodies of their dead comrades and were appalled to find that the Confederates had stripped the dead men of anything of use. "Those that had a bloody shirt were allowed to wear them but they were turned over their heads," observed Sergeant Ballentine. "This was the most brutish thing I have seen since the war began so it is now do or die for every man." The next day, the Federal horsemen moved around Early's flank and tried to draw the Southerners into renewing the fight, but they wanted no part of it. "They will not fight where the odds are against them."[35]

Even though most of the regiment was about to muster out, the Lancers had just been through quite a test. "All the fighting has been done by our Cavalry Division," noted an officer of the 1st New York Dragoons on September 1, "so you can imagine we are all worn out."[36] Although Sheridan had been given the task of scattering Early's army, he had so far left all the hard work to his horse soldiers. "We have had a dozen fights with the rebels since we went into the valley," observed Clement Hoffman of Company E.[37] The imminent discharge of the Lancers made them cringe every time they went out; nobody wanted to die only a few days before going home.

Because the men of the Lancers had widely varying discharge dates, "we now applied to be sent to Pleasant Valley, to muster out those entitled to discharge, and reorganize the regiment upon the nucleus composed of those who had re-enlisted, the '62 men, and such recruits as we had received from time to time."[38] On September 8, this request was granted. "This news was welcome to us," observed Ballentine.[39] The Lancers moved out that day, after completing a final scouting mission. They had earned the respect of their fellow troopers in the Reserve Brigade, and would be especially missed by their comrades of the 1st New York Dragoons. "About noon I received word from Colonel Gibbs that the 6th Pennsylvanias were about to leave for Pleasant Valley near Harper's Ferry to muster out their men whose terms of service had expired and reorganize the Regiment," recounted Maj. Howard M. Smith of the Dragoons. "The 6th is the only Regiment of the Brigade that we have ever had much fellow feeling for. They have always stood by us in every fight we have been in and could always be depended on. We were sorry to lose them indeed." When Major Smith learned that the Lancers would be leaving for good, he rounded up the regimental band of the Dragoons and escorted the Pennsylvanians out of camp with a song. "As they passed by our camp our boys gave them three hearty cheers which they returned with a will. The Regiments parted with the very best of feelings."[40]

"Of course the Sixth has to stand the brunt of every fight and the boys who can take that business by contract," observed Henry Cowan. "Some of the men whose time are up and did not re-enlist are going home over 200 are in the hospital wounded a large number killed and but few missing. At present we could show a front of 100 men."[41] The regiment, now commanded by Maj. Charles L. Leiper, reported to the Remount Camp at Pleasant Valley, Maryland, where "those men of the Sixth Pennsylvania who are to be discharged in September and October will at once be dismounted and the horses turned over to men of the Reserve Brigade in dismounted camp, veterans being mounted first."[42] The remaining veterans had no idea what further service the government had in mind for them.

Leiper assumed command of the camp, and turned over command of the regiment to Capt. J. Hinckley Clark. "What is left of us turned over our horses and arms &c. to new regiments who take our place in the field," added Cowan. "I hope our ranks will be filled up soon again and we will cross the river and give them another show for their money."[43] The men spent several days turning in their horses, weapons, and government equipment, and preparing to go home. A few days later, Major Starr returned from doing recruiting duty in Washington and assumed command of the Remount Camp. Leiper then took command of the regiment until he was sent to Philadelphia on recruiting duty. Lt. Charles B. Coxe received a promotion to captain and assumed command of Company L on September 12.[44]

The Pleasant Valley remount camp was the result of changes in the management of cavalry the previous year. In late July 1863, a few weeks after the Battle of Gettysburg, the War Department had formed the Cavalry Bureau, an organization specifically designed to provide mounts for the Union cavalry. New units would receive horses supplied by the Cavalry Bureau, and regiments already serving on the line could also obtain fresh mounts through the efforts of the Cavalry Bureau. The army established depots and remount camps where the horses and men would be trained.[45] While this system was far from perfect, it provided adequate mounts for the Federal cavalry, meaning that the losses sustained during the brutal Overland Campaign were made good. While the Confederate cavalry suffered greatly from the dismounting of its troopers, the Union cavalry maintained its effective strength, due at least in part to the successful efforts of the Cavalry Bureau to have an adequate supply of replacement horses at all times.[46] One of the largest and most important remount camps was established at Pleasant Valley, Maryland, at the foot of South Mountain, and became home for the men of the Lancers, while they waited either to receive their discharges or to receive and train fresh mounts.

"A remount camp is a rendezvous for all straggling cavalrymen, whether coming from the front with worn-out horses, or returning to duty from hospitals, or arriving as recruits," candidly observed Chaplain Gracey. "Every cavalry soldier looking for a refitting-place goes to remount camp; there he knows that if he wants to go he will be sent to his regiment, and if he wants to skulk, he has a better chance there than anywhere else; if a recruit, he goes there simply because he is sent." Fearing that such influences would taint his regiment, Major Starr went about a mile away from the main camp site to establish the camp of the Lancers, where the remaining members of the regiment stayed until November 15.[47]

Clement Hoffman of Company E, who enlisted in September 1861, had just over a week to go before the expiration of his term of service. "Our regiment is to lay here until all the old three years men's time runs out, so as to discharge them as our time runs out. Every man is discharged on the day three years from the time that he enlisted," he reported to his mother on September 10. "My time is out on the 20th and I expect to get my discharge that day."[48] Hoffman received his discharge on September 20 as predicted and returned to Philadelphia, where he collected his bounty and back pay and then returned to civilian life.[49]

Pvt. John T. Baynes of Company H, returned to duty in September after recovering his leg wound at Trevilian Station. He was promoted to quartermaster sergeant on October 1. A few days later, he wrote his sister, reflecting the attitude of many Union soldiers. "I think that Uncle Abe will be able to discharge the most of us next spring or early next summer if things continue the same for a few months longer as the hated rebellion is tottering even to its base and the fall cannot be far distant. Even the rebel papers speak despondingly of late, only a few months ago they were boasting of their glorious victories but 'the times have changed.'" Baynes correctly predicted Lincoln's reelection and reiterated his grim determination to see things through to the end.[50]

On September 13, Capt. Emlen N. Carpenter, captured at Todd's Tavern and held prisoner in South Carolina, wrote his mother from captivity. Carpenter was one of the original company commanders of the Lancers, dating back to the regiment's formation in 1861. "The Regt's time expires on the 4th of October. I despair of getting out—if and when I do all of the vacancies in the Regt. will be filled & I will be mustered out as an officer without a command unless I can get some other position," he complained. "I am sorry for my rank was so high in the Regt. that I might have looked for promotion. I hardly thought Major [Treichel] would stay with the Regt.—how is it that Major [Starr] commands—I heard he was seriously wounded." By virtue of his seniority, Carpenter would have been entitled to a promotion to lieutenant colonel in the fall of 1864, but he never received that promotion due to his incarceration. Carpenter, confined with his brother Quincy, escaped and made his way back to Maj. Gen. William T. Sherman's invading army during the winter of 1865. While Carpenter received a brevet promotion to lieutenant colonel, he never returned to command men of the 6th Pennsylvania Cavalry.[51]

In early October 1864, Henry Cowan of Company H complained about the lack of activity. "I expected before this to have went over to see the folks in Dixie," he noted. "We are waiting every day for horses. Our regiment has been so reduced in numbers that we were ordered to the rear for sixty days to recruit." Reflecting on Sheridan's successes at Winchester and Fisher's Hill, Cowan wrote to a friend who lived near Shepherdstown Ford, "I believe Sheridan has ruined Early's Army so that they will not bother you for a while. Our armies are victorious everywhere. I hope to live to see this war end and the north and south united by links inseparable."[52] Although Cowan's comments reflected the general consensus among the Federals, Early's army still had a few tricks up its sleeve.

On September 26, Confederate guerrillas captured and brutally attacked thirty-year-old Dr. John B. Coover, the popular and competent surgeon of the 6th Pennsylvania Cavalry. Not long before his death, Dr. Coover was appointed Sheridan's Medical Inspector. However, Coover had received his orders to muster out, and was preparing to go home, his term of service having expired. While the doctor and a Federal wagon train were riding to Harpers Ferry, the guerrillas had attacked Coover's column, and the doctor was mortally wounded.[53] He was admitted to the Field Hospital at Sandy Hook, Maryland, on September 27, 1864, and died September 28, 1864 from a gunshot wound in the abdomen.[54]

A correspondent from the *Philadelphia Inquirer* left an account of Coover's wounding:

> A small wagon train was approaching Harper's Ferry from Winchester, and while about half-way between Charlestown and Halltown, an attack was made by guerrillas, which resulted in the shooting and subsequent death of Surgeon John B. Coover, of the Sixth Pennsylvania Cavalry.[55] "The train left Winchester during the afternoon and was overtaken by the darkness. It appears that the deceased Surgeon, in company with an orderly and another medical officer, lagged behind the train and became a mark at once for the guerrillas, who are always prowling about directly after the shades of evening fall, and if appearances are propitious, even before the "golden sun spanned the horizon's girth.[55]

The correspondent continued, "Dr. Coover, who was perhaps some few hundred yards in the rear of the main escort, was shot in the bowels, the ball passing through his body. His comrade saved him from being captured and brought him safely to Harper's Ferry. He was soon transferred to the Sandy Hook Hospital, where he died on Tuesday night." The newspaperman blamed Coover's death on his escort of inexperienced troopers: "It is stated that the escort party in advance of Surgeon Coover, at the time he was shot, started off on a run, it being composed of green troops who had not yet smelt gunpowder."[56]

In November, members of the Independent Loudoun Virginia Rangers, a loyal scout unit attached to the Union cavalry, captured the perpetrator, a deserter from the 61st New York Infantry known as "French Bill" Loge. Relying upon authority granted them by Sheridan, the Rangers hanged French Bill within hours of capturing him. French Bill's execution came as little consolation to the family of the beloved surgeon.[57]

"I think we will have to go to the front soon," remarked Hamilton Ballentine on October 2. "There is nothing talked of in camp but Abe and McClelland. The nights are getting cold and sleep is impossible. If you do happen to go to sleep you will not do so for long for some poor devil who cannot sleep will propose 3 cheers for Mac to stir things up and in 2 second all the camp will be in an uproar. Some hang up the culprit and others put him in a nosebag and so there is no danger of anyone's sleeping his brains away." At the same time, the men got only half rations, and they had not been paid. The remaining veterans grew quite discontented with their plight, longing for activity, for something different than the boring routine of camp life.[58]

On November 8, the *Philadelphia Inquirer* published a lengthy letter from the regiment's camp in Pleasant Valley. "We are laying in camp, doing nothing but camp duty," reported the correspondent. The letter reported on the discharge of the bulk of the regiment's strength and the consolidation of the remaining companies. With Major Leiper in Philadelphia on recruiting duty, Capt. Albert P. Morrow, "a gallant soldier and a gentleman," commanded the regiment. "Last winter there was about one hundred and fifty men who re-enlisted, and they, in conjunction with the new men received, leave quite a respectable number remaining," the reporter wrote.

Things in camp moved slowly. "Between watching for the appearance of the paymaster with his greenbacks, and canvassing the prospects of the candidates for the Presidency, camp life passes agreeably by," declared the correspondent. "The coming election is principal topic of conversation, and there is as much interest depicted on the features of the boys, as they gather around the camp fires, canvassing the prospects of 'Little Mac' or 'Honest Abe,' as we imagine to have existed at Chicago amongst the 'scene shifters' and 'party chums' there gathered." The correspondent concluded by declaring that among the Lancers, as with most other veterans, Lincoln was highly favored over McClellan, in spite of the men's lingering affection for their old commander.[59]

The men found ways to pass the time. Cpl. Edgar H. Klemroth of Company A spent much of his free time drawing wonderfully detailed scenes of the Shenandoah Valley, its residents, and the vicious fighting that took place that fall.[60] On November 15, the last of the Lancers received their discharges and headed for Philadelphia and home, eager to resume their lives. The few members of the regiment still remaining at Pleasant Valley missed out on the heavy combat that had marked the 1864 Valley Campaign; they did not return to the Army of the Shenandoah until January 1865. The Lancers instead spent the winter near Hagerstown, Maryland.[61] There were only enough men to fill five small companies remaining. After consolidation, the companies still active were H, I, K, L, and M. With only the shell of a regiment remaining, three companies would remain on guard duty in Hagerstown. The men would continue to do this dull duty until their ranks could be filled out again and the full complement of twelve companies could be fielded.[62]

With Morrow in command of the regiment in the field, Maj. Charles L. Leiper had been sent to Philadelphia on recruiting duty. He had reopened the regimental recruiting office at 533 Chestnut Street, and was looking for recruits "for this celebrated Regiment of Major-General Sheridan's command." A newspaper ad indicated that "the long experience of the Officers and the splendid reputation earned by the Sixth Pennsylvania Cavalry in the field, render this a most desirable Regiment for Veterans of Cavalry or Infantry desiring to re-enlist." All governmental bounties would be paid. Leiper's efforts proved successful, as scores of new recruits signed up. Sadly, almost none of them received sufficient training to join the regiment in the field, and the Lancers went into the war's final months with their ranks badly depleted.[63]

On November 18, responding to reports of guerrilla activity near Hagerstown, Sheridan ordered the Lancers to leave Pleasant Valley. Sheridan sent two dismounted companies of the 6th Pennsylvania Cavalry to Pennsylvania to protect the Carlisle Barracks, while the rest marched to Hagerstown to perform provost duty in and about the town. Major Leiper was placed in command of the defenses of Hagerstown and received specific orders: "A great many horses are being taken from this army and Virginia by officers and men, soldiers and citizens, and sold in Hagerstown. You will endeavor to break up this business. . . . Arrest all officers and soldiers, cavalry, found in Hagerstown without proper permission, and send them to dismounted camp at Pleasant Valley."[64]

Guard duty at Carlisle Barracks was pleasant enough, if boring. The men had a cook-house, a dining room, a laundry, real beds, and everything they needed to be comfortable while still on duty. "I suppose this will last until our regiment is full when we will take our place in line in the field," complained a bored Henry Cowan on November 23. "Probably that will not be until next spring. Meanwhile we will have a chance to whiten our complexion and fatten up."[65] On November 29, the two companies—H and K—were relieved from their duty at the Carlisle Barracks, and rejoined the balance of their regiment at Hagerstown.[66]

By December 10, the Lancers had been relieved of their duties in Hagerstown, and were instead picketing and guarding the Potomac River fords near Williamsport.[67] They remained on this duty for much of the winter, intercepting Union deserters and suppressing the passage of contrabands fleeing north.[68] Only five small companies of men remained with the regiment—about 125 men—with Major Leiper in command. With the discharge of most of its veterans, this once proud regiment was now only a shadow of its former self.[69] "Now I would not be a soldier in the likes of these times but I have two more years to go," grumped Ballentine on December 22. "Pleasure and enjoyment and then I will enlist with my mother-in-law's daughter for life."[70] Little did Ballentine realize that he and the remaining veterans would have one final shot at achieving their prior glory.

Chapter Eleven

THE END OF THE LINE
FOR THE LANCERS

THE LAST REMAINING MEMBERS OF the 6th Pennsylvania Cavalry started 1865 near Hagerstown, right where they had ended the old. Even though the men of the regiment were not engaged in active duty in the field, casualties still occurred, including to those who had already received their discharges. Pvt. Richard J. Gibbs, who had served in Company E for three years, was in Philadelphia, still recuperating from three terrible wounds received at the Battle of Old Church on May 30, 1864. Gibbs had been shot through the neck and both arms, and had spent the balance of his time in the service recovering in various hospitals. When his term ended in October and he was well enough to go home to Philadelphia, he received his discharge and transferred to the Refreshment Saloon Hospital in the City of Brotherly Love.[1]

Still in the hospital, Gibbs was celebrating the arrival of the new year with a friend. Some time between 11:00 and midnight, a bullet struck him in the right elbow, passing through to the wrist. "The ball has not yet been extracted, and much fear is entertained that he will lose his arm," reported the *Philadelphia Inquirer*. Gibbs was a veteran of all of the regiment's notable campaigns, and was wounded five times. "Of all his wounds this is the most painful to him," declared the newspaper reporter, who concluded with great understatement, "There is always much danger in the practice of firing off the old year."[2]

The men continued picketing through the frigid winter. "We have just come off duty for the last 24 hours and that was about the hardest night I have ever put in," complained Sergeant Ballentine of Company K on January 8. "It rained all day yesterday and at night it began to snow and freeze and blow. In fact it was weather not to be sneezed at." However, Ballentine knew that changes were in the air. The remaining veterans received horses the next day. That always meant that a new campaign could not be far off.[3]

In January, the Lancers received a contingent of one hundred fresh recruits, their first new soldiers in many months. On January 18, a detachment of twenty-three men escorted the army's paymaster train from Martinsburg, West Virginia to Hagerstown. Just the opportunity to get out of camp and do something productive appealed to the men, who eagerly embraced each such occasion.[4]

The Lancers broke their winter camp near Hagerstown on January 26 and marched to Winchester, where they rejoined the Army of the Shenandoah on January 29. Major Leiper assumed temporary command of the Reserve Brigade.[5] The march was arduous. January 29 was bitter cold, and the roads were icy. Men and horses slipped, and men could be seen painfully sprawled in the roadway. The column took three days to cover seventy miles. Their bivouacs were crude and uncomfortable. "We could not hunt wood anywhere. There was not enough to stake our horses. We could not drive the little wood we did find into the ground," shuddered Ballentine. "We tied the lines around our legs, rolled our blankets tight around us and laid ourselves down on a good hard bed of snow. Of course, it was not as pleasant as we could wish," he concluded, with great understatement.[6]

After their ordeal on the march, the Lancers prepared a second set of winter quarters at Winchester, and remained there until February 27. Six hundred new recruits arrived during this month. These men were all raw and untrained, and were far from ready to take the field with the veteran cavalrymen of Sheridan's command. In addition, they had no horses, meaning that they would not be able to take the field until they received adequate mounts.[7] Major Leiper kept the men hard at work, drilling them twice a day in the freezing cold. "We have just one half hour free from reveille to retreat," complained one trooper. "It is perfectly sickening."[8]

Sheridan reviewed the cavalry on February 8. "It looked fine but the cavalry corps is small compared to what it was a year ago," observed Sgt. Hamilton Ballentine. "General Sheridan paid particular talent to our regiment."[9] On February 10, Leiper received a well-deserved promotion to lieutenant colonel, and Capt. Albert P. Morrow, who started the war as a sergeant, was promoted to major.[10] Twenty-two-year-old Capt. Charles B. Coxe, who had commanded Company L since September 1864, also received a promotion to major a few weeks later.[11] Not all of the men were pleased with the new group of officers. Sergeant Ballentine, who had turned down an officer's commission several times during the war, was not impressed. "We have 3 new officers just from their mama's titties," he sniffed on February 8, 1865. "They look more like baby turkeys on drill than officers. All they can say is 'Right dress' or 'Right turn.' In fact it is no wonder that the war has gone on for 4 years."[12]

As Grant planned his spring offensive for 1865, he knew the end of the war was in sight. The Confederacy's resources were stretched to their breaking point, and desertions plagued Lee's army. One good, coordinated push by all of the Federal forces in the field would bring the war to an end. Since Sheridan took command of the Middle Military District, Grant had wanted Sheridan to cross the Blue Ridge and bring his army to bear on the siege lines at Petersburg. For months, Sheridan found excuse after excuse to ignore or disobey Grant's wishes.

Finally, Grant grew weary of Sheridan's resistance. "On the 8th of February I ordered Sheridan, who was in the Valley of Virginia, to push forward as soon as the weather would permit and strike the canal west of Richmond at or about Lynchburg," wrote Grant.[13] Little Phil delayed his departure, claiming the weather prevented him from carrying out the lieutenant general's orders. "The weather here still continues very bad," he wrote on February 12, "The deep snow is still on the ground and very cold. It is utterly impossible to do anything here in such weather."[14] Sheridan was playing for time, hoping to creatively apply Grant's instructions.

On February 20, Grant clarified his wishes. As soon as the weather permitted, Sheridan was to take his cavalry and move on the important railroad junction town of Lynchburg and cut the rail lines there. From Lynchburg, he was to destroy the railroads and canals in all directions, and then "strike south, heading the streams in Virginia to the westward of Danville, and push on and join Sherman." If Sheridan could not make his way to Sherman, he was to return to Winchester. Nothing in Grant's unambiguous orders gave Sheridan authority to march to join the Army of the Potomac. Grant wanted Little Phil to act quickly, because coordinated assaults were being launched on all fronts, and "Sherman with a large army eating out the vitals of South Carolina—is all that will be wanted to leave nothing for the rebellion to stand upon."[15]

These orders made Sheridan very unhappy. He realized that the end was at hand. When he wrote his memoirs, Little Phil admitted that he had decided "that it was useless to adhere to my alternate instructions to return to Winchester, I now decided to destroy more thoroughly the James River Canal and the Virginia Central Railroad, and then join General Grant in front of Petersburg." He also admitted that since "the war was nearing its end, I desired my cavalry to be in at the death."[16] The Federal horsemen spent their last days in their winter camps struggling to achieve the highest level of discipline and efficiency for the new campaign season.[17] "Sabres are being sharpened in every regiment, and 2 horse shoes furnished to every man," reported Henry Cowan on February 23. "This looks like preparing for action." Cowan was correct.[18]

Sheridan finally broke his winter camp on February 27, departing Winchester with the First and Third Cavalry Divisions and a mounted brigade from the Army of West Virginia under command of Col. Charles R. Capehart. Torbert had again taken medical leave, and Merritt replaced him at the head of Sheridan's Cavalry Corps. Brig. Gen. Thomas C. Devin now commanded the First Division, and newly promoted Brig. Gen. Alfred Gibbs of the 19th New York Cavalry led the Reserve Brigade. Major Morrow commanded the Lancers during this expedition. "A magnificent force of cavalry it was," observed a Regular officer. "Ten thousand gallant troopers, men of intelligence, free citizens of a free country, fighting for a cause which could but strengthen and confirm every courageous impulse. They had been educated, trained, and seasoned by years of exacting service against an enemy whose courage and tenacity of purpose had won the admiration of the world." The ranks of the Reserve Brigade were badly depleted, however, and the entire brigade numbered 1,000 men or less.[19] Although the men had grown restless over the long winter, the orders to march were not entirely welcome. "We had been there about six weeks, and had built log cabins and were very nicely fixed, and the thought of being compelled to leave them in such inclement weather was anything but pleasant," complained Saddler Edgar Strang of Company M.[20]

Having broken camp, the Federals faced a difficult march. It was cold and raw, and the skies were heavy and gray, threatening more rain. "For several days the roads had been in process of preparation for a soft, it not an easy march, by a continuous fall of rain, which also melted the snow on the mountains, swelling the streams in the valleys until they were almost impassable," recalled Chaplain Gracey.[21] "By this time marching had become almost impossible," remembered Strang, "the heavy rain had made the ground so soft that the horses sank to their knees in mud, and it was with great difficulty that our artillery and wagon train were moved at all."[22]

The blueclad horsemen, however, advanced quickly over the macadamized Valley Turnpike, covering thirty-five miles in heavy rain on the first day.[23] General Devin ordered the Lancers to push on and seize and hold the bridge across Stony Creek at Edenburg. They carried out this order with only slight opposition from the enemy. The next morning, they resumed their march for Mt. Jackson, skirmishing all the way with a small force of the dogged Confederate cavalry. Devin ordered the Lancers to push on to Mt. Jackson and seize and hold the bridge across the North Fork of the Shenandoah River if it had not been destroyed. Reaching Mt. Jackson, they discovered that the bridge had been destroyed, forcing the men to ford the badly flooded North Fork of the Shenandoah.[24] Seven troopers drowned in the raging torrent, including a member of the 6th Pennsylvania Cavalry. After crossing, they rode through New Market to Sparta, where they rested for a couple of hours.[25]

The following day, March 1, the Union cavalrymen covered another thirty miles, bivouacking a few miles from Staunton. Brig. Gen. Thomas C. Devin and his division headed for Staunton to reconnoiter on a dark and rainy night. They punched through Early's line of pickets, rode through the town, and continued for another seven miles beyond, to Christian's Creek, where they destroyed a trestle of the Virginia Central Railroad and returned.[26]

The next day, March 2, Bvt. Maj. Gen. George Custer's 3rd Cavalry Division pounced upon the ragtag remnants of Early's once-proud army at Waynesboro, scattering it and effectively clearing the Valley of remaining Confederate forces. Early and his staff escaped by swimming the Shenandoah River. The Reserve Brigade did not participate in this attack; it was guarding Sheridan's wagons.[27] "In this engagement we captured eleven guns, two hundred wagons and teams, seventeen battle flags, and sixteen hundred prisoners, all of which were sent back to Winchester," Chaplain Gracey recalled.[28]

Sheridan then captured Charlottesville and also destroyed the locks along the James River Canal in the vicinity of Lynchburg. His men turned their attention to the Virginia Central and Richmond, Fredericksburg and Petersburg railroads, destroying tracks and bridges. They also destroyed large quantities of fine Virginia tobacco and factories where cloth for Confederate uniforms was made.[29] Sheridan liberally applied Grant's orders and decided not to join Sherman in North Carolina. Instead, he announced, "After finishing the Fredericksburg road I will join you, unless otherwise directed."[30]

The Federal cavalry faced a difficult cross-country march over terrible roads turned to a sea of sucking mud by the heavy rains. "We were in the saddle the greater part of the time night and day, and the men became so exhausted that they would fall asleep in the saddle at night, and it was no unusual thing to hear a splash and find some horse and rider in the canal," remembered Strang.[31] Along the way, they visited familiar spots, such as Trevilian Station, where they again tore up the Virginia Central Railroad. They destroyed lengthy sections of the railroad and burned trestles over the South Anna River. Pvt. John W. Wells of Company B was killed in an enemy ambush on March 16 while on a foraging mission near Beaver Dam Station.[32]

On March 14, Grant acquiesced to the inevitable. "I am disposed now to bring your cavalry over here and unite it with what we have," instructed the lieutenant general. "When you start I want no halt made until you make the intended raid, unless rest is necessary; in that case take it before crossing the James."[33] The Federals marched again on March 17, passing by way of Harrison's Landing and Bottom's Bridge. They spent five days—March 19-24—at White House Landing on the Pamunkey River, resting and preparing for the hard work that remained unfinished on the south side of the James River. "The expedition had been eminently successful," noted a Lancer, "and had been accomplished with but slight loss to our force, and great loss to the enemy in the shape of canals and railroads." While the Lancers rested at White House Landing, Capt. Charles B. Coxe received a promotion to major.

On March 25, Sheridan and his command left White House Landing and made their way to Petersburg, arriving the next day. When the Lancers arrived near Petersburg on March 26, Leiper rejoined the regiment and assumed command, with another new promotion, his second in just a month. This time, the twenty-two-year-old officer was promoted to colonel. Morrow also received a promotion to lieutenant colonel, and Capts. Abraham D. Price and Bernard H. Herkness were promoted to major. The regiment now had a full slate of field-grade officers, for the first time since April 1863.[34]

With these promotions in place, as of March 26, 1865, the roster of officers of the 6th Pennsylvania Cavalry was as follows:

> Colonel Charles L. Leiper
>
> Lieutenant Colonel Albert P. Morrow
>
> Majors Abraham D. Price, Charles B. Coxe, Bernard H. Herkness
>
> Adjutant Charles A. Newhall; Quartermaster J. W. McElhenny; Commissary Charles White
>
> Surgeons D. D. Swift, Joseph J. Yocum

Chaplain Samuel L. Gracey

Captains T. Campbell Oakman, William R. Wright, Isaac F. Moffett, Charles A. Vernon, Samuel R. Colladay, Andrew L. Lanigan, Edward Whiteford, J. H. Workman, Edward I. Hazel, Archer Maris, Lewis Miller, Jr., Robert M. Sheppard

1st Lieutenants Michael Golden, William Scott, John Laird, Abiah T. Smedley, Joseph D. Price, Daniel D. Hurtz, Henry J. Toudy, William Carey, James Magee.

Unfortunately, many of these officers were not ready to take the field. Just before breaking camp, Colonel Leiper wrote to Governor Curtin. Leiper was unhappy with most of his officers, and he took the unusual step of asking Curtin to commission civilians as officers, and not men from the ranks. "In no single instance has any of the original officers disgraced themselves or the regiment," he observed. By contrast, "The sergeants who were promoted were first class men as sergeants, but after their promotion they have invariably . . . become inefficient and have to be driven to do anything, except fight." Leiper reported that many of the current batch of officers had "no idea of discipline and of the simplest duties of an officer. . . . We are obliged to keep them, because if they were court-martialed, this regiment would be left with but three-four officers, and that number would be insufficient to work it."[35]

What remained of the 6th Pennsylvania Cavalry was now just a "skeleton of a regiment. . . . Meanwhile, our regiment was getting ready for the fray as best it could," noted a Lancer. "We were not very strong, except in faith and self-reliance, only 100 men being found to stand to horse on the morning of the 29th, when, at the sounding of 'the general,' we fell in and waited for the order to march. But this small number was mainly owing to the dearth of horses, for at dismounted camp, we had plenty of men, and we might have thrown a strong front still if horses could bear the work which our cavalry had been called upon to do." Without adequate mounts, the large contingent of fresh recruits could not take the field, meaning that the Lancers would have to go into the new campaign with only a fragment of a regiment.[36]

Sheridan and his nine thousand bedraggled horsemen arrived at Petersburg just in time for the breakout that led to the war's final campaign. "The reunited corps was to enter upon the campaign as a separate army, I reporting directly to General Grant," commented Sheridan in his memoirs, "the intention being to reward me for foregoing, of my own choice, my position as a department commander by joining the armies at Petersburg."[37]

The day that Sheridan's cavalry broke its camp, it again began raining. "The country we marched over was low land, not much above sea level, and the road soon became extremely muddy." Mule teams would sink into the thick muck, sometimes miring so badly that they could not be rescued. "On several occasions I saw mules shot in a bunch and another team rushed into place on top of their dead carcasses," recalled an officer of the 1st U.S. Cavalry. "The mud holes were finally filled in that way so as to make it possible to make a crossing. If one mule team did not make foundation enough, another was added." The Federal horse soldiers slogged on, spurred on by the knowledge that the end of their travail was in sight.[38]

The Army of the Potomac fought a successful action along the Boydton Plank Road on March 29, 1865, extending Lee's Petersburg lines to the breaking point. Maj. Gen. Gouverneur K. Warren's Fifth Corps infantry made first contact and bore the brunt of a savage fight. Sheridan and his troopers marched along the route of the Weldon Railroad, passing from Reams Station across Rowanty Creek, and on to Dinwiddie Court House, where they briefly skirmished with Confederate cavalry.

Dinwiddie Court House was a small village about thirteen miles from Petersburg, which had, before the war, "claimed two hundred inhabitants; and, although the county seat, it seemed to have contained when in its prime not over half a dozen dwellings."[39] The local road network, however, made Dinwiddie Court House a strategic spot. It provided the gateway to the crucial crossroads of Five Forks, which the Confederates had to hold in order to protect the South Side Railroad and the right flank and rear of Lee's army. The Federal troopers realized the area around Five Forks would be the site of the next major engagement with Lee's army.

About 9 o'clock on March 30, Sheridan ordered Merritt to reconnoiter toward Five Forks. A stream called Gravelly Run, badly swollen by the heavy rains, became a formidable obstacle, but the Union horsemen waded across it. They deployed into line of battle after encountering a small brigade of enemy cavalry in the woods to their front. "The enemy was in our front, then, and we were to have the honor of opening the campaign," proudly noted a member of the Lancers. "Colonel Leiper immediately advanced his men, and rapid firing at once ensued, and was sustained until we drew close to the opposing force, when prudence called a halt for assistance, the enemy greatly outnumbering us."[40] Soon, the 2nd Massachusetts, the 1st U.S., and 7th Michigan Cavalry Regiments came up to aid the Lancers, and Leiper, commanding this impromptu brigade, advanced again. "The Second Massachusetts and Sixth Pennsylvania also met the enemy, whom they were unable to drive, but firmly held their position."[41]

The Federal horsemen were left in an exposed position, so Merritt withdrew them. They resumed their position along Gravelly Run, having killed or captured forty of the enemy with few losses of their own. "It was a horrid day, and enough of itself to quench the ardor of anybody, but the men behaved in the most spirited way, and Colonel Leiper added a fresh leaf to his laurels, and was brevetted a Brigadier-General for his conduct and good management on the field." That afternoon, the Lancers supported the 6th New York Cavalry in a skirmish, "and when the miserable evening fell, we very uncomfortably went into camp to find rations all soaked, and blankets all wet, and spongy beds under leaking shelters," shuddered Chaplain Gracey. "Those who had the heart to whistle, whistled 'Home, Sweet Home,' and the rest of us lay still under the trickling canvas, hungry, cold, tired, coveting our neighbor's house."[42]

On March 31, Warren moved toward an important intersection along White Oak Road, where his men had an indecisive fight with Confederate infantry. While Warren made his movement, Sheridan's troopers had a prolonged fight with Maj. Gen. George E. Pickett's grayclad infantry at Dinwiddie Court House, where his dismounted horse soldiers successfully held off a desperate attack by Pickett's Division. The Lancers began the day in reserve, but when the Confederates found a gap in the Federal line and exploited it, the Lancers went into battle.[43] "The enemy were now seeking to break up our force and drive us away from Dinwiddie," observed Gracey, "and send us reeling back upon the Army of the Potomac. They were making good headway, they thought, in this intent, when we were ordered to the rescue." A heavy fight broke out in which Lt. James Magee was killed, and Lieutenant Colonel Morrow was severely wounded in the thigh. "I carried him off the field and saved him from the Rebs," claimed Hamilton Ballentine. "I got a bullet through my hat at the same time."[44] A number of enlisted men were also lost. "Lieutenant Magee had just been promoted," noted Chaplain Gracey, "he had distinguished himself on many fields and had won an excellent name for all soldierly qualities. He fell in front of his men, doing his duty manfully, and bearing his part in upholding the honor of his regiment and the cause for which he fought."[45]

The Confederate infantry nearly dealt Sheridan a crushing blow. For once, Sheridan had to call for reinforcements. Little Phil and his cavalry slept on their arms on the battlefield. That night, Sheridan reported to Meade that the enemy's infantry was now isolated and ripe for the picking. Meade then suggested to Grant that the Fifth Corps be sent to Sheridan "to smash up the force in front" of the cavalry. Grant promptly approved the request and placed the Fifth Corps under Sheridan's direct command for an assault on the crucial road junction at Five Forks.[46]

Sheridan did not want either Warren or the Fifth Corps. Instead, he preferred the old familiar Sixth Corps, with which he felt very comfortable. Sheridan rode to headquarters to register his complaints. "His plea was that the Sixth Corps had been with the cavalry in the Shenandoah Campaign; officers and men knew and trusted each other; that the Fifth Corps were strangers; and when hard pressed, said he had no confidence in Warren, under such circumstances. He would not like to be subordinated to [Sheridan] and he expected nothing but trouble." Grant heard out his subordinate's complaints, but made it clear that Warren and the Fifth Corps, and not Wright and the Sixth Corps, would be sent to Sheridan.[47]

Grant, looking to mollify his unhappy subordinate and concerned about Warren's caution himself, "notified General Sheridan that he was authorized to relieve General Warren, if, in his judgment, it was for the best interests of the service to do so; that I was afraid he would fail him in a critical moment."[48] While Grant respected the corps commander's many good qualities, the lieutenant general believed that Warren had "a defect which was beyond his control, that was very prejudicial to his usefulness in emergencies like the one just before us. He could see every danger at a glance before he had encountered it. He would not only make preparations to meet the danger which might occur, but he would inform his commanding officer what others should do while he was executing his move."[49]

Sheridan eagerly awaited his chance to pitch into the fray. On the night of March 31, Sheridan grew increasingly anxious and excited. As he discussed his plans for the coming fight with one of Grant's staff officers, Col. Horace Porter, Little Phil became very animated. When Porter inquired about fodder and supplies, Sheridan gave a characteristic response. "Forage?" he asked. "I'll get all the forage I want. I'll haul it out if I have to set every man in the command to corduroying roads, and corduroy every mile of them from the railroad to Dinwiddie. I tell you, I'm ready to strike out tomorrow and go to smashing things." Porter observed that the pacing Sheridan "chafed like a hound in the leash."[50] Sheridan's anxiety only grew.

The next morning, April 1, 1865, Sheridan planned to march on Five Forks with his cavalry, led by Merritt and Crook. At 3 a.m., Sheridan gave Warren his marching orders for the day. After reporting on the enemy's dispositions, Sheridan informed Warren that he intended to attack near the J. Boisseau house in the morning. "Possibly they may attack Custer at daylight; if so, attack instantly and in full force. Attack at daylight anyhow, and I will make an effort to get the road this side of Adams's house, and if I do, you can capture the whole of them," instructed Sheridan. "Any force moving down the White Oak Road, will be in the enemy's rear, and in all probability get any force that may escape you by a flank movement. Do not fear my leaving here. If the enemy remains, I shall fight at daylight."[51] Warren's infantry would support the attack of the dismounted horse soldiers.

Little Phil's battle blood was up. The depleted Lancers led the Union advance to Five Forks, where the Pennsylvanians dismounted and spearheaded Sheridan's attack on the Confederate breastworks. Only forty-eight officers and men remained in the ranks of the regiment as it went into battle that morning. There were not even enough men remaining to provide horse-holders for the dismounted men heading into battle. "Every man was willing and eager to do his part, and the horses were given in charge to officers' servants and such other peaceful followers as could be borrowed for the occasion."[52] They faced both difficult terrain and a stubborn enemy. "It is a section of country more difficult for cavalry operations than it is possible to imagine; the fields all quicksands, the woods all jungle; and there were heavy casualties among Merritt's men," observed Sheridan's adjutant, Lt. Col. Frederic C. Newhall.[53]

The dismounted Union cavalry pitched into Maj. Gen. George E. Pickett's infantry and Maj. Gen. Fitzhugh Lee's cavalry while Sheridan impatiently waited for the Fifth Corps to come up and join the attack. About 1 p.m., Sheridan ordered Warren to bring up the Fifth Corps and join the fighting around Five Forks. Warren joined Sheridan at the front. Sheridan laid out his plan for winning the battle, "telling Warren how the

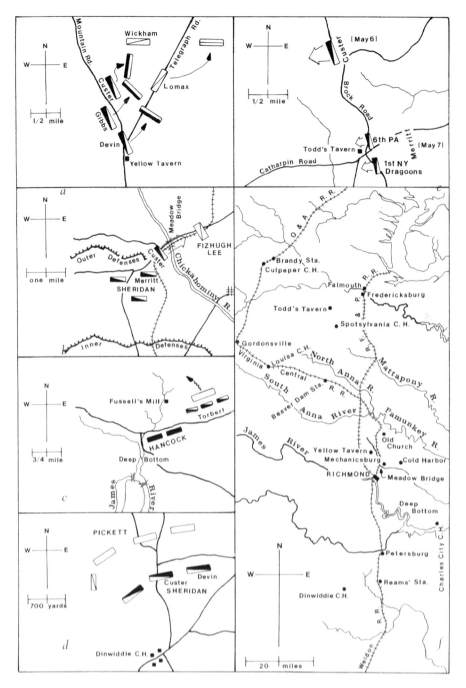

Map 11. *The Lancers's final battles and skirmishes: a. Yellow Tavern,*
b. Meadow Bridge, c. Deep Bottom, d. Dinwiddie Court House,
e. Todd's Tavern, f. the Eastern Theater.

enemy was posted, explaining with considerable detail, and concluding by stating that I wished his troops to be formed on the Gravelly Church Road, with two divisions to the front, aligned obliquely to the White Oak Road, and one in reserve, opposite the centre of these two." Sheridan later claimed, "General Warren seemed to understand me clearly, and then left to join his command."[54]

In spite of his clear understanding, Warren did not move quickly enough to satisfy Sheridan, whose "disappointment grew into disgust." Sheridan spurred over to Warren's location and "expressed my fears that the cavalry might expend their ammunition before the attack could be made, that the sun would go down before the battle could be begun, or that troops from Lee's right, which, be it remembered, was less than three miles away from my right, might, by striking my rear, or even by threatening it, prevent the attack on Pickett."[55] Sheridan believed that Warren was apathetic, and his limited patience had about run out.

After thoroughly examining the ground, Warren opened the attack at 4 o'clock. When his foot soldiers went in, Sheridan was not happy with their dispositions and tried to recall them. Warren was not at the head of his column, where Little Phil expected him to be. Instead, the corps commander was off looking for one of his division commanders, Brig. Gen. Samuel W. Crawford, whose troops had wandered off course, away from the battlefield. Warren went to bring Crawford's errant division to bear in the massed attack. His absence from the front proved to be the last straw for Sheridan. "Crawford's division had moved off in a northerly direction, marching away from Ayres, and leaving a gap between the two divisions," observed Horace Porter. "Sheridan became exceedingly annoyed at this circumstance, complained that Warren was not giving adequate personal supervision to the infantry, and sent nearly all his staff-officers to the Fifth Corps to see that the mistakes made were corrected."[56] Sheridan then relieved Warren of command of the Fifth Corps. Warren spent years trying to restore his reputation.[57]

Nevertheless, Warren's men carried the day, shattering the Confederate line and driving the panicked Southerners from the field in a wild rout. The corps commander had a horse shot out from under him during the final assault on the enemy line. Although he did not move as quickly as Sheridan might have liked, Warren's Fifth Corps provided the impetus for a decisive victory at Five Forks. When Warren's attack cracked the enemy line, the dismounted cavalrymen joined in, helping to sweep Pickett's infantrymen from the field.[58]

"We got up our horses then and went into camp on the battlefield, congratulating each other on the glorious victory and on the safety of our little party; for in spite of the stirring fight and the random firing through which we had passed, nobody of ours was killed, and a good Providence seemed to have watched over us that day," recounted a member of the Lancers. Five Forks proved to be the last battle in which the 6th Pennsylvania Cavalry took part. "General Merritt, thinking us too weak to do a regiment's duty in the brigade, ordered us to his headquarters as escort and guard, and we marched

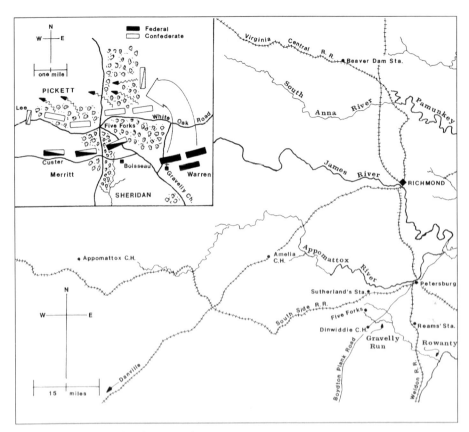

Map 12. Battle of Five Forks.

with him for the rest of the campaign, our carbines swung idly over our shoulders from Five Forks to Appomattox Court House." Although the Lancers were finished fighting, important work remained to be done by them, including many long, grueling hours in the saddle.[59]

After Sheridan's decisive victory at Five Forks, the war's final drama began. With the Union army firmly astride the Boydton Plank Road and around his flank, Robert E. Lee had no choice but to evacuate the siege lines at Petersburg after a significant skirmish at Sutherland's Station on the South Side Railroad cut the final Confederate rail line to the west. Lee had to abandon his lines before his last remaining route of retreat was cut. "I see no prospect of doing more than holding our position here until night," the Confederate commander wrote to Secretary of War John C. Breckinridge, "I am not certain I can do that. If I can I shall withdraw tonight north of the Appomattox, and, if possible, it will be better to withdraw the whole line tonight from the James River. I advise that all preparations be made for leaving Richmond tonight. I will advise you later according to circumstances."[60]

After cutting the railroad at Sutherland's Station, Grant ordered a full-scale assault all along the siege lines at Petersburg.[61] "The cannonade was the most frightful I ever heard," recalled an officer of the Reserve Brigade. "The heavens were lit up as with lighting from the exploding of shells. The very earth we lay on that night trembled with the concussions."[62] Lt. Gen. A. P. Hill, the veteran commander of the Army of Northern Virginia's Third Corps, was killed in action that day. The Union assault shattered the Confederate lines, forcing Lee to abandon Petersburg.

On April 2, the Lancers were detailed to Reserve Brigade headquarters for temporary duty. That day, they moved toward the South Side Railroad, destroyed nearly half a mile of track, marched west, and overtook Confederate infantry near Exeter Mills. They sparred with the enemy foot soldiers, and then bivouacked on the skirmish line. This excursion proved to be the last independent mission of the 6th Pennsylvania Cavalry.[63]

As the Confederates streamed west, away from the trench lines at Petersburg, Sheridan's troopers led the pursuit. The withdrawal of Lee's army meant that Richmond had to be evacuated. Lee recognized the inevitable. "It is absolutely necessary that we should abandon our position tonight, or run the risk of being cut off in the morning," he wrote. "I have given all the orders to officers on both sides of the river, and have taken every precaution that I can to make the movement successful. It will be a difficult operation, but I hope not impracticable."[64] Confederate President Jefferson Davis and his cabinet fled, leaving the Rebel capital to capture by the Northern armies.[65]

Lee tried to escape to the west, where he hoped to find desperately needed provisions at Amelia Court House. After resupplying his threadbare army, he would turn south and try to join Gen. Joseph E. Johnston's command in North Carolina. Johnston was fleeing from Sherman's army, hoping to link up with Lee near Danville. Perhaps the combined fragments of the two armies could then turn on their pursuers. Sheridan commanded the left wing and led the chase across the Virginia countryside, "thundering on with his cavalry."[66]

By April 8, Sheridan's cavalry had cut off Lee's line of retreat. As Gen. Joshua Chamberlain, commander of a Fifth Corps brigade, recalled, "Sheridan is square across the enemy's front, and with that glorious cavalry alone is holding at bay all that is left of the proudest army of the Confederacy. It has come at last,—the supreme hour. No thought of human wants or weakness now: all for the front; all for the flag, for the final stroke to make its meaning real—these men of the Potomac and James, side by side, at the double in time and column, now one and now the other in the road or the fields beside."[67]

The small remnant of the Lancers made their final charge that day. They charged several trains of supplies, capturing them and helping themselves to anything of interest before destroying the rest. It was the last moment of glory for the veterans of the regiment, although they had no way of knowing it.[68]

That night, Lee held a council of war. His army would try to break through the Yankee cavalry. If it turned out that Union infantry also blocked their route of march, Lee would have no choice but to surrender his army.[69] When the council of war adjourned, Lee penned a response to Grant's dispatch of that morning, saying that he had not proposed a surrender of the Army of Northern Virginia, but rather that he wanted to explore the terms for one. "To be frank, I do not think the emergency has arisen to call for the surrender of this army; but as the restoration of peace should be the sole object of all, I desired to know whether your proposals would lead to that end." Lee offered to meet Grant between the lines the next morning at 10 o'clock.[70]

The following day, April 9, Grant replied to Lee's note. "As I have no authority to treat on the subject of peace the meeting proposed for 10 a.m. today could lead to no good," he wrote. "I will state, however, general, that I am equally anxious for peace with yourself, and the whole North entertain the same feeling. The terms upon which peace can be had are well understood. By the South laying down their arms they will hasten that most desirable event, save thousands of human lives, and hundreds of millions of property not yet destroyed."[71]

Lt. Gen. John B. Gordon's Second Corps, supported by Fitz Lee's cavalry division, spearheaded Lee's effort to punch through Sheridan's lines at Appomattox Court House. On the morning of April 9, Gordon's initial volleys drove back the pickets of Brig. Gen. Charles F. Smith's cavalry brigade. "We had nothing to oppose Lee but cavalry and nobly they did their work. We fought them dismounted. They tried hard to break our lines and poured in the shot and shell with their musketry until the air seemed full of it," wrote a Yankee trooper.[72] Spurred by their initial success, the Confederates continued to press the attack, pushing the Federal cavalry back to the next ridge. "It was plain as could be to us that the fighting was drawing nearer," wrote a member of the 19th New York Cavalry, "the bullets began every once in a while to crash among the tree-tops overhead. This made us very anxious, & much speculation was indulged in as to how many and what Infantry were already up, for overestimating as we did Lee's strength . . . & feeling certain that we had all of it cope with, we felt sure we would be thrashed."[73]

Sgt. Michael J. Golden of Company K was the last member of the 6th Pennsylvania Cavalry to suffer a combat wound. Joining one of Maj. Gen. George Crook's Second Division brigades, Golden, on the left of the Union line, charged and wounded himself in the face with his own saber which rebounded from the branch of a tree as he slashed away at a Rebel, who was galloping away. Golden's wound, although somewhat embarrassing, was trivialized by the events of April 9, 1865.[74]

Just as it appeared that the thin line of cavalry pickets would break, Union infantrymen arrived on the scene. The horse soldiers opened ranks and fell back, so that the advancing Rebels could see the foot soldiers behind them. "In 20 minutes we could have slaughtered all the Rebs," claimed Sergeant Ballentine.[75] Gordon realized that further attacks were futile and reported to Lee that Federal infantry had arrived on the scene.

"Heard heavy firing in several directions," wrote a Confederate soldier in his diary. "Just before we halted all the firing suddenly ceased. All the men were jubilant as we concluded we had whipped the enemy and put their guns out of commission."[76] Further, Meade's Army of the Potomac was moving to attack Lee's eastern flank, and the Confederates found themselves hopelessly trapped between the pincers of a powerful Union infantry force. Soon, a flag of truce came through the lines.[77] As the cheers of the Yankee soldiers echoed through the valley, Sheridan rode up and down his lines on Rienzi, waving his hat and crying out, "God bless you boys! God bless you boys!"[78]

Left with no choice, Lee agreed to a meeting with Grant.[79] When Grant arrived at Appomattox Court House, Sheridan and Ord awaited him. "How are you Sheridan?" inquired the lieutenant general.

"First-rate, thank you; how are you?" responded Sheridan.

"Is Lee over there?" asked Grant, pointing up the road toward the village.

"Yes," replied Sheridan, "He is in that brick house waiting to surrender to you."

"Well, then, we'll go over," Grant said nonchalantly.[80] They did, and Lee surrendered to Grant in the parlor of Wilmer McLean's home.

"Peace, then, had come at last. No more need for pickets and scouts; no more weary raids and dusty marches; no more need for fighting on foot in tangled woods; no more wounded, and no more killed," observed Chaplain Gracey with gratitude. "The Great Rebellion being dead, some troopers that we know of had much better chance of their lives thenceforth, and were duly thankful, let us hope, as they went to bed that night." Cpl. Edgar H. Klemroth of Company A, who was performing courier duty that morning, watched Lee and Grant come and go from the McLean house, and understood the significance of these events. "What a glorious night was that 9th of April! Both sides— Yanks and Johnnies—alternately would yell and hurrah," he recalled. "It seemed too good to believe that, after those four awful years of strife, there would no more sudden alarm, no more freezing nights in little pup tents in winter, no more long marches in the broiling sun and dust of summer." That night, the homesick men of both sides sang "Home, Sweet Home," and tears flowed freely.[81] The Lancers quietly celebrated the surrender of Lee's army and the welcome prospect of returning to their homes and loved ones.[82]

The next day, April 10, Grant and Lee rode out and met between their lines for about forty-five minutes. They remained mounted, sat under a tree, and talked, although the specific topic of their discussion was never recorded. Corporal Klemroth, who was watching from a distance of only twenty to thirty feet away, and who was an accomplished artist, pulled out his sketch pad and drew the conference between Lee and Grant. His sketch was eventually published in a veterans' newspaper years after the war.[83]

"We have great times with the Rebs since we are all together," declared Hamilton Ballentine on April 11. "The Rebs are riding around without officers by themselves all through our camp and we are doing the same. Firing had scarcely ceased an hour when they were all through the camp." Now that they were countrymen again, the veterans of both armies began trying to heal the country's wounds.[84]

On April 12, Bvt. Maj. Gen. Joshua L. Chamberlain received the formal surrender of the Army of Northern Virginia. Sergeant Ballentine had a clear view of the surrender ceremony. He watched the tattered remnant of the Army of Northern Virginia march up and stack arms. "In spite of the 4 years of bloody encounters I have had with them I could not help feeling sorry for them," he wrote. Sheridan led the Cavalry Corps off toward Danville in an attempt to join Sherman's army in North Carolina. "Gen. Merritt and staff with the remnant of the 6th Penna. left Appomattox Court House."[85] Because Sheridan did not want to go on this expedition, it started late, made little progress, and produced little in the way of tangible results.[86]

The news of the assassination of President Abraham Lincoln on April 14, 1865, shocked the men of the Lancers. "How sad the Nation feels today on account of the assassination of our beloved President just at a time when he could see the end of the war in the distance," wrote Pvt. John T. Baynes of Company K on April 20. "When he was down here at City Point he visited each Corps Hospital shaking hands with the sick and wounded telling them to cheer up as the war was nearly over. Who would have thought that in so short a time he would have been brutally murdered by the hand of a dastardly assassin leaving the country to mourn his loss. In his death we have lost one who the whole nation looked up to for support and guidance." Baynes also reported, "I have not yet got a horse although as near as I can understand we are to get the next lot that comes as our regiment is at General Merritt's Hd/Qrs and of course we will be wanted there too as the regiment is very small at present."[87]

That same day, the 6th Pennsylvania was detached from the Reserve Brigade, and temporarily assigned to duty at Cavalry Corps headquarters. They would not rejoin the Reserve Brigade; the Lancers spent the rest of this expedition at Cavalry Corps headquarters.[88] However, Gen. Joseph E. Johnston surrendered before the Union horsemen made it to North Carolina, meaning that Sheridan and his command only made it as far as Danville before turning back. "You ought to have heard Sheridan's boys swear at Johnston for not holding out one day longer," exclaimed Sergeant Ballentine. "He knew Sheridan was coming and was dangerous."[89]

After resting in Danville for a few days, the Union horsemen then returned to Petersburg. "We are again back at Petersburg after a nine days ride, which I rather enjoyed," reported Maj. Charles B. Coxe on May 7. "The rumor is that we are to stay here ten days & then march to Alexandria, which appears to be the point where the armies are to assemble."[90] Eight hundred new recruits joined the regiment there, too late to have made the unit combat effective during the war's last campaign.[91] The remaining veterans welcomed the brief respite after the long trek to Danville. "We will take up our line of march for Washington about day after tomorrow and then it will not be a great while before we are mustered out," reported Private Baynes on May 9. "Since we have got back to Petersburg the time seems to slip around very slowly for there is nothing to keep us busy at as we do no picket duty whatever."[92]

The Cavalry Corps marched to Washington, D.C., where several days of grand reviews of the victorious Union armies were planned for mid-May. The weather had turned hot and dry, meaning that the roads would be very dusty. However, even the dust could not dampen the spirits of men who knew that they would soon be heading back to their homes and families.[93] "We returned to Washington, making one of the most delightful marches of our three years' service," fondly recalled a Lancer.[94] Along the way, they passed many of the battlefields where they had fought, suffered, and watched their friends die, including Yellow Tavern, Trevilian Station, and Brandy Station, where the Lancers first found undying glory nearly two years earlier.

The men were ready to go home. "The war is now over and the word 'home' is now in every man's mouth," said Ballentine on May 18. "The old vets like myself have very heavy hanging lips this last 2 or 3 days as there is an order for them to be consolidated and reorganized to remain in the service. Merritt says our regiment is a good one and that he will not let it go." The frustrated veteran declared his intention to leave whether the high command sanctioned it or not. The grand review was yet to come, and while Ballentine had no intention of missing that event, he wanted to go home.[95]

The Grand Review of the Army of the Potomac, which was held on May 23, presented a spectacle such as few had ever seen. "For an entire day Pennsylvania Avenue was a solid mass of soldiers: cavalry first, our division at the very head, the infantry and artillery, corps after corps, an army the equal of which the world had never seen marching up that avenue all that day," proudly recalled an officer of the 1st U.S. Cavalry, "both sides of the street lined with admiring spectators and then passing in review before the president, the cabinet, and General Grant."[96] Sheridan had been ordered to Texas, where tensions with Mexico's puppet emperor, Maximilian, threatened to flare into war, so Wesley Merritt now commanded the Army of the Potomac's Cavalry Corps.

The Lancers proudly participated in this spectacle, rejoining the Reserve Brigade for the review.[97] "We shared in all the glory of the Grand Review," recorded Chaplain Gracey. "Here, as the 6th Pennsylvania Cavalry turned out of Pennsylvania Avenue, where the great throng had greeted us with such a splendid outburst of applause, it may be said that our glorious old regiment ended its career; with the cheers of the crowd still ringing about us we furled up the tattered colors which had streamed over us for so long."[98]

Not to be outdone, the returned and discharged veterans of the regiment held their own grand review in Philadelphia on June 10. They gathered at Camp Cadwalader, with the First City Troop leading the way for General Meade and his staff. Immediately after Meade and his staff came a detachment of Lancers, who occupied a place of honor in the great parade. They were followed by other former soldiers in a parade through the streets of Philadelphia. It was a grand spectacle that did honor to the men who served and also gave the faithful of the City of Brotherly Love an opportunity to show their gratitude. Thus, even those who had already left the service had their moment in the sun at the end of the terrible conflict.[99]

After the Grand Review, the Lancers were sent across the Potomac River to Cloud's Mill, Virginia. "We are constantly expecting to receive orders to be disbanded," reported Henry Cowan on June 2. "I will be with you soon." Unfortunately, Cowan was wrong. Not only was the long awaited discharge not imminent, a new and unwanted task instead awaited the veterans of the 6th Pennsylvania Cavalry.[100]

"News of Consolidation of the 17th Penn Cav and making the regiment over to be called the 2nd Provisional Cav.," noted a veteran of the regiment on June 18.[101] Their small contingent was consolidated with the remnants of the 17th Pennsylvania Cavalry to form the 2nd Pennsylvania Provisional Cavalry. General Leiper commanded this new regiment, which then traveled cross-country to Louisville, Kentucky. "We marched to Harpers Ferry by land and then took cars to [Parkersburg, West Virginia,]" reported Baynes on July 9.[102] They embarked on steamboats on July 9, and finally arrived at Louisville on July 12. "After reporting there was ordered across the River to [Jeffersonville, Indiana] where we found the 2nd New York Provisional Cavalry also," he wrote a few days later. "I think yet we will all be mustered out and sent home this fall for certain for I cannot see what good we are doing at present. When we was ordered down here I think it was the intention to send us down to Texas but they have got more troops there now that they know what to do with."[103] The men passed their days waiting for the welcome news that it was, at long last, time to go home. "We have nothing to do but ride around," complained a bored Henry Cowan on July 23.[104] "News of our being mustered out is still going around. Expect to turn in our Horses soon and march for the city of Harrisburg to be mustered out and discharged there, hope it is true," noted a veteran on July 27.[105]

A day or two later, the men learned that they would be going home in just over a week. They would perform provost duty for an upcoming election, and once the election was over, they would be relieved in order to mustered out.[106] "Still in camp and likely to stay there now till mustered out. For we turned in our horses today, so no more rides for us now," reported a Lancer on August 1.[107] The men were miserable, idly passing the time and counting the days and trying to avoid the swarms of flies plaguing them. "Weather very warm still in camp. A great many of the men are sick, and will be worse if we don't move out of here soon," observed one unhappy veteran on August 2, "for the place is to foul to live in."[108] The men spent their days preparing muster rolls, getting their equipment ready to turn in, and eagerly waiting to see their loved ones again.

On August 7, 1865, the mustering officer excused them from further duty and sent them home, rejoicing. "The KY Election came off today several of the men went out to guard the polls.," gleefully reported Francis Ballinger. "Were *mustered* out today."[109] "I think we will start on our way tomorrow or next day," declared Hamilton Ballentine. "We have all our papers and books squared away and our discharges made out."[110] The men of the 2nd Pennsylvania Provisional Cavalry "drifted slowly out of the service."[111] The long, fratricidal war was finally and truly over, and with it ended the storied career of one of the finest mounted units of the Civil War, the 6th Pennsylvania Cavalry.

In 1868, Chaplain Gracey wrote a valediction of the accomplishments and sacrifices of the Lancers. "It is a long road we have traveled since leaving [Philadelphia], and the soldier who returns in 1865 is not much like the recruit of 1861," he wrote. "He has parted with his picturesque lance, and carried a practical carbine in place of it; he wears his cap on the side of his head, and the visor turned up with a jaunty air; his short blue blouse is a perfect fit, and his tight drawn belt does not give to the pistols weight; his trousers are close about the thigh, and spring over the foot a little; his saber is strapped under his saddle-girth, and he knows how to sit his horse; he is neat and straight and feels himself to be a man; he has self respect and pride in his regiment; and when he is mustered out of service he is a better civilian than ever he was before." He concluded, "But there are many who started with us, and many who joined us later, who have fallen by the way. Let us give our last thought to the memory of these, as we bid farewell to the gallant old regiment, and put away the torn standard and the trusty arms."[112]

Chapter Twelve

REQUIEM

WITH THEIR SERVICE FINALLY ENDED, the men of the 6th Pennsylvania Cavalry returned to Philadelphia, their families, and their lives. Many of them had been away from home for nearly four years. Their lives and careers had been disrupted. Many had suffered financial hardship as a result of their service. Certainly, their personal relationships had suffered. Eighteen hundred men were mustered into the regiment, including the six hundred new recruits who were mustered in 1865 but never served in the field with the regiment. Of the approximately 1,200 men who did serve, a total of 574 were casualties during the four years of war. These men paid the price for their service: 7 officers and 71 enlisted men were killed or mortally wounded in battle, and 3 officers and 86 enlisted men died of disease. A total of 167 of the men who answered the clarion call of war did not come home.[1] In addition, 11 officers and 222 enlisted men were wounded in battle, and 6 officers and 204 enlisted men were captured.[2] Nearly half of the men who served either died of disease or were killed, wounded, or captured. These figures represent some of the highest casualty figures of any Union cavalry regiment assigned to the Army of the Potomac. The Lancers paid a high price for their service and fealty to the Union. Among the survivors, many would never be the same again.[3]

Although their service during the war began with jeers of "turkey drivers," "broomstick soldiers," and "Lances Rushers," the men of the 6th Pennsylvania Cavalry gradually earned the respect of the men and officers of the Army of the Potomac. By war's end, they had a reputation for being one of the finest mounted units to serve in the Civil War. Maj. Gen. George B. McClellan, the man responsible for the regiment being armed with lances, referred to the 6th Pennsylvania Cavalry as "the eyes and ears of the Army."[4] Just a few months after the end of the war, Maj. Gen. George Stoneman, the first commander of the Army of the Potomac's Cavalry Corps, called the Lancers "one of the finest Regts. in the world."[5] Brig. Gen. John Buford, the tough, hard-bitten old Regular cavalryman who commanded them for most of 1863, came to call the Lancers "my Seventh Regulars" out of respect for their superb performance at the Battle of Brandy Station.[6]

In 1866, Maj. Gen. Philip H. Sheridan, who drove the Federal cavalry to glory during the last year of the war, wrote of the Lancers, "No organization in either the regular or volunteer service enjoyed a more enviable reputation in every respect, and its services were of so valuable a character to the government that every endeavor was made by me after its muster out in 1864 to have an organization formed, the nucleus of which should be such officers and men of the original regiment as were desirous of again entering the service."[7] Maj. Gen. George G. Meade, commander of the Army of the Potomac for the last two years of the war, "had a high appreciation of the intelligence and courage of our men, and valued their services at their full worth."[8] Meade's nephew, William M. Graham, a captain and commander of the battery of horse artillery assigned to the Reserve Brigade, who retired as a brigadier general after many years of service in the Army, was similarly impressed. "I saw a great deal of the regiment during the Gettysburg campaign and always regarded it as the best volunteer cavalry regiment I ever saw," he declared in 1889.[9]

No Union cavalry unit had to master more weapons than the 6th Pennsylvania. When McClellan suggested that they be armed with lances, the men not only had to master the normal weapons carried by the cavalry—saber, pistol, and carbine—they also had to master a strange, clumsy, and cumbersome nine-foot-long pole. They had to learn to fight mounted with lances, sabers, and pistols, and they also had to learn to fight dismounted. Because the Lancers were fragmented and their companies scattered among so many different infantry commands until the fall of 1862, they were disadvantaged by not serving together as a cohesive unit. Once the Lancers received permission to serve as a full regiment, they often acted as an independent command, on detached duty at Cavalry Corps headquarters. When the 6th Pennsylvania Cavalry finally turned in their lances and became part of the Reserve Brigade, they performed admirably. By July 1863 and the Battle of Gettysburg, they were fully integrated into the Army of the Potomac's Cavalry Corps and earned the permanent respect of their comrades in arms. Forgotten were the derisive early war nicknames.

By the fall of 1863, the 6th Pennsylvania Cavalry were one of the most reliable units in the Army of the Potomac's Cavalry Corps. Time after time, the Lancers received the most difficult assignments. Again and again, they led the way for the Cavalry Corps as the Northern horse soldiers went into battle. They earned the respect of professional horse soldiers such as Stoneman, Buford, Sheridan, Pleasonton, Merritt, and Gibbs. By the end of their combat career at Five Forks, the tiny remnant of the regiment had established as distinguished a battle record as any unit in the Cavalry Corps: they had fought in nearly thirty battles, and they had been in dozens of skirmishes. They also participated in dozens of reconnaissance missions and other expeditions, including all the major raids of the Cavalry Corps.[10]

Many members of the Lancers became pillars of Philadelphia society in the years after the war. A few select examples amply demonstrate this fact. Frank Furness, the regiment's sole Medal of Honor recipient, resumed his architectural career, becoming the leading North American architect of the 1870s and 1880s. His innovative work became one of the primary inspirations for Frank Lloyd Wright. Furness designed and built more than six hundred buildings in his long and successful career, including palatial homes for several of his old comrades-in-arms from the Lancers.[11] Although his radical designs eventually fell from favor, he remains one of the most influential architects in American history.[12] Furness died in 1912, and was buried in Philadelphia's famous Laurel Hill Cemetery, where his grave overlooks the Schuylkill River. He rests under a marker that proudly proclaims his status as a recipient of the Medal of Honor.

William W. Frazier returned to Philadelphia, founded his own business, and made a vast fortune refining Cuban sugarcane. When he died at age ninety-two in August 1921, he was estimated to have been worth between $30 million and $40 million, and was one of the wealthiest men in the United States. He was the owner of Overbrook Farms, a thousand-acre estate on York Road in Willow Grove, and was also a financier and educator. He was the founder and principal donor of the Jenkintown Club, an organization for the education and advancement of young men. "For years he entertained the surviving members of the Sixth Pennsylvania Cavalry annually at his summer home at Rydal," noted his obituary. The town of Frazier, Pennsylvania, was named for him. He was the last survivor of the regiment's original officer corps.[13]

Frederic C. Newhall, the former regimental adjutant who served on Pleasonton's and Sheridan's staffs for most of the second half of the war, also got into the sugar business. Newhall, whose family members were world-famous cricket players, owned his own sugar refining company for several years. When his business failed, Newhall represented the American Sugar Refining Company in London. He was also one of the founders of the Germantown Cricket Club. In 1866, Newhall wrote an account of the Appomattox Campaign as "A Staff Officer," although his true identity was not difficult to ascertain.[14] Newhall, who was known for his staunch loyalty to family and friends, had two objectives for this work. First, and foremost, he chronicled the last days of Sheridan's cavalry, memorializing those heady days of March and April 1865. Newhall's second and less blatant motivation was to defend his idol Sheridan from claims that Little Phil had unjustly relieved Maj. Gen. Gouverneur K. Warren of command of the Fifth Corps at the Battle of Five Forks. Newhall also authored a number of well-regarded articles about his service. He remained active in veterans' affairs until his death of cancer in 1898 at the age of fifty-eight, and was buried in Laurel Hill Cemetery, just a few steps from the grave of Ulric Dahlgren.[15]

In 1885, remembering the regimental guidon that was lost in the charge on the guns at St. James Church on June 9, 1863, Newhall penned a letter to then-Lieut. Gen. Philip H. Sheridan. "The 6th Regt. Penna. Cavalry has a very large and fine veteran association," he wrote. "They have heard that the flag of the regt. is in the room of abandoned and captured property in the War Dept. at Washington. If this is so, cannot we have it to awaken old memories at annual occasions." Sheridan, rewarding the loyalty of his former adjutant, recommended that the request be granted, and the Secretary of War approved it. The next day, an officer carried the flag to Newhall and personally delivered it to him. The flag stayed in the Newhall family until the 1970s, when it was sold to a collector.[16]

After illness forced him to resign his commission in the Lancers in April 1863, Richard H. Rush accepted a commission as colonel and commander of the Invalid Reserve Corps. The Invalid Reserve Corps consisted of men of former service who were sick or wounded but were still fit for garrison or guard duty, and also commanded the prisoner of war camp and training depot at Rock Island, Illinois. Depending on the severity of their disabilities, these men typically served either as guards or as hospital clerks, cooks, or nurses. In 1864, he was appointed president of the board for examination of officers for several months, and then commanded a brigade of troops assigned to the defenses of Washington from March until July 1864. He resigned his commission on July 1, 1864, and returned to Philadelphia.[17] After doing so, he threw his support to his long-time friend and West Point classmate, George B. McClellan, who was the Democratic nominee for president that year.[18]

Perhaps for political reasons, including his close linkage to McClellan, Rush was passed over for promotion to brigadier general on three occasions, even though he had frequently been recommended for that position. He returned to private life and refused to participate in veterans' activities, perhaps as a result of bitterness resulting from being passed over for promotion.[19] Although a Democrat by birth and affiliation and a member of a family that had a long history of politicking, he took no active part in postwar politics and never held any political office. Rush died on October 17, 1893, at the age of sixty-eight, and, after a small funeral held in his Pine Street home, was buried in Laurel Hill Cemetery. He left six children.[20]

Chaplain Samuel L. Gracey left the regiment in 1864, when he was assigned to serve as chaplain for the prisoner of war camp at Rock Island, Illinois. He rejoined the Lancers in 1865, just in time for the unit to be mustered out of service. He returned home to Philadelphia, where he wrote a well-respected history of the Lancers, *Annals of the Sixth Pennsylvania Cavalry*, which was based on his wartime diary and which was published in 1868.[21] The book "contains many items of interest to any one who participated in its campaigns," noted a former sergeant of Company F seven years after the book's publication.[22] Gracey then acted as pastor for a number of congregations until 1890, when he was appointed U.S. consul to China, a post he held for various periods until 1897. Gracey received the Decoration of the Double Dragon from the Chinese government for his service in the Boxer Rebellion. He died in Boston in 1911, and his remains were brought home to Philadelphia. He was laid to rest in Mt. Moriah Cemetery, under a simple gravestone that reads, "Soldier-Clergyman-Diplomat."[23]

Albert P. Morrow found glory in another field of endeavor. After receiving a brevet to colonel of volunteers in March 1865, Morrow realized that he was destined to be a soldier. On July 28, 1866, Morrow was commissioned as a captain in the newly formed 7th

U.S. Cavalry, quite an accomplishment for a young man with no formal military training. Another company commander in the 7th U.S. Cavalry was Myles W. Keogh, with whom Morrow had served on the staff of General John Buford. Morrow's commissioning into the 7th U.S. reunited these two old friends and comrades in arms.[24] Morrow served on frontier duty with his regiment at Fort Hays, Kansas until he was transferred to the 9th U.S. Cavalry and promoted to major in March 1867. The 9th U.S. Cavalry consisted of African American soldiers, and was one of the famous "buffalo soldier" regiments that served in the West with great distinction during the latter nineteenth century.

Morrow participated in various expeditions against hostile Indians, including the 1876 Sioux Campaign and an 1878 campaign against the Ute Indians. In the fall of 1880, he was sent to France to witness maneuvers of the French army, and did not return to the United States until January 1881, when he was promoted to lieutenant colonel and appointed aide-de-camp to the commanding general-of-the-army, William T. Sherman. He served in that capacity until June 1, 1883, when he was relieved of that duty and returned to his regiment in Arizona. He was promoted to colonel of the 3rd U.S. Cavalry on February 18, 1891, and served in Texas until he retired from active duty in August 1892. During a long and successful career as an Indian fighter, Morrow received many commendations. After his retirement, Morrow was active in the Military Order of the Loyal Legion of the United States (MOLLUS), Colorado Commandery, and died on January 20, 1911.[25]

Theodore J. Wint had a similar story. Wint, who was born near Scranton on March 8, 1845, enlisted as a private in the Lancers at age sixteen in 1861. He lied about his age in order to do so. He was captured at Brandy Station in June 1863 and was not exchanged until September, when he returned to duty with the regiment.[26] By June 1864, he wore a sergeant's chevrons, and he was then commissioned first lieutenant on July 1, 1864. He served honorably until the expiration of his term of service on September 30, 1864, when he mustered out of the volunteer service as a nineteen-year-old lieutenant. On February 20, 1865, he enlisted as a private in the General Mounted Service of the U.S. Army, and served in this role until November 24, 1865, when he received a commission as a second lieutenant in the 4th U.S. Cavalry. In May 1866, he was promoted to first lieutenant, serving as regimental adjutant from August 1868 to December 31, 1871. On April 21, 1872, he was promoted to captain, and then in May 1892, he was promoted to major and transferred to the 10th U.S. Cavalry, another famous "buffalo soldier" regiment consisting of African American soldiers led by white officers.

In April 1899, he was promoted to lieutenant colonel and was again transferred, this time to the 6th U.S. Cavalry. He was promoted to colonel on February 2, 1891, and to brigadier general on June 9, 1902. Wint served in the frontier Indian Wars (1866 to 1888) (where he served with great distinction), in Cuba, during the Spanish-American War (1898) (where he was badly wounded in battle while leading the assault on San

Juan Hill), China (1900-1901), the Philippine insurrection (1901-1904) (where he distinguished himself by capturing one of the leaders of the insurgency), and the Army of Cuban Pacification (1906-1907). Ironically, while operating in both Cuba and the Philippines, Wint served under the command of General Joseph Wheeler, a former Confederate cavalry officer who again donned the blue uniform of the United States Army. The U.S. Army's Philippines fortifications were named Fort Wint in his honor. "A fighting record from start to finish is the story of General Wint's life," observed a newspaper reporter.[27]

General Wint died suddenly of heart disease at the relatively young age of sixty-two on March 21, 1907, while still on active duty in the field. Accompanied by four troops of the 13th Cavalry and the 4th Battery of Field Artillery, he was buried in Arlington National Cemetery, where a handsome monument marks his grave. His honorary pallbearers included Maj. Gen. Frederick D. Grant, the son of the late President Ulysses S. Grant. Other than the six months from the end of his term of service with the Lancers in 1864 and his reenlistment in the U.S. Army in 1865, Wint spent his entire adult life as a soldier, a remarkable career that spanned forty-six years. "He was a fine soldier, and would have made a major general soon if he had lived," lamented Secretary of War William Howard Taft upon learning of Wint's death. "Wint was a quiet man that did things." No member of the Lancers achieved higher military rank than did General Wint.[28]

George Meade also remained in the Regular Army after the end of the war, receiving a brevet to lieutenant colonel of volunteers. In 1867, he received Regular Army brevets to lieutenant colonel and colonel. Young Meade eventually rose to the rank of captain, serving in the 1st Artillery, 22nd Infantry, and 31st Infantry, serving on his father's staff for most of his postwar career. In 1874, two years after his father's death, Meade resigned his commission and returned to Philadelphia, where he became a successful stockbroker. He was active in a number of patriotic organizations, and spent much of his life defending his father's actions at the Battle of Gettysburg.[29] After suffering from kidney problems, Meade died on February 2, 1897, at the age of fifty-three. He was buried in Laurel Hill Cemetery, not far from his father and several other members of the Lancers, including Furness, James H. Starr, and Richard H. Rush.[30]

Rudolph Ellis, who served in the First City Troop and as captain of Company B of the Lancers, came back to Philadelphia upon the expiration of his term of service in the fall of 1864. He returned to private life and immediately established himself in the banking business, becoming the senior member of a very successful brokerage firm called R. Ellis & Company, where he was associated with the J. P. Morgan family interests in Pennsylvania. In 1901, he became president of Fidelity Trust Company, a major banking institution. He also served as a director of the Pennsylvania Railroad and several other Philadelphia banking institutions. Ellis was a member of MOLLUS and the Lancers' alumni association, and was involved in several social clubs, including the Germantown

Cricket Club and the Radnor Hunt Club. In 1912, Ellis donated $100,000 to establish the Rudulph Ellis Gratuity Fund of the Fidelity Trust Company, to be used for the relief of sick employees of the bank, and also to provide a pension for retired employees. "Mr. Ellis was the instigator of the gift, the greatest ever given to employees of any firm in the city," noted his obituary. He died in September 1915 at the age of seventy-eight.[31]

Maj. Charles Brinton Coxe, who had been born into a very affluent family and who was a cousin of Maj. Gen. George Brinton McClellan, grew even more wealthy after the war. His grandfather, Tench Coxe, had started an anthracite coal mining empire in northeastern Pennsylvania, and Charles Coxe became a partner in a venture called Coxe Brothers and Company with several of his brothers. Within a few years, the company owned nine huge collieries. Within twenty years of the company's founding, it was the largest anthracite coal producer in the United States. In 1866, Coxe became an honorary member of the First Troop Philadelphia City Cavalry, rejoining some of his old comrades from the Lancers in re-fighting their battles. When he died at the young age of thirty on January 3, 1873, Charles B. Coxe was one of the wealthiest men in the United States. He was buried in venerable Christ Church Burial Ground in the oldest section of Philadelphia, not far from the graves of his wealthy grandfather, Benjamin Franklin, and Colonel Rush's patriot ancestor, Dr. Benjamin Rush.[32]

Capt. William Redwood Wright, who became commander of Company B at the precocious age of nineteen, also became a wealthy banker and member of Philadelphia's social elite after the war. He joined his grandfather's successful shipping firm and then became very active in Democratic politics in Philadelphia. In 1888 and 1892, he was Democratic candidate for the position of presidential elector, but was unsuccessful in winning either election. He was appointed city and county treasurer of Philadelphia in 1891, and held office for about a year. After resigning as treasurer, Wright and his brother founded a very successful banking firm called S. L. & W. R. Wright, which he ran until his death at sixty-eight in 1914. He was also a prominent member of the Germantown Cricket Club, where he maintained his long-time friendship with Fred Newhall. He also belonged to a prominent social club called "The Famous State in Schuylkill," which maintained its headquarters on the Schuylkill River's Boathouse Row and was considered high society. Wright's beautiful home, Waldheim, was donated to Philadelphia's LaSalle University, but was demolished during the Depression years. Its foundation can still be found on LaSalle's campus.[33]

After resigning his commission as a major in 1864 as a result of wounds received in combat, Benoni Lockwood briefly returned to Philadelphia. In 1866, he relocated to New York City, where he spent the rest of his life. He was a principal in the successful insurance agency of Frame, Hare & Lockwood, which was established as the American office of the London Assurance Corporation in 1873. Lockwood was elected vice president of the Board of Fire Underwriters in 1902, and was then elected president of that organization two years later. His wife, Florence, was the sister of Thomas Bayard, the

Secretary of State during Grover Cleveland's presidency, meaning that he was well-connected politically. He was a member of MOLLUS and the City and Downtown Clubs of New York. He died in New York on April 27, 1909, and was buried at Swan's Point Cemetery in Providence, Rhode Island.[34]

John P. Rausenberger of Company C devoted much of his postwar life to serving the poor. After the war, he worked for a time in a meat and provision store, and later opened his own stores, first in Philadelphia, and later in Camden, New Jersey. However, in 1869, he suffered a terrible injury while getting off a train. His foot was so badly crushed that it had to be amputated. However, the injury did not slow him down. In 1879, he opened a store in Germantown, which he ran for fifteen years. He retired in 1893, at the age of fifty. In 1900, he was elected a member of the local school board, and the next year, he was elected to the Germantown city council. In 1902, he was appointed superintendent of the local almshouse. He outlived his wife by fifteen years, and died on July 24, 1924, at the age of seventy-six. He was buried at Ivy Hill Cemetery in Germantown.[35]

Dr. William Moss, the regiment's original surgeon, returned home to Philadelphia after completing his service as United States Service. He resumed his private practice as a surgeon, and was "prominent in the medical profession and social circles of this city for many years," as a local newspaper observed. "He was a prominent member of Mickve Israel Synagogue, and was married to Miss Mary Noronha, who died several years ago." His daughter, Mary Moss, was a well-known novelist and literary critic. Dr. Moss died at the age of seventy-seven on October 30, 1907, after a long and productive life.[36]

Charles L. Leiper's military career ended with his discharge in 1865. Leiper was just twenty-two years old, and he was a brevet brigadier general of volunteers, the only member of the Lancers to achieve that rank.[37] He became a successful manufacturer of textiles and owned his own business. He was active in various veterans' associations, including the Grand Army of the Republic and MOLLUS. He served as the president of the Rush's Lancers alumni association for many years, and was also very active in various civic associations in and around Philadelphia.[38] Leiper died on May 14, 1899, and was buried at Middletown Presbyterian Churchyard, in Delaware County. Many of his former comrades in arms attended his funeral. His active and honorary pallbearers were all former members of the Lancers, including Charles E. Cadwalader, M.D., Frank Dorsey, William W. Frazier, Frank Furness, Michael Golden, William J. Roney, W. W. Sweisfort, George Sykes, William Treas, William P. C. Treichel, John Wagner, and William Redwood Wright.[39] Furness designed a handsome granite monument to mark the grave. The monument contains the following inscription: "1861-1865—Sixth Pennsylvania Cavalry Lancers. In memory of Brevet Brigadier General Charles L. Leiper, Colonel Sixth Pennsylvania Cavalry. Erected by surviving members of the regiment, May 1900." It was one of Furness' finest works. More than two thousand people attended the dedication of the monument, including most of the surviving members of the regiment.[40]

James H. Starr, the Harvard-trained lawyer who commanded the regiment for much of 1864, received a brevet to colonel of volunteers for his valor during the 1864 Valley Campaign. At the close of the war, he took an active role in the reorganization of the Pennsylvania National Guard, and served as division inspector, assistant adjutant general, and judge advocate general of the First Division of the Guard. In March 1875, he was offered command of a division, but declined the appointment. In 1876, he was appointed Marshal of the Department of Public Order for the Centennial Exhibition, which was held in Philadelphia, and organized the police force. Starr also continued to practice law throughout his service in the National Guard, and was an early supporter of municipal reform. He ran for prothonotary of the District Court in 1872, and served as an assistant attorney general for a time. "He was much respected as a lawyer and as a man and in the military circles was held in very high esteem as an accomplished, brave, and faithful soldier," proclaimed the *Philadelphia Times*.[41]

"He never fully recovered from the severe strain made upon his constitution by the war," recalled a Harvard classmate. "On the evening of 22 August, 1881, he had a severe chill, succeeded by fever, and, after much suffering, he died from typhoid-pneumonia at half past one p.m., 1 September." A large number of the Lancers, with Colonel Rush at their head, were drawn up in open ranks upon the path leading to the church door, and Cadwalader, Frazier, Leiper, George Meade, Newhall, and Treichel served as his pallbearers. Starr was buried in Laurel Hill Cemetery, just a few steps from the grave of his former commander, Colonel Rush.[42]

George E. Clymer, who resigned his commission as major in early 1863, briefly returned to his hometown of Reading, where he and his brothers operated a successful iron furnace. He spent the years 1866-1868 in the mining business in New Mexico and Nevada. In 1870, Clymer severed his ties with his brothers, and relocated to his wife's hometown of Cincinnati, where he acquired an interest in the Swift Iron and Steel Works of Newport, Kentucky, of which his father-in-law was the president. In 1874, Clymer became vice president of the company. In 1884, after the death of his wife, he returned to Reading and again became involved with the family's iron furnace business. After the death of one of his brothers, Clymer bought out his remaining brother's interest in the business, which he ran successfully until his retirement in 1893. Clymer died on July 6, 1895, and was buried in Charles Evans Cemetery in Reading.[43]

Postwar financial success was not reserved to the officers of the regiment. In the fall of 1864, following his discharge from the Lancers, Charles H. Masland was employed at a dye house owned by John Tingley in Germantown, Philadelphia. After two years, Charles, his brother James, and Sgt. Joe Scargle, his close friend and fellow Lancer, formed a partnership and purchased the business from Tingley. In 1868, the brothers purchased an abandoned vinegar plant and converted it into a dye house. They named the plant Allegheny Dye Works, and conducted business under the name of C. H. Masland and Brother. They used this name until Charles bought out his brother, when the name was changed to C. H. Masland. The business prospered.

After selling the dye works in 1886, Masland purchased the Anchor Carpet Mills, and changed the name to C. H. Masland Sons. Eventually four of Masland's sons had a hand in running this company, which flourished and by the early 1900s was a successful venture employing many workers. Philadelphia, however, was the scene of many bitter union battles, prompting the officers of the company to decide to build a new plant and eventually its corporate headquarters in Carlisle, Pennsylvania, in 1919. The company eventually became the largest supplier of automotive carpet in the United States before it was sold to Burlington Industries in 1986. Charles Henry Masland remained in Philadelphia for the rest of his life, living to the ripe old age of ninety-three, one of the last survivors of the Lancers. He was the final president of the regimental alumni association.[44]

Of course, not all the men who served in the Lancers equaled the accomplishments of the men profiled above. Several profiles of the postwar lives of common soldiers illustrate what the lives of most looked like.

William W. Maree, a Delaware native, had enlisted in Company A of the Lancers in 1861 at the age of twenty. He served out his term of service and took his discharge in August 1864, returning home to Delaware, where he resumed his farming career. In a ceremony presided over by Chaplain Gracey, he married Mary Robinson Bennett on March 2, 1868. Their union produced nine children. However, an influenza epidemic took Mary's life at the age of forty-two, leaving him to raise his seven remaining children alone (the youngest was six at the time of Mary's death). He was active in the regimental veterans' association and the Grand Army of the Republic, and regularly attended reunions of the Lancers (he appears in the photograph of the 1912 reunion). The hernia that he suffered during the Peninsula Campaign when his horse was shot out from under him and landed on him caused him health problems for the rest of his life, and his eyesight eventually failed. William Maree died at age seventy-two on May 6, 1914, and was buried in Hickory Grove Cemetery in Saint Georges, Delaware.[45]

The men of the Lancers understandably were very proud of their service and of their accomplishments during the Civil War. The Rush's Lancers Veterans' Association was established as soon as the men returned home to Philadelphia.[46] By-laws were drawn up. The Preamble to the By-laws declared:

> We the honorably discharged Soldiers of the 6th Penna. Cavalry, (Rush's Lancers) having aided in maintaining the honor and integrity of the National Government during the late Rebellion, do unite together, to establish a permanent association for the purpose of strengthening and preserving those kind and fraternal feelings which bind together Soldiers, and also to perpetuate the history of the 6th Penna. Cavalry Regiment, as regards its services in suppressing the Rebellion from 1861 to 1865; also to assist such of our former comrades in arms, as need our help and pro-

tection, and to extend needful aid to the widows and orphans of our comrades who have fallen in the discharge of our duties.

Only honorably discharged members of the Lancers who could prove their service in the regiment were eligible for membership. Officers were elected, and annual reunions were planned.[47]

The Lancers held regular reunions at Frazier's estate in Willow Grove, coming together annually on June 9, marking the anniversary of their great moment at the Battle of Brandy Station. For more than five decades, the veterans maintained this tradition. In the 1920s, they changed the date of their reunion to September 17, the anniversary of their bold charge at Antietam. As one former member of the regiment proudly proclaimed in 1897, "to the credit of its officers be it said, the interest in the association does not wane in the least."[48]

In 1888, the veterans gathered at Gettysburg to celebrate the dedication of their regimental monument, which marks the position held by the dismounted skirmishers during the fighting on the afternoon of July 3, 1863. The Veteran Association sent out handsome engraved invitations that included a depiction of the unit's trademark crossed lances insignia, and which stated, "The Veteran Association of the Sixth Pennsylvania Cavalry request the honor of your company at the dedication of their monument, on the Battlefield of Gettysburg, on Sunday, October fourteenth, 1888." George Meade, who was the chairman of the committee responsible for erecting the monument, received a veritable blizzard of letters from former members of the regiment in response.[49]

The main regimental monument sits on the Emmitsburg Road, a few hundred feet south of the stone Currens house that marked the farthest advance by Merritt's brigade that day. Frank Furness designed a unique and memorable monument. Made of granite, it features six full-scale replicas of the lances carried by the men of the 6th Pennsylvania Cavalry. The monument was dedicated on the twenty-fifth anniversary of the battle. Fred Newhall gave a rousing speech that summarized the service of the Lancers during the Gettysburg Campaign, and other dignitaries spoke of the service and sacrifices of the Lancers. A small volume was published to commemorate the occasion. Nearly one hundred former members of the regiment attended the dedication of the monument, although Colonel Rush's absence was conspicuous.[50]

Three years later, a second, smaller monument was also dedicated on the battlefield. This monument, to Companies E and I, the Army of the Potomac's headquarters escort squadron, stands just outside the Widow Leister house, along Taneytown Road, near the Visitor's Center at Gettysburg. This monument contains the following inscription: COS. "E" AND "I", 6TH PENNA. CAVALRY, "LANCERS." RESERVE BRIG.: 1ST DIV. CAV'LY CORPS. ON DUTY AS ESCORT TO MAJ. GEN'L GEORGE G. MEADE, COMD'G ARMY OF THE POTOMAC. ERECTED BY THE SURVIVORS OF THE REGIMENT. General Leiper headed the committee, which also included Emlen N.

Carpenter, W. J. Cramer, Frank D. Dorsey, William W. Frazier, Frank Furness, H. Robeson, George Meade, and W. W. Sweisfort. A. W. Meachen came up with the concept for the monument, which Furness then perfected. The survivors raised the necessary funds, and another dedication ceremony was held on June 8, 1891. John S. Moore of Company E, and Irvine G. Whitehead gave speeches. The fifty-three veterans who attended enjoyed themselves immensely, and a photograph of them clustered around the monument survives.[51]

Two years later, the Lancers reconvened on the battlefield at Gettysburg. They held a large, widely attended campfire outside the Adams County courthouse, and spent two days reminiscing and touring the battlefield with old friends. Unfortunately, Colonel Rush had died a few days earlier, and did not attend this gathering.[52] These visits continued for several years until the ranks of veterans thinned too much for the tradition to go on.

In 1899, the 33rd annual national veterans' encampment of the Grand Army of the Republic was held in Philadelphia. Fifty thousand old soldiers attended the event. Frank Furness chaired the GAR decoration committee, and he designed a triumphal "Avenue of Fame" along Broad Street, lined by sixty-two "battle columns." Like the victorious Roman legions of yore, the old veterans of the GAR would enjoy a grand march down Broad Street before adoring crowds of admirers. The 6th Pennsylvania's Veterans' Association held a reception for their old comrades-in-arms at their headquarters on Walnut Street, gleefully mingling with other grizzled veterans of the Civil War.[53]

On September 8, 1899, the several hundred surviving veterans of the Lancers gathered at their old headquarters on Walnut Street. With Furness leading them, they held their last march, retracing their steps on the day when they left Philadelphia in the fall of 1861. The veterans marched to City Hall, where they passed in review. Col. Albert P. Morrow, wearing his old uniform as a captain in the 6th Pennsylvania Cavalry, and William W. Frazier were among the dignitaries on the reviewing stand that day. "With an enthusiasm which made their step almost as spry as in the old days when they rushed to answer the 'boots and saddles' call on the eve of battle, the survivors of the Sixth Pennsylvania Cavalry Lancers Veteran Association—Rush's Lancers—turned out yesterday on review," reported a Philadelphia newspaper.[54] Another noted, "Throughout the entire route of the parade the distinguished followers of Rush were received with much enthusiasm by the hundreds of spectators who lined the street."[55]

In 1900, a contingent of the surviving Lancers attended Memorial Day services at Trinity Reformed Church in downtown Philadelphia. William W. Frazier gave a speech about the regiment and its officers, and W. J. Roney discussed the role played by the regiment's noncommissioned officers and privates. A large contingent of the veterans attended the services, paying tribute to their fallen comrades. Their ranks were thinning rapidly with each passing year.[56] In 1904, 211 veterans traveled to Gettysburg for a reunion, spending a pleasant evening around the campfire, and also visited the handsome monument on the Emmitsburg Road.[57]

The regimental monuments at Gettysburg. (Author)

By 1907, only 196 veterans remained. The Alumni Association held its forty-second reunion at Capt. Rudulph Ellis' estate, Foxhall Farm, on June 9. One hundred seven of the veterans attended. They heard stirring speeches and swapped war stories. "Rallying around a single yellow banner bearing the names of forty famous battlefields where lay their honored dead; inspired still with that love of country and martial spirit that made them willing to lay down their lives to save the Union in the war of the Rebellion, all that remained of the grey-haired survivors of the Sixth Pennsylvania Cavalry assembled at Foxhall Farm, near Bryn Mawr, yesterday, on the occasion of their forty-second reunion," announced the *Philadelphia Press.* Bvt. Maj. Gen. David M. Gregg attended, and Maj. Gen. James H. Wilson was the principal speaker. Their ranks were thinning, but the Lancers continued to turn out to commemorate their great day at Brandy Station. The only question was, how many more times would they be able to reunite?[58]

Two years later, when the celebrated the forty-seventh anniversary of the Battle of Brandy Station, only 102 remained. Capt. William Redwood Wright hosted the 1909 reunion at his home in Philadelphia's Germantown section, which was attended by fifty-two of the old veterans. "The survivors came from many parts of Pennsylvania and one journeyed from Ohio," reported a local newspaper. "War songs were sung and war stories told." William Rotch Wister, who presented the regimental flag in October 1861, addressed the veterans, who included George W. Frazier, Frank Furness, Albert P.

The surviving veterans of the 6th Pennsylvania Cavalry at the dedication of the monument to Cos. E and I, taken at General Meade's headquarters, Gettysburg, PA, October 8, 1891. (Author)

Morrow, Ellis Pugh, and James Stall. Several judges and General St. Clair Mulholland attended the festivities. Their ranks thinned further with the passage of each day.[59]

The Lancers celebrated the fifty-fourth anniversary of the Battle of Brandy Station on June 9, 1917. The United States was about to go to war again, this time against the Central Powers of Europe. Soon enough, more eager, patriotic young men would be going off to die for a glorious cause in lands far from home. Three officers—William W. Frazier, Michael A. Golden, and Thomas W. Neill—attended, as did fifty-three surviving enlisted men. Although the clouds of war were rapidly gathering, the veterans nevertheless enjoyed their fellowship and basked in each other's company again. Nobody knew how many more reunions they would have.[60]

By 1931, only five members of the regiment still survived. Charles H. Masland, the youngest of the four, was eighty-nine years old. They held their annual reunion dinner at the home of the son of William W. Frazier, Benjamin West Frazier, who served as the secretary of the Veterans' Association, though he was not himself a veteran. "In welcoming the veterans, Mr. and Mrs. Frazier were continuing a yearly custom of long standing," noted a newspaper account. "Until his death in 1921, Captain Frazier for a great many years had been host to his old comrades at their annual reunion, held at his farm at Willow Grove." The other survivors included Lewis Warley, the oldest at ninety-six, Edgar H. Klemroth, John H. Miller, and John Sterrett. After viewing their tattered regimental colors and the guidon of Frazier's old Company B, the old veterans exchanged recollections of their battles and skirmishes. Maj. James Starr, son of the former commander of the regiment, also attended, as did relatives of a few other veterans.[61] "The memory of 'Rush's Lancers' is to be perpetuated by an endowment for maintenance of free beds in hospitals, which obtained its nucleus through a gift of $5000 by the late

The surviving veterans of Rush's Lancers, taken at Devil's Den on the Gettys-burg battlefield during the October 1912 reunion. (Author)

Major Charles J. Coxe, a veteran of the regiment," reported a Philadelphia newspaper. "This regimental fund has more than doubled."[62]

A wonderful photograph of that final reunion remains.[63] In it, the five surviving members, joined by Benjamin Frazier, stand rigidly at attention. One holds his saber at the salute position, and two others hold their lances. Sixty-five years had passed since war's end, but these old men retained their military bearing, still proudly bore their weapons. For a moment, the years melted away, and the five surviving Lancers were young once again, eager to ride into glory and into legend, with the hell-for-leather charge at the guns at St. James Church not yet within contemplation. Soon, that magical moment ended, and the last remnants of the 6th Pennsylvania Cavalry slowly faded into history's warm embrace. So ended the story of one of the finest cavalry regiments of the American Civil War.

Campaigns of the
Sixth Pennsylvania Cavalry

THE SIXTH PENNSYLVANIA CAVALRY was also known by its nickname or local designation of Rush's Lancers. In addition to this name, the regiment, like almost all Civil War units, was frequently known by an alternate designation derived from the name of its commanding officer. Names of this type used by or for the regiment are shown below.

Richard H. Rush's Cavalry
Charles L. Leiper's Cavalry
John H. McArthur's Cavalry
C. Ross Smith's Cavalry
Albert P. Morrow's Cavalry
Robert Morris, Jr.'s Cavalry
John H. Gardner's Cavalry
George H. Clymer's Cavalry
Henry C. Whelan's Cavalry
J. Henry Hazeltine's Cavalry
William P. C. Treichel's Cavalry
James Starr's Cavalry
Abraham D. Price's Cavalry
Charles B. Coxe's Cavalry
Bernard H. Harkness's Cavalry

On December 10, 1861, the Sixth Pennsylvania Cavalry was ordered to Washington, D.C., where it joined the Army of the Potomac. It served on provost duty with that Army until the following May, remaining with the Army of the Potomac until August 1864. It then joined the Army of the Shenandoah. In November 1864, the regiment returned to service in that Army for the remainder of its career. Listed below are the specific higher command assignments of the regiment.

Emory's Brigade, Cooke's Cavalry Division, Cavalry Reserve, Army of the Potomac
Dec. 1861–July 1862

Emory's Second Brigade, Cavalry Division, Army of the Potomac
July 1862–Aug. 1862

Third Brigade, Pleasonton's Cavalry Division, Army of the Potomac
July 1862–Nov. 1862

Headquarters, Left Grand Division, Army of the Potomac
Nov. 1862–Feb. 1863

Reserve Brigade, Cavalry Corps, Army of the Potomac
Feb. 1863–June 1863

Reserve Brigade, First Division, Cavalry Corps, Army of the Potomac
June 1863–Aug. 1864

Third (Reserve) Brigade, First Cavalry Division, Cavalry Corps, Army of the Shenandoah
Aug. 1864–Nov. 1864

Third (Reserve) Brigade, First Cavalry Division, Cavalry Corps, Army of the Potomac
Nov. 1864–June 1865

The Sixth Pennsylvania Cavalry participated in a large number of various engagements during its career. These are identified below.

Scout to Hunter's Mills, VA	March 19, 1862
Advance from Fortress Monroe to Yorktown, VA	May 3–5, 1862
Reconnaissance to New Castle and Hanovertown Ferry, VA	May 22, 1862
Reconnaissance to Hanover Court House, VA	May 24, 1862
Skirmish, Hanover Court House, VA (Company C)	May 25, 1862
Operations about Hanover Court House, VA	May 27–29, 1862
Skirmish, Hanover Court House, VA (Company A)	May 27, 1862
Occupation, Ashland, VA	May 30, 1862
Reconnaissance to Hanover Court House, VA	June 10–12, 1862
Operations against Stuart's Raid about White House, VA	June 12–15, 1862
Skirmish, Garlick's Landing, Pamunkey River, VA	June 13, 1862
Seven Days Battles, VA	June 25–July 1, 1862
Affair, Beaver Dam Station, VA (Companies B, C, G, and H)	June 26, 1862
Battles, Gaines's Mill, Cold Harbor, Chickahominy, VA	June 27, 1862
Battle, Glendale, Frazier's Farm, Charles City Crossroads, New Market Crossroads, Willis Church, VA	June 30, 1862
Battle, Malvern Hill, Crew's Farm, VA (Company F)	July 1, 1862
Skirmishes, Falls Church, VA	Sept. 2–4, 1862
Maryland Campaign	Sept. 6–22, 1862
Skirmish, South Mountain, MD	Sept. 13, 1862
Skirmish, Jefferson, MD	Sept. 13, 1862
Battle, Crampton's Gap, South Mountain, MD (Companies B, G, and I)	Sept. 14, 1862
Battle, Antietam, Sharpsburg, MD (Companies B, G, and I)	Sept. 16–17, 1862
Action, Sharpsburg, Shepherdstown, and Blackford's Ford (Boteler's Ford) and Williamsport, MD	Sept. 19, 1862
Operations in Loudoun, Fauquier, and Rappahannock Counties, VA	Oct. 26–Nov. 10, 1862
Actions, Bloomfield and Upperville, VA	Nov. 2–3, 1862
Battle, Fredericksburg, VA	Dec. 12–15, 1862
Skirmish, Occoquan River, VA (Companies B and G)	Dec. 19, 1862

Burnside's "Mud March," VA (Companies A, D, and E)	Jan. 20–24, 1863
Chancellorsville Campaign	April 27–May 6, 1863
Stoneman's Raid, VA (Company L)	April 29–May 8, 1863
Skirmish, Raccoon Ford, VA (detachment)	April 30, 1863
Engagement, Brandy Station and Beverly Ford, VA	June 9, 1863
Reconnaissance to Ashby's Gap, VA (Company A)	June 14, 1863
Gettysburg Campaign	June 9–July 24, 1863
Skirmish, Greencastle, PA	June 20, 1863
Battle, Gettysburg, PA	July 1–3, 1863
Action, Williamsport, MD	July 6, 1863
Action, Boonsboro, MD	July 8, 1863
Skrimishes at and near Funkstown, MD	July 10–13, 1863
Skirmish, Aldie, VA (detachment)	July 11, 1863
Skirmishes, Kelly's Ford, VA	July 31–Aug. 1, 1863
Action, Brandy Station, VA	Aug. 1, 1863
Advance from the Rappahannock to the Rapidan, VA	Sept. 13–17, 1863
Bristoe Campaign	Oct. 9–22, 1863
Skirmish, Manassas Junction, VA	Oct. 17, 1863
Skirmish, Bristoe Station, Kettle Run, VA	Oct. 18, 1863
Advance to the line of the Rappahannock, VA	Nov. 7–8, 1863
Mine Run Campaign, VA	Nov. 26–Dec. 2, 1863
Demonstration on the Rapidan, VA	Feb. 5–7, 1864
Custer's Raid in Albemarle County, VA	Feb. 26–Mar. 1, 1864
Skirmish near Charlottesville, VA	Feb. 29, 1864
Skirmish, Burton's Ford, Rapidan River, VA	March 1, 1864
Skirmish, Stannardsville, VA	March 1, 1864
Wilderness Campaign	May 4–June 12, 1864
Engagement, Todd's Tavern, VA	May 7–8, 1864
Sheridan's Raid from Todd's Tavern to the James River, VA	May 9–24, 1864
Engagement, Ground Squirrel Church, South Anna River, and Yellow Tavern, Richmond, VA (separate detachments involved in separate actions)	May 11, 1864
Engagement, Meadow Bridge, Chickahominy River, VA	May 12, 1864
Combat, Mechanicsville, VA	May 12, 1864
Operations on the line of the Pamunkey River, VA	May 26–28, 1864
Action, Hanovertown, Pamunkey River, VA	May 27, 1864
Skirmish, Hanovertown Ferry, VA	May 27, 1864
Operations on the line of the Totopotomoy Creek, VA	May 28–31, 1864
Engagement, Old Church, VA	May 30, 1864
Action, Mattadequin Creek, VA	May 30, 1864

Combat, Bethesda Church, VA	May 31–June 1, 1864
Engagement, Cold Harbor, VA	May 31–June 1, 1864
Skirmish, McClellan's [Bottom's] Bridge, VA	June 2, 1864
Skirmishes, Haw's Shop, VA	June 4–5, 1864
Sheridan's Trevilian Raid, VA	June 7–24, 1864
Battle, Trevilian Station, Central R.R., VA	June 11–12, 1864
Action, Newark (Mallory's Cross Roads), VA	June 12, 1864
Action, Black River (Tunstall's Station) and White House (St. Peter's Church), VA	June 21, 1864
Action, Jones' Bridge, VA	June 23, 1864
Siege operations against Petersburg and Richmond, VA	July 4–30, 1864
Demonstration on the North Side of the James River and Engagements at Deep Bottom (Darbytown), Strawberry Plains, and New Market Road, VA	July 27–29, 1864
Engagement, Charles City Cross Roads, VA	July 27–28, 1864
Engagement, Malvern Hill, VA	July 28, 1864
Sheridan's Campaign in the Shenandoah Valley, VA	Aug. 7–Nov. 28, 1864
Action near Stone Chapel, VA	Aug. 10, 1864
Action, Toll Gate near White Post, VA	Aug. 11, 1864
Action near Newtown, VA	Aug. 11, 1864
Skirmish near Strasburg, VA	Aug. 14, 1864
Skirmish, Summit Point, WV	Aug. 21, 1864
Skirmish, Summit Point, WV	Aug. 23–24, 1864
Action near Kearneysville, WV	Aug. 25, 1864
Skirmishes, Leetown and Smithfield, WV	Aug. 28, 1864
Engagement, Smithfield, Crossing of the Opequon, WV	Aug. 29, 1864
Sheridan's Expedition from Winchester, VA	Feb. 27–March 25, 1865
Engagement, Waynesboro, VA	March 2, 1865
Appomattox Campaign, VA	March 28–April 9, 1865
Skirmishes on the line of Hatcher's and Gravelly Runs, VA	March 30, 1865
Engagement, Dinwiddie Court House, VA	March 30–31, 1865
Battle, Five Forks, VA	April 1, 1865
Action, Scott's Cross Roads, VA	April 2, 1865
Skirmish, Tabernacle Church (Beaver Dam Creek), VA	April 4, 1865
Engagement, Sailor's Creek, VA	April 6, 1865
Engagement, Appomattox Station, VA	April 8, 1865
Engagement, Clover Hill, Appomattox Court House, VA	April 9, 1865
Surrender, Appomattox Court House, VA	April 9, 1865
Expedition from Burkesville and Petersburg to Danville and South Boston, VA	April 23–29, 1865

On May 2, 1865, the regiment was ordered from Danville to Washington, D.C. On May 23, 1865, it took part in the Grand Review of Eastern Armies held there. The regiment was consolidated with the First and Seventeenth Pennsylvania Cavalry Regiments on June 17, 1865, to form the Second Pennsylvania Provisional Cavalry. This regiment was moved to Louisville and Lebanon, Kentucky, a short time later. It was mustered out of Federal service at Lebanon on August 7, 1865.

NOTES

PREFACE

1 Samuel L. Gracey, *Annals of the Sixth Pennsylvania Cavalry* (Philadelphia: E. H. Butler & Co., 1868), 159.

2 The cavalry charge was trained in three types: in-line, in-column, and as foragers. It was most important to keep the horses straight and moving toward the objective. The charge consisted of the commands: "Forward, Guides right (or left), March!" After twenty paces, the command was "Trot March!" and after another sixty paces, "Gallop March!" After another eighty paces, the final command was "CHARGE!" The area of ground to be covered by the charge should be short as possible, so as to arrive in good order and without fatiguing the horses. J. R. Poinsett, *Cavalry Tactics, Second Part, School of the Trooper, of the Platoon and of the Squadron Mounted* (Washington, D.C.: J. and G. S. Gideon Printers, 1841), 173.

3 Gracey, *Annals*, 159.

CHAPTER 1. FORMATION OF THE SIXTH PENNSYLVANIA CAVALRY

1 J. Matthew Gallman, *Mastering Wartime: A Social History of Philadelphia During the Civil War* (New York: Cambridge University Press, 1990), 1.

2 To find a detailed narrative of the first three centuries of the City of Brotherly Love's history, see Russell Weigley, *Philadelphia: A 300-Year History* (New York: W. W. Norton, 1982).

3 For a detailed discussion of the national bank crisis, see Robert V. Remini, *Andrew Jackson and the Bank War: A Study in the Growth of Presidential Power* (New York: W. W. Norton, 1967).

4 Gallman, *Mastering Wartime*, 253-254.

5 Ibid., 1.

6 Ibid., 2.

7 Ibid., 3.

8 Diary of Sarah Butler Wister, entry for April 15, 1861, Wister Papers, Historical Society of Pennsylvania, Philadelphia.

9 Nicholas B. Wainwright, ed., *A Philadelphia Perspective: The Diary of Sidney George Fisher* (Philadelphia: Historical Society of Pennsylvania, 1967), 386.

10 Nicholas B. Wainwright, "Education of an Artist: The Diary of Joseph Boggs Beale," *Pennsylvania Magazine of History and Biography* (October 1973), 500, entry for April 30, 1861.

11 Frank H. Taylor, *Philadelphia in the Civil War* (Philadelphia: privately published, 1879), 48-184.

12 John C. Waugh, *Class of 1846* (New York: Warner Books, 1994), xiv-xvi.

13 Francis B. Heitman, *Historical Register and Dictionary of the United States Army, from Its Organization, September 29, 1789, to March 2, 1903*, 2 vols. (Washington, D.C.: U.S. Government Printing Office, 1903), 1.852.

14 Statement of Richard Henry Rush, W. M. Meredith Papers, Misc. Correspondence, Historical Society of Pennsylvania, Philadelphia.

15 George Archibald McCall to Peter McCall, May 27, 1861, Cadwalader Collection, Collection No. 1454, Historical Society of Pennsylvania, Philadelphia.

16 Joseph Blaschek, "The Story of Rush's Lancers," *National Tribune*, June 24, 1897.

17 Thomas A. Newhall to William Meredith, October 11, 1861, Collection No. 1199, J. K. Stoddard Collection, Correspondence of the Newhall Family, Historical Society of Pennsylvania, Philadelphia; Gracey, *Annals*, 359-60; Richard H. Rush to William M. Meredith, October 11, 1861, Meredith Papers, Historical Society of Pennsylvania, Philadelphia.

18 William H. Egle, ed., *Andrew Gregg Curtin: His Life and Services* (Philadelphia: Avil Printing Co., 1895), 417-420.

19 Richard H. Rush service records, Entry for October-November, 1861, National Archives and Records Administration, Washington, D.C. (hereafter NARA).

20 *Philadelphia Public Ledger*, September 1, 1861; *Philadelphia Sunday Dispatch*, September 1, 1861. The pay scale listed in the ad was as follows: $22 per month for sergeant major, chief bugler and quartermaster sergeant; $21 per month for orderly sergeant; $18 per month for other sergeants; $16 per month for farriers and blacksmiths; $15 per month for corporals and buglers; $13 for privates.

21 Regimental recruiting poster owned by Mitchell E. McGlynn, Alexandria, Virginia.

22 Lewis J. Boos memoir, Civil War Papers, Box 9, Historical Society of Pennsylvania, Philadelphia (hereafter Boos Memoir, HSP), 1.

23 *Philadelphia Inquirer*, September 4, 1861.

24 *Philadelphia Public Ledger*, September 10, 1861.

25 Gracey, *Annals*, 19.

26 *Philadelphia Inquirer*, September 25, 1861.

27 For a detailed description of what was involved with raising, equipping, and training a regiment of cavalry, see Stephen Z. Starr, *The Union Cavalry in the Civil War*, 3 vols. (Baton Rouge: Louisiana State University Press, 1979), 1:47-165.

28 Gracey, *Annals*, 35.

29 Hamilton S. Ballentine to William S. Ballentine, March 27, 1863, Hamilton S. Ballentine Letters, Richard Carlile Collection, Dayton, Ohio (hereafter Ballentine Letters). All letters cited below as "Ballentine to Ballentine" were from Hamilton to William.

30 Michael J. Lewis, *Frank Furness: Architecture and the Violent Mind* (New York: W. W. Norton, 2001), 47.

31 *First Troop Philadelphia City Cavalry* (Philadelphia: Published by the Troop, 1991), 1.

32 *Philadelphia Inquirer*, August 15, 1861.

33 The First City Troop remains an ongoing, active unit today. It proudly claims the longest continuous service of any American military unit. Today, its troopers ride tanks and armored personnel carriers, but its men continue to perform the traditional roles of horse cavalry, scouting, and screening.

34 *Philadelphia Inquirer*, August 15, 1861.

35 *First Troop*, 6-7. The thirteen officers were Robert Morris, Jr., Edwin L. Tevis, G. Irvine Whitehead, Charles E. Richards, James H. Haseltine, Charles E. Cadwalader, Charles L. Leiper, Rudulph Ellis, Emlen N. Carpenter, Osgood Welsh, Charles B. Coxe, T. Campbell Oakman, and Thomas W. Neill. The First City Troop proudly claims Co. E of the Sixth Pennsylvania Cavalry in its direct line.

36 James H. Stevenson, *"Boots and Saddles": A History of the First Volunteer Cavalry of the War, Known as the First New York (Lincoln) Cavalry, and also as The Sabre Regiment, Its Organization, Campaigns and Battles* (Harrisburg, Pa.: Patriot Publishing, 1879), 13-18.

37 Edward J. Nichols, *Toward Gettysburg: A Biography of General John F. Reynolds* (State College: Penn State University Press, 1958), 73.

38 Taylor, *Philadelphia in the Civil War*, 23-24. Landis was married to a sister of Maj. Gen. John F. Reynolds of Lancaster, who was killed in action at Gettysburg on July 1, 1863. Ironically, Chapman Biddle commanded one of Reynolds's infantry brigades.

39 Heitman, *Historical Register*, 1:652; see, also, James R. Arnold, *Jeff Davis's Own: Cavalry, Comanches and the Battle for the Texas Frontier* (New York: John Wiley & Sons, 2000), 335. McArthur received a promotion to major in September 1862, as a reward for surviving the suicidal charge of the 5th U.S. at Gaines's Mill in June 1862. In the spring of that year, McArthur fell victim to typhoid fever but recovered in time to lead the regiment in the Peninsula Campaign. However, he had a relapse in the fall and had to resign his commission in November, less than sixty days after receiving the promotion to major. Arnold, *Jeff Davis's Own*, 335.

40 George Meade, *The Life and Letters of George Gordon Meade*, George Gordon Meade, ed., 2 vols. (New York: Charles Scribner's Sons, 1913), 1:xv-1.

41 "Death of a Prominent Surgeon," *Germantown Guide*, November 2, 1907.

42 Gracey, *Annals*, 36.

43 Eric J. Wittenberg, ed., *"We Have It Damn Hard Out Here": The Civil War Letters of Sgt. Thomas W. Smith, Sixth Pennsylvania Cavalry* (Kent, Ohio: Kent State University Press, 1999), 26.

44 *Philadelphia Inquirer*, September 30, 1861.

45 Gracey, *Annals*, 34.

46 Ibid., 357.

47 Ibid., 34, 357.

48 C. M. Ruff to Montgomery Meigs, August 12, 1861, "Horses, 1861," Box 839, Quartermaster Consolidated Correspondence, File 1794-1915, NARA.

49 Gracey, *Annals*, 20; *Philadelphia Inquirer*, September 25, 1861.

50 Gracey, *Annals*, 358.

51 *Philadelphia Inquirer*, October 3, 1861.

52 Richard H. Rush to Andrew G. Curtin, October 2, 1861, "Muster Rolls & Related Records, 1861-1866, 70th Regt.-6th Cavalry," Records of the Department of Military Affairs, RG 19, Office of the Adjutant General, Pennsylvania State Archives, Harrisburg, Pennsylvania.

53 *Philadelphia Inquirer*, October 7, 1861.

54 *Philadelphia Sunday Dispatch*, October 6, 1861.

55 Ibid., October 27, 1861.

56 RG 94, #120, Histories of Commands from Organization to March 31st, 1863, NARA.

57 *Philadelphia Inquirer*, October 18, 1861.

58 *The War of the Rebellion: A Compilation of the Official Records of the Union and Confederate Armies*, 128 vols. in 3 series (Washington, D.C.: U.S. Government Printing Office, 1880-1901), Series 3, Vol. 1, 606 (hereafter O.R.; unless otherwise noted, all future references are to series 1 of the Official Records).

59 *Philadelphia Inquirer*, October 30, 1861.

60 Gracey, *Annals*, 23.

61 *Philadelphia Inquirer*, October 31, 1861.

62 Ibid.

63 Ibid.

64 Ibid., November 4, 1861.

65 "Lancers and Dragoons," *Army and Navy Journal*, November 14, 1863.

66 Blaschek, "The Story of Rush's Lancers."

67 *Philadelphia Sunday Dispatch*, November 3, 1861.

68 Gracey, *Annals*, 26 and 360.

69 Ibid., 360.

70 Lewis, *Frank Furness*, 32. Unfortunately, the drawing did not survive the war.

71 Blaschek, "The Story of Rush's Lancers."

72 "Lancers and Dragoons."

73 Robert F. O'Neill, Jr., "The Federal Cavalry on the Peninsula," in William J. Miller, ed., *The Peninsula Campaign of 1862: Yorktown to the Seven Days* (Campbell, Calif.: Savas Publishing, 1997), 3:87; O.R. series 3, vol. 1, 622.

74 *Philadelphia Inquirer*, November 23, 1861.

75 Richard H. Rush to Andrew G. Curtin, November 21, 1861, Pennsylvania State Archives, Harrisburg, Pennsylvania.

76 Gracey, *Annals*, 362.

77 The 6th Pennsylvania suffered its first casualty on November 24. Private Jacob James, a member of Company F, broke his leg when his horse fell on top of him during mounted drills. The horseman was taken to Episcopal Hospital, where his injured leg was treated. *Philadelphia Inquirer*, November 25, 1861.

78 Robert Milligan to Dear Levi, November 23, 1861, Sue Clark Knight Papers, Wisconsin Historical Society, Madison, Wisconsin.

79 *Philadelphia Sunday Dispatch*, December 1, 1861.

80 *Philadelphia Inquirer*, December 4, 1861.

81 Gracey, *Annals*, 26-27.

82 Sydney L. Wright Memoir, Collection No. 2096, Wright Family Papers, William Redwood Wright Section Folder, Historical Society of Pennsylvania, Philadelphia.

83 *Philadelphia Inquirer*, December 7, 1861.

84 Ibid., December 10, 1861.

85 Ibid., December 14, 1861.

86 Ballentine to Ballentine, December 2, 1861.

CHAPTER 2. LEARNING TO BE SOLDIERS

1 Henry Inch Cowan to his parents, December 10, 1861, Henry Inch Cowan Papers, Annenberg Rare Book and Manuscript Library, University of Pennsylvania, Philadelphia (hereafter Cowan Papers).

2 Gracey, *Annals*, 37.

3 *Philadelphia Sunday Dispatch*, January 26, 1862.

4 Charlton L. Bonham to his parents, January 7, 1862, in Charlton L. Bonham pension file, RG 94, NARA.

5 Gracey, *Annals*, 38.

6 Theodore Sage to Dear Sister, December 24, 1861, Harrisburg Civil War Roundtable Collection, United States Army Military History Institute, Carlisle, Pennsylvania.

7 Cowan to his parents, December 25, 1861.

8 Gracey, *Annals*, 38.

9 *Philadelphia Inquirer*, January 2, 1862.

10 *Philadelphia Sunday Dispatch*, February 2, 1862.

11 Wittenberg, *We Have It Damn Hard Out Here*, 7-8.

12 *Philadelphia Sunday Dispatch*, January 26, 1862.

13 *Philadelphia Inquirer*, February 1, 1862.

14 Cowan to his parents, January 18, 1862.

15 Cowan to his parents, January 8, 1862.

16 Emlen N. Carpenter to Dear Mr. Henszey, January 25, 1862, Alexander R. Chamberlin Collection, United States Army Military History Institute, Carlisle, Pennsylvania.

17 *Philadelphia Inquirer*, February 1, 1862.

18 *Philadelphia Sunday Dispatch*, February 2, 1862.

19 *Philadelphia Inquirer*, February 1, 1862.

20 Ballentine to Ballentine, February 16, 1862; Gracey, *Annals*, 39; Wittenberg, *We Have It Damn Hard Out Here*, 13.

21 *Philadelphia Inquirer*, February 8, 1862; Gracey, *Annals*, 300-301; *Philadelphia Sunday Dispatch*, February 23, 1862.

22 *Philadelphia Sunday Dispatch*, February 2, 1862.

23 Shelby Foote, *The Civil War: A Narrative*, 3 vols. (New York: Vintage Books, 1986), 1:242.

24 Wittenberg, *We Have It Damn Hard Out Here*, 11-12.

25 Milligan to Dear Levi, February 8, 1862, Sue Clark Knight Papers, Wisconsin Historical Society.

26 Wittenberg, *We Have It Damn Hard Out Here*, 15.

27 *Philadelphia Inquirer*, February 1, 1862.

28 Gracey, *Annals*, 39-40.

29 Wittenberg, *We Have It Damn Hard Out Here*, 15.

30 Cowan to his parents, February 23, 1862.

31 Ibid.

32 Cowan to his parents, March 5, 1864.

33 Carpenter to Henszey, March 2, 1862; *Philadelphia Sunday Dispatch*, February 23, 1862.

34 John Booth to his father, January 8, 1862, included in John Booth pension file, RG 94, NARA.

35 Cowan to his parents, March 4, 1862.

36 W. W. H. Davis, *History of the 104th Pennsylvania Regiment from August 22nd, 1861, to September 30th, 1864* (Philadelphia: J. B. Rogers, 1866), 40.

37 *Philadelphia Sunday Dispatch*, February 23, 1862.

38 Ballentine to Ballentine, March 1, 1862.

39 Cowan to his parents, March 9, 1862. Sadly, the full content of this stirring speech has been lost to history, and only the fragment quoted by Cowan survives.

40 Gracey, *Annals*, 40.

41 Gracey, *Annals*, 40.

42 Boos memoir, 2.

43 Ballentine to Ballentine, March 13, 1862.

44 Wittenberg, *We Have It Damn Hard Out Here*, 16-17.

45 Ballentine to Ballentine, March 16, 1862.

46 Milligan to Dear Levi, March 20, 1862.

47 Gracey, *Annals*, 41.

48 Ballentine to Ballentine, March 16, 1862.

49 Wittenberg, *We Have It Damn Hard Out Here*, 18.

50 Cowan to his parents, March 20, 1862.

51 Ballentine to Ballentine, March 29, 1862.

52 Ibid., April 5, 1862.

53 Cowan to his parents, April 2, 1862.

54 Boos memoir, 3.

55 Charles H. Masland to his parents, March 18, 1862, Charles H. Masland letters, Frank Masland collection, Carlisle, Pennsylvania.

56 Wittenberg, *We Have It Damn Hard Out Here*, 19-20.

57 Gracey, *Annals*, 41.

58 Wittenberg, *We Have It Damn Hard Out Here*, 20.

59 Ballentine to Ballentine, April 5, 1862.

60 Wittenberg, *We Have It Damn Hard Out Here*, 20.

61 For a detailed discussion of the duel of the *Monitor* and *Merrimack*, see James L. Nelson, *Reign of Iron: The Story of the First Battling Ironclads, the Monitor and the Merrimack* (New York: William Morrow, 2004).

62 Masland to his parents, April 12, 1862.

63 Ballentine to Ballentine, April 5, 1862.

64 Cowan to his father, April 15, 1862.

65 Masland to his parents, April 12, 1862.

66 Carpenter to Henszey, June 20, 1862.

67 O.R. vol. 11, part 3, 36.

68 Benjamin W. Crowninshield, "Sheridan at Winchester," *Atlantic Monthly*, 42 (1878): 684.

69 Ezra J. Warner, *Generals in Blue* (Baton Rouge: Louisiana State University Press, 1964), 142-143.

70 O'Neill, *The Federal Cavalry*, 49.

71 Col. Alexander Biddle to Dear Julia, October 22, 1862, Rush/Williams/Biddle Family Papers, Series IV: Biddle Family, Box 30, Rosenbach Museum and Library, Philadelphia.

72 See, e.g., Eugene C. Tidball, *No Disgrace to My Country: The Life of John C. Tidball* (Kent, Ohio: Kent State University Press, 2002), 249.

73 Ibid.

74 "A Boy Spy in Dixie: At Army Headquarters," *National Tribune*, April 26, 1888.

75 Ibid.

76 Cowan to his father, April 15, 1862.

77 Hamilton Ballentine described the daily routine: "Our daily calls are as follows: Reveille sounds at 5:00, Stable call at 5:30 when we feed and clean our horses, 6:00 Sick call when the sick, lame and lazy pay their respects to the 1st Serg't and have their names put on the Shisher's list in hopes of being marked off duty by the doctor, 7:00 water call, 7:30 fatigue. Then we prepare for drill or we take our horses to pasture. We generally take them to the banks of the James River. 11:30 Recall sounds, 12:00 dinner call, 1:00 Boots and Saddles sounds for mounted drill; 4:00 Recall, 4:30 Guard Mount, 5:00 water and stable call, 6:00 Retreat then supper, 8:00 Roll call and 9:00 Tattoo." Ballentine also noted that between all of those calls, they had duties to perform which left the men with very little time to themselves. Ballentine to Ballentine, April 26, 1862.

78 *Philadelphia Inquirer*, April 19, 1862.

CHAPTER 3. THE LANCERS IN MCCLELLAN'S 1862 PENINSULA CAMPAIGN

1 Christian Geisel to his sister, April 22, 1862, Christian Geisel Papers, Pennsylvania State Archives, Harrisburg, Pennsylvania (hereafter Geisel Papers).

2 Masland to his parents, May 5, 1862.

3 Geisel to his sister, May 12, 1862.

4 Cowan to his parents, May 3, 1862. Confederate Brig. Gen. Felix K. Zollicoffer, who was terribly nearsighted, mistakenly rode into Union lines at the January 18, 1862, Battle of Mill Springs, giving Cowan something to mock.

5 Cowan to his parents, May 12, 1862.

6 Gracey, *Annals*, 43.

7 O.R. vol. 11, part 1, 633.

8 Wittenberg, *We Have It Damn Hard Out Here*, 25.

9 Ibid., 25-26. Gregg, an extremely competent cavalry officer, commanded a division of the Army of the Potomac's Cavalry Corps in 1863-1864.

10 Alexander Biddle to Julia Biddle, January 19, 1863.

11 Wittenberg, *We Have It Damn Hard Out Here*, 30.

12 Report for Company D, RG 94, #120, History of Commands from Organization to March 31, 1863, NARA.

13 Wittenberg, *We Have It Damn Hard Out Here*, 31.

14 Masland to his parents, May 12, 1862.

15 Wittenberg, *We Have It Damn Hard Out Here*, 31.

16 John P. Kepner to his family, May 12, 1862, John P. Kepner Papers, Virginia Historical Society, Richmond.

17 Gracey, *Annals*, 44. Specifically, this was the place where George Washington courted General Lee's grandmother, Martha Custis.

18 Robert Milligan to Dear Sir, May 17, 1862, Milligan service records, NARA.

19 Ibid. Milligan resigned from the regiment in January 1863 on a Surgeon's Certificate of Disability, resulting from illness contracted in the field. Milligan service records.

20 Gracey, *Annals*, 44.

21 Robert Milligan to Dear Levi, May 18, 1862.

22 Cowan to his parents, May 21, 1862.

23 O.R. vol. 11, part 1, 650.

24 Richard H. Rush to Col. Tyler, May 23, 1862, Lewis Leigh Collection, U.S. Army Military History Institute, Carlisle, Pennsylvania.

25 Judith W. McGuire, *Diary of a Southern Refugee During the War by a Lady of Virginia* (New York: E. J. Hale & Son, 1867), 135-136.

26 Ibid., 147-148. In June, describing the concern of the local citizenry for a wounded Federal officer, Col. Gouverneur K. Warren noted, "Captain Royall seemed to be very much liked by people in the country, many of whom inquired kindly after him, and Mrs. Braxten sent a note to the commanding officer of the Confederate forces, which came to me and which I inclose." O.R. vol. 11, part 1, 1031. It seems highly unlikely that any of the local residents would have asked about the well-being of any of the Lancers.

27 *Supplement to the Official Records of the Union and Confederate Armies*, 100 vols. in 3 series (Wilmington, N.C.: Broadfoot Publishing, 1994), 2:357.

28 Masland to his parents, May 24, 1862.

29 Wittenberg, *We Have It Damn Hard Out Here*, 36.

30 Ibid., 34-35.

31 Theodore Sage to Dear Parents, May 24, 1862.

32 Wittenberg, *We Have It Damn Hard Out Here*, 41.

33 O.R. vol. 11, part 1, 668. This was a ferry across the Pamunkey River, northeast of the town of Hanover Court House. Stephen W. Sears, *To the Gates of Richmond: The Peninsula Campaign* (New York: Ticknor & Fields, 1992), 116.

34 Ibid., 114.

35 For a detailed discussion of the Battle of Hanover Court House, see Michael C. Hardy, *Battle of Hanover Court House: Turning Point of the Peninsula Campaign, May 27, 1862* (Jefferson, N.C.: McFarland, 2006).

36 *Richmond Enquirer*, May 28, 1862.

37 Fitz-John Porter, "Hanover Court-House and Gaines's Mill," in Robert U. Johnson and Clarence C. Buel, eds., *Battles and Leaders of the Civil War*, 4 vols. (New York: Century Publishing, 1884-88), 2:322 (hereinafter referred to as *B&L*).

38 Allan Paul Speer, ed., *Voices from Cemetery Hill: The Civil War Diary, Reports, and Letters of Colonel William Henry Asbury Speer (1861-1864)* (Johnson City, Tenn.: Overmountain Press, 1997), 55-56.

39 Cowan to his parents, June 1, 1862.

40 *New York Times*, June 4, 1862.

41 *Philadelphia Inquirer*, June 14, 1862.

42 Given this success, it is something of a mystery why McClellan did not plan and execute more operations of a similar nature.

43 Wittenberg, *We Have It Damn Hard Out Here*, 39.

44 Ibid.

45 O.R. vol. 12, part 1, 683.

46 Sidney Morris Davis, *Common Soldier, Uncommon War: Life as a Civil War Cavalryman*, Charles F. Cooney, ed. (Bethesda, Md.: SMD Group, 1994), 148.

47 Alexander Biddle to Julia Biddle, January 17, 1863.

48 O.R. vol. 12, part 1, 736.

49 Gracey, *Annals*, 46.

50 Richard H. Rush to Gov. Andrew G. Curtin, May 31, 1862, quoted in Gracey, *Annals*, 47.

51 Ibid.

52 Memorandum of Richard H. Rush, May 31, 1862.

53 Statement of Col. Richard H. Rush, June 3, 1862, NARA.

54 O.R. vol. 11, part 1, 997; August V. Kautz, "Reminiscences of the Civil War," August V. Kautz Papers, USAMHI, 13-14. When he penned his report of this expedition, Kautz wrote, "I could collect no satisfactory information that a force was organizing or existed on the north side of the river, as I supposed in my instructions. Having complied with my instructions I returned to camp with my command this afternoon."

55 Gracey, *Annals*, 49.

56 McGuire, *Diary of a Southern Refugee*, 141-142.

57 Sears, *To the Gates of Richmond*, 168.

58 Emlen N. Carpenter to Mr. Henszey, June 20, 1862.

59 Wittenberg, *We Have It Damn Hard Out Here*, 44.

60 O.R. vol. 11, part 1, 1014; Gracey, *Annals*, 51.

61 O.R. vol. 11, part 1, 1016-1019.

62 Quoted in Gracey, *Annals*, 51-52.

63 *James Starr, Late Colonel Sixth Pennsylvania Cavalry: A Memoir Prepared for the Twenty-Fifth Anniversary of the Class of 1857 in Harvard College, June 28, 1882* (Privately published, 1882), 6.

64 Quoted in Gracey, *Annals*, 51-52.

65 Emlen N. Carpenter to Mr. Henszey, June 20, 1862.

66 John Esten Cooke, "The Ride Around McClellan," *Philadelphia Weekly Times*, July 19, 1879, quoted in Gracey, *Annals*, 51-52.

67 O.R. vol. 11, part 1, 1017.

68 Albert P. Morrow, III, "The Soldier: Albert Payson Morrow, Son of Hugh and Anna Leslie Garnett Morrow, 1842-1911," unpublished manuscript.

69 Wittenberg, *We Have It Damn Hard Out Here*, 45; Gracey, *Annals*, 120.

70 Gracey, *Annals*, 55-56.

71 Wittenberg, *We Have It Damn Hard Out Here*, 46.

72 Gracey, *Annals*, 56-57.

73 William W. Blackford, *War Years with Jeb Stuart* (New York: Charles Scribner's Sons, 1945), 72-73.

74 *A Trooper's Adventures in the War for the Union* (New York: Hurst & Co., 1863), 557.

75 Gracey, *Annals*, 64.

76 Lt. Col. Abraham K. Arnold, "The Cavalry at Gaines' Mill," *Journal of the United States Cavalry Association*, 2 (1889): 358-359.

77 Charles F. James to Dear Sir, January 3, 1899, copy in files, Richmond National Battlefield, Richmond, Virginia.

78 *Philadelphia Inquirer*, July 15, 1862.

79 Masland to his parents, July 5, 1862.

80 Philip St. George Cooke, "The Charge of Cooke's Cavalry at Gaines's Mill," in *B&L*, 4:345. Years after the war, Wesley Merritt wrote, "I thought at the time, and subsequent experience has convinced me, that your cavalry and the audacity of its conduct at that time, together with the rapid firing of canister at short range by the battery mentioned, did much, if not everything, toward preventing the entire destruction of the Union army at Gaines's Mill."

81 O.R. vol. 11, part 2, 45.

82 Quoted in Gracey, *Annals*, 65.

83 O.R. vol. 11, part 2, 226.

84 *Philadelphia Press*, July 21, 1862.

85 Gracey, *Annals*, 77-78. These men included Dr. Ellis, Sgts. Richard M. Sheppard and Harvey Sanderson, Cpl. Jacob K. Long, Bugler Robert B. Beers, and Pvts. William F. Adams, William Marel, William Spears, William Ripley, Thomas L. P. Russell, Albert Konegan, and David Page. *Philadelphia Inquirer*, July 15, 1862.

86 Boos memoir, 4-7; Louis J. Boos service and pension records, NARA.

87 Gracey, *Annals*, 65-67.

88 Robert Knox Sneden, *Eye of the Storm: A Civil War Odyssey*, Nelson D. Lankford, ed. (New York: Free Press, 2000), 76.

89 Gracey, *Annals*, 69-71.

90 Tidball, *No Disgrace to My Country*, 248-249.

91 O.R. vol. 51, part 1, 716-717.

92 General Orders No. 1, Cavalry Division, July 8, 1862, RG 393, General Orders, Special Orders, Sept. 1861-Aug. 1862, NARA.

93 Gracey, *Annals*, 81.

94 Ibid., 80-81.

95 Gracey, *Annals*, 80-81; Sneden, *Eye of the Storm*, 88.

96 William S. Riddell service and pension records, RG 94, NARA. Sgt. Thomas W. Smith had a similar story, suffering with recurring bouts of malaria for years.

97 Lewis, *Frank Furness*, 38.

98 Gracey, *Annals*, 81-82; *Philadelphia Inquirer*, July 19, 1862.

99 Wittenberg, *We Have It Damn Hard Out Here*, 52-53.

100 Charles E. Cadwalader to his brother, July 19, 1862, Collection 1454, Charles E. Cadwalader letters to various persons, Historical Society of Pennsylvania, Philadelphia.

101 *Philadelphia Inquirer*, July 17, 1862.

102 Ballentine to Ballentine, July 24, 1862.

103 Christian Geisel to his sister, August 5, 1862.

104 Wittenberg, *We Have It Damn Hard Out Here*, 52; Gracey, *Annals*, 82; John Booth pension and service files, RG 94, NARA.

105 Geisel to his sister, August 5, 1862.

106 O.R. vol. 11, part 3, 326.

107 Gracey, *Annals*, 83-84; Wittenberg, *We Have It Damn Hard Out Here*, 50.

108 Diary of Samuel P. Heintzelman, entries for August 12 and 14, 1862, Heintzelman Papers, Library of Congress, Washington, D.C.

109 Wittenberg, *We Have It Damn Hard Out Here*, 50-51.

110 O.R. vol. 12, part 3, 737.

111 Averell, "With the Cavalry on the Peninsula," in *B&L*, 2:429.

CHAPTER 4. THE LANCERS IN THE MARYLAND AND FREDERICKSBURG CAMPAIGNS OF 1862

1 Wittenberg, *We Have It Damn Hard Out Here*, 59.

2 Ballentine to Ballentine, September 5, 1862.

3 Charlton L. Bonham to his parents, September 10, 1862, in Charlton L. Bonham pension file, RG 94, NARA.

4 O.R. vol. 19, part 1, 180.

5 Gracey, *Annals*, 87.

6 Wittenberg, *We Have It Damn Hard Out Here*, 59.

7 Gracey, *Annals*, 94.

8 Ibid., 214.

9 Stephen W. Sears, *Landscape Turned Red: The Battle of Antietam* (New York: Ticknor & Fields, 1983), 111-115.

10 O.R. vol. 19, part 1, 825-826.

11 Gracey, *Annals*, 90.

12 David L. Thompson, "In the Ranks of Antietam," *B&L*, 2:556.

13 O.R. vol. 19, part 1, 450.

14 Ibid., 815, 825.

15 Timothy J. Reese, *Sealed With Their Lives: The Battle for Crampton's Gap* (Baltimore: Butternut & Blue, 1998), 24-25.

16 George M. Neese, *Three Years in the Confederate Horse Artillery* (New York: Neale Publishing Co., 1911), 118.

17 Robert Milligan to Dear Levi, October 7, 1862, Milligan Papers.

18 Gracey, *Annals*, 91.

19 Milligan to Dear Levi, October 7, 1862.

20 Gracey, *Annals*, 97.

21 J. Gregory Acken, ed., *Inside the Army of the Potomac: The Civil War Experience of Captain Francis Adams Donaldson* (Mechanicsburg, Pa.: Stackpole, 1998), 122.

22 Report of John C. Tidball, September 21, 1862, Henry J. Hunt Papers, Manuscripts Division, Library of Congress, Washington, D.C.

23 Emlen N. Carpenter to Mr. Henszey, October 5, 1862.

24 Gracey, *Annals*, 100.

25 Robert Milligan to Dear Levi, October 7, 1862.

26 Charles Francis Adams, Jr., *Autobiography* (Boston: Houghton Mifflin, 1916), 152-153.

27 Sears, *Landscape Turned Red*, 271.

28 Ballentine to Ballentine, October 19, 1862.

29 Milligan to Dear Levi, October 7, 1862.

30 Cowan to his parents, September 23 and 29, 1862.

31 O.R. vol. 19, part 2, 55.

32 David G. Douglas and Robert L. Brown, eds., *A Boot Full of Memories: Captain Leonard Williams, 2nd S.C. Cavalry* (Camden, S.C.: Gray Fox, 2004), 150-151.

33 O.R. vol. 19, part 2, 52.

34 Charles E. Cadwalader to Richard H. Rush, October 16, 1862, Cadwalader Collection, Collection #1454, Charles E. Cadwalader Miscellaneous Box, Historical Society of Pennsylvania, Philadelphia; Gracey, *Annals*, 109-110; Wright, narrative.

35 O.R. vol. 19, part 2, 41.

36 R. Channing Price to his mother, October 15, 1862, in Robert J. Trout, ed., *With Pen and Saber: The Letters and Diaries of J.E.B. Stuart's Staff Officers* (Mechanicsburg, Pa.: Stackpole, 1995), 107.

37 Henry B. McClellan, *I Rode with Jeb Stuart* (Bloomington: Indiana University Press, 1958), 152.

38 O.R. vol. 19, part 2, 42.

39 McClellan, *I Rode with Jeb Stuart*, 152-153.

40 Cowan to his parents, October 16, 1862.

41 O.R. vol. 19, part 2, 42. Colonel Rush reported that Stuart's column consisted of the 1st, 3rd, 4th, 5th, 9th, and 10th Virginia Cavalry, the 1st and 2nd North Carolina Cavalry, the Cobb Legion, and the Jeff Davis Legion. However, Scott told Rush that Stuart had between 4,000 and 5,000 sabers, not less than 2,000, as he actually had.

42 John W. Thompson, IV, *Horses, Hostages, and Apple Cider: J.E.B. Stuart's 1862 Pennsylvania Raid* (Mercersburg, Pa.: Privately published, 2002), 84-85.

43 O.R. vol. 51, part 1, 41-42; vol. 19, part 2, 41.

44 Gracey, *Annals*, 106.

45 Ballentine to Ballentine, October 19, 1862.

46 Cowan to his parents, October 21, 1862.

47 Gracey, *Annals*, 110-111.

48 Ibid., 111.

49 Meade, *Life and Letters*, 1:325.

50 Ibid., 1:336.

51 Carpenter to Henszey, November 7, 1862.

52 Ballentine to Ballentine, November 13, 1862.

53 Geisel to his sister, November 7, 1862.

54 Carpenter to Henszey, November 7, 1862.

55 O.R. vol. 21, 824.

56 Cowan to his parents, November 10, 1862.

57 Ballentine to Ballentine, November 24, 1862.

58 Albert P. Morrow to Dear Jessie, December 9, 1862, Albert P. Morrow letters, Paul Polizzi collection, Rochester, N.Y.

59 Ballentine to Ballentine, December 8, 1862.

60 Gracey, *Annals*, 113.

61 Cowan to his parents, December 21, 1862.

62 Gracey, *Annals*, 113.

63 Meade, *Life and Letters*, 1:339.

64 Morrow to Dear Jessie, December 25, 1862.

65 Ibid.; O.R. vol. 21, 129-142.

66 Cowan to his parents, December 21, 1862.

67 Morrow to Dear Jessie, December 25, 1862.

68 Lewis, *Frank Furness*, 39.

69 Gracey, *Annals*, 118.

70 *Philadelphia Inquirer*, January 8, 1863; O.R. vol. 21, 694.

71 Morrow to Dear Jessie, December 26, 1862.

Chapter 5. The Stoneman Raid

1 Emlen N. Carpenter to Dear Mr. Henszey, January 2, 1863, Alexander R. Chamberlin Collection.

2 Ibid., January 9, 1863.

3 Gracey, *Annals*, 123.

4 Morrow to My Dearest Jessie, January 13, 1863, Morrow letters.

5 Cowan to his parents, February 8, 1863, Cowan Papers.

6 Carpenter to Henszey, January 24, 1863.

7 *Philadelphia Inquirer*, January 30, 1863.

8 Ballentine to Ballentine, January 25, 1863, Ballentine Letters.

9 O.R. vol. 21, 1004-1005.

10 Clement Hoffman to his mother, February 12, 1863, Clement Hoffman letters, United States Army Military History Institute, Carlisle, Pennsylvania. Hoffman's letters are especially interesting, as he was that rare breed of man, a fighting Quaker. His letters are filled with the

plain language of the pacifist sect, but yet Hoffman, along with many other members of the Society of Friends, fought hard during the Civil War, hoping to end slavery forever.

11 Meade, *Life and Letters*, 1:318.

12 O.R. vol. 25, part 1, 51.

13 Theophilus F. Rodenbough, ed., *From Everglade to Canon with the Second Dragoons* (New York: D. Van Nostrand, 1875), 285.

14 Gracey, *Annals*, 128.

15 Meade, *Life and Letters*, 1:354.

16 Christian Geisel to Dear Sister, March 10, 1863, Geisel Papers.

17 Gracey, *Annals*, 130.

18 General Orders No. 6, February 17, 1863, RG 393, General Orders and Special Orders, Cavalry Corps, Feb.-Dec. 1863, 87, NARA.

19 Cowan to his parents, February 20, 1863.

20 Morrow to My Dear Jessie, March 25, 1863.

21 Ballentine to Ballentine, February 21, 1863.

22 Cowan to his parents, March 15, 1863.

23 Meade, *Life and Letters*, 1:358.

24 "Personal Recollections—The Stoneman Raid of '63," in Theophilus F. Rodenbough, ed., *From Everglade to Canon with the Second Dragoons* (New York: D. Van Nostrand, 1875), 273.

25 Ballentine to Ballentine, March 5, 1863.

26 Walter H. Hebert, *Fighting Joe Hooker* (Indianapolis: Bobbs-Merrill, 1944), 186.

27 Cowan to his parents, March 24, 1863.

28 Cowan to his brother, April 5, 1863.

29 Ballentine to Ballentine, March 17, 1863, Ballentine Letters.

30 Ibid., March 27, 1863.

31 Silas D. Wesson, Diary 1861-1864, entry for April 6, 1863, *Civil War Times Illustrated Collection*, United States Army Military History Institute, Carlisle, Pennsylvania.

32 Alexander Biddle to Julia Biddle, April 6, 1863, Rush/Williams/Biddle Family Papers.

33 Richard N. Griffin, ed., *Three Years a Soldier: The Diary and Newspaper Correspondence of Private George Perkins, Sixth New York Independent Battery, 1861-1864* (Knoxville: University of Tennessee Press, 2006), 94.

34 *Philadelphia Inquirer*, April 9, 1863.

35 Ibid., April 8, 1863.

36 George Stoneman to Joseph Hooker, undated letter from 1863, Box 12, Folder B, Joseph Hooker Papers, Huntington Library, San Marino, California.

37 Joseph Hooker to Samuel P. Bates, April 2, 1878, Samuel P. Bates Papers, Pennsylvania State Archives, Harrisburg; O.R. vol. 25, part 1, 1066.

38 Stoneman to Hooker, undated 1863 letter.

39 Cowan to his parents, April 11, 1863.

40 O.R. vol. 25, part 1, 1089.

41 Gracey, *Annals*, 133.

42 Ben F. Fordney, *Stoneman at Chancellorsville* (Shippensburg, Pa.: White Mane, 1998), 17.

43 Charles S. Wainwright, *A Diary of Battle: The Personal Journals of Colonel Charles S. Wainwright, 1861-1865*, ed. Allan Nevins (New York: Harcourt, Brace & World, 1962), 182.

44 Ballentine to Ballentine, April 23, 1863.

45 Ibid.

46 Gracey, *Annals*, 134.

47 Ballentine to Ballentine, April 23, 1863.

48 Gracey, *Annals*, 136.

49 O.R. vol. 25, part 1, 1057.

50 Wittenberg, *We Have It Damn Hard Out Here*, 81.

51 O.R. vol. 25, part 1, 782.

52 Geisel to his sister, April 27, 1863, Geisel Papers.

53 Walter S. Newhall to his father, April 26, 1863, Newhall Family Papers, Historical Society of Pennsylvania, Philadelphia.

54 Richard H. Rush to Col. Andrew J. Alexander, April 25, 1863, Richard H. Rush service records, NARA. Rush resigned his commission in the 6th Pennsylvania on September 30, 1863, after accepting a commission as colonel in the Invalid Corps, which he commanded for most of the rest of the war. Richard H. Rush to Lorenzo Thomas, September 30, 1863, Richard H. Rush service records, NARA.

55 Gracey, *Annals*, 135.

56 Cowan to his parents, May 15, 1863.

57 Gracey, *Annals*, 137.

58 John B. Coover to John B. Coover, May 22, 1863, John B. Coover letters, George F. Scott Collection, Mt. Carmel, Pennsylvania.

59 Gracey, *Annals*, 139-140.

60 Ibid., 138-139.

61 Fordney, *Stoneman at Chancellorsville*, 31.

62 Report of Brig. Gen. W. H. F. Lee, *Southern Historical Society Papers*, 3 (1877): 181.

63 Gracey, *Annals*, 142.

64 Ballentine to Ballentine, May 12, 1863.

65 O.R. vol. 25, part 1, 1060.

66 Ibid., 171.

67 Darius N. Couch, "The Chancellorsville Campaign," in Robert U. Johnson and Clarence C. Buel, eds., *Battles and Leaders of the Civil War*, 4 vols. (New York: Century, 1880-1901), 3:161.

68 Hoffman to his mother, May 17, 1863, Harrisburg Civil War Roundtable Collection.

69 Wittenberg, *We Have It Damn Hard Out Here*, 87.

70 Ibid., 88.

71 Ernest B. Furgurson, *Chancellorsville 1863: The Souls of the Brave* (New York: Alfred A. Knopf, 1992), 364-365.

72 Coover to Coover, May 22, 1863.

73 Edgar B. Strang, *General Stoneman's Raid, Or, the Amusing Side of Army Life* (Philadelphia: Privately published, 1911), 17-18, 24-25.

74 Richard Bowles, Jr., "Shannon Hill Encounter," *Goochland County Historical Society Magazine*, 17 (1985): 44-45.

75 Gracey, *Annals*, 149.

76 Ballentine to Ballentine, May 12, 1863.

77 O.R. vol. 25, part 1, 1089.

78 Gracey, *Annals*, 150.

79 Ballentine to Ballentine, May 12, 1863.

80 Ibid.

81 O.R. vol. 25, part 1, 1089.

82 Gracey, *Annals*, 149-150.

83 George Stoneman to Joseph Hooker, May 7, 1863, Box 12, Folder B, Hooker Papers.

84 O.R. vol. 25, part 1, 1063.

85 Gracey, *Annals*, 151.

86 O.R. vol. 25, part 1, 1063.

87 "Personal Recollections—The Stoneman Raid of '63," 282.

88 O.R. vol. 25, part 1, 1090.

89 Christian Geisel to Dear Sister, May 20, 1863.

90 Ballentine to Ballentine, May 12, 1863.

91 Meade, *Life and Letters*, 1:375.

92 Gracey, *Annals*, 154.

93 O.R. vol. 25, part 1, 1064.

94 Meade, *Life and Letters*, 1:371-372.

95 Geisel to his sister, May 30, 1863.

96 Coover to Coover, May 22, 1863.

97 Edward P. Tobie, *History of the First Maine Cavalry* (Boston: First Maine Cavalry Association, 1887), 144.

98 Henry R. Pyne, *The History of First New Jersey Cavalry* (Trenton, N.J.: J. A. Beecher, 1871), 147.

99 Charles B. Coxe to John B. Cadwalader, Jr., May 12, 1863, Charles B. Coxe Papers, Historical Society of Pennsylvania, Philadelphia.

100 O.R. vol. 25, part 2, 533.

101 Ibid.

102 Hoffman to his Mother, May 17, 1863.

103 O.R. vol. 25, part 2, 463 and 468-469; Joseph Hooker to Samuel P. Bates, December 24, 1878, Bates Papers.

104 Meade, *Life and Letters*, 1:381.

105 See O.R. vol. 25, part 2, 513, and vol. 27, part 3, 11, for the orders granting Stoneman his medical leave and placing Pleasonton in temporary command of the Cavalry Corps. On June 5, 1863, Hooker directed Stoneman to report to the adjutant general of the army for further instructions. On July 28, Stoneman was appointed chief of the newly formed Cavalry Bureau, an administrative post similar to the old position of chief of cavalry.

106 Alexander Biddle to Julia Biddle, June 21, 1863.

107 Wittenberg, *We Have It Damn Hard Out Here*, 91-92.

108 Blaschek, "The Story of Rush's Lancers."

109 Coxe to Cadwalader, May 12, 1863.

110 Clement Hoffman to his mother, June 23, 1863.

111 Montgomery Meigs to Rufus Ingalls, June 22, 1863, RG 393, Part 1, Army of the Potomac, 1861-1865, entry 3976, Letters Received 1863, Box 10, NARA.

112 "Lancers and Dragoons," *Army and Navy Journal*, November 14, 1863.

113 Cowan to his parents, May 15, 1863.

114 Gracey, *Annals*, 153; see also Albert P. Morrow service records, RG94, NARA. Morrow's service records indicate that he was arrested for being away without leave upon reporting at Camp Parole on June 6, but after it was determined that his absence was the result of having been a prisoner of war, those charges were dismissed immediately.

115 Gracey, *Annals*, 155.

CHAPTER 6. THE BATTLE OF BRANDY STATION

1 O.R. vol. 25, part 2, 528. This was just one of a number of extremely accurate intelligence reports which Col. Sharpe would generate over the course of the coming Gettysburg Campaign.

2 Ibid., part 1, 32.

3 Ibid., part 2, 536. The Confederate concentration observed by Gregg's scouts was the beginning of the great massing of Confederate cavalry at Brandy Station. This massing of horse would have far-reaching implications for both sides (see Chapter 7 for full discussion).

4 Ibid., 537.

5 Ibid., 571-572.

6 Ibid., vol. 27, part 3, 8. The Jones whom Buford refers to is Brig. Gen. William E. "Grumble" Jones, a classmate from the West Point class of 1846. Buford and Jones would tangle many times in the coming months. Ironically, neither would survive the war, Jones dying in action in June 1864, a few days short of a year later. Their careers paralleled each other in many ways, even in their deaths.

7 Ibid., 14

8 McClellan, *The Campaigns of Stuart's Cavalry*, 261; see also Blackford, *War Years with Jeb Stuart*, 211-212.

9 William N. McDonald, *A History of the Laurel Brigade* (Baltimore: Sun Job Printing Office, 1907), 132.

10 O.R. vol. 27, part 3, 24-25.

11 Heros von Borcke and Justus Scheibert, *The Great Cavalry Battle of Brandy Station*, trans. Stuart T. Wright and F. D. Bridgewater (1893; reprint, Gaithersburg, Md.: Olde Soldier Books, 1976), 35.

12 O.R. vol. 27, part 3, 27-28.

13 Daniel A. Grimsley, *Battles in Culpeper County, Virginia, 1861-1865* (Culpeper, Va.: Raleigh Travers Green, 1900), 3.

14 Chiswell Dabney to Dear Father, June 14, 1863, quoted in Trout, *With Pen and Saber*, 213.

15 Henry C. Whelan to James F. McQuesten, June 11, 1863, Box 15, Folder A, Hooker Papers.

16 Grimsley, *Battles in Culpeper County*, 8.

17 Daniel E. Sutherland, *Seasons of War: The Ordeal of a Confederate Community, 1861-1865* (New York: Free Press, 1995), 241-42.

18 McClellan, *The Campaigns of Stuart's Cavalry*, 262.

19 John Blue, *Hanging Rock Rebel: Lt. John Blue's War in West Virginia and the Shenandoah Valley*, Dan Oates, ed. (Shippensburg, Pa.: Burd Street Press, 1994), 198.

20 Alfred Pleasonton to John Buford, June 8, 1863, Order Book of the Chief of Cavalry for 1863, Civil War Miscellaneous Collection, United States Army Military History Institute, Carlisle, Pennsylvania.

21 Abner Hard, *History of the Eighth Cavalry Regiment, Illinois Volunteers* (reprint, Dayton, Ohio: Morningside, 1984), 242.

22 Gracey, *Annals*, 156-157.

23 Moore, ed., *The Rebellion Record*, 8:16.

24 Hard, *History of the Eighth*, 243.

25 John Buford to Lt. Col. A. J. Alexander, June 13, 1863, Hooker Papers.

26 Hard, *History of the Eighth*, 243.

27 Blue, *Hanging Rock Rebel*, 198.

28 Maj. James F. Hart, in the *Philadelphia Weekly Times*, June 26, 1880, quoted in McClellan, *Life and Campaigns*, 266.

29 Henry Norton, *Deeds of Daring, or History of the Eighth N.Y. Volunteer Cavalry* (Norwich, N.Y.: Chenango Telegraph Printing House, 1889), 65; McClellan, *Life and Campaigns*, 265; Edward G. Longacre, *The Cavalry at Gettysburg* (Lincoln: University of Nebraska Press, 1986), 67.

30 Buford to Alexander, June 13, 1863.

31 O.R. vol. 27, part 2, 749.

32 Dennis E. Frye, *12th Virginia Cavalry* (Lynchburg, Va.: H. E. Howard, 1988), 36.

33 Ibid.

34 Richard L. T. Beale, *History of the Ninth Virginia Cavalry in the War Between the States* (Richmond, Va.: B. F. Johnson Publishing, 1899), 85.

35 Buford to Alexander, June 13, 1863.

36 Ballentine to Ballentine, June 10, 1863, Ballentine Letters.

37 Rear Adm. John A. Dahlgren, *Memoir of Ulric Dahlgren* (Philadelphia: J. B. Lippincott, 1872), 147-148. For more on this extraordinary young man's extensive role in the Gettysburg Campaign, see Eric J. Wittenberg, "Ulric Dahlgren in the Gettysburg Campaign," *Gettysburg: Historical Articles of Lasting Interest*, no. 22 (January 2000): 96-111.

38 Major Henry C. Whelan to Charles C. Cadwalader, 6th Pennsylvania Cavalry, June 11, 1863, Cadwalader Family Collection, Historical Society of Pennsylvania, Philadelphia.

39 Cowan to his parents, June 10, 1863, Cowan Papers.

40 Fairfax Downey, *Clash of Cavalry: The Battle of Brandy Station* (New York: David McKay, 1959), 103.

41 Gracey, *Annals*, 160.

42 Charles L. Leiper pension records.

43 O.R. vol. 27, part 2, 763, 770.

44 See the Register of Captured Flags, 1861-1865, RG 394, NARA, which indicates that the Regimental Guidon of the 6th Pennsylvania Cavalry was recovered in Richmond at the end of the war. Thanks to Howard Michael Madaus, the renowned vexillologist, for bringing this to light, and for explaining this theory to me. Thanks also to Mitchell E. McGlynn of Alexandria, Virginia, who owns the flag today, and who first pointed this story out to me.

45 Ballentine to Ballentine, June 10, 1863.

46 Lt. Col. W. H. Carter, *From Yorktown to Santiago with the Sixth U.S. Cavalry* (1900; reprint, Austin, Tex.: State House Press, 1989), 84.

47 Dr. John B. Coover to his sister, June 10, 1863, Coover letters.

48 Neese, *Three Years*, 172.

49 Whelan to Cadwalader, June 11, 1863.

50 Ballentine to Ballentine, June 10, 1863.

51 O.R. vol. 27, part 2, 772-773.

52 Capt. Frank Robertson to My Dear Kate, June 12, 1863, quoted in Trout, *With Pen and Saber*, 208.

53 Trout, *With Pen and Saber*, 209; Thomas C. Devin to Capt. A. J. Cohen, June 1863, Hooker Papers.

54 McClellan, *Campaigns of Stuart's Cavalry*, 267.

55 Diary entry for June 9, 1863, Jasper Cheney, Co. A, 8th New York Volunteer Cavalry, Civil War Times Illustrated Collection, U.S. Army Military History Institute, Carlisle, Pennsylvania.

56 Buford to Alexander, June 13, 1863.

57 McClellan, *Campaigns of Stuart's Cavalry*, 282.

58 Whelan to McQuesten, June 11, 1863.

59 Whelan to Cadwalader, June 11, 1863.

60 G. W. Beale, *A Lieutenant of Cavalry in Lee's Army* (Boston, 1918; reprint, Baltimore: Butternut & Blue, 1994), 96.

61 Ballentine to Ballentine, June 10, 1863.

62 Whelan to Cadwalader, June 11, 1863.

63 Cowan to his parents, June 10, 1863.

64 Wesley Merritt, "Recollections of the Civil War," in Rodenbough, *From Everglade to Canon*, 287.

65 Lt. Albert O. Vincent to Lt. J. Hamilton Bell, June 16, 1863, Hunt Papers.

66 Buford to Alexander, June 13, 1863.

67 Merritt, "Recollections," 289.

68 Beale, *A Lieutenant of Cavalry*, 96.

69 Buford to Alexander, June 13, 1863.

70 Hampton S. Thomas, *Some Personal Reminiscences of Service in the Cavalry of the Army of the Potomac* (Philadelphia: L. R. Hammersley, 1889), 9.

71 O.R. vol. 27, part 3, 876.

72 Frederick C. Newhall, "The Battle of Beverly Ford," in *Annals of the War: Written by Leading Participants North and South* (reprint, Dayton, Ohio: Morningside, 1986), 143.

73 Buford to Alexander, June 13, 1863.

74 Newhall, "The Battle of Beverly Ford," 144.

75 O.R. vol. 27, part 1, 1045.

76 Coover to his sister, June 10, 1863.

77 O.R. vol. 27, part 1, 903-904.

78 Cowan to his parents, June 10, 1863.

79 Ballentine to Ballentine, June 10, 1863.

80 Lewis Miller to Colonel Thomas, September 13, 1863, Muster Rolls and Related Records, 1861-66, 70th Regiment—6th Cavalry, Records of the Department of Military Affairs, RG 19, Pennsylvania State Archives, Harrisburg, Pennsylvania.

81 Frederic C. Newhall, "Address at Dedication of Monument Sixth Regiment of Cavalry," *Pennsylvania at Gettysburg*, 2 vols. (Harrisburg, Pa.: B. Slingerly, 1904), 2:824.

82 Ballentine to Ballentine, June 10, 1863.

83 Whelan to Cadwalader, June 11, 1863.

84 Whelan to McQuesten, June 11, 1863.

85 Coover to his sister, June 10, 1863.

86 Buford to Alexander, June 13, 1863.

87 Whelan to Cadwalader, June 11, 1863.

88 Newhall, "Dedication," 2:825.

89 Brian Stuart Kesterson, ed., *The Last Survivor: The Memoirs of George William Watson* (Washington, W.Va.: Night Hawk Press, 1993), 35.

90 Whelan to McQuesten, June 11, 1863.

91 Charles J. Whiting to Theodore C. Bacon, June 12, 1863, Box 15, Folder A, Hooker Papers.

92 Dahlgren to his father, June 12, 1863.

93 William Brooke-Rawle to his mother, June 12, 1863, William Brooke-Rawle Papers, Civil War Museum and Library, Philadelphia.

94 *Pottstown News*, January 16, 1915.

95 William F. Smith to C. Ross Smith, June 9, 1875, Mitchell E. McGlynn Collection, Alexandria, Virginia.

96 Meade, *Life and Letters*, 1:384. Young George Meade missed the battle as he had already assumed his new duties on his father's staff. "George is quite disgusted with his luck," recounted his father, "but I tell him a live dog is better than a dead lion." Ibid.

97 *Philadelphia Evening Bulletin*, June 13, 1863.

98 Hoffman to his mother, June 23, 1863.

99 Norton, *Deeds of Daring*, 66.

100 Coover to his sister, June 10, 1863.

101 McClellan, *Campaigns of Stuart's Cavalry*, 234.

102 John N. Opie, *A Rebel Cavalryman with Lee, Stuart, and Jackson* (Chicago: W. B. Conkey, 1899), 157.

103 Noble D. Preston, *History of the Tenth Regiment of Cavalry, New York State Volunteers, August 1861-August 1865* (New York: D. Appleton & Co., 1892), 85.

104 O.R. vol. 27, part 3, 58.

105 Charles Francis Adams, *A Cycle of Adams Letters, 1861-1865*, Worthington C. Ford, ed., 2 vols. (Boston: Houghton Mifflin, 1920), 2:32. Like his famous ancestors, Charles Francis Adams was never afraid to say what was on his mind.

CHAPTER 7. THE GETTYSBURG CAMPAIGN

1 General Orders No. 19, June 13, 1863, RG 393, General Orders and Special Orders, Cavalry Corps, Feb.-Dec. 1863, 137, NARA.

2 Robert F. O'Neill, Jr., *The Cavalry Battles at Aldie, Middleburg and Upperville: Small but Important Riots* (Lynchburg, Va.: H. E. Howard, 1993), 25.

3 Ballentine to Ballentine, June 23, 1863, Ballentine Letters.

4 Clement Hoffman to Dear Mother, June 23, 1863, USAMHI.

5 Wittenberg, *We Have It Damn Hard Out Here*, 99. By this time, significant portions of Lee's army were already in Pennsylvania. For example, a column of Lt. Gen. Richard S. Ewell's Second Corps had already embarked on a raid to Harrisburg, and another column, under command of Maj. Gen. Jubal A. Early, had passed through the small town of Gettysburg, marching east toward the town of York, thirty-two miles away. The mention of the militias near "Harrisburgh" refers to Darius N. Couch, who had asked to be relieved of command of the Second Corps in disgust over Hooker's performance at Chancellorsville. Couch was sent to command the Department of Pennsylvania, where he mustered the Pennsylvania militia forces to resist the Confederate advance toward Harrisburg.

6 Dorastus McCord to his sisters, June 30, 1863, Spanish-American War Survey, USAMHI.

7 Clement Hoffman to Dear Mother, July 5, 1863.

8 Cadwalader to his mother, July 10, 1863, Historical Society of Pennsylvania, Philadelphia.

9 O.R. vol. 27, part 3, 373.

10 The only full-length biography of Wesley Merritt is Don E. Alberts, *Brandy Station to Manila Bay: A Biography of General Wesley Merritt* (Austin, Tex.: Presidial Press, 1980).

11 E. R Hagemann, ed., *Fighting Rebels and Redskins: Experiences in Army Life of Colonel George B. Sanford, 1861-1892* (Norman: University of Oklahoma Press, 1968), 225.

12 Theophilus F. Rodenbough, "Some Cavalry Leaders," in *The Photographic History of the Civil War*, ed. Francis Trevelyan Miller, 10 vols. (New York: Review of Reviews Co., 1911), 10:278.

13 James H. Kidd, *Personal Recollections of a Cavalryman in Custer's Michigan Brigade* (Ionia, Mich.: Sentinel Printing Co., 1908), 238-39.

14 The Widow Leister House was located near the copse of trees near the point of the Confederates' farthest advance during Pickett's Charge.

15 Wittenberg, *We Have It Damn Hard Out Here*, 99. For more on the heavy fighting on the Union left on the afternoon of July 2, see Harry W. Pfanz, *Gettysburg: The Second Day* (Chapel Hill: University of North Carolina Press, 1987).

16 Clement Hoffman to Dear Mother, July 5, 1863.

17 Wittenberg, *We Have It Damn Hard Out Here*, 99.

18 Smith describes Pickett's Charge, the "high water mark" of the Confederacy. Smith is mistaken when he states that Longstreet personally led the attack. He did not.

19 Gracey, *Annals*, 179.

20 E. D. Swain, ed., *Crumbling Defenses; Or Memoirs and Reminiscences of John Logan Black, C.S.A.* (Macon, Ga.: J. W. Burke Co., 1960), 41.

21 Frederic C. Newhall, "Address," *Dedication of the Monument to the Sixth Penna. Cavalry on the Battlefield of Gettysburg* (Philadelphia: privately published, 1888), 21.

22 Ibid. The Currens house has been altered by a large addition, but it still stands at the corner of the Emmitsburg Pike and Ridge Road.

23 Eugene R. Bertrand to John B. Bachelder, March 26, 1864, included in David L. Ladd and Audrey J. Ladd, eds., *The Bachelder Papers: Gettysburg in Their Own Words*, 3 vols. (Dayton, Ohio: Morningside, 1995), 1:119-120.

24 Gracey, *Annals*, 179.

25 Col. Laurin L. Lawson, *History of the Sixth Field Artillery, 1793-1932* (Harrisburg, Pa.: Telegraph Press, 1933), 57.

26 Dr. Samuel J. Crockett to Bachelder, December 27, 1882, *The Bachelder Papers*, 2:916.

27 Betrand to Bachelder, *The Bachelder Papers*, 1:119.

28 Isaac Rothermel Dunkelberger, "Reminiscences," Michael Winey Collection, USAMHI.

29 Swain, *Crumbling Defenses*, 42.

30 Evander M. Law, "The Struggle for Round Top," in *B&L*, 3:328.

31 Ibid.

32 Swain, *Crumbling Defenses*, 42.

33 For more about the charge and death of Brig. Gen. Elon J. Farnsworth, see Eric J. Wittenberg, *Gettysburg's Forgotten Cavalry Actions* (Gettysburg, Pa.: Thomas Publications, 1998), 20-68.

34 Lawson, *History of the Sixth Field Artillery*, 57.

35 Wesley Merritt, "Personal Reminiscences of the Civil War," in *B&L*, 3:295.

36 O.R. vol. 27, part 2, 400.

37 Dunkelberger, "Reminiscences."

38 Newhall, "Dedication Address," 21. The monument was designed by Capt. Frank Furness of Company F.

39 For more about Dahlgren's role in the Gettysburg Campaign, see Eric J. Wittenberg, "Ulric Dahlgren in the Gettysburg Campaign," *Gettysburg Magazine* 22 (January 2000): 96-111.

40 Ballentine to Ballentine, July 8, 1863.

41 Newhall, "Address," 18.

42 Diary of Ulric Dahlgren, entry for July 3, 1863, John A. Dahlgren Papers, Library of Congress, Washington, D.C.

43 Newhall, "Address," 18-19.

44 Gracey, *Annals*, 189.

45 Samuel P. Bates, *History of Pennsylvania Volunteers, 1861-5*, 10 vols. (Harrisburg, Pa.: State Printer, 1869-1871), 4:748.

46 Dahlgren diary, entry for July 4, 1863.

47 McHenry Howard, *Recollections of a Maryland Confederate Soldier and Staff Officer Under Johnston, Jackson, and Lee* (Baltimore: Williams & Wilkins, 1914), 210-211.

48 Ballentine to Ballentine, July 8, 1863.

49 John D. Imboden, "The Confederate Retreat from Gettysburg," in *B&L*, 3:423.

50 Gracey, *Annals*, 190.

51 John A. Dahlgren, *Memoir of Ulric Dahlgren* (Philadelphia: J. B. Lippincott, 1872), 167.

52 Dahlgren diary, entry for July 5, 1863. On the morning of July 4, Kilpatrick's Third Division pulled out of Gettysburg and began its pursuit of the Confederates. That night, Kilpatrick engaged a small force of Rebel cavalry in Monterey Pass in a midnight fight marked by torrential rains and vivid flashes of lightning. Brushing aside the grayclad cavalry, the Federal troopers ransacked the Confederate wagon train and began marching toward Hagerstown. At Smithsburg, just south of the Mason-Dixon Line, Kilpatrick ran into the main body of the Army of Northern Virginia's cavalry. A sharp but short fight took place at Smithsburg, with Maj. Gen. J.E.B. Stuart in personal command of the Rebel cavalry. The engagement broke off, and Kilpatrick continued his advance toward Boonsboro before continuing on to Hagerstown the next day.

53 Newhall, "Address," 19.

54 Imboden, "The Confederate Retreat," 3:425.

55 W. A. Popkins, "Imboden's Brigade at Gettysburg," *Confederate Veteran* 22 (1914): 552.

56 Gracey, *Annals*, 190-191.

57 Ibid., 190.

58 Ibid., 191.

59 George H. Chapman diary, entry for July 4, 1863, George H. Chapman Papers, Indiana Historical Society, Indianapolis, Indiana.

60 Dunkelberger, "Reminiscences."

61 Ibid.

62 *Philadelphia Inquirer*, July 9, 1863.

63 Ibid.

64 *National Tribune*, March 6, 1884, and *New York at Gettysburg*, 3:943. John Farrington, "137th Regiment Volunteer Infantry," in New York State Monuments Commission for the

Battlefields of Gettysburg and Chattanooga, *Final Report on the Battlefield at Gettysburg*, 3 vols. (Albany: J. B. Lyon Co., 1900).

65 Dunkelberger, "Reminiscences." For a detailed discussion of this episode, see Eric J. Wittenberg, "And Everything Is Lovely and the Goose Hangs High: John Buford and the Hanging of Confederate Spies During the Gettysburg Campaign," *Gettysburg Magazine* 18 (January 1998): 5-14.

66 G.O. 73, 24 March 1863, which included Public Law 54 (12 Stat. 735), Section 21. U.S. law had recognized an officer's right to conduct drumhead courts-martial and to hang spies since the time of the Revolutionary War. For a detailed discussion of this subject, including the definition of a spy, what must be demonstrated in order to prove that a person is a spy, and the various forms of punishment proscribed for convicted spies, see William Woolsey Winthrop, *Military Law*, 2 vols. (Washington, D.C.: W. H. Morrison, 1888), 1:1098-1106.

67 Davis, *Common Soldier, Uncommon War*, 450; Dunkelberger, "Reminiscences"; *National Tribune*, April 4, 1884.

68 Gracey, *Annals*, 185.

69 O.R. vol. 27, part 1, 928.

70 Imboden, "The Confederate Retreat," 427.

71 O.R. vol. 27, part 1, 940.

72 Ibid., 928.

73 Ibid.

74 Gracey, *Annals*, 184.

75 Ibid., 185.

76 Imboden, "The Confederate Retreat," 428.

77 *Aurora Beacon*, August 20, 1863.

78 Dunkelberger, "Reminiscences."

79 O.R. vol. 27, part 2, 761; Richard L. Armstrong, *Seventh Virginia Cavalry* (Lynchburg, Va.: H. E. Howard, 1992), 57.

80 Gracey, *Annals*, 186.

81 Ballentine to Ballentine, July 8, 1863.

82 Gracey, *Annals*, 189-192.

83 Henry Norton, *Deeds of Daring: or History of the Eighth New York Volunteer Cavalry* (Norwich, N.Y.: Chenango Telegraph Printing House, 1889), 70-71.

84 O.R. vol. 27, part 1, 941.

85 Neese, *Three Years in the Confederate Horse Artillery*, 196.

86 Edward G. Longacre, *The Cavalry at Gettysburg* (East Rutherford, N.J.: Fairleigh-Dickinson University Press, 1986), 261.

87 Hillman A. Hall, ed., *History of the Sixth New York Cavalry (Second Ira Harris Guards), Second Brigade-First Division-Cavalry Corps, Army of the Potomac, 1861-1865* (Worcester, Mass.: Blanchard Press, 1908), 148.

88 Jasper Cheney diary, entry for July 10, 1863, Civil War Miscellaneous Collection, USAMHI.

89 *Aurora Beacon*, August 20, 1863.

90 Gracey, *Annals*, 188.

91 John Watts DePeyster, *The Decisive Conflicts of the Late Civil War* (New York: MacDonald & Co., 1867), 96.

92 Gracey, *Annals*, 189.

93 James Bell to Gusta Ann Hallock, July 11, 1863, A. P. Huntington Library, San Marino, California.

94 Wittenberg, *We Have It Damn Hard Out Here*, 99.

95 O.R. vol. 27, part 1, 929.

96 Ibid., 944; Merritt, "Reminiscences," 296.

97 Gracey, *Annals*, 188.

98 *Aurora Beacon*, August 20, 1863.

99 Hard, *History of the Eighth Cavalry Regiment*, 266.

100 O.R. vol. 27, part 1, 937.

101 Merritt, "Reminiscences," 297.

102 O.R. vol. 27, part 1, 945.

103 Ibid., 937-938; Hard, *Eighth Cavalry Regiment*, 267.

104 Merritt, "Reminiscences," 297-298.

105 O.R. vol. 27, part 1, 930.

106 Daniel Peck, *Dear Rachel: The Civil War Letters of Daniel Peck*, Martha Gerber Stanford and Eleanor Erskin, eds. (Freeman, S.D.: Pine Hill Press, 1993), 51.

107 Casualty return for the First Cavalry Division, Theodore C. Bacon Papers, Connecticut Historical Society, Hartford.

108 Michael Donlon to Patrick Donlon, July 27, 1863, Michael Donlon letters, Civil War Miscellaneous Collection, USAMHI.

109 *Aurora Beacon*, August 20, 1863.

110 Ballentine to Ballentine, July 28, 1863.

111 Wittenberg, *We Have It Damn Hard Out Here*, 101.

CHAPTER 8. IN THE FIELD AND IN WINTER CAMP WITH THE ARMY OF THE POTOMAC

1 *Philadelphia Press*, August 7, 1863.

2 Ballentine to Ballentine, August 4, 1863, Ballentine Letters.

3 Gracey, *Annals*, 194.

4 Ballentine to Ballentine, August 4, 1863.

5 Wittenberg, *We Have It Damn Hard Out Here*, 102-103.

6 Ballentine to Ballentine, August 4, 1863.

7 Wiliam M. Graham to George G. Meade, Jr., August 10, 1889, author's collection.

8 Ballentine to Ballentine, August 4, 1863.

9 Gracey, *Annals*, 194-955.

10 William P. C. Treichel service and pension records.

11 Ballentine to Ballentine, August 4, 1863.

12 O.R. vol. 27, part 1, 824-827.

13 James H. Hazeltine service records.

14 Gracey, *Annals*, 218; Winfield S. Hancock to Benjamin F. Davis, May 21, 1863; John Buford to Alpheus S. Williams, August 3, 1863, both included in Whiteford pension file, NARA.

15 George G. Meade to Andrew G. Curtin, August 22, 1863, Whiteford pension file.

16 Whiteford service records.

17 *Philadelphia Press*, August 10, 1863.

18 Gracey, *Annals*, 195.

19 Ballentine to Ballentine, August 7, 1863.

20 *Philadelphia Press*, August 10, 1863.

21 Gracey, *Annals*, 196.

22 Christian Geisel to Dear Sister, October 15, 1863, Geisel Papers.

23 RG 108, Records of the Headquarters of the Army 1828-1903, Register of Letters Received, August 1863-September 1865, Vol. 1, 259, NARA.

24 Ibid.

25 Wittenberg, *We Have It Damn Hard Out Here*, 104.

26 Clement Hoffman to his mother, August 26, 1863.

27 "Oration of Major Gerard Irvine Whitehead, Sixth Pennsylvania Cavalry," in *Dedication of the Monument of the Sixth Penna. Cavalry "Lancers" at the Headquarters of General Meade on the Battlefield of Gettysburg June 8, 1891* (Philadelphia: privately published, 1892), 12.

28 Wittenberg, *We Have It Damn Hard Out Here*, 105.

29 Smith to his brother, October 10, 1863.

30 Ballentine to Ballentine, August 21, 1863.

31 Cowan to his parents, September 9, 1863, Cowan Papers.

32 Gracey, *Annals*, 196.

33 Cowan to his parents, September 21, 1863.

34 Gracey, *Annals*, 198. Even the Richmond newspapers eulogized Major Morris. "DEATH OF A FEDERAL OFFICER.—Maj. Rob't Morris, of the 6th Pennsylvania cavalry, captured at Brandy Station on the 6th of June, died suddenly in the Libby prison hospital on Wednesday night. He had been apparently well until Wednesday morning, when he was, at his own request, taken to the hospital, being somewhat unwell, and desiring to take medicine. He did not appear seriously ill, but looked rather cheerful, and walked about the hospital during the day. He was found yesterday morning dead in his bed, having died evidently in a cateleptic fit. His remains were interred last evening in Oakwood cemetery, and were attended to the grave by the captive officers of his regiment. Major Morris, of Revolutionary memory, and was only twenty-six years of age." *Richmond Enquirer*, August 14, 1863. After the end of the war, Morris was disinterred and his remains removed to his native Philadelphia. Today, he rests in the graveyard of St. James the Less Episcopal Churchyard.

35 Miller to Col. Thomas, September 13, 1863.

36 Cowan to his parents, September 9, 1863.

37 Cadwalader to his mother, September 4, 1863, Cadwalader Collection.

38 Hageman, *Fighting Rebels and Redskins*, 211-212. Captain Sanford did not identify the officer by name, only as Captain T. However, there was only one officer to serve in the Lancers during its entire tenure of service whose last name began with the letter "T": Treichel.

39 Cadwalader to his mother, October 16, 1863.

40 Hoffman to his mother, October 26, 1863.

41 Ballentine to Ballentine, October 21, 1863.

42 Ibid.

43 Gracey, *Annals*, 198.

44 Smith to his brother, October 16, 1863.

45 O.R. vol. 29, part 1, 427. Obviously, the details of the infantry battle at Bristoe Station go beyond the scope of this book. For a more detailed discussion of this battle, see William D. Henderson, *The Road to Bristoe Station: Campaigning with Lee and Meade, August 1-October 29, 1863* (Lynchburg, Va.: H. E. Howard, 1987).

46 John A. Sloan, *Reminiscences of the Guilford Grays* (Washington, D.C.: R. C. Polkinhorn, 1883), 74.

47 Gracey, *Annals*, 199.

48 Smith to his brother, October 16, 1863.

49 Gracey, *Annals*, 200.

50 O.R. vol. 29, part 1, 352.

51 *New York Tribune*, October 20, 1863.

52 Smith to his brother, October 16, 1863.

53 Ballentine to Ballentine, October 21, 1863.

54 Gracey, *Annals*, 200.

55 *James Starr*, 7.

56 Gracey, *Annals*, 201.

57 O.R. vol. 29, part 2, 400.

58 Ibid., 346.

59 Gideon Welles, *Diary of Gideon Welles*, 3 vols. (Boston: Houghton-Mifflin, 1911), 1:438-440.

60 O.R. vol. 29, part 2, 375.

61 Geisel to his sister, October 30, 1863.

62 *Philadelphia Inquirer*, November 7, 1863.

63 Theodore Sage service records, NARA. A detailed discussion about the exploits of the 43rd Battalion and the Union efforts to bring Mosby to bay goes far beyond the scope of this study. For detailed accounts of the exploits of Mosby's command, see Hugh C. Keen and Horace Mewborn, *43rd Battalion, Virginia Cavalry, Mosby's Command* (Lynchburg, Va.: H. E. Howard, 1993) and Jeffry D. Wert, *Mosby's Rangers* (New York: Simon & Schuster, 1990).

64 Cowan to his parents, November 11, 1863.

65 Gracey, *Annals*, 204-205.

66 Ibid., 207.

67 Coover to his sister, November 15, 1863.

68 William Harbeson pension and service records.

69 *Philadelphia Inquirer*, November 18, 1863.

70 C. Ross Smith service records.

71 Cowan to his parents, November 21, 1863.

72 A detailed discussion of the aborted Mine Run Campaign goes far beyond the scope of this study. For a more detailed analysis of the Mine Run Campaign, see Martin F. Graham and George F. Skoch, *Mine Run: A Campaign of Lost Opportunities, October 21, 1863-May 1, 1864* (Lynchburg, Va.: H. E. Howard, 1987).

73 Ballentine to Ballentine, December 4, 1863.

74 Gracey, *Annals*, 207.

75 Ballentine to Ballentine, December 4, 1863.

76 Ibid., December 11, 1863.

77 Ibid.

78 Gracey, *Annals*, 301-302.

79 Ibid., 302.

80 Albert P. Morrow, ed., *Journal of Leslie G. Morrow, 1864* (Yorba Linda, Calif.: Privately published, 1988), 15.

81 Howard M. Smith to his mother, January 17, 1864, Howard M. Smith Papers, Manuscripts Division, Library of Congress, Washington, D.C.

82 Capt. Emlen N. Carpenter to Dear Mr. Henszey, December 8, 1863.

83 Wittenberg, *We Have It Damn Hard Out Here*, 108-109.

84 Capt. Emlen N. Carpenter to Dear Mr. Henszey, December 29, 1863.

85 Ballentine to Ballentine, December 30, 1863.

86 Morrow, *Journal of Leslie G. Morrow*, 15.

87 Carpenter to Henszey, December 29, 1863.

88 Geisel to his sister, January 7, 1864.

89 John T. Baynes to Dear Stephen, April 19, 1864, in Richard C. Baynes, comp., *The Life and Ancestry of John Thistlethwaite Baynes (1833-1891)* (Irvine, Calif.: Richard C. Baynes, 1987), 38.

90 *James Starr*, 7.

91 Gracey, *Annals*, 222.

92 Ibid., 221.

93 Geisel to his sister, January 7, 1864.

94 O.R. vol. 33, 892.

95 Strang, *Sunshine and Shadows*, 42.

96 Morrow, *Journal of Leslie G. Morrow*, 15.

97 O.R. vol. 33, 783.

98 Ibid., 666.

99 For a detailed description of the regular routine of the Lancers that winter, see the diary for the year 1864 of Trooper Charles H. Coller of Company C, Wiley Sword Collection, USAMHI. The entries for the month of January provide the basis for the statements set forth in this paragraph.

100 Lewis, *Frank Furness*, 45.

101 Hoffman to his mother, January 6, 1864.

102 O.R. vol. 33, 139.

103 Ibid., 140.

104 Howard M. Smith to his mother, February 9, 1864.

105 Coller diary, entries for February 6 and 7, 1864.

106 Ibid., entries for February 13, 15, and 20, 1864.

107 Gracey, *Annals*, 223.

108 There are two book-length treatment of the Kilpatrick-Dahlgren Raid, one of which is now quite dated: Virgil Carrington Jones, *Eight Hours Before Richmond* (New York: Henry Holt, 1957). A more recent treatment focuses more on the controversies surrounding the raid and not the tactics: Duane P. Schultz, *The Dahlgren Affair: Terror and Conspiracy in the Civil War* (New York: W. W. Norton, 1998). For a shorter but more modern treatment of the tactical aspects of the raid, see Bruce M. Venter, "The Kilpatrick-Dahlgren Raid on Richmond, February 28-March 4, 1864," *Blue & Gray*, 20, no. 3 (Winter 2003): 6-22, 44-50.

109 O.R. vol. 33, 164-165.

110 Coller diary, entries for February 28 and 29 and March 1, 1864.

111 This refers to Maj. William P. C. Treichel.

112 According to Chaplain Samuel L. Gracey, the contingent from the 6th Pennsylvania Cavalry was commanded by Capt. Benoni Lockwood, not Major Treichel.

113 Actually, this is Greene County Court House.

114 This may also be Orange County Court House. It is somewhat unclear.

115 1st U.S. Cavalry, also of the Reserve Brigade.

116 The Rivanna River.

117 This refers to Pennsylvanian Capt. Joseph Penrose Ash of the 5th U.S. Cavalry, who was killed in action in the cavalry battle near Todd's Tavern, Virginia, on May 8, 1864. Francis E. Heitman, *Historical Register and Dictionary of the U.S. Army*, 2 vols. (Washington, D.C.: U.S. Government Printing Office, 1903), 1:173.

118 Custer reported that two Confederate cavalry brigades involved in this charge, that of Brig. Gen. Williams C. Wickham, along with another unidentified brigade, commanded in person by J.E.B. Stuart. Custer further reported that Stuart personally led a charge by the 1st and 5th Virginia Cavalry. O.R. vol. 33, 162.

119 This refers to Sgt. Samuel Wright of Philadelphia, who also served in Smith's Company I.

120 Actually, this is Burton's Ford over the Rapidan River.

121 This is actually the Robinson River.

122 Contrabands were runaway slaves, who often latched on to the coattails of the advancing Federal armies. Their presence was generally tolerated by the Yankee soldiers, but not appreciated.

123 Wittenberg, *We Have It Damn Hard Out Here*, 113-116.

124 O.R. vol. 33, 163.

125 Gracey, *Annals*, 227.

126 O.R. vol. 33, 163.

127 Theodore Sanford Garnett, *Riding with Stuart: Reminiscences of an Aide-de-Camp*, Robert J. Trout, ed. (Shippensburg, Pa.: White Mane, 1994), 41-42. Garnett refers to Capt. Charles Gratton, Stuart's chief of ordnance.

128 O.R. vol. 33, 163.

129 Ibid., 783.

130 Clement Hoffman to his mother, March 15, 1864.

131 O.R. vol. 33, 641.

132 Bruce Catton, *Grant Takes Command* (Boston: Little, Brown, 1968), 163.

133 Charles B. Coxe to John Cadwalader, Jr., December 10, 1863, Charles Coxe Letters, Historical Society of Pennsylvania, Philadelphia.

134 *New York Times*, March 29, 1864.

135 O.R. vol. 33, 732.

136 "This evening an order has arrived relieving General Pleasonton, which, although I did not originate it, yet was, I presume, brought about by my telling the Secretary that the opposition that I had hitherto made to his removal I no longer should make," reported General Meade in a letter to his wife. "As the Secretary has been desirous of relieving him ever since I have had command, and I have been objecting, he has taken the first chance to remove him as soon as my objections were withdrawn." Meade, *Life and Letters*, 2.182-183.

137 Henry E. Davies, *General Sheridan* (New York: D. Appleton & Co., 1895), 92-93. Lt. Gen. Ulysses S. Grant, the new commander-in-chief of the Union armies, went out of his way not to criticize Pleasonton in his memoirs. Speaking of Pleasonton's relief from command of the Cavalry Corps, Grant wrote, "It was not a reflection on that officer, however, for I did not know but that he had been as efficient as any other cavalry commander." Ulysses S. Grant, *Personal Memoirs* (New York: Library of America, 1990), 481.

138 O.R. vol. 33, 806.

139 Hagemann, *Fighting Rebels and Redskins*, 224.

140 John W. Wells to his parents, April 17, 1864, included in John W. Wells pension file.

141 Morrow, *Journal of Leslie G. Morrow*, 15.

142 Cowan to his parents, April 17, 1864.

143 Hoffman to his mother, April 16, 1864.

144 Ballentine to Ballentine, April 21, 1864.

145 Cowan to his parents, April 25, 1864.

146 Gracey, *Annals*, 218.

147 Ibid., 222; William P. C. Treichel service records. Lt. Col. C. Ross Smith did not assume command of the regiment because he remained on detached duty with Cavalry Corps headquarters.

Chapter 9. 1864: Campaigning with Grant and Sheridan

1 Allan Nevins, ed., *A Diary of Battle: The Personal Journals of Colonel Charles S. Wainwright, 1861-1865* (New York: Harcourt, Brace & World, 1962), 341.

2 Davies, *General Sheridan*, 93-95.

3 Roy Morris, Jr., *Sheridan: The Life and Wars of General Phil Sheridan* (New York: Crown, 1992). For more on Sheridan's critical role in the Battle of Chattanooga, see Wiley Sword, *Mountains Touched with Fire* (New York: St. Martin's Press, 1995).

4 Horace Porter, *Campaigning with Grant* (Bloomington: University of Indiana Press, 1961), 23.

5 Kidd, *Personal Recollections of a Cavalryman*, 298.

6 Morris, *Sheridan*, 1.

7 Gracey, *Annals*, 231.

8 Louis Henry Carpenter, "Sheridan's Expedition Around Richmond, May 9-25, 1864," *Journal of the United States Cavalry Association* 1 (1888): 301.

9 Edward Laight Wells, *Hampton and His Cavalry in 1864* (Richmond, Va.: B. F. Johnson Publishing Co., 1899), 95.

10 Wittenberg, *We Have It Damn Hard Out Here*, 120.

11 O.R. vol. 36, part 1, 787.

12 Philip H. Sheridan, *Personal Memoirs of P. H. Sheridan*, 2 vols. (New York: Charles L. Webster & Co., 1888), 1:354-345.

13 Cowan to his parents, May 3, 1864, Cowan Papers.

14 O.R. vol. 33, 941.

15 Wittenberg, *We Have It Damn Hard Out Here*, 120.

16 Coller diary, entry for April 29, 1864.

17 Christian Geisel to Dear Sister, May 3, 1864.

18 Ballentine to Ballentine, April 30, 1864, Ballentine Letters.

19 Baynes, *Life and Ancestry*, 38.

20 Gracey, *Annals*, 302.

21 Ballentine to Ballentine, May 15, 1864.

22 O.R. vol. 36, part 2, 944-945.

23 Geisel to Dear Sister, May 3, 1864.

24 1864 Diary of John P. Kepner, entry for May 4, 1864, Virginia Historical Society, Richmond.

25 Cowan to his parents, May 15, 1864.

26 Gordon C. Rhea, *The Battles for Spotsylvania Court House and the Road to Yellow Tavern, May 7-12, 1864* (Baton Rouge: Louisiana State University Press, 1997), 30-37.

27 A. O. Abbott, *Prison Life in the South: At Richmond, Macon, Savannah, Charleston, Columbia, Charlotte, Raleigh, Goldsborough, and Andersonville, During the Years 1864 and 1865* (New York: Harper, 1865), 15.

28 James R. Bowen, *Regimental History of the First New York Dragoons During the Three Years of Active Service in the Great Civil War* (privately published, 1900), 143.

29 Fitzhugh Lee to Dear General, December 20, 1866, Eleanor S. Brockenbrough Library, Museum of the Confederacy, Richmond, Virginia.

30 Cowan to his parents, May 15, 1864.

31 Gracey, *Annals*, 235. Starr was shot in the face. The pistol ball carried away part of his jaw bone, all of the teeth on the upper left side of his mouth, and all but one on the upper right side, leaving a "discharging wound." Starr served out the balance of the war, receiving a brevet to lieutenant colonel for his valor at Todd's Tavern. Starr pension records, RG 94, NARA.

32 *Philadelphia Inquirer*, May 18, 1864.

33 See Kirk, Carpenter, and Coxe service records, NARA.

34 Gracey, *Annals*, 236.

35 Lewis, *Frank Furness*, 46.

36 Clement Hoffman to his mother, May 17, 1864.

37 *Philadelphia Inquirer*, May 10, 1864.

38 Andrew A. Humphreys, *The Virginia Campaign of 1864 and 1865*, 2 vols. (New York: Charles Scribner's Sons, 1881), 1:60-72.

39 Porter, *Campaigning with Grant*, 83-84.

40 Sheridan, *Personal Memoirs*, 1:368-369. In fact, Sheridan had a legitimate point. Of all the commanders of the Army of the Potomac, Meade probably had the least understanding of both the proper role and proper usage of cavalry. His record as an army commander is replete with examples of clear misunderstanding of the proper usage for his mounted arm. Instead of using it as a striking force, his focus was almost entirely on using it to scout and screen, which, while important, is a less effective use of a large and powerful force such as the one commanded by Sheridan in the spring of 1864.

41 Porter, *Campaigning with Grant*, 84. While there is no evidence that Meade specifically intended to relieve Sheridan and replace him with Brig. Gen. David M. Gregg, the senior division commander, this may have been the case. Sheridan was not Meade's choice, and the two men had already had some friction in their relationship. Meade probably saw Sheridan's actions as a direct challenge to his authority, and reacted strongly. Further, Sheridan had failed in his mission to clear the way for the infantry's advance on Spotsylvania via Todd's Tavern. Grant obviously did not agree with the army commander's assessment, something that undoubtedly angered Meade a great deal. An early account, written by Bvt. Lt. Col. Carswell McClellan, a cavalry staff officer, accused Sheridan of being both a liar and insubordinate, and that his insubordination in refusing to obey the lawful orders of his commanding officer, Meade, was rewarded by Grant, who permitted him to cut loose from the army in independent command. See Carswell McClellan, *Notes on the Personal Memoirs of P. H. Sheridan* (St. Paul, Minn.: Press of Wm. E. Banning, Jr., 1889), 25.

42 Sheridan, *Personal Memoirs*, 1:370-371.

43 Coller diary, entry for May 9, 1864.

44 Carpenter, "Sheridan's Expedition Around Richmond," 305.

45 Stephen Z. Starr, *The Union Cavalry in the Civil War*, 3 vols. (Baton Rouge: Louisiana State University Press, 1981), 2:97.

46 O.R. vol. 36, part 1, 184.

47 Gracey, *Annals*, 242.

48 O.R. vol. 36, part 1, 846-847.

49 Hageman, *Fighting Rebels and Redskins*, 233.

50 Leiper Moore Robinson memoir, Virginia Historical Society, Richmond, 12.

51 Gracey, *Annals*, 242-243.

52 O.R. vol. 36, part 1, 813.

53 Ibid., 156.

54 Bowen, *First New York Dragoons*, 155.

55 O.R. vol. 36, part 1, 813.

56 Ballentine to Ballentine, May 15, 1864.

57 Bown, *First New York Dragoons*, 157.

58 Howard Smith to his mother, May 18, 1864.

59 O.R. vol. 36, part 1, 847.

60 Ibid., 184.

61 Ibid., 847.

62 Christian Geisel to Dear Sister, May 17, 1864.

63 Ballentine to Ballentine, May 15, 1864.

64 Hageman, *Fighting Rebels and Redskins*, 234.

65 Gracey, *Annals*, 244.

66 Ibid., 243-245.

67 Edgar H. Klemroth, "Fight at Yellow Tavern: Custer Charged and Captured a Battery," *National Tribune*, September 4, 1919.

68 Hoffman to his mother, May 17, 1864.

69 Alonzo V. Foster, *Reminiscences and Record of the 6th New York V.V. Cavalry* (Brooklyn: privately published, 1892), 75; Edward P. Tobie, *History of the First Maine Cavalry* (Boston: First Maine Cavalry Assoc., 1887), 266.

70 Coller diary, entry for May 12, 1864.

71 Ballentine to Ballentine, May 15, 1864.

72 Charles McK. Loeser, "Personal Recollections—A Ride to Richmond in 1864," in Rodenbough, *From Everglade to Canon*, 306.

73 Cowan to his parents, May 15, 1864.

74 Geisel to his sister, May 17, 1864. See also Gordon C. Rhea, *To the North Anna River: Grant and Lee, May 13-25, 1864* (Baton Rouge: Louisiana State University Press, 2000), 46-56. Rhea's account is the only detailed tactical treatment of the important engagement at Meadow Bridge.

75 O.R. vol. 36, part 1, 185.

76 Ballentine to Ballentine, May 15, 1864.

77 Hoffman to his mother, May 17, 1864.

78 Sgt. Lawrence Pennington, who was killed at the Battle of Trevilian Station on June 11, 1864.

79 William H. Rinehart. Interestingly, the regimental muster roll lists Rinehart as being a private, and does not reflect a promotion to sergeant.

80 Wittenberg, *We Have It Damn Hard Out Here*, 123.

81 Emory M. Thomas, *Bold Dragoon: The Life of J. E. B. Stuart* (New York: Random House, 1986), 297. For a detailed study of Sheridan's Richmond Raid and the Battle of Yellow Tavern, see Carpenter, "Sheridan's Expedition Around Richmond," and Theophilus F. Rodenbough, "Sheridan's Richmond Raid," *B&L*, 4:188-193.

82 Festus P. Summers, ed., *A Borderland Confederate* (Pittsburgh: University of Pittsburgh Press, 1962), 80; Tracy Power, *Lee's Miserables: Life in the Army of Northern Virginia from the Wilderness to Appomattox* (Chapel Hill: University of North Carolina Press, 1998), 57.

83 G. T. Cralle, "The Bold Horsemen," *Richmond Dispatch*, January 1, 1900.

84 Manly Wade Wellman, *Giant in Gray: A Biography of Wade Hampton of South Carolina* (New York: Charles Scribner's Sons, 1949), 140. Southern historian Douglas Southall Freeman observed, "In combat [Hampton] undeniably was the peer if he was not the superior of Fitz Lee, though Hampton was not as resourceful as Fitz in finding provender for the horses. Fitz, on the other hand, had been closer to Stuart personally and had much of 'Jeb's' joy of battle. The difficulty was that Hampton and Fitz Lee were secret rivals. They never were pitted against each other. Outwardly, they were on good terms. At heart, Fitz Lee represented and Wade Hampton challenged the Virginia domination of the cavalry Corps, and, some would say, of the entire Army of Northern Virginia. Advancement of one man over the other might, at the moment, be demoralizing. Time must try and perhaps time would resolve the differences between the two." Douglas Southall Freeman, *Lee's Lieutenants: A Study in Command*, 3 vols. (New York: Charles Scribner's Sons, 1944), 3:436.

85 O.R. vol. 36, part 2, 1001 ("until further orders, the three Divisions of Cavalry serving with this Army will constitute separate commands and will report directly to and receive orders from these headquarters"). Lloyd Halliburton, ed., *Saddle Soldiers: The Civil War Correspondence of General William Stokes of the 4th South Carolina Cavalry* (Orangeburg, S.C.: Sandlapper, 1993), 139 ("Since Stuart has been killed I hear there will be no more Cavalry Corps, but that each of the Major Generals will have a division and report direct to General Lee").

86 O.R. vol. 36, part 1, 815.

87 Carpenter, "Sheridan's Expedition Around Richmond," 321.

88 Ballentine to Ballentine, May 15, 1864.

89 Geisel to his sister, May 22, 1864. Captured by the Confederates, he was taken away. The wound eventually became infected, and Geisel died of disease, far from home.

90 Gracey, *Annals*, 251.

91 George R. Agassiz, ed., *Meade's Headquarters, 1863-1865: Letters of Colonel Theodore Lyman from the Wilderness to Appomattox* (Boston: Atlantic Monthly Press, 1922), 131.

92 Gracey, *Annals*, 254.

93 O.R. vol. 36, part 1, 848.

94 Ibid.; Charles L. Leiper pension and service records.

95 O.R. vol. 36, part 1, 848.

96 Richard J. Gibbs pension file, NARA. Gibbs remained hospitalized until well after his discharge in October 1864.

97 Coller diary, entry for May 30, 1864.

98 Gracey, *Annals*, 255.

99 Ibid.

100 O.R. vol. 26, part 1, 849.

101 Ibid., 805.

102 Ibid., 851; Gracey, *Annals*, 255.

103 Lewis, *Frank Furness*, 47-48.

104 O.R. vol. 36, part 1, 18-22. The fighting at Cold Harbor and Petersburg foreshadowed the ghastly trench warfare of World War I, featuring direct frontal assaults against strongly entrenched enemy positions marked by appalling casualties.

105 Grant, *Personal Memoirs*, 588.

106 Gracey, *Annals*, 258.

107 John D. Imboden to I. Marshall McCue, October 1, 1883, John D. Imboden Papers, Museum of the Confederacy, Richmond, Virginia. For more on the campaign in the Valley, see Richard R. Duncan, *Lee's Endangered Left: The Civil War in Western Virginia, Spring of 1864* (Baton Rouge: Louisiana State University Press, 1998).

108 O.R. vol. 37, part 1, 485-486.

109 Ibid., 591.

110 Edward G. Longacre, *Mounted Raids of the Civil War* (South Brunswick, N.J.: A. S. Barnes, 1975), 122. For more on Grierson's spectacular raid, see D. Alexander Brown, *Grierson's Raid: A Cavalry Adventure of the Civil War* (Urbana: University of Illinois Press, 1954). A similar diversion by a brigade of mounted infantry under command of Col. Abel Streight earlier in the campaign also drew off Maj. Gen. Nathan Bedford Forrest's cavalry, thereby allowing Grant freedom of maneuver. Unfortunately, Streight's raid was nowhere near as successful as that of Grierson.

111 For a detailed discussion of the Battle of Piedmont, see Scott C. Patchan, *The Forgotten Fury: The Battle of Piedmont, Virginia* (Fredericksburg, Va.: Sergeant Kirkland's Museum and Historical Society, 1996).

112 O.R. vol. 36, part 1, 22.

113 O.R. vol. 36, part 3, 598.

114 Sheridan, *Personal Memoirs*, 1:415.

115 O.R. vol. 36, part 1, 795. This may be a bit of twenty-twenty hindsight on Sheridan's part.

116 O.R. vol. 37, part 1, 598.

117 Sheridan, *Personal Memoirs*, 1:417-418. The precise location of Carpenter's Ford is impossible to pin down today, as that crossing is now under water, part of the Lake Anna dam complex built for flood control, reservoir, and recreational purposes during the latter half of the twentieth century.

118 O.R. vol. 36, part 1, 795; *New York Herald*, June 21, 1864.

119 Henry Pyne, *Ride to War: The History of the First New Jersey Cavalry* (New Brunswick, N.J.: Rutgers University Press, 1961), 217.

120 William P. Lloyd, *History of the First Regiment Pennsylvania Reserve Cavalry, From Its Organization, August 1861, to September 1864, With List of Names of All Officers and Enlisted Men Who Have Ever Belonged to the Regiment, and Remarks Attached to Each Name, Noting Change* (Philadelphia: King & Baird, 1864), 97.

121 *New York Herald*, June 21, 1864.

122 *Philadelphia Press*, July 4, 1864.

123 Ballentine to Ballentine, June 22, 1864.

124 Gracey, *Annals*, 258-259.

125 Frank Furness Medal of Honor File, RG 94, File No. F164VS1862, NARA. Furness' Medal of Honor application was also endorsed by Col. Albert P. Morrow, who went on to enjoy a lengthy career in the Regular Army in the years following the Civil War.

126 Fitzhugh Lee to Dear General, December 20, 1866.

127 Baynes, *Life and Ancestry*, 40-41.

128 Robert W. Mitchell to Jeremiah Geissinger, July 12, 1864, included in Abraham Geissinger pension file.

129 Gracey, *Annals*, 262-263.

130 O.R. vol. 36, part 1, 186.

131 Memorandum of Maj. James D. Ferguson on the Virginia Campaign, Jedediah Hotchkiss Papers, Library of Congress, Manuscripts Division, Washington, D.C.

132 O.R. vol. 36, part 1, 809.

133 Howard M. Smith diary, entry for June 12, 1864.

134 Gracey, *Annals*, 263.

135 Ibid., 265.

136 Wittenberg, *We Have It Damn Hard Out Here*, 126.

137 William P. C. Treichel service and pension records.

138 Ballentine to Ballentine, July 3, 1864.

139 Coover to his sister, June 23, 1864.

140 Wittenberg, *We Have It Damn Hard Out Here*, 126.

141 Hoffman to his mother, June 23, 1864.

142 O.R. vol. 40, part 2, 512.

143 Sheridan, *Personal Memoirs*, 1:444.

144 Howard M. Smith diary, entry for June 29, 1864.

145 Smith to his sister, July 6, 1864.

146 Cowan to his parents, July 4, 1864.

147 Hageman, *Fighting Rebels and Redskins*, 250.

148 Smith to his sister, July 6, 1864.

149 Strang, *Sunshine and Shadows*, 54.

150 Cowan to his parents, July 4, 1864.

151 O.R. vol. 40, part 1, 289.

152 Strang, *Sunshine and Shadows*, 54-55.

153 Moses Harris, "With the Reserve Brigade," *Journal of the United States Cavalry Association* 3 (1890): 10.

154 Gracey, *Annals*, 271.

155 Ballentine to Ballentine, July 22, 1864.

156 O.R. vol. 40, part 3, 409.

157 Coller diary, entry for July 22, 1864.

158 O.R. vol. 40, part 3, 437-438, 505, 532.

159 Hageman, *Fighting Rebels and Redskins*, 253.

160 Ibid.

161 Smith to his sister, August 2, 1864.

162 Sheridan, *Personal Memoirs*, 1:448. There is no comprehensive study of the First Battle of Deep Bottom, and one is needed. For the best treatment to date, see Bryce A. Suderow, "Glory Denied: The First Battle of Deep Bottom, July 27th-29th, 1864," *North & South* 3, no. 7 (September 2000): 17-33.

163 Gracey, *Annals*, 272.

164 Coller diary, entry for July 28, 1864.

165 Cowan to his parents, August 3, 1864.

166 Smith to his sister, August 2, 1864.

167 Lanigan service records.

168 Gracey, *Annals*, 273.

169 Ibid., 274.

170 Suderow, "Glory Denied," 31.

171 Sheridan, *Personal Memoirs*, 1:448.

172 Ballentine to Ballentine, August 4, 1864.

173 Sheridan, *Personal Memoirs*, 1:451.

174 Gracey, *Annals*, 277.

175 Coover to his sister, August 3, 1864.

CHAPTER 10. THE LANCERS GO TO THE SHENANDOAH VALLEY

1 The best source on Early's movement to Lynchburg is Richard R. Duncan, *Lee's Endangered Left: The Civil War in Western Virginia, Spring of 1864* (Baton Rouge: Louisiana State University Press, 1998).

2 For a more detailed examination of the Battle of Monocacy and of Early's march on Washington, see Benjamin Franklin Cooling, *Jubal Early's Raid on Washington 1864* (Baltimore: Nautical and Aviation Pub. Co. of America, 1989) and Benjamin Franklin Cooling, *Monocacy: The Battle That Saved Washington* (Shippensburg, Pa.: White Mane, 1997).

3 O.R. vol. 37, part 2, 558.

4 Wesley Merritt, "Sheridan in the Shenandoah Valley," in *B&L*, 4:501.

5 Grant, *Personal Memoirs*, 2:321.

6 Leiper service records.

7 O.R. vol. 43, part 1, 697-698.

8 Ibid., 54.

9 Sheridan noted in his memoirs, "The transfer of Torbert to the position of chief of cavalry left Merritt . . . in command of the First Cavalry Division. He had been tried in the place before, and from the day he was selected as one of a number of young men to be appointed general officers, with the object of giving life to the Cavalry Corps, he filled the measure of expectation." Sheridan, *Memoirs*, 1:474.

10 O.R. vol. 43, part 1, 487.

11 Gracey, *Annals*, 280.

12 Harrison, "Personal Recollections," 339.

13 Hageman, *Fighting Rebels and Redskins*, 257.

14 Gracey, *Annals*, 281-282.

15 Ibid., 283.

16 Ibid., 284.

17 Ibid., 288.

18 Henry C. Cowan to Mary Virginia Shell, September 15, 1864, Helen L. and Mary Virginia Shell Papers, 1858-1875, Perkins Library, Duke University, Durham, North Carolina.

19 James E. Taylor, *With Sheridan up the Shenandoah Valley in 1864: Leaves from a Special Artist's Sketchbook and Diary* (Cleveland, Ohio: Morningside House, 1989), 259.

20 Charles Richard Williams, ed., *The Diary and Letters of Rutherford B. Hayes, Nineteenth President of the United States*, 5 vols. (Columbus, Ohio: Ohio Historical Society, 1922), 2:500.

21 Gracey, *Annals*, 291.

22 Harrison, "Personal Recollections," 345.

23 Letter by Charles L. Leiper of December 5, 1864, in John Wagner pension file.

24 Ballentine to Ballentine, September 2, 1864.

25 *The Germantown Guide*, July 1924.

26 Gracey, *Annals*, 290-295.

27 Coover to his sister, August 30, 1864.

28 Ballentine to Ballentine, September 2, 1864.

29 O.R. vol. 43, part 1, 489.

30 Ballentine to Ballentine, September 2, 1864.

31 Harrison, "Personal Recollections," 347.

32 Cowan to Shell, September 15, 1864.

33 Cowan to his parents, September 1, 1864, Cowan Papers.

34 Coller diary, entry for August 29, 1864.

35 Ballentine to Ballentine, September 2, 1864.

36 Howard M. Smith to his mother, September 1, 1864.

37 Hoffman to his mother, September 10, 1864.

38 Gracey, *Annals*, 296-297.

39 Ballentine to Ballentine, September 15, 1864.

40 Howard M. Smith to his mother, September 12, 1864. The Dragoons were transferred out of the Reserve Brigade that day, joining Col. Thomas C. Devin's brigade.

41 Cowan to his parents, September 10, 1864, Cowan Papers.

42 O.R. vol. 43, part 2, 52.

43 Cowan to Shell, September 15, 1864.

44 Charles B. Coxe service records.

45 O.R., series 3, vol. 3, 580.

46 An extended discussion of the merits and weaknesses of the Cavalry Bureau goes far beyond the scope of this book. For further information, readers should see Stephen Z. Starr, *The Union Cavalry in the Civil War*, 3 vols. (Baton Rouge: Louisiana State University Press, 1981), 2:4-19.

47 Gracey, *Annals*, 297.

48 Hoffman to his mother, September 10, 1864.

49 Clement Hoffman service records.

50 Baynes, *Life and Ancestry*, 43.

51 Carpenter to his mother, September 13, 1864, Carpenter letters, USAMHI; Gracey, *Annals*, 307-308. Carpenter actually escaped in July 1864 and made it to within five miles of the Union lines before being recaptured. The Carpenter brothers escaped a second time in October 1864 and were recaptured in a miserable South Carolina swamp. The brothers were moved to a prison camp in Columbia. Learning of the approach of Sherman's army, the Carpenters and a few others cut holes in the wooden ceiling of a frame building, concealed themselves in the ceiling, and waited until the Rebels departed in the wake of Sherman's army. The brothers came down from their hiding place, and headed out to meet the vanguard of Sherman's army, which was closing in on Columbia in mid-February. A friend of Emlen Carpenter's, serving on Sherman's staff, recognized Carpenter and welcomed the escapees. Carpenter received orders

to report to Maj. Gen. O. O. Howard, and served on Howard's staff through the Carolinas Campaign. Soon after Sherman's army entered Fayetteville on March 11, Carpenter received a leave of absence and returned to Philadelphia, where he received his discharge. Gracey, *Annals*, 308-309.

52 Cowen to Shell, October 10, 1864.

53 Gracey, *Annals*, 299.

54 See Coover service records.

55 William H. Cunningham, "The Shenandoah Valley," *Philadelphia Inquirer*, October 3, 1864.

56 Ibid.

57 Briscoe Goodhart, *History of the Independent Loudoun Virginia Rangers, U.S. Cav. Scouts, 1862-65* (Washington, D.C.: Press of McGill & Wallace, 1896), 174-176.

58 Ballentine to Ballentine, October 2, 1864.

59 *Philadelphia Inquirer*, November 8, 1864. Henry Cowan of Company K reported that the Republican electors received 114 votes, and the Democratic electors received 36, for a Republican majority of 78 votes. Cowan to his parents, November 9, 1864, Cowan Papers.

60 Klemroth's sketch book survived, and is part of the manuscripts and archives collection at the Main Library at Michigan State University, in East Lansing, Michigan. While almost none of it has been published, Klemroth's drawings chronicle the Valley Campaign and the last days in service of most of a fine cavalry regiment.

61 Gracey, *Annals*, 297.

62 Cowan to his parents, November 21, 1864.

63 *Philadelphia Inquirer*, November 8, 1864.

64 O.R. vol. 43, part 2, 641, 647.

65 Cowan to his parents, November 23, 1864.

66 O.R. vol. 43, part 2, 708.

67 Ibid., 830.

68 Ibid., 845-846.

69 Ibid., 791, 825, 856.

70 Ballentine to Ballentine, December 22, 1864.

CHAPTER 11. THE END OF THE LINE FOR THE LANCERS

1 Richard J. Gibbs pension records, RG 94, NARA.

2 *Philadelphia Inquirer*, January 3, 1865. It is not known what happened to Gibbs as a result of this wound. Because he had already been discharged from the Army, there is no mention of it in his pension file, and the author has been unable to locate any further information to indicate Gibbs's fate. We do know that the wound was not fatal, since he successfully applied for—and received—an invalid pension for his 1864 combat wounds in 1868.

3 Ballentine to Ballentine, January 8, 1865, Ballentine Letters.

4 Cowan to his parents, January 20, 1865, Cowan Papers.

5 O.R. vol. 46, part 1, 124.

6 Ballentine to Ballentine, January 30, 1865.

7 The six hundred new recruits of the 6th Pennsylvania Cavalry did not receive mounts until mid-April 1865, after the surrender of the Army of Northern Virginia on April 9. The dismounted recruits spent the interim period guarding the Baltimore & Ohio Railroad from Mosby's guerrillas. On April 12, 1865, they were ordered to report to the Remount Camp in Pleasant Valley to receive their horses. O.R. vol. 46, part 3, 726.

8 Ballentine to Ballentine, February 8, 1865.

9 Ibid.

10 Gracey, *Annals*, 317.

11 Charles B. Coxe service records.

12 Ballentine to Ballentine, February 8, 1865.

13 Grant, *Personal Memoirs*, 676.

14 O.R. vol. 46, part 2, 545.

15 Ibid., 606.

16 Sheridan, *Personal Memoirs*, 2:119.

17 Hageman, *Fighting Rebels and Redskins*, 311.

18 Cowan to his parents, February 23, 1865.

19 Harris, "With the Reserve Brigade," 4:4 and 10.

20 Strang, *Sunshine and Shadows*, 76.

21 Gracey, *Annals*, 318.

22 Strang, *Sunshine and Shadows*, 76.

23 Gracey, *Annals*, 318.

24 O.R. vol. 46, part 1, 488.

25 Gracey, *Annals*, 318-319.

26 Ibid., 319.

27 Veil, *Memoirs*, 58.

28 Gracey, *Annals*, 320.

29 Veil, *Memoirs*, 61.

30 O.R. vol. 46, part 2, 918.

31 Strang, *Sunshine and Shadows*, 79.

32 Wells pension records.

33 O.R. vol. 46, part 2, 980.

34 Gracey, *Annals*, 323.

35 Charles L. Leiper to Andrew G. Curtin, February 12, 1865, Muster Rolls & Related Records, 1861-1865, 70th Regiment, 6th Pennsylvania Cavalry, Records of the Dept. of Military Affairs, RG 19, Records of the Office of the Adjutant General, Pennsylvania State Archives, Harrisburg.

36 Gracey, *Annals*, 326.

37 Sheridan, *Personal Memoirs*, 2:124.

38 Veil, *Memoirs*, 61.

39 Henry E. Tremain, *The Last Hours of Sheridan's Cavalry* (New York: Bonnell, Silver & Bowers, 1904), 20.

40 Gracey, *Annals*, 329.

41 O.R. vol. 46, part 1, 1128.

42 Gracey, *Annals*, 330.

43 For a detailed narrative of the battles at Dinwiddie Court House and Five Forks, see Chris Calkins, *The Appomattox Campaign, March 29-April 9, 1865* (Conshohocken, Pa.: Combined Publishing, 1999), 9-27. This book is probably the best account of the war's last campaign.

44 Ballentine to Ballentine, April 15, 1865.

45 Gracey, *Annals*, 335.

46 O.R. vol. 46, part 2, 341-342.

47 Sylvanus Cadwallader, *Three Years with Grant, as Recalled by War Correspondent Sylvanus Cadwallader*, Benjamin P. Thomas, ed. (New York: Knopf, 1955), 301.

48 Transcript of the Court of Inquiry of Gouverneur K. Warren, 2 vols., in *Supplement to the Official Records of the Union and Confederate Armies*, 100 vols. (Wilmington, N.C.: Broadfoot Publishing, 1995), 9:1028.

49 Grant, *Personal Memoirs*, 702.

50 Horace Porter, "Five Forks and the Pursuit of Lee," in *B&L*, 4:710.

51 Porter, *Campaigning With Grant*, 419-420.

52 Gracey, *Annals*, 377.

53 Frederic C. Newhall, *With General Sheridan in Lee's Last Campaign* (Philadelphia: J. B. Lippincott, 1866), 93.

54 Sheridan, *Personal Memoirs*, 2:160.

55 Ibid., 161.

56 Porter, *Campaigning With Grant*, 440-441.

57 Newhall wrote his book for two reasons. First, and foremost, he chronicled the Civil War's final campaign in the Eastern Theater. However, Newhall's less obvious motivation was to defend Sheridan's removal of Warren, Which he continued to do for the rest of his life. Years after the events Warren finally received a court of inquiry, which found that Sheridan was not justified in relieving Warren of command.

58 For a detailed study of the Battle of Five Forks, see Edwin C. Bearss and Chris Calkins, *The Battle of Five Forks* (Lynchburg, Va.: H. E. Howard, 1985).

59 Gracey, *Annals*, 340.

60 O.R. vol. 46, part 3, 1378.

61 For a detailed examination of the breakthrough at Petersburg, see A. Wilson Greene's excellent *Breaking the Backbone of the Rebellion: The Final Battles of the Petersburg Campaign* (Mason City, Iowa: Savas, 2000).

62 Veil, *Memoirs*, 63.

63 O.R. vol. 46, part 1, 1128.

64 Ibid., part 3, 1379.

65 Calkins, *The Appomattox Campaign*, 55-59.

66 Porter, *Campaigning With Grant*, 452-453.

67 Chamberlain, *The Passing of the Armies*, 231-232.

68 Ballentine to Ballentine, April 11, 1865.

69 Calkins, *The Appomattox Campaign*, 155-156.

70 O.R. vol. 46, part 3, 641.

71 Ibid., 664.

72 James McLean, *California Sabers: The 2nd Massachusetts Cavalry in the Civil War* (Bloomington: University of Indiana Press, 2000), 271.

73 Bowen, *Nineteenth New York Cavalry*, 282.

74 Gracey, *Annals*, 349-350.

75 Ballentine to Ballentine, April 11, 1865.

76 Power, *Lee's Miserables*, 280.

77 O.R. vol. 46, part 1, 1109.

78 Edward G. Longacre, *Lincoln's Cavalrymen: A History of the Mounted Forces of the Army of the Potomac* (Mechanicsburg, Pa.: Stackpole, 2000), 332.

79 Sheridan, *Personal Memoirs*, 2:196-198.

80 Ibid., 2:200; Porter, *Campaigning With Grant*, 469-470.

81 Edgar H. Klemroth, "An Artist at Appomattox," *National Tribune*, April 21, 1927.

82 Gracey, *Annals*, 353.

83 Klemroth, "An Artist at Appomattox."

84 Ballentine to Ballentine, April 11, 1865.

85 Ibid., April 15, 1865.

86 For additional information on the Danville Expedition, which is beyond the scope of this work, see Chris Calkins, *The Danville Expedition of May and June 1865* (Danville, Va.: Blue & Gray Education Society, 1998), 5-15.

87 Baynes, *Life and Ancestry*, 47.

88 O.R. vol. 46, part 1, 125.

89 Ballentine to Ballentine, May 6, 1865.

90 Charles B. Coxe to John Cadwalader, May 7, 1865, Cadwalader Collection, HSP.

91 Cowan to his parents, May 18, 1865, Cowan Papers.

92 Baynes, *Life and Ancestry*, 48.

93 Ibid., 48-49.

94 Strang, *Sunshine and Shadows*, 79.

95 Ballentine to Ballentine, May 18, 1865.

96 Veil, *Memoirs*, 66.

97 O.R. vol. 46, part 3, 1191.

98 Gracey, *Annals*, 353.

99 *Philadelphia Inquirer*, June 10, 1865.

100 Cowan to his parents, June 2, 1865.

101 Francis L. Ballinger diary, entry for June 18, 1865, Geoff and Jill Jones Collection, Shasta Lake, California.

102 Baynes, *Life and Ancestry*, 50.

103 Ibid., 51.

104 Cowan to his parents, July 23, 1865.

105 Ballinger diary, entry for July 27, 1865.

106 Baynes, *Life and Ancestry*, 52.

107 Ballinger diary, entry for August 1, 1865.

108 Ibid., entry for August 2, 1865.

109 Ibid., entry for August 7, 1865.

110 Ballentine to Ballentine, August 7, 1865.

111 Gracey, *Annals*, 354.

112 Ibid., 364.

CHAPTER 12. REQUIEM

1 Frederick H. Dyer, *A Compendium of the War of the Rebellion: Compiled and Arranged from Official Records of the Federal and Confederate Armies, Reports of the Adjutant Generals of the Several States, the Army Registers, and Other Reliable Documents and Sources*, 3 vols. (Des Moines: Dyer Publishing Co., 1908), 3:1561.

2 Taylor, *Philadelphia in the Civil War*, 164.

3 As an example, Capt. Emlen N. Carpenter's health was so shattered by the trials and tribulations of his service that he never fully recovered his strength, and died young. See Carpenter service records.

4 "Richard H. Rush," *Twenty-Fifth Annual Reunion of the Association of the Graduates of the United States Military Academy at West Point, New York, June 12th, 1894* (Saginaw, Mich.: Seemann & Peters, 1894), 42.

5 George Stoneman to George Meade, November 28, 1865, Gregory Acken Collection, Middleton, New Jersey.

6 Whelan to Cadwalader, June 11, 1863; *Philadelphia Press*, August 6, 1863.

7 Philip H. Sheridan to Samuel L. Gracey, February 5, 1866, in Gracey, *Annals*.

8 *Dedication of the Monument of the Sixth Penna. Cavalry*, 12.

9 Graham to Meade, August 10, 1889.

10 Dyer, *Compendium*, 3:1560-61. A detailed list of the engagements of the 6th Pennsylvania Cavalry is included in the Appendix to this book.

11 Commissions for his old comrades-in-arms included William W. Frazier and Rudulph Ellis, among several others.

12 A detailed examination of Furness' architectural work strays far beyond the scope of this study. Those interested in Furness' architectural legacy should refer to George E. Thomas, Michael J. Lewis, and Jeffrey A. Cohen, *Frank Furness: The Complete Works* (New York: Princeton Architectural Press, 1991), and James F. O'Gorman, *The Architecture of Frank Furness* (Philadelphia: Philadelphia Museum of Art, 1973). A large collection of Furness' papers, including many of his architectural designs, can be found at the University of Pennsylvania in Philadelphia.

13 "Rush's Lancers Meet Once More," *National Tribune*, October 8, 1931; *Philadelphia Public Ledger*, August 25, 1931.

14 *With General Sheridan in Lee's Last Campaign* (Philadelphia: J. B. Lippincott & Co., 1866). In the 1890s, most of the book was serialized, this time under Newhall's own name, in a veterans' publication called the *First Maine Bugle*.

15 *Philadelphia Public Ledger*, August 25, 1898.

16 Newhall to Sheridan, July 13, 1886, 3496 AGO 1886, RG 94, NARA and endorsements thereto. Vexillologist Howard Michael Madaus purchased it in the 1970s, and eventually sold it to Mitchell E. McGlynn of Burke, Virginia, who remains its steward. Thanks to both Madaus and McGlynn for making me aware of this fascinating vignette in the history of the Lancers.

17 George W. Cullum, *Biographical Register of the Officers and Graduates of the U.S. Military Academy at West Point, N.Y. from Its Establishment in 1802 to 1890*, 2 vols. (Boston: Houghton, Mifflin & Co., 1891), 2:276.

18 Stephen W. Sears, Stephen, ed., *The Civil War Papers of George B. McClellan: Selected Correspondence, 1860-1865* (New York: Ticknor & Fields, 1989), 607-608.

19 When Rush was invited to the dedication of the regimental monument on the Gettysburg battlefield, he wrote: "Col. R. H. Rush presents his compliments and thanks to the V. A. Association, 6th Pennsylvania Cavalry, for the honor of their invitation, to be with them at the dedication of their monument at Gettysburg, and very much regrets that he cannot accept." Richard H. Rush to George Meade, October 11, 1888, author's collection.

20 *Philadelphia Record*, October 20, 1893; *Philadelphia Inquirer*, October 19, 1893; *Germantown Guide*, October 21, 1893. Almost nothing is known about Rush's postwar life. Extensive research has failed to determine how he spent the years 1865-1893. Most sources simply indicate that he returned to private life and say nothing further.

21 Samuel L. Gracey, *Annals of the Sixth Pennsylvania Cavalry* (Philadelphia: E. H. Butler & Co., 1868).

22 Smith to Smith, June 9, 1865.

23 Benedict Maryniak, *Inventory of Federal Chaplains of the Civil War*, unpublished manuscript, Buffalo, New York.

24 In December 1865, Keogh wrote of Morrow: "He served in our staff with Maj. Genl. Buford. I liked him much he was considered quite a handsome fellow and was a very gallant soldier—as we would say in the Green Isle—'The Devil among the women.'" Myles W. Keogh to his brother, December 24, 1865, Myles W. Keogh Papers, National Library, Dublin, Ireland. Keogh met an unfortunate end, dying with his commander, Lt. Col. George A. Custer, in the June 1876 Battle of the Little Big Horn.

25 "Record of Colonel Albert P. Morrow," William Redwood Wright Section Folder, Sidney L. Wright Collection, Historical Society of Pennsylvania.

26 See Wint's service records, which indicate that he was eighteen years old at the time of his enlistment.

27 *Philadelphia Inquirer*, March 22, 1907.

28 Ibid.; "Gen. Wint Dead," *New York Times*, March 22 and 26, 1907; Heitman, *Historical Register*, 1:1051; Carter, *From Yorktown to Santiago*, 312; *Washington Post*, March 25, 1907.

29 Meade wrote a book defending his father's conduct of the battle. See George Meade, *Did General Meade Desire to Retreat at the Battle of Gettysburg?* (Philadelphia: Porter & Coates, 1883).

30 Blake A. Magner, ed., *At Peace with Honor: The Civil War Burials of Laurel Hill Cemetery, Philadelphia, Pennsylvania* (Collingswood, N.J.: C. W. Historicals 1997), 31-32.

31 *Philadelphia Public Ledger*, September 23, 1915.

32 Biography of Charles B. Coxe, Coxe Family Papers, Historical Society of Pennsylvania, Philadelphia; Allan M. Heller, *Philadelphia Area Cemeteries* (Atglen, Pa.: Schiffer, 2005), 15-22.

33 Justin Couples, "'Waldheim' and Its Inhabitants," http://www.lasalle.edu/commun/history/articles/waldheim.htm

34 *Philadelphia Public Ledger*, April 27, 1909; David Outerbridge to the author, May 3, 2004.

35 *Germantown Guide*, July 1924.

36 Ibid., November 2, 1907.

37 Roger D. Hunt and Jack R. Brown, *Brevet Brigadier Generals in Blue* (Gaithersburg, Md.: Olde Soldier Books, 1989), 354.

38 *Chester Times*, May 15, 1899.

39 *Philadelphia Public Ledger*, May 18, 1899.

40 Ibid., May 28, 1900.

41 *Philadelphia Times*, September 3, 1881.

42 *James Starr*, 11.

43 *Reading Eagle*, July 13, 1895.

44 Frank Masland to the author, May 3, 2004.

45 William W. Maree service and pension records; *Wilmington Every Evening*, May 7, 1914. Thanks to Ervil J. Francis of Wilmington, Delaware, for sharing this information with the author.

46 Blaschek, "The Story of Rush's Lancers."

47 See *By-Laws of the Association of Veterans of the Sixth Pa. Cavalry* (Philadelphia: Privately published, n.d.).

48 Blaschek, "The Story of Rush's Lancers."

49 See copy of invitation to the dedication of the monument, as well as a number of letters to Meade responding to the invitation, in the author's collection. All of these items came from the Meade collection, which remained in the family until 2004, when it was all auctioned off.

50 See *Dedication of the Monument of the Sixth Penna. Cavalry "Lancers" on the Battlefield of Gettysburg, October 14, 1888* (Philadelphia: James Beale, Printer, 1889).

51 See *Dedication of the Monument of the Sixth Penna. Cavalry "Lancers" at the Headquarters of General Meade on the Battlefield of Gettysburg June 8, 1891* (Philadelphia: Privately published, 1892).

52 *North American*, October 23, 1893.

53 *Philadelphia Inquirer*, September 5, 1899.

54 Ibid., September 9, 1899.

55 *Philadelphia Times*, September 9, 1899.

56 Program for Memorial Day Services, Trinity Reformed Church, Sunday Evening, May 27th, 1900, including visitation of Sixth Pennsylvania Cavalry (Lancers) Veteran Association, Pamphlets Collection, HSP.

57 *Gettysburg Star and Sentinel*, October 5, 1904.

58 "Capt. Rudulph Ellis Casts Off Financial Cares to Play Host for Old Comrades of the Sixth," *Philadelphia Press*, June 10, 1907.

59 "Rush's Lancers' Reunion," *Germantown Independent Gazette*, June 1909.

60 Program of the 54th anniversary of the Battle of Beverly Ford, Reunion and Banquet, Sixth Pennsylvania Cavalry Lancers Association, June 9, 1917.

61 "Rush's Lancers Meet Once More."

62 *Philadelphia Inquirer*, September 18, 1930.

63 The author has studied this photograph, but unfortunately its whereabouts are now not known.

BIBLIOGRAPHY

PRIMARY SOURCES

Newspapers

American Tribune
Army and Navy Journal
Atlanta Journal
Aurora Beacon
Chester Times
Every Evening (Wilmington, Delaware)
Germantown Guide
Germantown Independent Gazette
Gettysburg Star and Sentinel
National Tribune
New York Herald
New York Times
New York Tribune
North American
Philadelphia Evening Bulletin
Philadelphia Inquirer
Philadelphia Press
Philadelphia Public Ledger
Philadelphia Record
Philadelphia Sunday Dispatch
Philadelphia Weekly Times
Pottstown News
Reading Eagle
Reading Times
Richmond Dispatch
Richmond Enquirer
Rock Island Argus

Unpublished Manuscripts

Gregory Acken Collection, Middleton, New Jersey
      George Stoneman letter of November 28, 1865
Alderman Library, University of Virginia, Charlottesville, Virginia
      Beverly Whittle Diary for 1864
Thomas A. Canfield Collection, Richfield, New York
      George Meade Correspondence
Christopher Biache Collection, Trenton, New Jersey
      Christian Geisel Letters
      Christian Geisel Diary for 1863
Civil War Museum and Library, Philadelphia, Pennsylvania
      George Meade Photographic Scrapbook Collection

Daniel H. Morgan Letters
William Brooke-Rawle Papers
Connecticut Historical Society, Hartford, Connecticut
Theodore C. Bacon Papers
Germantown Historical Society, Germantown, Pennsylvania
Naaman K. Ployd Scrapbook
Historical Society of Pennsylvania, Philadelphia
Lewis Boos memoir
Cadwalader Family Papers
Coxe Family Mining Papers
Charles B. Coxe Papers
Civil War Papers
W. M. Meredith Papers
Newhall Family Papers
J. K. Stoddard Collection
Wister Family Papers
Wright Family Papers
Henry E. Huntington Library, San Marino, California
James Bell Letters
Joseph Hooker Papers
Indiana Historical Society, Indianapolis, Indiana
George H. Chapman Diary for 1863
Geoff and Jill Jones Collection, Shasta Lake, California
Frank Ballinger Diary for 1865
Richard Lewis Collection, Lexington, Virginia
Oliver Willets Letters
Library of Congress, Manuscripts Division
Dahlgren Family Papers
Samuel P. Heintzelman Papers
Jedediah Hotchkiss Papers
Henry J. Hunt Papers
Howard M. Smith Letters
Frank Masland Collection, Carlisle, Pennsylvania
Charles H. Masland Letters
Mitchell E. McGlynn Collection, Burke, Virginia
Various documents and correspondence
Special Collections, Main Library, Michigan State University, East Lansing, Michigan
Edgar H. Klemroth Papers
Eleanor Brockenbrough Library, Museum of the Confederacy, Richmond, Virginia
John D. Imboden Papers
Fitzhugh Lee Narrative of Operations, 1864-1865
National Archives, Washington, D.C.
Frank Furness Medal of Honor File, RG 94, File No. F164VS1862
Quartermaster Consolidated Correspondence File
RG 92 Records of the Quartermaster General
RG 93 Combined Service Records, Sixth Pennsylvania Cavalry

RG 93 Combined Pension Records, Sixth Pennsylvania Cavalry

RG 94 Records of the Adjutant General's Office, 1780'S-1917

RG 94.2.1 Correspondence

RG 94.2.2 Orders, muster rolls, and returns

RG 94.2.4 Records relating to volunteers and volunteer organizations

RG 94.6 Records of the Volunteer Service (VS) Division 1861-89

RG 108 Records of the Headquarters of the Army, 1828-1903

RG 108.4 Records of the Cavalry Bureau

RG 108.4.1 Records of the Chief of Cavalry

RG 108.4.3 Records of the Cavalry Depot, Giesboro, DC

RG 156 Records of the Office of the Chief of Ordnance

RG 156.5 Records of Ordnance Department Units (Civil War to World War I) 1861-1911

RG 393 Records of United States Army Continental Commands, 1821-1920

RG 393 Letters Received 1863, Entry 3976

RG 393.4 Records of Named Departments 1821-1920

RG 393.7 Records of Posts 1820-1940

RG 393.8 Records of Armies 1832-1865

RG 393.9 Records of Army Corps, 1861-66

RG 393.13.8 Records of Cavalry Depots and Depot Camps

RG 394 Register of Captured Flags, 1861-1865

RG 394 Records of the Adjutant General's Office, 1780's-1917

National Library, Dublin, Ireland

Myles W. Keogh Papers

Pearce Civil War Collection, Special Collections, Navarro College, Corsicana, Texas

Thomas W. Smith Letters

Pennsylvania State Archives, Harrisburg, Pennsylvania

Samuel P. Bates Papers

Christian Geisel Papers

"Muster Rolls & Related Records, 1861-1866, 70th Regt.-6th Cavalry," Records of the Department of Military Affairs, RG-19, Office of the Adjutant General

Perkins Library, Duke University, Durham, North Carolina

Helen L. Shell and Mary Virginia Papers, 1858-1875

Paul Polizzi Collection, Rochester, New York

Albert P. Morrow Letters

Richmond National Battlefield, Richmond, Virginia

Charles F. James Letter

Rosenbach Museum and Library, Philadelphia, Pennsylvania

Rush/Williams/Biddle Family Papers

George F. Scott Collection, Mt. Carmel, Pennsylvania

John B. Coover Letters

United States Army Military History Institute, Carlisle, Pennsylvania

Alexander R. Chamberlin Collection

Civil War Miscellaneous Collection

Civil War Times Illustrated Collection

Harrisburg Civil War Roundtable Collection

Clement Hoffman Letters
August V. Kautz Papers
Lewis Leigh Collection
Theodore Sage Letters
Wiley Sword Collection
Michael Winey Collection
Architectural Archives, University of Pennsylvania, Philadelphia, Pennsylvania
Frank Furness Papers
Rare Books and Manuscripts Library, University of Pennsylvania, Philadelphia, Pennsylvania:
Henry Inch Cowan Papers
Virginia Historical Society, Richmond, Virginia
John Price Kepner Papers
Leiper Moore Robinson Memoir
James Ewell Brown Stuart Papers
Archives, Virginia Polytechnic Institute, Blacksburg, Virginia
Fenwick Civil War Materials Collection:
Charles Gulager Sketchbook, 1862-1864
Wisconsin Historical Society, Madison, Wisconsin
Sue Clark Knight Papers
Eric J. Wittenberg Collection, Columbus, Ohio
Miscellaneous correspondence
Miscellaneous regimental muster rolls

Published Sources

"A Boy Spy in Dixie: At Army Headquarters." *National Tribune*, April 26, 1888.

A Trooper's Adventures in the War for the Union. New York: Hurst & Co., 1863.

Abbott, Allen O. *Prison Life in the South: At Richmond, Macon, Savannah, Charleston, Columbia, Charlotte, Raleigh, Goldsborough, and Andersonville, During the Years 1864 and 1865.* New York: Harper, 1865.

Acken, J. Gregory, ed. *Inside the Army of the Potomac: The Civil War Experience of Captain Francis Adams Donaldson.* Mechanicsburg, Pa.: Stackpole, 1998.

Adams, Charles Francis, Jr. *A Cycle of Adams Letters, 1861-1865.* Edited by Worthington C. Ford. 2 vols. Boston: Houghton Mifflin, 1920.

———. *Autobiography.* Boston: Houghton Mifflin, 1916.

Agassiz, George R., ed. *Meade's Headquarters, 1863-1865: Letters of Colonel Theodore Lyman from the Wilderness to Appomattox.* Boston: Atlantic Monthly Press, 1922.

Arnold, Lt. Col. Abraham K. "The Cavalry at Gaines' Mill." *Journal of the United States Cavalry Association* 2 (1889).

Averell, William Woods. "With the Cavalry on the Peninsula." In Robert U. Johnson and Clarence C. Buel, eds., *Battles and Leaders of the Civil War.* 4 vols. New York: Century Publishing Co., 1884-1888. 2:429-433.

Baynes, Richard C., comp. *The Life and Ancestry of John Thistlethwaite Baynes (1833-1891).* Irvine, Calif.: Richard C. Baynes, 1987.

Beale, G. W. *A Lieutenant of Cavalry in Lee's Army.* Boston: Houghton Mifflin, 1918.

Beale, Richard L.T. *History of the Ninth Virginia Cavalry in the War Between the States.* Richmond, Va.: B. F. Johnson Publishing, 1899.

Blackford, William W. *War Years with Jeb Stuart*. New York: Charles Scribner's Sons, 1945.

Blaschek, Joseph. "The Story of Rush's Lancers." *National Tribune*, June 24, 1897.

Blue, John. *Hanging Rock Rebel: Lt. John Blue's War in West Virginia and the Shenandoah Valley*. Edited by Dan Oates. Shippensburg, Pa.: Burd Street Press, 1994.

Borcke, Heros von, and Justus Seibert. *The Great Cavalry Battle of Brandy Station*. Translated by Stuart T. Wright and F. D. Bridgewater. 1893; reprint, Gaithersburg, Md.: Olde Soldier Books, 1976.

Bowen, James R. *Regimental History of the First New York Dragoons During the Three Years of Active Service in the Great Civil War*. Privately published, 1900.

Boykin, Edward M. *The Falling Flag: Evacuation of Richmond, Retreat and Surrender at Appomattox*. New York: E. J. Hale & Son, 1874.

By-Laws of the Association of Veterans of the Sixth Pa. Cavalry. Philadelphia: privately published, n.d.

Cadwallader, Sylvanus. *Three years with Grant, as Recalled by War Correspondent Sylvanus Cadwallader*. Edited by Benjamin P. Thomas. New York: Knopf, 1955.

"Capt. Rudulph Ellis Casts Off Financial Cares to Play Host for Old Comrades of the Sixth," *Philadelphia Press*, June 10, 1907.

Carpenter, Louis Henry. "Sheridan's Expedition Around Richmond, May 9-25, 1864." *Journal of the United States Cavalry Association*, 1 (1888): 300-324.

Chamberlain, Joshua L. *The Passing of the Armies: An Account of the Final Campaign of the Army of the Potomac, Based Upon Personal Reminiscences of the Fifth Army Corps*. New York: G. P. Putnam, 1915.

Conway, Dr. W. S. "Gen. Custer's Raid on Charlottesville, Virginia, February 28th, 1864." *Atlanta Journal*, March 29, 1902.

Cooke, John Esten. "The Ride Around McClellan." *Philadelphia Weekly Times*, July 19, 1879.

Cooke, Philip St. George. "The Charge of Cooke's Cavalry at Gaines's Mill." In Robert U. Johnson and Clarence C. Buel, eds., *Battles and Leaders of the Civil War*. 4 vols. New York: Century Publishing Co., 1884-1888. 2:344-345.

Conrad, Thomas Nelson. *The Rebel Scout: A Thrilling History of Scouting Life in the Southern Army*. Washington, D.C.: National Publishing Co., 1904.

Couch, Darius N. "The Chancellorsville Campaign." In Robert U. Johnson and Clarence C. Buel, eds., *Battles and Leaders of the Civil War*. 4 vols. New York: Century, 1880-1901.

Cunningham, William H. "The Shenandoah Valley," *Philadelphia Inquirer*, October 3, 1864.

Dahlgren, Rear Adm. John. *Memoir of Ulric Dahlgren*. Philadelphia: J. B. Lippincott, 1872.

Davis, Sidney Morris. *Common Soldier, Uncommon War: Life as a Civil War Cavalryman*. Edited by Charles F. Cooney. Bethesda, Md.: SMD Group, 1994.

Davis, W. W. H. *History of the 104th Pennsylvania Regiment from August 22nd, 1861, to September 30th, 1864*. Philadelphia: J. B. Rogers, 1866.

Dedication of the Monument of the Sixth Penna. Cavalry "Lancers" on the Battlefield of Gettysburg, October 14, 1888. Philadelphia: James Beale, Printer, 1889.

Dedication of the Monument of the Sixth Penna. Cavalry "Lancers" at the Headquarters of General Meade on the Battlefield of Gettysburg June 8, 1891. Philadelphia: privately published, 1892.

Douglas, David G. and Robert L. Brown, eds. *A Boot Full of Memories: Captain Leonard Williams, 2nd S. C. Cavalry*. Camden, S.C.: Gray Fox, 2003.

Farrington, John. "137th Regiment Volunteer Infantry." In New York State Monuments Commission for the Battlefields of Gettysburg and Chattanooga, *Final Report on the Battlefield at Gettysburg*. 3 vols. Albany: J. B. Lyon Co., 1900, 3:936-950.

Forsyth, George A. *Thrilling Days in Army Life*. New York: Harper & Bros., 1900.

Foster, Alonzo V. *Reminiscences and Record of the 6th New York V.V. Cavalry*. Brooklyn: privately published, 1892.

Garnett, Theodore Sanford. *Riding with Stuart: Reminiscences of an Aide-de-Camp*. Edited by Robert J. Trout. Shippensburg, Pa.: White Mane, 1994.

"Gen. Wint Dead." *New York Times*, March 22, 1907.

Goodhart, Briscoe. *History of the Independent Loudoun Virginia Rangers, U.S. Cav. Scouts, 1862-65*. Washington, D.C.: Press of McGill & Wallace, 1896.

Gracey, Samuel L. *Annals of the Sixth Pennsylvania Cavalry*. Philadelphia: E. H. Butler & Co., 1868.

Grant, Ulysses S. *Personal Memoirs*. New York: Library of America, 1990.

Grimsley, Daniel A. *Battles in Culpeper County, Virginia, 1861-1865*. Culpeper, Va.: Raleigh Travers Green, 1900.

Hagemann, E. R., ed. *Fighting Rebels and Redskins: Experiences in Army Life of Colonel George B. Sanford, 1861-1892*. Norman: University of Oklahoma Press, 1968.

Hall, Hillman A., ed. *History of the Sixth New York Cavalry (Second Ira Harris Guards), Second Brigade-First Division-Cavalry Corps, Army of the Potomac 1861-1865*. Worcester Mass.: Blanchard Press, 1908.

Halliburton, Lloyd, ed. *Saddle Soldiers: The Civil War Correspondence of General William Stokes of the 4th South Carolina Cavalry*. Orangeburg, S.C.: Sandlapper Publishing, 1993.

Hard, Abner. *History of the Eighth Cavalry Regiment, Illinois Volunteers*. Reprint, Dayton, Ohio: Morningside, 1984.

Harris, Moses. "With the Reserve Brigade." *Journal of the United States Cavalry Association* 3 (1890): 10-20, 235-247, and 363-370.

———. "With the Reserve Brigade." *Journal of the United States Cavalry Association* 4 (1891): 3-26.

Harris, Samuel. *Personal Reminiscences of Samuel Harris*. Chicago: Robinson Press, 1897.

Harrison, William H. "Personal Recollections—Deep Bottom to Winchester." In Theophilus F. Rodenbough, ed., *From Everglade to Canon with the Second Dragoons*. New York: D. Van Nostrand, 1875, 329-353.

Howard, McHenry. *Recollections of a Maryland Confederate Soldier and Staff Officer Under Johnston, Jackson, and Lee*. Baltimore: Williams & Wilkins Co., 1914.

Humphreys, Andrew A. *The Virginia Campaign of 1864 and 1865*. 2 vols. New York: Charles Scribner's Sons, 1881.

Imboden, John D. "The Confederate Retreat from Gettysburg." In Robert U. Johnson and Clarence C. Buel, eds., *Battles and Leaders of the Civil War*. 4 vols. New York: Century, 1880-1901, 3:420-429.

Kennon, L. W. V. "The Valley Campaign of 1864: A Military Study." In *The Shenandoah Campaigns of 1862 and 1864 and the Appomattox Campaign of 1865: Papers of the Military Historical Society of Massachusetts*. Vol. 6. Boston: Military Historical Society of Massachusetts, 1907, 31-57.

Kesterson, Brian Stuart, ed. *The Last Survivor: The Memoirs of George William Watson*. Washington, W.Va.: Night Hawk Press, 1993.

Kidd, James H. *Personal Recollections of a Cavalryman in Custer's Michigan Brigade*. Ionia, Mich.: Sentinel Printing Co., 1908.

Klemroth, Edgar H. "An Artist at Appomattox." *National Tribune*, April 21, 1927.

————. "Fight at Yellow Tavern: Custer Charged and Captured a Battery." *National Tribune*, September 4, 1919.

Ladd, David L., and Audrey J. Ladd, eds. *The Bachelder Papers: Gettysburg in Their Own Words.* 3 vols. Dayton, Ohio: Morningside, 1995.

Law, Evander M. "The Struggle for Round Top." In Robert U. Johnson and Clarence C. Buel, eds., *Battles and Leaders of the Civil War.* 4 vols. New York: Century, 1880-1901, 3:318-330.

Lloyd, William P. *History of the First Regiment Pennsylvania Reserve Cavalry, From Its Organization, August 1861, to September 1864, With List of Names of All Officers and Enlisted Men Who Have Ever Belonged to the Regiment, and Remarks Attached to Each Name, Noting Change.* Philadelphia: King & Baird, 1864.

Loeser, Charles McK. "Personal Recollections—A Ride to Richmond in 1864." In Theophilus F. Rodenbough, ed., *From Everglade to Canon with the Second Dragoons.* New York: D. Van Nostrand, 1875: 304-314.

McClellan, Henry B. *I Rode with Jeb Stuart.* Bloomington: Indiana University Press, 1958.

McDonald, William N. *A History of the Laurel Brigade.* Baltimore: Sun Job Printing Office, 1907.

McGuire, Judith W. *Diary of a Southern Refugee During the War by a Lady of Virginia.* New York: E. J. Hale & Son, 1867.

Meade, George Gordon. *Did General Meade Desire to Retreat at the Battle of Gettysburg?* Philadelphia: Porter & Coates, 1883.

————. *The Life and Letters of George Gordon Meade.* Edited by George Gordon Meade. 2 vols. New York: Charles Scribner's Sons, 1913.

Memorial Day Services: Sunday Evening, May 27th, 1900: Visitation of Sixth Pennsylvania Cavalry (Lancers) Veterans Association. Philadelphia: Trinity Reformed Church, 1900.

Merritt, Wesley. "Recollections of the Civil War." In Theophilus F. Rodenbough, ed., *From Everglade to Canon with the Second Dragoons.* New York: D. Van Nostrand, 1875: 283-303.

Moore, Frank, ed. *Rebellion Record: A Diary of American Events with Documents, Narratives, Illustrative Incidents, Poetry, Etc.* 11 vols. and supplement. New York, 1861-1868.

Morrow, Albert P., ed. *Journal of Leslie G. Morrow, 1864.* Yorba Linda, Calif.: Privately published, 1988.

Neese, George M. *Three Years in the Confederate Horse Artillery.* New York: Neale Publishing Co., 1911.

Nevins, Allan, ed. *A Diary of Battle: The Personal Journals of Colonel Charles S. Wainwright, 1861-1865.* New York: Harcourt, Brace & World, 1962.

Newhall, Frederic C. "Address at Dedication of Monument Sixth Regiment of Cavalry." *Pennsylvania at Gettysburg.* 2 vols. Harrisburg, Pa.: B. Slingerly, 1904.

————. "The Battle of Beverly Ford." In *Annals of the War: Written by Leading Participants North & South.* Reprint, Dayton, Ohio: Morningside, 1986: 134-146.

————. *With General Sheridan in Lee's Last Campaign.* Philadelphia: J. B. Lippincott & Co., 1866.

Norton, Henry. *Deeds of Daring, or History of the Eighth N.Y. Volunteer Cavalry.* Norwich, N.Y.: Chenango Telegraph Printing House, 1889.

Opie, John N. *A Rebel Cavalryman with Lee, Stuart, and Jackson.* Chicago: W. B. Conkey, 1899.

Peck, Daniel. *Dear Rachel: The Civil War Letters of Daniel Peck.* Edited by Martha Gerber Stanford and Eleanor Erskin. Freeman, S.D.: Pine Hill Press, 1993.

"Personal Recollections—The Stoneman Raid of '63." In Theophilus F. Rodenbough, ed., *From Everglade to Canon with the Second Dragoons.* New York: D. Van Nostrand, 1875: 270-282.

Poinsett, J. R. *Cavalry Tactics, Second Part, School of the Trooper, of the Platoon and of the Squadron Mounted.* Washington, D.C.: J. and G. S. Gideon Printers, 1841.

Popkins, W. A. "Imboden's Brigade at Gettysburg." *Confederate Veteran* 22 (1914): 552.

Porter, Fitz-John. "Hanover Court-House and Gaines's Mill." In Robert U. Johnson and Clarence C. Buel, eds., *Battles and Leaders of the Civil War.* 4 vols. New York: Century Publishing Co., 1884-1888. 2:319-343.

Porter, Horace. *Campaigning with Grant.* Bloomington: University of Indiana Press, 1961.

———. "Five Forks and the Pursuit of Lee." In Robert U. Johnson and Clarence C. Buel, eds., *Battles and Leaders of the Civil War.* 4 vols. New York: Century Publishing Co., 1884-1888. 4:708-722.

Preston, Noble D. *History of the Tenth Regiment of Cavalry, New York State Volunteers, August 1861-August 1865.* New York: D. Appleton & Co., 1892.

Pyne, Henry R. *The History of First New Jersey Cavalry.* Trenton, N.J.: J. A. Beecher, 1871.

Regimental History of the First New York Dragoons, With a List of Names, Post-Office Address, Casualties of Officers and Men, and Number of Prisoners, Trophies, &., Captured from Organization to Muster-out. Washington, D.C.: Gibson Bros., 1865.

"Report of Brig. Gen. W. H. F. Lee." *Southern Historical Society Papers,* 3 (1877).

Rodenbough, Theophilus F., ed. *From Everglade to Canon with the Second Dragoons.* New York: D. Van Nostrand, 1875.

———. "Some Cavalry Leaders." In *The Photographic History of the Civil War,* ed. Francis Trevelyan Miller. 10 vols. New York: Review of Reviews Co., 1911: 10:262-288.

Roberts, Ellwood. *Biographical Annals of Montgomery County, Pennsylvania.* 2 vols. New York: T. S. Benham, 1904.

Rosser, Thomas L. *Riding with Rosser.* Edited by S. Roger Keller. Shippensburg, Pa.: Burd Street Press, 1998.

"Rush's Lancers' Reunion." *Germantown Independent Gazette,* June 1909.

"Rush's Lancers Meet Once More." *National Tribune,* October 8, 1931.

Schaff, Morris. *The Sunset of the Confederacy.* Boston: John W. Luce & Co., 1912.

Sears, Stephen W., ed. *The Civil War Papers of George B. McClellan: Selected Correspondence, 1860-1865.* New York: Ticknor & Fields, 1989.

Sheridan, Philip H. *Personal Memoirs of P. H. Sheridan.* 2 vols. New York: Charles L. Webster & Co., 1888.

Sloan, John A. *Reminiscences of the Guilford Grays.* Washington, D.C.: R. C. Polkinhorn, 1883.

Smith, Robert S. "Personal Recollections—Fisher's Hill to Cedar Creek." In Theophilus F. Rodenbough, ed., *From Everglade to Canon with the Second Dragoons.* New York: D. Van Nostrand, 1875: 354-367.

Sneden, Robert Knox. *Eye of the Storm: A Civil War Odyssey.* Edited by Nelson D. Lankford. New York: Free Press, 2000.

Speer, Allen Paul, ed. *Voices from Cemetery Hill: The Civil War Diary, Reports, and Letters of Colonel William Henry Asbury Speer (1861-1864).* Johnson City, Tenn.: Overmountain Press, 1997.

Stevenson, James H. *"Boots and Saddles": A History of the First Volunteer Cavalry of the War, Known as the First New York (Lincoln) Cavalry, and also as The Sabre Regiment, Its Organization, Campaigns and Battles.* Harrisburg, Pa.: Patriot Publishing Co., 1879.

Strang, Edgar B. *General Stoneman's Raid, Or, the Amusing Side of Army Life.* Philadelphia: Privately published, 1911.

————. *Sunshine and Shadows of the Late Civil War*. Philadelphia: Privately published, 1898.

Summers, Festus P., ed. *A Borderland Confederate*. Pittsburgh: University of Pittsburgh Press, 1962.

Supplement to the Official Records of the Union and Confederate Armies. 100 vols. in 3 series. Wilmington, N.C.: Broadfoot, 1994.

Swain, E. D., ed. *Crumbling Defenses; Or Memoirs and Reminiscences of John Logan Black, C.S.A.* Macon, Ga.: J. W. Burke, 1960.

Taylor, Emerson Gifford, ed. *Gouverneur Kemble Warren: The Life and Letters of an American Soldier*. Boston: Houghton Mifflin, 1932.

Taylor, James E. *With Sheridan up the Shenandoah Valley in 1864: Leaves from a Special Artist's Sketchbook and Diary*. Dayton, Ohio: Morningside House, 1989.

Thomas, Hampton S. *Some Personal Reminiscences of Service in the Cavalry of the Army of the Potomac*. Philadelphia: L. R. Hammersley, 1889.

Thompson, David L. "In the Ranks of Antietam." In Robert U. Johnson and Clarence C. Buel, eds., *Battles and Leaders of the Civil War*. 4 vols. New York: Century Publishing Co., 1884-1888. 2:660-662.

Tobie, Edward P. *History of the First Maine Cavalry*. Boston: First Maine Cavalry Association, 1887.

Tremain, Henry Edwin. *The Last Hours of Sheridan's Cavalry*. New York: Bonnell, Silver & Bowers, 1904.

Trout, Robert J., ed. *With Pen and Saber: The Letters and Diaries of J.E.B. Stuart's Staff Officers*. Mechanicsburg, Pa.: Stackpole, 1995.

Wainwright, Charles S. *A Diary of Battle: The Personal Journals of Colonel Charles S. Wainwright, 1861-1865*. Edited by Allan Nevins. New York: Harcourt, Brace & World, 1962.

Wainwright, Nicholas B., ed. *A Philadelphia Perspective: The Diary of Sidney George Fisher*. Philadelphia: Historical Society of Pennsylvania, 1967.

————. "Education of an Artist: The Diary of Joseph Boggs Beale." *Pennsylvania Magazine of History and Biography* (October 1973).

The War of the Rebellion: A Compilation of the Official Records of the Union and Confederate Armies. 128 vols. in 3 series. Washington, D.C.: U.S. Government Printing Office, 1880-1901.

Welles, Gideon. *Diary of Gideon Welles*. 3 vols. Boston: Houghton Mifflin, 1911.

Wells, Edward Laight. *Hampton and His Cavalry in 1864*. Richmond, Va.: B. F. Johnson Publishing Co., 1899.

Williams, Charles Richard, ed. *The Diary and Letters of Rutherford B. Hayes, Nineteenth President of the United States*. 5 vols. Columbus, Ohio: Ohio Historical Society, 1922.

Wittenberg, Eric J., ed. *"We Have It Damn Hard Out Here": The Civil War Letters of Sgt. Thomas W. Smith, Sixth Pennsylvania Cavalry*. Kent, Ohio: Kent State University Press, 1999.

SECONDARY SOURCES

Periodical Articles

Bowles, Richard, Jr. "Shannon Hill Encounter." *Goochland County Historical Society Magazine* 17 (1985): 36-49.

Brennan, Patrick. "'I'd Rather Die Than Be Whipped': Jeb Stuart's Fatal Stand at the Battle of Yellow Tavern." *North & South* 7, no. 4 (June 2004): 56-73.

Cavanaugh, Phil. "6th Pennsylvania Cavalry Uniforms." *Military Collector & Historian* 23 (Summer 1971): 57-59.

Longacre, Edward G., ed. "Henry Whelan's 'Race for Life' at Brandy Station." *Civil War Times Illustrated* 17 (Jan l979): 3238.

Pohanka, Brian C., ed. "I Was There." *Civil War* 8 (July-August 1990): 10.

Suderow, Bryce A. "Glory Denied: The First Battle of Deep Bottom, July 27th-29th, 1864." *North & South* 3, no. 7 (September 2000): 17-33.

Todd, Frederick P. and Harry G. Larter. "6th Pennsylvania Cavalry (Rush's Lancers) 1862." *Military Collector and Historian* 6 (1954): 102.

Venter, Bruce M. "The Kilpatrick-Dahlgren Raid on Richmond, February 28-March 4, 1864." *Blue & Gray* 20, no. 3 (Winter 2003): 6-22, 44-50.

Wittenberg, Eric J. "And Everything Is Lovely and the Goose Hangs High: John Buford and the Hanging of Confederate Spies During the Gettysburg Campaign." *Gettysburg Magazine* 18 (January 1998): 5-14.

———. "Ulric Dahlgren in the Gettysburg Campaign." *Gettysburg: Historical Articles of Lasting Interest* 22 (January 2000): 96-111.

Books

Adamson, Jason. *Rush Genealogy: Capt. Peter Rush of Pa., and His Descendants.* Turlock, Calif.: Privately published, 1965.

Alberts, Don E. *Brandy Station to Manila Bay: A Biography of General Wesley Merritt.* Austin, Tex.: Presidial Press, 1980.

Arnold, James R. *Jeff Davis's Own: Cavalry, Comanches and the Battle for the Texas Frontier.* New York: John Wiley & Sons, 2000.

Bates, Samuel P. *History of the Pennsylvania Volunteers, 1861-5.* 5 vols. Harrisburg: B. Slingerly, 1869.

———. *Martial Deeds of Pennsylvania.* Philadelphia: T. H. Davis & Co., 1875.

Bearss, Edwin C., and Chris Calkins. *The Battle of Five Forks.* Lynchburg, Va.: H. E. Howard, 1985.

Brown, D. Alexander. *Grierson's Raid: A Cavalry Adventure of the Civil War.* Urbana: University of Illinois Press, 1954.

Calkins, Chris. *The Appomattox Campaign, March 29-April 9, 1865.* Conshohocken, Pa.: Combined Publishing, 1999.

———. *The Danville Expedition of May and June 1865.* Danville, Va.: Blue & Gray Education Society, 1998.

Carter, Lt. Col. W. H. *From Yorktown to Santiago with the Sixth U.S. Cavalry.* 1900; reprint, Austin, Tex.: State House Press, 1989.

Catton, Bruce. *Grant Takes Command.* Boston: Little, Brown, 1968.

Conrad, W. P., and Ted Alexander. *When War Passed This Way.* Shippensburg, Pa.: Beidel, 1982.

Cooling, Benjamin Franklin. *Jubal Early's Raid on Washington 1864.* Baltimore: Nautical & Aviation Pub. Co. of America, 1989.

———. *Monocacy: The Battle That Saved Washington.* Shippensburg, Pa.: White Mane, 1997.

Crouch, Richard E. *"Rough-Riding Scout": The Story of John W. Mobberly, Loudoun's Own Civil War Guerrilla Hero.* Arlington, Va.: Elden Editions, 1994.

Cullum, George W. *Biographical Register of the Officers and Graduates of the U.S. Military Academy at West Point, N.Y., from Its Establishment, in 1802, to 1890.* 2 vols. Boston: Houghton Mifflin, 1890.

Davies, Henry E. *General Sheridan.* New York: D. Appleton & Co., 1895.

DePeyster, John Watts. *The Decisive Conflicts of the Late Civil War*. New York: MacDonald & Co., 1867.

Downey, Fairfax. *Clash of Cavalry: The Battle of Brandy Station*. New York: David McKay, 1959.

Duncan, Richard R. *Lee's Endangered Left: The Civil War in Western Virginia, Spring of 1864*. Baton Rouge: Louisiana State University Press, 1998.

Dyer, Frederick H. *A Compendium of the War of the Rebellion: Compiled and Arranged from Official Records of the Federal and Confederate Armies, Reports of the Adjutant Generals of the Several States, the Army Registers, and Other Reliable Documents and Sources*. 3 vols. Des Moines: Dyer Publishing Co., 1908.

Egle, William H., ed. *Andrew Gregg Curtin: His Life and Services*. Philadelphia: Avil Printing Co. 1895.

Foote, Shelby. *The Civil War: A Narrative*. 3 vols. New York: Vintage, 1986.

Fordney, Ben F. *Stoneman at Chancellorsville*. Shippensburg, Pa.: White Mane, 1998.

Freeman, Douglas Southall. *Lee's Lieutenants: A Study in Command*. 3 vols. New York: Charles Scribner's Sons, 1944.

Frye, Dennis E. *12th Virginia Cavalry*. Lynchburg, Va.: H. E. Howard, 1988.

———. "'I Resolved to Play a Bold Game': John S. Mosby as a Factor in the 1864 Valley Campaign." In Gary W. Gallagher, ed., *Struggle for the Shenandoah: Essays on the 1864 Valley Campaign*. Kent, Ohio: Kent State University Press, 1991.

Furgurson, Ernest B. *Chancellorsville 1863: The Souls of the Brave*. New York: Knopf, 1992.

Gallman, J. Matthew. *Mastering Wartime: A Social History of Philadelphia During the Civil War*. New York: Cambridge University Press, 1990.

Graham, Martin F., and George F. Skoch. *Mine Run: A Campaign of Lost Opportunities, October 21, 1863–May 1, 1864*. Lynchburg, Va.: H. E. Howard, 1987.

Greater Chambersburg Chamber of Commerce. *Southern Revenge: Civil War History of Chambersburg, Pennsylvania*. Chambersburg, Pa.: Chamber of Commerce, 1989.

Greene, A. Wilson. *Breaking the Backbone of the Rebellion: The Final Battles of the Petersburg Campaign*. Mason City, Iowa: Savas, 2000.

———. "Stoneman's Raid." In Gary W. Gallagher, ed., *Chancellorsville: The Battle and Its Aftermath*. Chapel Hill: University of North Carolina Press, 1996.

———. "Union Generalship in the 1864 Valley Campaign." In Gary W. Gallagher, ed., *Struggle for the Shenandoah: Essays on the 1864 Valley Campaign*. Kent, Ohio: Kent State University Press, 1991.

Griffin, Richard N. ed., *Three Years a Soldier: The Diary and Newspaper Correspondence of Private George Perkins, Sixth New York Independent Battery, 1861–1864*. Knoxville: University of Tennessee Press, 2006.

Hardy, Michael C. *Battle of Hanover Court House: Turning Point of the Peninsula Campaign, May 27, 1862*. Jefferson, N.C.: McFarland, 2006.

Harper, Douglas, comp. *Index of Civil War Soldiers and Sailors from Chester County, Pennsylvania*. Chester, Pa.: Chester County Historical Society, 1995.

Heatwole, John L. *The Burning: Sheridan's Devastation in the Shenandoah Valley*. Charlottesville, Va.: Rockbridge Publishing, 1998.

Hebert, Walter H. *Fighting Joe Hooker*. Indianapolis: Bobbs-Merrill, 1944.

Heitman, Francis B. *Historical Register and Dictionary of the U.S. Army*. 2 vols. Washington, D.C.: U.S. Government Printing Office, 1903.

Heller, Allan M. *Philadelphia Area Cemeteries*. Atglen, Pa.: Schiffer, 2005.

Henderson, G. F. R. *The Science of War: A Collection of Essays & Lectures, 1892-1903*. Edited by Capt. Neill Malcolm. London: Longmans, Green & Co., 1905.

Henderson, William D. *The Road to Bristoe Station: Campaigning with Lee and Meade, August 1-October 29, 1863*. Lynchburg, Va.: H. E. Howard, 1987.

History of the First Troop Philadelphia City Cavalry, From Its Organization November 17th, 1774 to Its Centennial Anniversary November 17, 1874. Trenton, N.J.: Trenton-Princeton, 1874.

History of the First Troop Philadelphia City Cavalry: 1948-1991, Together with an Introductory Chapter Summarizing Its Earlier History and the Rolls, Complete from 1774. Philadelphia: published by the Troop, 1991.

Hoke, Jacob. *The Great Invasion of 1863; or, General Lee in Pennsylvania*. Dayton, Ohio: W. J. Shuey, 1887.

Holland, Lynwood M. *Pierce M. B. Young: The Warwick of the South*. Athens: University of Georgia Press, 1964.

Hunt, Roger D., and Jack R. Brown. *Brevet Brigadier Generals in Blue*. Gaithersburg, Md.: Olde Soldier Books, 1989.

James Starr, Late Colonel Sixth Pennsylvania Cavalry: A Memoir Prepared for the Twenty-Fifth Anniversary of the Class of 1857 in Harvard College, June 28, 1882. Privately published, 1882.

Jones, Virgil Carrington. *Eight Hours Before Richmond*. New York: Henry Holt, 1957.

Keen, Hugh C., and Horace Mewborn. *43rd Battalion, Virginia Cavalry, Mosby's Command*. Lynchburg, Va.: H. E. Howard, 1993.

Lawson, Col. Laurin L. *History of the Sixth Field Artillery, 1793-1932*. Harrisburg, Pa.: Telegraph Press, 1933.

Lewis, Michael J. *Frank Furness: Architecture and the Violent Mind*. New York: W. W. Norton, 2001.

Longacre, Edward G. *General John Buford: A Military Biography*. Conshohocken, Pa.: Combined Books, 1995.

———. *Lee's Cavalrymen: A History of the Mounted Forces of the Army of Northern Virginia, 1861-1865*. Mechanicsburg, Pa.: Stackpole, 2002.

———. *Lincoln's Cavalrymen: A History of the Mounted Forces of the Army of the Potomac*. Mechanicsburg, Pa.: Stackpole, 2000.

———. *Mounted Raids of the Civil War*. South Brunswick, N.J.: A. S. Barnes, 1975.

———. *The Cavalry at Appomattox: A Tactical Study of Mounted Operations during the Civil War's Climactic Campaign, March 27-April 9, 1865*. Mechanicsburg, Pa.: Stackpole Books, 2003.

———. *The Cavalry at Gettysburg*. Lincoln: University of Nebraska Press, 1986.

Magner, Blake A., ed. *At Peace with Honor: The Civil War Burials of Laurel Hill Cemetery, Philadelphia, Pennsylvania*. Collingswood, N.J.: C. W. Historicals, 1997.

Mahr, Theodore C. *The Battle of Cedar Creek: Showdown in the Shenandoah, October 1-30, 1864, Early's Valley Campaign*. Lynchburg, Va.: H. E. Howard, 1992.

Maryniak, Benedict. "Inventory of Federal Chaplains of the Civil War." Unpublished manuscript. Buffalo, New York.

McClellan, Carswell. *Notes on the Personal Memoirs of P. H. Sheridan*. St. Paul: Press of Wm. E. Banning, Jr., 1889.

McLean, James. *California Sabers: The 2nd Massachusetts Cavalry in the Civil War*. Bloomington: University of Indiana Press, 2000.

Montgomery, Norton L. *History of Berks County, Pennsylvania*. Philadelphia: Everts, Peck & Richards, 1886.

Morris, Roy, Jr. *Sheridan: The Life and Wars of General Phil Sheridan*. New York: Crown, 1992.

Morrow, Albert Payson, III. "The Soldier: Albert Payson Morrow, Son of Hugh and Anna Leslie Garnett Morrow, 1842-1911." Unpublished manuscript.

Nichols, Edward J. *Toward Gettysburg: A Biography of General John F. Reynolds*. State College: Penn State University Press, 1958.

O'Gorman, James F. *The Architecture of Frank Furness*. Philadelphia: Philadelphia Museum of Art, 1973.

O'Neill, Robert F., Jr. "The Federal Cavalry on the Peninsula." In William J. Miller, ed., *The Peninsula Campaign of 1862: Yorktown to the Seven Days*. Campbell, Calif.: Savas, 1997.

Patchan, Scott C. *The Forgotten Fury: The Battle of Piedmont, Virginia*. Fredericksburg, Va.: Sergeant Kirkland's Museum and Historical Society, 1996.

Pfanz, Harry W. *Gettysburg: The Second Day*. Chapel Hill: University of North Carolina Press, 1987.

Power, Tracy. *Lee's Miserables: Life in the Army of Northern Virginia from the Wilderness to Appomattox*. Chapel Hill: University of North Carolina Press, 1998.

Reese, Timothy J. *Sealed with Their Lives: The Battle for Crampton's Gap*. Baltimore: Butternut & Blue, 1998.

Rhea, Gordon C. *Cold Harbor: Grant and Lee, May 26-June 3, 1864*. Baton Rouge: Louisiana State University Press, 2002.

———. *The Battle of the Wilderness, May 5-6, 1864*. Baton Rouge: Louisiana State University Press, 1994.

———. *The Battles for Spotsylvania Court House and the Road to Yellow Tavern, May 7-12, 1864*. Baton Rouge: Louisiana State University Press, 1997.

———. *To the North Anna River: Grant and Lee, May 13-25, 1864*. Baton Rouge: Louisiana State University Press, 2000.

"Richard H. Rush." *Twenty-Fifth Annual Reunion of the Association of the Graduates of the United States Military Academy at West Point, New York, June 12th, 1894*. Saginaw, Mich.: Seemann & Peters, 1894: 41-42.

Schultz, Duane P. *The Dahlgren Affair: Terror and Conspiracy in the Civil War*. New York: W. W. Norton, 1998.

Sears, Stephen W. *Landscape Turned Red: The Battle of Antietam*. New York: Ticknor & Fields, 1983.

———. *To the Gates of Richmond: The Peninsula Campaign*. New York: Ticknor & Fields, 1992.

Sheridan Monument Commission. *Unveiling of the Equestrian Statue of General Philip H. Sheridan, Capitol Park, Albany, New York, October 7, 1916, by the Citizens of Albany and the State of New York*. Albany: Press of J. B. Lyon Company, 1916.

Starr, Stephen Z. *The Union Cavalry in the Civil War*. 3 vols. Baton Rouge: Louisiana State University Press, 1976-1979.

Sutherland, Daniel E. *Seasons of War: The Ordeal of a Confederate Community, 1861-1865*. New York: Free Press, 1995.

Sword, Wiley. *Mountains Touched with Fire*. New York: St. Martin's Press, 1995.

Taylor, Frank H. *Philadelphia in the Civil War*. Philadelphia: privately published, 1879.

Thiele, T. F. "The Evolution of Cavalry in the American Civil War, 1861-1865." Ph.D. diss., University of Michigan, 1951.

Thomas, Emory M. *Bold Dragoon: The Life of J.E.B. Stuart*. New York: Random House, 1986.

Thomas, George E., Michael J. Lewis, and Jeffrey A. Cohen. *Frank Furness: The Complete Works*. New York: Princeton Architectural Press, 1991.

Thomason, John W. *Jeb Stuart*. New York: Charles Scribner's Sons, 1929.

Thompson, John W., IV. *Horses, Hostages, and Apple Cider: J.E.B. Stuart's 1862 Pennsylvania Raid*. Mercersburg, Pa.: Privately published, 2002.

Tidball, Eugene C. *No Disgrace to My Country: The Life of John C. Tidball*. Kent, Ohio: Kent State University Press, 2002.

Warner, Ezra J. *Generals in Blue*. Baton Rouge: Louisiana State University Press, 1964.

Waugh, John C. *Class of 1846*. New York: Warner Books, 1994.

Wellman, Manly Wade. *Giant in Gray: A Biography of Wade Hampton of South Carolina*. New York: Charles Scribner's Sons, 1949.

Wert, Jeffry D. *From Winchester to Cedar Creek: The Shenandoah Campaign of 1864*. Carlisle, Pa.: South Mountain Press, 1987.

———. *Mosby's Rangers*. New York: Simon & Schuster, 1990.

Whittaker, Frederick. *A Complete Life of Gen. George A. Custer, Major-General of Volunteers, Brevet Major-General U.S. Army, and Lieutenant-Colonel Seventh U.S. Cavalry*. New York: Sheldon & Co., 1876.

Winthrop, William Woolsey. *Military Law*. 2 vols. Washington, D.C.: W. H. Morrison, 1888.

Wittenberg, Eric J. *Gettysburg's Forgotten Cavalry Actions*. Gettysburg, Pa.: Thomas Publications, 1998.

———. *Glory Enough for All: Sheridan's Second Raid and the Battle of Trevilian Station*. Washington, D.C.: Brassey's, 2001.

———. *The Union Cavalry Comes of Age: Hartwood Church to Brandy Station, 1863*. Washington, D.C.: Brassey's, 2003.

Wittenberg, Eric J., J. David Petruzzi, and Michael F. Nugent. *One Continuous Fight: The Retreat from Gettysburg, July 4-14, 1863*. Columbus, Ohio: Ironclad Publishing, 2006.

Women's Club of Mercersburg. *Old Mercersburg*. New York: Frank Allaben Genealogical Co., 1912.

INDEX

Acknowledgments

I have spent nearly twelve years studying and researching the men and deeds of the 6th Pennsylvania Cavalry, also known as Rush's Lancers. My interest dates to my earliest studies of Civil War cavalry actions, and is linked inexorably to my own Philadelphia roots. One troop, Company G, came from my hometown of Reading, Pennsylvania. I am also an alumnus of Dickinson College, which was founded by Dr. Benjamin Rush, the prominent Philadelphia patriot, in 1773. One half of Dickinson's campus is called the Benjamin Rush campus, and I have nurtured an interest in the Rush family since beginning my studies at Dickinson in 1979. Col. Richard H. Rush, the organizer of the Lancers, was Dr. Rush's grandson, and that connection has always intrigued me. His regiment, constituted as it was of the cream of Philadelphia society, has also fascinated me for years. I discovered their exploits when I first visited their monument on the battlefield at Gettysburg as a teenager, prompting me to want to learn more about this regiment and their funny-looking weapons. My years of research have ultimately led to this book.

As with every project of this nature, I owe enormous debts of gratitude to many people who helped over more than a decade.

I appreciate the assistance of the following individuals, all of whom provided me with valuable primary source material: Gregory Acken, Chris Biache, Dennis J. Boylan, Ben Brockenbrough, Ben F. Fordney, Clark B. "Bud" Hall, Howard M. Madaus, Frank Masland, Matthew McCausland, Mitchell E. McGlynn, Albert P. Morrow, Albert P. Morrow, III, Hugh Morrow, James D. Nolan, Ronn Palm, Paul Polizzi, Marc Riddell, Richard A. Sauers, Patrick Schroeder, George F. Scott, Bryce A. Suderow, Wiley Sword, Terry Walbert, Roger D. Winthrop, Steve L. Zerbe, the late Brian C. Pohanka (friend, mentor, and advisor, who provided important material on Albert Payson Morrow, and who encouraged me to undertake this project), and numerous others who contacted me through my Web site, generously offering to provide me with primary source material pertaining to the service of their ancestors who served in the Lancers. Likewise, I am grateful to the many individuals who provided me with photographs of their forebears who served in the Lancers. Where possible, I have included those photographs in this book in an effort to bring their ancestors back to life in these pages.

I also am grateful to a handful of friends who reviewed my manuscript for me and provided useful feedback that ultimately made this a better book: David Arthur, Tom Clemens, Michael F. Nugent, Clark B. "Bud" Hall, Horace Mewborn, Robert F. O'Neill, Jr., J. David Petruzzi, and Tonia "Teej" Smith. I am particularly grateful to Prof. Michael J. Lewis of Williams College, the leading authority on the life and work of Frank Furness, who read this manuscript for me and provided me with a previously unpublished photograph of Furness that appears in this book. I also thank Tom Canfield of New York, who shares my fascination with the men of Rush's Lancers. Tom provided me with many of the illustrations, as well as quite a bit of valuable primary source material, and he reviewed the manuscript for me. I am grateful to Rick Carlile of Dayton, Ohio, for generously giving me permission to use quotations from the Hamilton S. Ballentine letters, which add a great deal of substance and flavor to the story. Likewise, I appreciate the superb maps of Blake Magner which grace these pages. Blake and I have worked together on half a dozen books now, and his maps always make my work better.

I also appreciate the efforts of Bruce H. Franklin of Westholme Publishing. I would also like to thank Noreen O'Connor-Abel, my copyeditor, who did such a fine job of getting this manuscript ready for publication and was a pleasure to deal with.

Finally, I must express my appreciation and gratitude to my long-suffering but much loved wife, Susan Skilken Wittenberg, who has tolerated my addiction to telling the stories of the horse soldiers of the Civil War for far longer than I probably have a right to ask for. I could not accomplish the things that I accomplish in the field of Civil War history without her unfailing and unflinching love and support, and for that I shall be eternally grateful.